COLLAPSE OF AN EMPIRE

COLLAPSE OF
AN EMPIRE
LESSONS FOR MODERN RUSSIA

YEGOR GAIDAR
TRANSLATED BY ANTONINA W. BOUIS

BROOKINGS INSTITUTION PRESS
Washington, D.C.

Copyright © 2007
THE BROOKINGS INSTITUTION
1775 Massachusetts Avenue, N.W., Washington, D.C. 20036
www.brookings.edu

This work, licensed by Yegor Gaidar, Institute for the Economy in Transition,
2006, was originally published in Russia in 2006 as
Gibel' imperii. Uroki dlya sovremennoy Rossii
[The Downfall of an Empire: Lessons for Contemporary Russia]

Library of Congress Cataloging-in-Publication data
Gaidar, E. T. (Egor Timurovich)
[Gibel' imperii : uroki dlia sovremennoi Rossii. English]
Collapse of an empire : lessons for modern Russia / Yegor Gaidar ; translated by
Antonina W. Bouis.
   p.   cm.
Includes bibliographical references and index.
ISBN-13: 978-0-8157-3114-6 (cloth : alk. paper)
ISBN-10: 0-8157-3114-0 (cloth : alk. paper)
1. Russia (Federation)—Politics and government—1991– 2. Authoritarianism—
Russia (Federation) 3. Soviet Union—Politics and government—1985–1991. I. Title.
DK510.763.G34913 2007
947.085—dc22   2007033505

1 3 5 7 9 8 6 4 2

Printed on acid-free paper

Typeset in Minion with Trajan display
Composition by Circle Graphics, Columbia, Maryland
Printed by R. R. Donnelley, Harrisonburg, Virginia

CONTENTS

ACKNOWLEDGMENTS

Brookings Institution Press acknowledges the generous gift of Daniel Yergin, chairman of Cambridge Energy Research Associates and a trustee of the Brookings Institution, to help cover the costs of this translation.

We also thank Brookings senior fellow Clifford G. Gaddy for his helpful advice and Antonina W. Bouis for her excellent work in translating the Russian text and assisting throughout the page proof stage. Janet Mowery provided outstanding support as she edited the manuscript. Carlotta Ribar also made valuable contributions through proofreading, and Mary Mortensen has pulled together a useful index.

INTRODUCTION

We don't have the strength for an empire!—and we don't
need it, may it fall from our shoulders: it weakens our
brains and sucks them out, and hastens our death.
                                        —Aleksandr Solzhenitsyn

If it befalls you to be born in an empire, it is best to live in a
distant province by the sea.
                                        —Joseph Brodsky

WE ARE NOT THE FIRST to suffer post-empire nostalgia, which permeates the Russian consciousness today. It has occurred in history more than once. The Soviet Union was not the first empire to collapse in the twentieth century, but it was the last. Not a single state formation that called itself an empire at the start of the twentieth century remains. In a number of key characteristics our country did not resemble the traditional colonial empire with overseas territories. The argument over whether it was in fact an empire will continue for a long time. There will be works proving Russia was an empire, demonstrating that the Russian people, under both the tsars and the Communist regime, in many ways supported the other peoples inhabiting our state. There will be examples given of Russian state figures of non-Russian ethnic descent—from Prince Bagration to Joseph Stalin. That specificity may have helped the Russian empire last longer than others that fell apart decades earlier.

However, the elite of the tsarist period regarded their country as an empire. They called it that. The leaders of the Soviet empire did not use the term, but they expanded it far beyond the official borders of the state called the USSR.[1] Today's proponents of the restoration of the empire appeal to the legacy of tsarist Russia through the period of Soviet history to the present time.

The examples of appeals to post-imperial nostalgia in contemporary Russia are numerous. Let me cite just a few. A political analyst close to the

Kremlin, Stanislav Belkovsky: "In 2004–08 the foundations of the Russian nation must be laid. Our nation has only one destiny—imperial."[2] The writer Alexander Prokhanov: "This is why great empires of the past are of a higher order than the great republics. They bore the concept of a united humanity capable of hearing and embodying God's will. That is why today's liberal, disgusting Russia is worse and more bastardized than the great Soviet Union, which was an empire and which we lost carelessly."[3] The geopolitician Alexander Dugin: "The Soviet state was perceived by the people as the construction of a 'New Empire,' a 'kingdom of light,' a 'haven of the spirit,' not as the creation of the most rational method for managing numerous individuals."[4] A vision of the collapse of the Soviet Union as the collapse of the last world empire of the twentieth century is widespread in the literature devoted to that period.[5] Russian president Vladimir Putin, in his state of the union address to the Federal Assembly in 2005, called the collapse of the Soviet Union the greatest geopolitical catastrophe of the century.[6]

The age of empires is in the past, but their study is fashionable now. This happens in history. It is related to the acuteness of ethnic conflicts and their spread in post-imperial periods.[7] The literature devoted to the death of empires is boundless. Montesquieu's *Considerations on the Causes of the Grandeur and Decadence of the Romans* and Edward Gibbon's six-volume history of the rise and fall of the Roman Empire reveal that the plots relating to the collapse of empires and the post-imperial syndrome are not new. A great book showing traces of post-imperial nostalgia appeared in Spain in the early seventeenth century. It is *Don Quixote* by Cervantes.

Knowing that others suffered from the same disease is small consolation. That happened long ago and to others. What is happening to us is the reality of today.

When Peter I took the title Emperor of All Russia, he was merely declaring that Russia was a great European state. Grandeur and empire at that time were synonymous. If you consider how often the word "empire" is used today in political discourse, it is difficult to understand why there is no generally accepted definition commensurate with the contemporary context. The Dal dictionary defines *empire* as a state whose head bears the title *emperor*, the highest rank for unlimited rulers.[8] According to the Ozhegov dictionary, an *empire* is a monarchic state headed by an *emperor*.[9] The academic dictionary of Russian gives two definitions for *empire*: a monarchic state headed by an *emperor* or a large imperialistic colonial state.[10] It is not difficult to see that all these definitions have very little in common with the meaning given to the word *empire* in contemporary Russia. The content of the term is elastic and

has been transformed through history. I would like to offer my own definition of the concept that is close to today's context. In this work I use *empire*
to mean a powerful multiethnic state formation in which the power (or at the
least the right to vote) is concentrated in the metropolis and in democratic
institutions (if they exist), though that power and those institutions do not
extend to the entire territory under its control.

The twentieth century saw a vivid manifestation of the variety of problems
faced by two types of empires: overseas (Britain, Holland, Portugal)[11] and territorially integrated (Austria-Hungary, Russia). In the latter, the colonies are
not separated from the metropolis by seas. The ethnic groups that dominate
in the metropolis and satellite territories live side by side and interact closely.

As history has shown, especially the experience of the second half of the
twentieth century, empires fall apart. The identification of state grandeur with
being an empire makes the adaptation to the loss of status of superpower a
difficult task for the national consciousness of the former metropolis. The
exploitation of the post-imperial syndrome is an effective way of obtaining
political support. The concept of empire as a powerful state that dominates
other nations is an easy-sell product, like Coca-Cola or Pampers. It does not
take intellectual effort to advertise it.

The problem for a country dealing with post-imperial syndrome is that it
is easy to evoke feelings of nostalgia for the lost empire. The calls for its
restoration are not practicable. It is not hard to say: "The restoration of the
empire is good for the people." Such a slogan is inevitably popular. But the
reality is that an empire cannot be revived.

There is one unique case: the restoration of the Russian empire in different, Communist, almost unrecognizable form in the period 1917–21. This is
an exception, and the whole point is that it was *in a different form*, which
would cause a strict analyst to use "restoration" only in quotation marks. The
USSR arose as a result of a fratricidal civil war, unprecedented terror, and the
death of millions of people. In the great majority of cases the restoration of
empires is impossible, in view of circumstances formed by long-standing
tendencies in socioeconomic development.

This contradiction is the root of many of the mistakes of previous metropolises in dealing with their formerly controlled territories. The decision of
England and France to invade Egypt in order to regain control over the Suez
Canal in 1956 is a painful reminder of what the Russian authorities tried to
do in Ukraine in 2004.

The actual formation of an empire is the product of fundamental changes in
the life of a society. Empires rise and fall under the influence of historical cir-

cumstances. Dreams of returning to another era are illusory. Attempts to do so end in defeat. The Russian failures in 2003–04 in Georgia, Ajaria, Abkhazia, Ukraine, and Moldova continued the "collection of errors" made by others long before. But it is difficult for the post-imperial consciousness to accept that. It is easier to believe that we were beaten not by the Georgians or the Ukrainians but by a "world conspiracy" that backs them. If we make decisions within that paradigm we will be miffed at everyone and make mistake after mistake.

The nostalgia for territorially integrated empires is stronger, longer lasting, and deeper than for overseas empires. The almost 3 million Sudeten Germans (the majority nationals in Austria-Hungary) had difficulty adapting to being a minority in the new Czech state. The rhetoric used in their situation was a key theme in Hitler's propaganda before the occupation of Czechoslovakia. When territorially integrated empires collapse (Austria-Hungary, Germany, Russia, Turkey, the USSR), problems like the ones faced by the Sudeten Germans take on massive proportions. Without that in mind, it is difficult to understand the sources of the wars between Serbs and Croats, the tragedy of Bosnia.

The decline of an empire, a gradual process that extends over years during which the elite and the public come to realize the hopelessness and uselessness of trying to preserve it, is much easier to handle for the society of the metropolis than a sudden collapse.[12]

A typical example is the end of the German Empire. Before autumn 1918, the German authorities assured the nation that victory was at hand. When the collapse of the German war machine became obvious in October and November and capitulation was inevitable, the people were not prepared. That is why the myths that "Germany was never beaten on a battlefield" and that "enemies stabbed the country in the back" were so readily believed. The latter—openly or covertly—refers to socialists. The collapse of the empire was blamed on Jewish revolutionaries and traitors in the pay of Moscow, who organized strikes in Germany at the end of the war. It was they, according to the authors of that version of events, who forced the kaiser to renounce the throne.[13] The phraseology was used by former leaders of the German army, who in September and October 1918 reported to the civilian authorities that it was impossible to continue the war and that peace had to be concluded at any price.

Many Germans quickly forgot how they had hated the monarchy in the final year of the war, the feelings they had in October 1918, when it became clear that the kaiser and the high command had deceived the people. They did not know that General Erich Ludendorff had demanded that the new chancellor of Germany, Prince Max of Baden, negotiate peace in October 1918 in order to avert a military catastrophe on the Western front. The monarchy of the Hohenzollerns would not have fallen apart as quickly as it did in November 1918 if the Germans had not already been convinced that the old regime was morally bankrupt.

Such things rapidly vanish from historical memory. The public does not want to remember. Who cares what really happened? A public humiliated by military defeat is easily enchanted by myths. Hitler said that the losses of August 1918 were nothing compared to the victories that the German army had won before that, and that they were not the cause of the capitulation. In his words, the defeat was caused by those who for decades had strived to destroy the political and moral pillars of the Germans, without which no nation can survive.[14]

These facts bring to mind Pushkin's words: "Ah, it is not hard to fool me, I am happy to be fooled." Scholars of the history of the Weimar Republic believe that its leaders were not prepared to make public materials about the responsibility of the German leadership in starting World War I and that it was one of the most important factors that led the republic to its end.[15] The myth of an innocent, unvanquished, loyal, and humiliated Germany was the weapon the leaders of the republic handed over to those who did not believe in democratic values.

The unexpectedness and speed with which apparently unshakable empires fall adds to the sense of unreality. Unreality is related to irrationality, where miracles are possible.[16] It is not difficult to convince the public that a state that collapsed so unexpectedly can be restored just as quickly. That is an illusion. And a dangerous one. It was paid for by the rivers of blood spilled during World War II.

The Soviet Union was a territorially integrated empire, one of the world's superpowers. A few years before its disintegration almost no one could have believed that what happened in the period 1988–91 was possible. After the collapse of the USSR, more than 20 million Russians ended up outside the borders of Russia. The elites in the majority of the countries where they had fled were not tactful and reasonable enough to properly solve the problems of people who found themselves an ethnic minority in a country that they used to consider their own. This increased the post-imperial syndrome in the metropolis, and has become one of the most difficult problems for contemporary Russia.[17]

It is a disease. Russia is going through a dangerous phase. We should not succumb to the magic of numbers, but the fact that there was a fifteen-year gap between the collapse of the German Empire and Hitler's rise to power and fifteen years between the collapse of the USSR and Russia in 2006–07 makes one think.

Igor Yakovenko notes: "The fall of the imperial state was not dealt with properly by the public consciousness. In Russia a responsible political force could not be found that would dare to declare that, from the point of view of self-preservation and reproduction of the Russian people, the collapse of the USSR was the luckiest event in the past half-century. There were influential political forces that started feeding and using nostalgic feelings for political purposes. Particularly unseemly is the fact that the imperial nostalgia is being exploited by politically savvy people who understand the impossibility and catastrophic consequences of any form of restoration."[18]

There is a medical phenomenon in which a person who has had a limb amputated perceives that limb to still be causing pain. The same phenomenon applies to the post-imperial consciousness. The loss of the USSR is a reality. It is a reality that has led to social pain caused by separated families, the suffering of fellow countrymen abroad, nostalgic reminiscences of former glory, longing for the geography of the homeland that has shrunk or been lost. It is not difficult to exploit that pain politically. Say a few words that make the point that "we were stabbed in the back," "it's all the fault of foreigners who have misappropriated our wealth," or "now we will take their property and live well again," and the deed is done. You do not have to make up the phrases; read any textbook on Nazi propaganda. Success is guaranteed.

Such populist tactics appealing to social pain are a political nuclear weapon. They are rarely used. Those who do exploit them end up tragically as a rule. Such leaders bring their countries to catastrophe. Unfortunately, for the past few years Pandora's box has been left open in Russia. The appeals to post-imperial nostalgia, nationalistic xenophobia, the usual anti-Americanism, and even to a not quite habitual anti-Europeanism have become fashionable and might soon become the norm. It is important to realize how dangerous this is for the country and the world.

Post-imperial nostalgia is curable. The experience of France, which had a difficult time losing its empire, shows that it takes several years of dynamic economic growth for the dangerous hysteria that almost blew up the democratic regime to evolve into a romantic nostalgia for the lost past. But they had to fight to preserve democracy during those years. In history there are moments when the role of an individual is particularly important. It is impossible to overestimate the significance of what Charles de Gaulle did in the early 1960s to keep radical nationalists from taking power. Things could have gone differently in Germany in the 1920s and 1930s.

Gibbon, a perceptive scholar of the fall of the Roman Empire, examined it from a long historical distance and did not settle for a single explanation.

When the historical distance is shorter, the task is even more difficult. But analysis of the problems that led to the collapse of the Soviet Empire and the post-imperial syndrome are too important for today's Russia and the world to leave to future historians.

Life has given me a few advantages over other scholars of fallen empires. I was a direct participant in events related to the collapse, one of the authors of the Belovezh accords, which established the fact of the collapse of the last twentieth-century empire, the Soviet Union. But this book is not a memoir; it is an attempt to analyze what surrounds the disintegration of empires and the problems they create. The significance of the Belovezh accords should not be overstated. They legalized the divorce that had taken place. States that cannot control their borders or their monetary, tax, and judicial systems and cannot suppress ethnic conflicts (which was true of the Soviet Union after the events in August 1991) do not exist.

As the Yugoslav experience shows, the divorce process can be bloody. The Belovezh accords of December 1991 did not remove the pain caused by the disintegration of the territorially integrated empire, but they helped avert bloodshed and nuclear catastrophe. As a result of the agreements, by May 1992 the majority of the most dangerous tactical nuclear weapons (because of the technology of the decision to employ them) that had been located in other republics had been moved to Russia.[19]

Let me repeat: I know more than many people about the practical issues related to the collapse of an empire and the problems faced by the authorities in the metropolis. But I would not have taken on this work if I did not see the political danger of exploiting the post-imperial syndrome in today's Russian politics, if I did not see the striking analogies between the rhetoric of people using post-imperial nostalgia in our country and the standard propaganda of the National Socialists in the last years of the Weimar Republic.

Parallels are frequently drawn between Russia and the Weimar Republic. I am among those who did so in Russian political discussions in the early 1990s. But not everyone understands their import. Few remember that the imperial state regalia and symbols were restored in Germany eight years after the empire's collapse, in 1926,[20] and in Russia, after nine years, in 2000. Not many more know that an important Nazi economic promise was to restore the bank deposits lost by the German middle class during the hyperinflation of 1922–23.[21]

The role of economic demagoguery in the Nazi rise to power in 1933 cannot be overestimated. Anti-Semitism, radical nationalism, and xenophobia were always elements in the thinking of the leaders of the Nationalist Socialist Workers Party of Germany. But before 1937, they were cautious in their use of slogans about these issues.[22] Appealing to the emotions of German property owners who had lost their deposits was an effective political tool. Today, the people who promise to restore the deposits made worthless during the Soviet financial catastrophe are repeating Goebbels's rhetoric of the 1930s word for word.

Once they came to power, the Nazis did not restore the deposits. They brought the country to war and yet another monetary catastrophe, for which the father of German economic reform, Finance Minister of the FRG Ludwig Erhard, who abolished price fixing in 1948, had to answer. But that came later.

In Russia, the peak of the post-imperial syndrome mixed with radical nationalism did not come immediately after the collapse of the USSR, as I had expected, but later. My colleagues and I understood, as we embarked on reforms in Russia, that the transition to the market and the adaptation to a new global position and to the existence of a new independent state would not be easy. But we had assumed that overcoming the transitional recession and the beginning of economic growth and an increase in real income for the population would allow people to replace the impossible dreams of empire restoration with the prosaic cares of personal well-being. We were mistaken.

Experience showed that in times of profound economic crisis, when it is not clear whether there will be enough money to feed the family until the next paycheck and whether there will be a next paycheck or whether you will be fired, most people do not worry about imperial grandeur. On the contrary, when economic security is growing and confidence that this year's salary will be greater than last year's, and that unemployment, if you are not living in a depressed region, will not affect you, and you see that life has changed but is returning to stability, you can come home and watch a Soviet film with your family in which our spies are better than theirs, where we always win, and the life depicted onscreen is cloudless, and then talk about how enemies have destroyed a great country and we'll still show them who's best.[23]

Appealing to imperial symbols of grandeur is a powerful tool for managing the political process. The more official Russian propaganda tries to present the Great Patriotic War as a chain of events leading to the preordained victory organized by the ruler, the faster memories of Stalinist repression vanish, and people forget that Stalin himself sanctioned the Molotov-Ribbentrop Pact and played a large role in starting the war. Positive feelings toward Stalin grew from 19 percent in 1998 to 53 percent in 2003. When asked, "If Stalin were alive and running for President of Russia, would you vote for him?" 26–27 percent of Russian residents replied yes.[24] This is a man who killed more of our fellow countrymen than anyone else in the long and complex history of Russia. I think that fact alone is enough to indicate the scale of the dangers associated with post-imperial syndrome in our country.

Trying to make Russia an empire again means imperiling its existence. The risk of movement in that direction is high. That is why it is so important to understand the empires of previous centuries, why they collapsed, and the key problems relating to their disintegration. The first few chapters cover this through an analysis of world experience, and the rest study the collapse of the last empire of the twentieth century, that of the Soviet Union.

The mechanism of the dismantling of empires was specific and covered the political and economic problems in the metropolis and former colonies. In the Soviet Union the crisis unfolded in the context of the eroding bases of the legitimacy of the totalitarian political regime and the fall in oil prices, on which the budget, the consumer market, and the payments balance depended in the early 1980s. The chapters devoted to the analysis of the causes of instability in authoritarian and totalitarian regimes and the problems faced by countries that depend on the market for raw materials are important for understanding the context of what happened in the early 1980s through the mid-1990s in the Soviet Union.

The fact that the Soviet Union was a multiethnic state in which Russians constituted only half of the population had a substantial influence on the tactics and development of events that led to its collapse. But more important was the fact that this was a society in which the imperium, the regime, dominated the organization of daily life. The conviction of the authorities and the society that the state could use unlimited force in order to suppress expressions of dissatisfaction was absolute. This form of state organization, which may appear stable superficially, is fragile because it does not have a flexible mechanism of adaptation that permits it to adjust to changing reality. A demonstration of related risks using the fate of the USSR as the model is the basic thrust of this book.

The unwillingness of the government of the Weimar Republic to tell the truth about the start of World War I was one of the main factors leading to its collapse. The truth about the reasons for and mechanisms of the collapse of the Soviet Union has not been told in a systematic way. Recent access to archival documents that can shed light on the unfolding of the crisis in the Soviet economy is becoming limited again. Nevertheless, the materials that were declassified in the early 1990s allow us to see what happened to us. The legend of a flourishing and mighty country destroyed by foreign enemies is a myth dangerous to the country's future. I will try to show how far from reality this view is. I would not like to see a repetition of the mistakes made by the

German Social Democrats in the 1920s. The cost of such mistakes in a world with nuclear weapons is too high.

This is the picture that dominates Russian public opinion: (1) twenty years ago there existed a stable, developing, and powerful country, the Soviet Union; (2) strange people (perhaps agents of foreign intelligence services) started political and economic reforms within it; (3) the results of these reforms were catastrophic; (4) in 1999–2000 people came to power who were concerned with the country's state interests; (5) life became better after that. This myth is as far from the truth as the one of an unconquerable and loyal Germany that was popular among the Germans in the late 1920s and 1930s.

The goal of this book is to show that this picture does not correspond to reality. Believing that myth is dangerous for the country and the world. Unfortunately, in this case the myth is supported by common sense. It would have been very hard to explain to a fifteenth-century European that the earth revolves around the sun and not the sun around the earth. Anyone could see the former was true by going outside. Weighty arguments were needed to persuade people to doubt what they saw.

When you try to argue against common sense, you should not skimp on evidence. My goal is to show the reader that the Soviet political and economic system was unstable by its very nature. It was just a question of when and how it would collapse. This thesis is correct. But it is difficult to grasp. That is why I am using many archival materials that demonstrate the development of events in the Soviet Union from 1985 to 1991. Some readers may find the quotations from official Soviet interagency correspondence excessive. I am working on the assumption that this is a case where an excess of documentary proof is a lesser evil than inadequate documentation. The reader can skip the quotations, after all.

I would like to thank N. Bazhov, Yu. Bobylev, L. Gozman, N. Glavatskaya, E. Vorobyov, V. Voinovich, V. Kudrov, L. Lopatnikov, V. Mau, A. Maximov, A. Moldavsky, B. Sarnov, S. Sinelnikov, E. Serova, V. Tsymbal, V. Yaroshenko, and Ye. Yasin for reading and commenting on the manuscript or individual chapters and for their indispensable advice. My gratitude goes to O. Lugovoy, V. Dashkeyev, and I. Mazaev for their invaluable help in gathering and analyzing historical statistics. I thank E. Mozgovaya, N. Zaitseva, T. Lebedeva, L. Mozgovaya, E. Vondareva, M. Krisan', and A. Kolesnikova for help with the technical work on the book. This book, like my previous works, could not have been written without the help of my beloved wife, Maria Strugatskaya.

Naturally, I as the author am responsible for any inaccuracies or mistakes.

CHAPTER I

THE GRANDEUR AND THE FALL OF EMPIRES

You can do anything with a bayonet except sit on it.
—Talleyrand

IN THE FIRST CENTURY B.C., the formation of a professional army and the resulting decline of the system of universal military service for free peasants undermined the republican institutions of ancient Rome and prepared the way for a regime in which the army served the ruler in power. The new state structure was called an empire (the term comes from the Latin *imperium,* power). Since Rome's power in those days extended over most of the known world, another meaning of the word developed: in Europe "empire" came to mean a multiethnic state created through conquest. After the fall of the western Roman Empire, its mores and traditions continued to influence what happened in the territories that had been part of the empire and were geographically close to the metropolis. These same influences were reflected in the ensuing course of European history.

Modern Economic Growth and the Era of Empires

The idea of empire—a powerful, authoritarian, multiethnic state, uniting numerous peoples, like the Christian Church—is part of the legacy inherited by medieval Europe from antiquity. James Bryce, a well-known scholar of the Holy Roman Empire, wrote: "Dying antiquity willed two ideas to later centuries: the idea of a universal monarchy and the idea of universal religion."[1] Aphorisms usually oversimplify. That is the case here. The influence of the institutions and Roman law was much more significant for European development than the idea of universal monarchy. However, the connection of the imperial ideal with Roman tradition is indisputable.

Many rulers tried to acquire the title of emperor. But through the centuries after the fall of the Roman Empire, only Byzantium was perceived by other European states as the heir to the Roman imperial tradition.[2] Byzantium referred to both the eastern and western parts of the Roman Empire. The rulers of Byzantium believed that they had only temporarily lost control over part of the empire's territory. When Charlemagne was crowned in 800 as emperor of the Holy Roman Empire, gaining recognition by the Byzantine authorities was a serious problem for him.[3]

The gradual weakening of Byzantium made its pretensions to the imperial title over the post-Roman space ever less convincing. After the Turks took Constantinople, the question of who held those rights became an issue again. The pretensions of the Russians to Moscow's role as the Third Rome, heir to the traditions of the Roman and Byzantine Empires, was in the spirit of the period, the late fifteenth and early sixteenth centuries. However, Russia was too far from the center of development to be taken seriously by Europe.

By the late fifteenth century, the Holy Roman Empire, which had been transformed many times in the ninth through fourteenth centuries and was in many ways ephemeral, was perceived by European royal courts as the only state with the legal right to call itself an empire. However, the idea of empire lives on and even today continues to exert an influence on European events.

Philip II sometimes called himself Emperor of India. We can see in the political polemics of the late sixteenth century the ideas of Spain's predestination as an empire and its holy mission to rule Europe. The Castilian elite in the late fifteenth century regarded the Roman Empire as a model to emulate and itself as its heirs. They were part of the chosen whose holy mission was to recreate a world empire.[4] Outside that context, it is difficult to understand why the Spanish kings needed to spend vast human and financial resources on wars in the sixteenth and seventeenth centuries, trying to expand Spain's dominance in the world.

By the fifteenth and sixteenth centuries, the economic and military growth of Europe and its supremacy over surrounding countries was indisputable. European nations began expanding to other continents. A powerful stimulus was the hope to replenish supplies of precious metals, a resource that permitted financing wars. It was only when the path to America's precious metals was laid that the continent became valuable for Spain.

That was the start of the European empires. It was a period of mercantile trade policies. States limited the import of refined and manufactured goods and stimulated the export of domestic products. Ownership of colonies expanded the controlled customs zone. Conquered countries could not regulate access to the products from the metropolis. The metropolis could have a limited trade policy toward its colonies. The expansion of colonial territories occurred simultaneously with a fierce struggle among empires, the redivision of holdings, and competition among trading companies that dealt with the colonies.

In the middle of the nineteenth century, China, Japan, and the Ottoman Porte (also known as the Sublime Porte) were not formally European colonies; however, after an agreement between Britain and Turkey on January 5, 1809, the opium wars of 1840–42, and the arrival of Commander Perry's squadron in Japan in 1853, the policy of low import tariffs was imposed on those countries as well.[5]

Even apologists for empires admit that the use of administrative force over conquered nations in that era was intended to support industrial development in the metropolis. In 1813 the textile and silk industry of India could have sold its products profitably on the British market at prices 50 to 60 percent lower than those commanded by English goods. But the customs duties (70 to 80 percent of the price) or direct bans of imported goods from India made it impossible. Had India been independent, it could have introduced prohibitive tariffs on British goods in response. India was the birthplace of the textile industry, which had existed there for six thousand years. Millions of people were employed in it. After it was colonized, hundreds of thousands of people lost work, people whose families had been weavers for generations. Cities such as Dacca and Mushirabad, formerly centers of the textile industry, went into decline. Sir Charles Trevelyan reported to a parliamentary committee that the population of Dacca shrank from 150,000 to between 30,000 and 40,000 over the twenty-year period 1813–33. Between 1814 and 1835, exports of British textiles into India grew from 1 million yards to 51 million yards annually. In that same period, Indian textile exports were reduced by approximately 400 percent, and by 1844 by another 500 percent.[6]

The start of simultaneous economic growth at the turn of the eighteenth and nineteenth centuries increased the economic, financial, and military gap between Europe and the rest of the world (with the exception of European immigrant colonies in the United States, Canada, Australia, and some other countries). The defeat of Russia, one of the largest agrarian powers in the world and close to Europe, in the Crimean War was visible proof of that.

The world in the middle of the nineteenth century was a harsh one, with no room for sentimentality. A rule known by the Romans operated here: *Vae victis,* woe to the vanquished. The treatment of vanquished peoples could not be called gentle by any stretch. In order to prove that, it is not necessary to cite the catastrophic population loss of the Americas after the Spanish conquest or the annihilation of the North American native Indians. We can recall the existence in the liberal British Empire of a ban on Indian nationals in government service.

The creation and collapse of the European empires is a component part of the process of unprecedented economic growth and socioeconomic change that began in northwestern Europe in the late eighteenth and early nineteenth centuries. Those changes opened the way to the economic, financial, and military expansion of the metropolis and the extension of its territorial control. Simultaneously, new connections increased the risk that the bases of any state's economic and political power could be undermined in a changing world.

In the mid-nineteenth century, the leading European countries, especially Britain, had no equals in using military power thousands of kilometers from their own borders. That ability is the basis for the formation of imperial policies. The British prime minister and leader of the Liberal Party William Gladstone wrote: "The imperial feeling is innate in every Englishman. It is part of our legacy, which appears with us and dies only after our death."[7]

By 1914, England controlled territory with approximately one-fourth of the world's population.[8] Its empire, backed by long-standing tradition, seemed indestructible to most contemporaries. But the preconditions for its collapse had been formed by the late nineteenth century in the new world order. Simultaneous economic growth and the large-scale concomitant changes in the relationships of economic power among nations made it inevitable.

Developing nations that embarked on the process of economic growth after England can use what A. Gerschenkron called the "advantages of backwardness."[9] In terms of population they often surpass states that began modern economic growth before them; and as they move along the path of industrialization, they can mobilize financial and human resources to form powerful armed forces. The economic, financial, and military rise of Germany and Japan in the late nineteenth and early twentieth centuries are telling examples.

In my book *Long Time,* I focused on the fact that, for the past century and a half, Russia has lagged approximately half a century, or two generations, behind the most highly developed countries that are leaders of modern economic growth.[10] In discussing Russia's problems today, it is useful to remember that the era of decline for world empires began approximately half a century ago.

All the countries that called themselves empires at the start of the twentieth century have rid themselves of their colonies, voluntarily or by force, and given them freedom. This would be difficult to explain as a coincidence. This experience is important for Russia. If Russia learns from it, it may be able to avoid repeating the mistakes that led to political defeat.

In the early twentieth century, contradictions between the harsh structure of control over territories that formed during British financial and military-naval hegemony in the nineteenth century, and the growing economic and military might of countries that had been left out when the world was being divided up, became an important factor in international politics. Peaceful regulation of this problem was not easy. Solving it by force would mean starting a chain of bloody wars. And that is what came to pass from 1914 to 1945.[11]

Crisis and the Dismantling of Overseas Empires

The empires of the eighteenth and nineteenth centuries are the product of the rise of Europe, the modern economic growth that created an asymmetry for decades in the financial, economic, and military forces in the world. But they were fragile formations that had difficulty adjusting to other concepts of rational political structure, to another system of forming armies, and to new forms of using force.

Over the course of the twentieth century, the world became a different place. The dominant ideology, within which the "white man's burden" was a given, was replaced by a picture of the world in which the separation of nations into masters and slaves is unacceptable. The relations between the metropolis and colonies that were organic for the nineteenth century became untenable in the mid-twentieth century. In the intellectual atmosphere of the 1940s to the 1960s it was impossible to explain why Britain should rule India and its other colonies.

Over time, ideas about what the metropolis can do to preserve its supremacy were transformed. The harsh world of the early nineteenth century had no sympathy for the weak. But the changing sociopolitical reality of the twentieth century dictated new rules of behavior. When Britain used harsh measures in Malaya in the early 1950s to suppress rebellion—taking hostages, destroying crops in intransigent villages—these practices were condemned in parliament and called crimes against humanity. What was acceptable in the early nineteenth century was no longer tolerated in the middle of the twentieth.

Russia was the only territorially integrated empire to survive World War I. After World War II, overseas empires began to fall, one after another— British, French, Dutch, Belgian, and Portuguese. At the start of the 1990s the last territorially integrated empire—the Soviet Union—collapsed, and so did Yugoslavia, a country that was not an empire in the literal sense of the word but that faced problems similar to those that bring about the collapse of territorially integrated empires.

The crisis of 1914–45 radically changed the world. The myth of the invincibility of Europeans, deeply rooted in the public mind in the late nineteenth and early twentieth centuries, but undermined by the Russo-Japanese War of 1904–05,[12] was completely discredited by the collapse of the European colonial empires in Southeast Asia during World War II. Europeans could no longer hope that their conquered peoples would continue to believe in the divine right of their conquerors to rule them.[13]

From the late 1940s to the early 1950s the very words "empire" and "imperialism" became unfashionable. In 1947, Clement Attlee, prime minister of England, said, "If at the present time imperialism, by which I mean the subjugation of some nations to the political and economic mastery of others, does exist somewhere, then such imperialism definitely does not exist in the British Commonwealth of Nations."[14]

A characteristic trait of empires is the lack of universal suffrage for its subjects.[15] Adam Smith wrote about the wisdom of offering the vote to the North American colonies. It did not become a topic of serious discussion among British politicians. But "no taxation without representation" was a key slogan of the American Revolution.

In the Hungarian part of Austria-Hungary, of the almost 11 million people over the age of 21, only 1.2 million could vote. The question of whether soldiers mobilized during World War I from non-Hungarian parts of the kingdom should be allowed to vote was hotly debated. The government was unable to make a decision. The Hungarian prime minister, Count Istvan Tisza, categorically refused to give the right to vote to soldiers who were not Hungarian. Attempts to federalize Austria-Hungary in order to save the monarchy came up against the stubborn refusal of the Hungarian political elite to make any concessions to Slavic peoples.[16] World experience shows that empire and political freedom—that is, the real democratic right to vote for all subjects—are incompatible.[17]

In the early 1950s, when France considered Algeria to be one of its departments, France refused to give Algerians a vote equal to that of Europeans. With voting controlled by two different electoral colleges, it took eight Muslim votes to equal one European vote. In 1954–58, the position of the French authorities changed. They recognized at last the inevitability of granting universal suffrage, understanding that they would not be able to hold on to Algeria without it. By then, however, nothing less than total independence was acceptable to the leaders of the liberation movement.[18]

Limiting suffrage in colonies was in line with the realities of the sixteenth and seventeenth centuries, when European empires were forming, and of the eighteenth and nineteenth centuries, when the conditions for modern economic growth were being established. However, it contradicts the perceptions of rational state order characteristic of the second half of the twentieth century. By that time, the conviction was entrenched that a regime that was not formed on the basis of universal suffrage and fair competition among political forces was illegitimate. The metropolis trying to save its colonies and the colonial elites was aware of that. There was only one way to preserve an empire: force the people living in the colonies to accept the regime as a given. But the empires kept confronting the problem that the statesman Talleyrand expressed to Napoleon in the following way: *You can do anything with a bayonet except sit on it.*

In the second half of the twentieth century the political rhetoric of those who favored maintaining colonies stressed not the advantages for the metropolis but the benefits to the colonies, arguing that the metropolis helped them create a legal system and a developed infrastructure. What also changed was the financial context of an empire's functioning. Before the end of World War I, the generally accepted perception was that the colonies should support themselves and pay for the colonial administration. Under the influence of the changing intellectual atmosphere in developed countries, that tradition had become obsolete by the 1920s. In the new paradigm, the metropolis had to expend financial resources to hasten the economic development of the colonies.[19] The authorities who wanted to prove that the empire was beneficial for its subjects had to invest even more in infrastructure and social programs in its territories.[20] This was done at the expense of metropolis taxpayers, who were dubious about this practice. The upkeep of the empire cost them more every year. Societies became convinced that solutions to many problems were being postponed in order to help the colonies. By the second half of the twentieth century, the elites and the public in empires realized that empires were too expensive to sustain. The moment that the political elites of the metropolis and the colonies stop believing that the situation is a given, the empire's fate is sealed. The only question is the form and time frame of its dismantling.

After World War II, an important factor in the dismantling of the colonial system was the opposition of the Soviet Union and its satellites on one side and NATO headed by the United States on the other. The Soviet Union, itself an empire, had reason to give financial, political, and military support to nationalist movements against traditional empires of European states. The

United States, as the leader of the military alliance against the Soviet Union, often treated Latin American countries the way European powers treated their colonies, but it never declared itself an empire or sent its representatives on a permanent basis to run dependent states.

For different reasons, neither the United States nor the Soviet Union liked traditional empires. At least they were not prepared to support them. Sometimes they directly encouraged their dismantling. That alone made maintaining empires impossible.[21] During the Suez Crisis of 1956, the British and French assumed that they could invade Egypt and restore control over the canal on their own without consulting the United States or the Soviet Union. They were wrong. They had to retreat and accept the fact that the canal would remain under Egyptian control.

A process is under way in the postwar world similar to one seen many times in history: a quick dissemination of military technology by wealthy states among their neighbors and potential enemies, giving them broad mastery of partisan warfare. Enormous human and financial resources are required for the metropolis to stand up to this challenge.

In the sixteenth century, for example, with Europe's obvious superiority in military technology, it took only several hundred conquistadores to conquer America. In the second half of the twentieth century, 400,000 French soldiers sent to Algeria were not enough to suppress a rebellion of 20,000 people who had the support of the civilian population. Likewise, Portugal's defense spending, which in 1971 constituted 43 percent of its budget, was untenable for the country. In the period from 1961 to 1974, 110,000 young Portuguese emigrated to avoid the draft. A 1967 decree increased the mandatory military service to four years. Unable to graduate enough officers from their military schools, the Portuguese authorities were forced to recruit junior officers who were promoted upon graduation from military departments in civilian universities. They became the nucleus of the movement that prepared the way for the overthrow of the authoritarian regime and the end of the colonial war.[22] And although Vietnam had never been a U.S. colony, America was pulled into the Vietnam War against the background of the collapse of the French colonial empire and the Cold War. By the time the United States was actively involved in the war, it was clear that controlling the territory and fighting off the partisans would require ten times their number in soldiers. The socioeconomic and political price for maintaining the colony was too high.

National pride is one of the most powerful tools for political mobilization in societies that do not have democratic traditions. Konstantin Leontiev knew very well that a feeling of national solidarity was a threat to an empire: "The idea of nationalities . . . in the form that it appears in the nineteenth century is an idea . . . with a lot of destructive force and nothing constructive."[23]

Appealing to the juxtaposition of the white exploiters and the abused and humiliated indigenous inhabitants of the colonies is an effective political ploy. When the myth of European invincibility was demolished, violent forms of struggle against colonialism became widespread. The participants could count on financial and military support from the Soviet bloc. The nascent independent states were a dependable rearguard for the partisans in countries that were still European colonies.

After World War II, the inevitability of the disintegration of colonial empires became self-evident. The only question was which metropolis would be quicker to realize it and manage to make the decolonialization process easier and less painful.

The British elite, unlike the French, did not survive the capitulation of 1940. Great Britain, which emerged as one of the victors in war, was prepared for the crisis that came with the disintegration of its empire. In 1945, England was one of the three world powers with an army of 4.5 million and held overseas territories scattered over many continents. The sun never set on the empire. But by the end of 1961 there was practically nothing left of it. Nevertheless, the British government, unlike the Russian one, does not see the loss of its empire as a geopolitical catastrophe. In most of the works devoted to the dissolution of colonial empires, England, which understood how the world worked in the second half of the twentieth century, is considered a model to emulate.[24]

The India Councils Act of 1909, even though it did not create radical changes in the organization of imperial rule, was an important milestone on the road to Indian independent statehood.[25] The decision on Indian independence was made during World War II, which in fact marked the end of the history of the British Empire. Further developments were merely an extended postscript. However, in the early 1950s the exploitation of nostalgia for empire was a strong political move, at least by the supporters of the Conservative Party, which identified itself with imperial grandeur. Discussion of the traditions of the past, the significance of empire for England, the inability to give it up, and the "treacherous policies" of the Laborites who were ready to dissolve it were important political components of conservative propaganda. The ideological basis for that policy was Churchill's statement of November 10, 1942: "We intend to hold on to our property. . . . I did not become the King's First Minister to preside over the liquidation of the British Empire."[26] He frequently expressed similar thoughts after his return to government in 1951.

Themes relating to the necessity of preserving the empire, the malign intentions of those who wished to dismantle it, and appeals to post-imperial nostalgia and anti-Americanism predominated in the policies of the Conservative Party in the early 1950s.[27] Many British politicians of the period saw the United States, not the Soviet Union, as their country's main foe. In 1951 it would have been impossible to explain to the majority of the Conservative Party, which had just won the election, that the empire's days were numbered.[28] But time has a way of putting things in perspective. The failure of the Suez campaign in 1956 and the efforts required to retain control on Cyprus in 1956 demonstrated that the dreams of maintaining the empire were romantic and unrealistic. In 1959 the Conservative government, which had sworn fidelity to the imperial ideal just a few years earlier, began forcing the dismantling of the empire. Iain Macleod, minister of colonial affairs, characterized the situation this way: "It has been said that after I became Colonial Secretary there was a deliberate speeding up of the movement towards independence. I agree, there was. And in my view any other policy would have led to terrible bloodshed in Africa. This is the heart of the agreement."[29]

In letting go of its empire, Britain had to deal with a decades-long and difficult terrorist war with Northern Ireland. The parallels with Russia, which in 1991 gave up the next-largest empire without bloodshed and then encountered the difficult Chechen problem, are obvious. No one has ever decolonialized painlessly.

An orderly, planned dismantling of empires corresponding to the metropolis's strategic plans is the exception, not the rule.[30] More often we see situations where the metropolis, unprepared to send soldiers to defend imperial holdings, finds itself in a political crisis, unable to elaborate a policy for the peaceful restructuring of its relations with former colonies. Here Portugal is a striking example: after the revolution of April 25, 1974, the army sent to the colonies lost all desire to fight, and the soldiers and junior officers could think of nothing but getting home quickly. In such a situation, long and complex negotiations about the transfer of power are beyond the government's capabilities.[31]

In France, because of the heavy legacy of its loss in 1940, the public adaptation to the new reality was slower than in England, and nostalgia for empire was stronger. The French political elite were certain that only their empire would allow the country to retain its status as a major power in the world.[32] The number of people who died in the fight for this was greater than in other European metropolises. But their struggle did not change the result, the dismantling of the empire.

As the European empires declined, the crisis of universal military service unfolded.[33] France expended the greatest effort to hold on to its colonies in the late 1940s and early 1950s; it spent more money and lost more lives. In Indochina between 1945 and 1954, 92,000 soldiers and officers of the expeditionary corps were killed, 140,000 wounded, and 30,000 captured. The war ended in defeat. Nevertheless, the French government did not send a single conscript from France to Indochina. It was politically impossible. French families were totally opposed to sending their sons to die in Indochina.

After the capitulation of the French at Dien Bien Phu, when 10,000 soldiers and officers surrounded them, the majority of the military leaders preferred to blame the civilian politicians for stabbing the army in the back. The loss in Southeast Asia, caused in part by France's refusal to send conscripts there, was an enormous factor in the independence movement in other French colonies, especially in Algeria. If the metropolis could not keep its territories in Asia, what guarantee was there that it could do so in northern Africa?

One of history's paradoxes is that the prime minister of France who concluded the war in Indochina with Ho Chi Minh in 1954 also initiated the large-scale increase of French forces in Algeria—Pierre Mendes-France. During parliamentary debates on November 12, 1954, he said, "Let no one expect any compromises from us, we will not compromise when it is a question of defending internal peace and the integrity of the republic. The departments of Algeria are part of the republic and have been France for an extended period of time. No separation is possible between Algeria and the main territory of France. Neither France nor any parliament nor any government will ever give up this fundamental principle."[34] The minister of internal affairs, later president of France, François Mitterrand, was just as adamant. He said, "Algeria is France."[35]

The number of Algerian rebels was smaller than the partisan forces in Vietnam. Algeria is geographically closer to France. More than a million French colonials lived there. They had an influential lobby in the metropolis. The country had significant oil and gas resources.

In May 1955, the French government took a step that the cabinets of ministers who were responsible for running the war in Indochina had not dared to take. They called in 8,000 reservists and announced their plans to extend the tour of duty of 100,000 recruits. In August of that year, they limited the allowable reasons for exemptions from the draft. In 1955, the number of French troops in France almost doubled, from 75,000 in January to 180,000 in December. In the fall of 1956, one-third of the French army was located in northern Africa. By the end of 1956, there were 400,000 French troops there.

Most of the young men drafted in accordance with the decree of August 22, 1952, were older than 23; many were married with children and embarking on careers. In 1914, when large numbers of middle-aged men had been drafted, it was done in an organized way without public resistance. The homeland was in danger; people understood that. In the mid-1950s, the French public and the world saw the war with Algeria as colonial and unjust. Never before had a conscript army been sent to fight such a war during peacetime. In September 1955, recruits being sent to Algeria started to riot. Mass protests took place in Vincennes, Nantes, and Marseilles.

Recruits as a rule did not take part in military action. That was done by the Foreign Legion and military professionals. The basic task of the recruited contingent was to protect the farms of the French colonists. Nevertheless, once recruits were sent to Algeria, public opinion about the war changed in France. Citizens of a democratic country, even those feeling nostalgic for former grandeur, did not want to send their children to fight for the phantom of empire. In 1960–61, polls showed that two-thirds of the French supported the independence of Algeria. In a referendum on January 8, 1961, 75.2 percent of the population voted to give the country's leadership freedom of action in solving questions of its implementation.[36]

In fact, neither France in 1960–61 nor Portugal in 1973–74, both of which had sent large contingents of drafted soldiers to their colonies, was confronted with the threat of direct military defeat. There was nothing like Dien Bien Phu in 1954 in the offing. The decision to dismantle their empires had other causes. Those included the domestic consequences of a long, expensive, and bloody war, the reason for which was becoming less apparent to the public. In the second half of the twentieth century, empires fell out of fashion. Modern society did not deem it necessary to die or to send its children to war in order to preserve the attributes of former grandeur.

The decision to reject the empire, supported by more than two-thirds of the voters, was not easy even in France with its long-standing democratic traditions. The minority, made up of former French colonials and professional soldiers who had fought in the war and felt betrayed by the civilian authorities, posed a serious threat to the stability of French democratic institutions in the period 1958–62. When in 1958 radical nationalists took control of Corsica, an official of the Ministry of Defense was asked if France intended to restore order through the use of force. "What force?" he replied, making it clear that the civilian authorities had no armed forces that could stop a rebellion.[37]

The fact that France managed to retain democratic institutions in the metropolis after the collapse of its empire was the result of several factors: the high level of development that makes authoritarian regimes that ignore the will of the majority seem archaic; the plans for European integration, in which France participated fully; and the authority and will of General de Gaulle, a man who could dissolve an empire and maintain control over the army and police.

In 1960–62, when the question of ending the war and granting independence to Algeria was being discussed, many observers expected a long period of political instability and disorder. They were disappointed. The country's continued dynamic economic growth and European integration removed the potential for a dangerous post-imperial syndrome. In France, as in Russia today, the peak of the post-imperial syndrome occurred in the years when the economy was booming. Experience shows that the illness can be cured.

Problems of Dissolving Territorially Integrated Empires

In agrarian states, many of which were not ethnically homogeneous, national differences were usually unimportant. What was fundamental was the division of society into the peasant majority and the privileged minority, specializing in force, state administration, and religion. The Habsburg monarchy in the middle of the sixteenth century included not only Castile and Austria but also such disparate components as Hungary, Czechia, Slovenia, Slovakia, Croatia, the Netherlands, Burgundy, and the Spanish colonies in America. The ethnic diversity of Russia, which had declared itself an empire in the early eighteenth century, needs no commentary here. Linguistic issues make it hard to determine whether the Ottoman Porte called itself an empire, but at the very least, European contemporaries referred to it as one.

Some agrarian monarchies had consistent policies of national unification. During the early Middle Ages, England and France were ethnically diverse countries. It took several centuries for each to create a single national identity. But the Austro-Hungarian Empire had subjects from very different language groups, and this strategy was not feasible.[38]

The beginning of modern economic growth and the radical changes it brought transformed society. New employment structures and higher educational attainment became entrenched. The bases of legitimacy for traditional political regimes were being eroded. Multiethnic, territorially integrated empires encountered more complex problems.

The spirit of the rising national consciousness in the early nineteenth century was nicely expressed by Johann Gottfried Herder, who wrote, "Providence has divided people by forests and mountains, seas and deserts, rivers and climatic zones, but first of all it divided people by language, tendencies, and character. . . . Nature brings up people in families, and the most natural state is one in which a single nation with one national character lives. . . . Thus it appears that nothing is as antithetical to the very goals of ruling as the natural growth of the state, the chaotic mix of various human breeds and tribes under one scepter. . . . Such kingdoms . . . are like the symbols of monarchy in the prophet's vision: lion's head, dragon's tail, eagle's wings, and bear's paws."[39] The rise of national consciousness and the demands for federalization based on nationality made the situation of territorially integrated empires particularly difficult.

An overseas empire created with the help of cannon can be abandoned. Problems remain with settlers who have to repatriated, but they touch only a narrow segment of society. One of the most serious complications for France in liquidating its overseas empire was the fate of a million French settlers in Algeria. Yet that was only some 2 percent of the population of France.

When the Portuguese empire was dissolved in the mid-1970s, the repatriated settlers in the metropolis made up approximately 10 percent of the total population, more than in any other overseas empire.[40] But the arrival of those outsiders did not become an explosive issue for the young Portuguese democracy and did not interfere with stabilization. In territorially integrated and multiethnic empires the issues relating to the resettlement of ethnic groups in the course of the empire's disintegration are more acute. This was seen in the empires that collapsed during World War I: the Russian, German, Austro-Hungarian, and Ottoman. Arming millions of peasants who were not necessarily loyal to the empire and sending them into the trenches for years without explaining why war was necessary made retaining the empire difficult. Military defeat, the collapse of the old order, and territorial disintegration were related processes.

The picture of anarchy born of the collapse of territorially integrated empires is well known from books and films about the Civil War in Russia (1918–20). But it is not a specifically Russian phenomenon. Here is a contemporary account of the collapse of the Austro-Hungarian Empire: "The green units (bands of deserters) have turned into bands of robbers. They took villages, castles, and railroad stations by storm and robbed them. They destroyed railway tracks. They kept trains in queues in order to rob them. The police and armed forces either joined the robbers or were unable to stop them. The new-found freedom rose in the smoke of burned houses and villages."[41] The most important argument for capitulation in the declaration by the State Council of Austria-Hungary was the fact that the army was multiethnic and its units, being neither Austrian nor Hungarian, were not prepared to fight for the empire.

The experience of dismantling empires after World War I is important for understanding the problems faced by the world in the late twentieth century. After the collapse of an authoritarian regime, a political and social vacuum forms. The policeman of the old regime is gone, and the new one has not yet arrived. Those who want power have no legitimizing tradition behind them, and there are no generally accepted rules of the political game. Conditions characteristic of great revolutions take shape: a weak government that is unable to collect taxes and pay people on the state payroll, maintain order, or guarantee that contractual obligations will be met.[42]

In those circumstances the exploitation of the simplest social instincts is a sure path to political success. Talking about national grandeur, about the injustices suffered by one's own ethnic group in history, or about territorial demands by neighbors will guarantee political success.[43] With weak democratic traditions and political parties, dependable weapons in the power struggle are radical nationalism, appeals to national self-identification and national injuries, and seeking out ethnic enemies. Austria-Hungary in 1918 provides a classic example of the use of such political tools by the leaders of the empire's ethnic elites.

Even on the eve of the empire's collapse, pan-Germanic circles in Austria were categorically opposed to its transformation into a federation. The *Neue Freie Presse,* which expressed their views, wrote a few days before the regime fell: "Germans in Austria will never permit the state to be pulled apart like an artichoke."[44]

The Polish poet Adam Mickiewicz wrote a century before its collapse that the Austro-Hungarian Empire had 34 million inhabitants, of which only 6 million were Germans who kept the remaining 28 million in subjugation. In 1830 the Austrian poet Franz Grillparzer noted that if the world were to confront unexpected trials, only Austria would fall into pieces as a result. The Austro-Hungarian elite understood the fragility of the empire and tried to protect it by engendering contradictions among the peoples it controlled, creating a situation in which the Hungarians hated the Czechs, the Czechs hated the Germans, and the Italians hated all of them. When collapse was inevitable, the mutual hostility made national problems in the successor states difficult to regulate.[45]

The attempts made by metropolis elites to make national identity the basis of statehood in multiethnic empires of the late nineteenth and early twentieth centuries actually radicalized anti-imperialist feelings among the national minorities. A leading Russian demographer, Professor Anatoly Vishnevsky, wrote:

> Ukrainian separatism in its argument with more moderate federalism had the same strong ally as the other separatists in the Russian empire—imperial

great-power centralism. Its harsh unitarist position, which permitted no deviation, constantly encouraged equally harsh demands from Ukrainian nationalists. Ukrainian nationalism objectively was incited by a sense of the subordinate position on the imperial economic and political stage of the new Ukrainian elite and generally of the stratum of the Ukrainian populace that had joined the movement. When Russian patriots, who recognized Ukrainians as part of the Russian people, refused to hear anything about the Ukrainian language, they were signing on to impose that disadvantaged and second-class position forever.[46]

One of the most important themes of Hungarian political propaganda in 1918 was the danger of losing privileged-nation status in Austria-Hungary. The main subject of Croatian propaganda was the unacceptability of Hungarian dominance and its territorial pretensions toward Croatia. For Austrian Germans the greatest problem at that time was the fate of the part of Czechoslovakia settled by Sudeten Germans, and for Czechoslovakia it was the preservation of territorial integrity.

These conflicts are hard to resolve rationally. From the point of view of reason it is difficult to explain which is more important—the preservation of Bohemia's integrity or the right of Sudeten Germans to join Germany. What should be done with Hungarian minorities in Yugoslavia and Romania? The occupation by Entente troops of the territories in question played an important part in the relatively peaceful resolution of these issues. But still there were armed conflicts. Things were much bloodier when other territorially integrated empires collapsed.

By 1870, on most of the territory of the future Bulgarian state, the Orthodox Bulgarians were almost outnumbered by Muslims, Turks, Bulgarian-speaking Pomaks, and the Crimean Tatars and Cherkessians who had moved there from Russia. Several million Turks from Bulgaria, Macedonia, and Trakia moved into Western Anatolia during the last quarter of the nineteenth century and the first quarter of the twentieth. By 1888 the percentage of Muslims in Bulgaria had shrunk to approximately 25 percent, and by 1920 it was only 14 percent. Similar processes took place in 1912–24 in Macedonia and Western Trakia.[47]

The final dismantling of the Ottoman Empire came with its defeat in World War I. In January 1920, the leaders of the Turkish nationalists were forced to acknowledge the right to self-determination of the territories of the empire where the Arab population predominated. But they insisted on preserving the integrity of the Turkish metropolis. The Greco-Turkish War followed the collapse of the Ottoman Empire. It resulted from disagreements over the borders of states forming in the post-imperial space. Victory in the war was a significant factor in the legitimization of the new Turkish state and made liquidation of the Muslim caliphate in 1924 relatively painless. However, even then, with the first attempts at democracy in the late 1920s and early 1930s, the legal opposition immediately exploited nostalgic feelings for the caliphate, Muslim values, and the lost empire.[48]

The imperial mission in Asia was a critical element in Russia's self-identification in the nineteenth century. Dostoevsky wrote: "In Europe we are spongers and slaves, but we will arrive in Asia as masters. In Europe we were Tatars, but in Asia we too are Europeans. Our mission as civilizers in Asia will entice our spirit and take us there, as soon as the movement starts. . . . A Russia would be created that would revive the old one and with time would resurrect and define its own paths."[49] But territorial expansion, the annexation of territories inhabited by peoples with fundamentally different traditions and languages, created risks at the first sign of a crisis in the regime.

The Civil War in Russia was not purely nationalistic; it had powerful ideological and social components. The question of land and *prodrazverstka,* the seizure of food from peasants for redistribution by the state, played no less a role than the nationality factor. Nevertheless, the nationality issue in Russian history from 1917 to 1921 must not be underestimated.[50]

Alain Besançon noted that the Russian Empire before World War I had a good chance of regulating social contradictions and problems of economic development, but it could not solve the nationalities question. This circumstance severely constrained the regime's evolution. The liberal, democratic, and modernizing alternative—the key to solving the issues of sociopolitical development—increased the probability of the empire's collapse.[51]

Russia is unique in restoring a failed empire, which it did in the period 1918–22. This required an unprecedented use of force and violence. But that was not the only factor in the Bolsheviks' success. Messianic Communist ideology shifted the center of political conflict from a confrontation between ethnic groups to a struggle among social classes. That struggle garnered support from people in the non-Russian regions, who fought for a new social order that would open the way to a brilliant future, and played a large role in forming the Soviet Union within borders resembling those of the Russian Empire. Russia succeeded owing to a unique combination of circumstances. No one else in the twentieth century managed to do it.

Austrian socialists, forced to adjust to the realities of political competition in a multiethnic empire, understood the potential of the national question for destabilizing the regime and saw that the active exploitation of ethnic issues was a bomb that could destroy its foundations.[52] V. I. Lenin's thesis of the right to self-determination to the point of secession radicalized the logic of the Austrian social democrats, who had wanted to undermine the imperial regime in order to restructure it as a federation.

After World War I, the European establishment accepted the idea that nations had the right to self-determination, and the principle was incorporated into the Treaty of Versailles. It was a way of dismantling the German, Austro-Hungarian, and Ottoman Empires. The document's authors had clearly not considered the long-term consequences of the propaganda associated with its ideas for other European empires.

In October 1914, Lenin spoke in Zurich to a social democratic audience on "war and social democracy," comparing the situation of Ukrainians in Russia and in Austro-Hungary. He said, "Ukraine has become for Russia what Ireland was for England; it was ruthlessly exploited, getting nothing in return." Lenin felt that the interests of the Russian and international proletariat required Ukraine to win state independence.[53]

He did not reject the principle of self-determination with the right to secession even after seizing power, when much of what he had preached before the revolution (freedom of speech, convening a National Assembly) had been forgotten. Why this remained part of Lenin's political catechism is the subject of much debate and will probably never be resolved completely. Probably the key is that he always regarded events in Russia in the context of preparation for world socialist revolution and understood what a powerful means of destabilization radical nationalism could be.[54]

I have already spoken of the most important difference between the collapse of territorially integrated empires and overseas empires: in the latter, colonial settlers can return to the metropolis, and the ensuing problems can usually be solved in a civilized manner.

The situation was more complex in territorially integrated empires. There the people were not colonial settlers who moved to the overseas colonies a generation or two earlier, but people whose ancestors had lived in the same place, next to other ethnic groups, for centuries. These were millions of people who considered themselves to be at the least equal citizens of the country and occasionally even the privileged stratum. When an empire collapses, the representatives of the metropolis sometimes become the ethnic minority and are discriminated against. More than 3 million Hungarians found themselves to be a minority in neighboring successor states: 1.7 million in Transylvania, which had seceded from Romania; around 1 million in Slovakia and trans-

Carpathian Russia, which joined Czechoslovakia; and approximately half a million in Vojvodina, which joined Yugoslavia. Almost 5 million Germans went from being representatives of the ruling nation in the Austrian half of the Austro-Hungarian monarchy and a number of eastern regions of the German Empire to being the ethnic minority in Czechoslovakia, Poland, and Italy.[55]

Questions inevitably arise: should it be possible for arbitrarily created borders of imperial regions to become the natural borders of new independent states? Should ethnic minorities have a say about where they live, as new states form after empires fall? The concept of self-determination has no answers for these questions. Understandably. It was created not to solve questions related to the fall of multiethnic empires but as a bomb to place beneath their foundations. Its creators were not particularly worried about what would happen once the socialist revolution came to pass. But these questions became real and often bloody.

The basis of the political ideology of movements for national independence and the destruction of empires is often hostility toward the formerly dominant ethnic group. That is not a political construction from which to expect political correctness toward the formerly privileged nation. This explains the support for radical nationalism among minorities, once representatives of the metropolis, in newly independent countries.

The Yugoslav Tragedy

In the late twentieth century, Yugoslavia became one of the states that illustrate the problems of dismantling a territorially integrated empire.[56] It fell apart almost simultaneously with the Soviet Union. What happened there is important for understanding the developments in the USSR in the late 1980s and early 1990s.

Yugoslavia, naturally, was not a great power or empire in the classic sense of the word. But some features of the country's state structure, beginning with its creation in 1918, made it resemble an empire. Both under the Karageorgevic dynasty and under Communist rule, it was a state with an authoritarian regime composed of ethnically heterogeneous but territorially integrated parts.

The idea of creating Yugoslavia as a commonwealth of Southern Slavic nations was first discussed in the late 1830s and early 1840s.[57] After World War I, both the southern Slavic national leaders and the heads of Entente countries concluded that the way to guarantee stability in the Balkans and prevent local wars was to create a state based on the Serbian monarchy.[58] The fragile balance of the national interests of the peoples living in Yugoslavia was destroyed in 1929 by political changes that limited the rights of non-Serbs and turned the country into a Serbian micro-empire.[59]

After World War II, Yugoslavia was reestablished. It had a relatively mild authoritarian Communist regime with an unusual construction. The Serbs were the largest ethnic group. The country's capital was also the Serbian capital. This led to the inevitable dominance of Serbs in the government and the army. For decades the head of the country was a Croatian who understood the need to struggle against Serbian nationalism in order to retain stability in a multiethnic country. He incorporated the struggle against Serbian nationalism into the constitution, appreciating that the preservation of the state's integrity depended on the reality of the federative structure.

Josip Tito's policy was directed at minimizing the risks of attempts to transform Yugoslavia into a Serbian empire. The authority and will of the leader who stood up to Hitler in 1941–45 and to Stalin in 1948–53 was needed to ensure this construction. S. L. Woodward, a perceptive scholar of the Yugoslavian crisis, wrote: "Yugoslav society was not held together by Tito's charisma, political dictatorship, or repression of national sentiments but by a complex balancing act at the international level and an extensive system of rights and of overlapping sovereignties. Far from being repressed, national identity and rights were institutionalized—by the federal system, which granted near statehood to the republics, and by the multiple rights of national self-determination for individuals."[60] This is true, but it is not all. This system could have worked only under strict control over any manifestation of political dissent. A crisis of legitimacy of the authoritarian regime would make the construction impossible.

As soon as the linchpin vanished—that is, the central authority's willingness to use whatever force was necessary to preserve power and the state's territorial integrity—Yugoslavia became ungovernable. The restraints that would have worked in a strong authoritarian regime, including the purely formal veto power of the republics and autonomous regions over decisions made by the federal government, never used under Tito, were unacceptable for running the country with a weakened government.

External problems added to the domestic ills. The most important element in Yugoslavia's stability after 1945 was the guarantee in the Yalta Agreement that it would not be under the control of either the Soviet Union or the West. Tito deftly used the advantages this conferred. After the reestablishment of relations between Moscow and Belgrade, which had been suspended during a conflict in the late 1940s and early 1950s, access to the Soviet and East European market and a clearing agreement with the Comecon countries helped boost the Yugoslav economy. At that time Yugoslavia was able to secure low-interest loans from the International Monetary Fund (IMF) and World Bank. Yugoslavia's foreign policy is best described by the old Russian proverb: "A gentle calf can suckle two cows."

Beginning in the late 1940s, Yugoslavia's national defense was based on using the conflict between the two military and political blocs in Europe. The Yugoslav leadership understood that they would not win a war if attacked by NATO or Warsaw Pact forces. However, by organizing partisan resistance, they could create problems for the attacking side and use the support of the opposing bloc. This led to military training for reservists as part of the plan to have an armed populace as the basis of national defense, which played a big role in the development of the Yugoslav crisis.

In 1989, informed analysts regarded Yugoslavia as a socialist country with the highest level of readiness to create a full-fledged market economy. In 1949 the Yugoslav leadership began consulting the IMF and implemented reforms designed to shape a "socialist" market economy. In 1955 it opened its borders to foreign travel by its citizens and to relatively free foreign trade. By 1965 negotiations were completed for the conditions of Yugoslavia's membership in the General Agreement on Tariffs and Trade (GATT). The country had a cooperation agreement with the European Community and with the European Zone of Free Trade before other socialist states even began discussing the possibility of concluding such agreements.

Even after the difficult decade of 1979–89, Yugoslavia's high living standard, the people's ability to work abroad, and its cultural pluralism seemed to make it the obvious leader (among states that had gone through a period of socialist development) to join the club of wealthy European states. The collapse of the Soviet Empire in Eastern Europe, which began in 1989, meant a shakeup in its unique position in the balance of power in the Balkans. Added to this was the erosion of communism as the basis for a legitimate regime.

Mikhail Gorbachev's policies, the end of the Cold War, and the disintegration of the Warsaw Pact and Comecon in the late 1980s changed Yugoslav foreign policy and the economic basis for Yugoslavia's existence. It lost its advantages as a state in a key region that was independent of both the Soviet Union and NATO. The collapse of the clearing trade within Comecon, into which it was integrated, was a blow to the Yugoslav economy. Another challenge was the loss of privileged-borrower status in international financial markets: it could no longer get inexpensive loans for political reasons. And domestic economic problems led to an economic crisis. Economic problems grew after the late 1970s. The rate of inflation increased and the rate of GDP growth fell (see table 1-1).

TABLE 1-1. GDP Growth Rate, Inflation, and Unemployment in
Yugoslavia, 1978–90

Percent

Year	GDP growth rate	Rate of inflation	Share of unemployed in the workforce
1978	9.0	14.1	12.0
1979	4.9	20.5	11.9
1980	2.3	30.3	11.9
1981	1.4	40.6	11.9
1982	0.5	31.8	12.4
1983	−1.4	40.8	12.8
1984	1.5	53.3	13.3
1985	1.0	73.5	13.8
1986	4.1	89.1	14.1
1987	1.9	120.3	13.6
1988	−1.8	194.6	14.1
1989	1.5	1,258.4	14.9
1990	...	580.6	16.4

Source: UN Statistics Division (http://unstats.un.org/unsd/cdb); B. R. Mitchell *International Historical Statistics. Europe 1750–1993* (London: Macmillan Reference, 1998).

It was becoming clear that the Yugoslav model of market socialism, based on labor self-management, did not work well in industrialized societies, and the well-known economic arguments against its viability reflected real problems in the Yugoslav economy.[61] Tito's death paralyzed the decisionmaking process related to taxes, the budget, and foreign trade. But the accumulated problems, including the growing foreign debt, demanded action from the federal authorities, who assumed the republics would agree to share the burden of adapting to worsening foreign economic conditions. But the republics could not agree on which belts to tighten or how much.

In 1989 the Ante Markovic government attempted to implement a package of economic reforms focused on an institutional transformation of the Yugoslav economy and on financial and monetary stabilization. An element of this program intended to integrate the Yugoslav market was the plan to repeal limitations on property rights for foreigners and on the right to repatriate income. On January 19, 1989, the premier introduced a bill in parliament that would liquidate the property rights system inherited from socialism. It did away with limits on the size of landholdings and their sale and expanded the rights of managers in hiring and firing workers. The Union of Communists of Yugoslavia lost the prerogative of approving the appointment of enterprise directors. The inflation rate, which in December 1989 was 50 percent a month, fell to almost zero by May 1990.[62]

The concentration of power on the federal level was a necessary prerequisite of this program. However, Tito's federal construction, which was intended to prevent Yugoslavia from turning into a Serbian empire, did not allow this to happen. The ability of the federal authorities to impose their decisions on the republics was minimized by the constitution.

Although intended to deal with the harsh economic reality and to save the country, the actions of the Markovic government led to the political crisis that brought about Yugoslavia's collapse. Two years later the country no longer existed. Its territory became a bloody battlefield of ethnic wars that took tens of thousands of lives and created millions of refugees. In the conflict between Serbia and Croatia, 20,000 people died, 200,000 became refugees, and 350,000 received displaced-person status. During the Bosnian war 70,000 died and 2 million became refugees or were resettled.[63]

The history of the 1990s Yugoslav crisis is well documented and is not the subject of this book.[64] I use it to demonstrate that in the collapse of an authoritarian regime in a multiethnic country, the topic of nationalism, both in the metropolis and in the parts of the federation that consider themselves oppressed, becomes predominant.

After the Balkan wars of 1912–13, there was an informal moral ban on discussing territorial claims. This taboo was violated only in the years preceding World War II. In an authoritarian regime, this ban was often strengthened by harsh political sanctions.[65] The liberalization of the regime and the democratic elections to the republican parliaments of 1990 made use of that weapon inevitable. It is too effective to ignore if one wants votes.

The Serbian leadership was the most important participant in the political process that exploited the ideas of radical nationalism. The Serbian Communist Party was led by Slobodan Milosevic: talented, charismatic, well educated, and with experience in market economics. Since Communist ideals no longer attracted voters, his only hope to retain control over the political situation in Serbia was to exploit the theme of Serbian nationalism, the oppressed situation of Serbs in Yugoslavia, and the problems of the Serbian minority in Kosovo, Bosnia, and Croatia.[66] It was not difficult then to garner political capital in Belgrade by talking about the artificiality of the republic's borders established by the Croatian Tito and the need to unite all Serbs in a single, territorially integrated state.

A draft document prepared by the Serbian Academy of Sciences in 1986 dwelled on the suppression of Serbs in Yugoslavia and set forth principles that could be used by politicians in a multiethnic country undergoing a crisis in its authoritarian regime. Excerpts, under the title "The Situation of Serbia and the Serbian People," appeared in the Belgrade newspaper *Evening News* in September 1986. The article's authors noted even then that this was a collection of ideas that would lead to a "fratricidal war and new bloodshed."[67] Appeals to national grandeur and national oppression are fuel for an atomic bomb in the political process of a country where the old regime is fading but there is a developed system of democratic institutions.[68]

The problem of young democracies that arise in multiethnic countries is that the slogans that are easiest to sell to unsophisticated voters are dangerous if implemented. It was a losing position politically in Belgrade in the late 1980s not to agree that "Serbia must be great" and "that we will not permit Serbs to be beaten anywhere." It was easy to sell the idea on the political market that Serbia was and would be great and that the leadership would never allow Serbs to be hurt in the other republics and autonomous structures. If a Serbian leader did not fill that niche, some other politician would do so to serve his own interests. In May 1989 the Serbian parliament elected Milosevic president. A referendum in December of that year showed 86 percent of the voters supported him.[69]

It would not have been difficult to predict that politicians in Zagreb, Ljubljana, and Sarajevo would latch on to those slogans enthusiastically, merely substituting "Croat," "Slovene," and "Bosnian Muslim" for "Serb." The moment the Serbian leadership agreed to accept the program of exploiting Serbian nationalism as a political ideology, the fate of Yugoslavia was sealed. In making territorial claims on their neighbors, the Serbian leaders opened the way to victory by nationalist leaders in the other republics who used the fear of Serbian domination and territorial expansion. Wars with Croatia, Bosnia, and Kosovo were inevitable. A process was set in motion that would cost tens of thousands of lives and lead to the forced resettlement of millions of people.

Political agitation based on pitting against one another people who had once lived together within borders arbitrarily imposed by a nondemocratic regime was the prologue to a bloody conflict. Twenty-five percent of Serbs in Yugoslavia lived outside Serbia. The propaganda of Serbian greatness influenced the treatment of Serbs in the republics where they were the minority. The response to the rhetoric and territorial claims on Croatia was repression of the Serbs living in that republic. The response to the repression was military action by the Yugoslav National Army (most of the junior officers were Serbs) to protect the Serbian minority. After that came war.

The political processes involved in the disintegration of an authoritarian regime affected the quality of economic policy. The democratic elections that began in the 1990s in the republics gave rise to what Rudi Dornbusch and Sebastian Edwards called economic populism.[70] Rival parties competed to promise the voters the best economic future, leading to the erosion of federal control over the budget and monetary policy. The inflation that had been stopped by spring 1990 took off again that fall. Of course, in view of the growing political chaos, this was a secondary factor.

The dissolution of empires in the twentieth century is a component of the process of global change that is called modern economic growth. That does not make it any easier for people caught in the mill of history. Appealing to their emotions is a powerful political tool. Think of Stalin's address to his "brothers and sisters." Coming from a man who killed millions of his fellow citizens, the words were blasphemous. And yet it was an astute political move, just like exploiting the problems of Russians who found themselves beyond the borders of Russia or appealing to post-imperial consciousness.

Historians and writers who incite radical nationalism and hostility toward neighboring peoples and who rehash long-ago injuries must realize that they are setting the stage for ethnic cleansing and the suffering of millions. Unfortunately, people rarely learn from their own experiences and almost never from the experiences of others. But if we do not draw lessons from what happened to our country and to other twentieth-century empires, we may become a threat to the world. That is the worst thing that could happen to Russia.

CHAPTER II

AUTHORITARIAN REGIMES

THE CAUSES OF INSTABILITY

The strongest is never strong enough to be always the master, unless he transforms strength into right, and obedience into duty.

—Jean-Jacques Rousseau
THE SOCIAL CONTRACT

AUTHORITARIAN REGIMES are political structures that are not based on traditional legitimacy or on a publicly accepted process of forming the government and parliament after competitive elections. Their leaders, having removed political rivals, suppressed the opposition, and taken control of mass media, often believe that they will be in power forever. They think that the means of oppression available to them will be enough to guarantee the stability of their regimes. This is an illusion that cost many dearly. Such forms of power are innately unstable. Their instability is not caused by attendant circumstances or accidents, but by their very nature.

Monarchies, which are based on tradition (future continuity in the form of government that existed in the time of fathers and grandfathers), can remain stable for centuries. The length of a dynastic cycle in the largest agrarian civilization, China, is three or four hundred years. Some republics and constitutional monarchies (a kind of democracy)[1] have exhibited an ability to adapt to unprecedented challenges from industrialization, urbanization, demographic changes, and the transformation of a democracy of taxpayers into a government structure based on universal suffrage. They have managed to preserve political stability for centuries.

Examples of authoritarian regimes that remained stable for more than seventy-five years (three generations) are rare. In this sense, Rome, the source of imperial tradition in Europe, is the exception. But its political structure interwove traits of authoritarian regime with agrarian monarchy.

Most states that can be called empires are either monarchies or democracies that limit the rights and freedoms of their colonies. Even in those cases when the metropolis was a democracy, indigenous inhabitants of the empire's conquered territories did not have the right to vote on issues affecting the entire empire. In this regard, the totalitarian Soviet Union and authoritarian Portugal, whose regimes were not based on monarchic traditions or democratic procedures in the metropolis, had common traits. For all their differences in scale, in both instances the collapse of the regime was simultaneous with the fall of the empire. The causes of the internal instability of authoritarian and totalitarian regimes are most important in discussing what happened to the Soviet Union in the 1980s and early 1990s.

This chapter deals with the instability of authoritarian regimes widely found in periods when the legitimacy of traditional monarchies is undermined by social transformation and the conditions for forming stable democracies are not yet in place.

Challenges in the Early Stages of Modern Economic Growth and Authoritarianism

One characteristic of agrarian society is long-term stability in the methods of organizing production, population distribution, and occupation.[2] Fidelity to tradition and following the example of ancestors are fundamental elements. Change means burned-out villages and trampled fields. For an agrarian society, monarchy, with its centuries of tradition and clear system of succession, is the natural political organization.

Mancur Olson wrote that in a dynastic regime the probability is not high that the oldest son of the king is the best qualified to rule. However, the citizens justly assume that they benefit when power is transferred by heredity because each successive head of state will care about the long-term future of the country and his heirs. Agreement on the next ruler is beneficial to all.[3] In a stable monarchy, after a king's death it is unusual to have wars of succession that bankrupt the peasantry. They happen, but as an exception to the rule. The stability of the ruling dynasty allows the sovereign to regard the country as a treasure that will belong to his children and grandchildren. This means he must care about his subjects and not exhaust them with outlandish taxes. The stability of the political system allows for the formation of behavioral norms related to the concept of a benign sovereign, a ruler who observes tradition and wants his country to flourish. Confucianism is a vivid example of an ideology on which such rule is based.

The rules of succession of power in agrarian societies and the role played by representative bodies (national assemblies, councils of nobles) in determining the order of succession after a monarch's death vary. But in the majority of agrarian societies, the eldest son inherits the throne.

Established in European city-states and then in territorially integrated political entities that were not cities, democratic systems of political and economic institutions supported by a taxpaying citizenry paved the way for an unprecedented economic upswing. This was the most serious challenge to traditional monarchy in the millennia-long history of the agrarian world.[4] Economic and social changes undermined tradition, the basis of political stability in hereditary monarchy.[5] If there is a place left for the monarch, it is in ceremonial functions and not in running the country.

By the early eighteenth century, the models to emulate were the most economically developed European countries—the Netherlands and Britain, countries with strong parliaments that controlled the executive power. It was there that Peter I traveled to learn the latest in technology. He did not intend to transplant Dutch or British institutions to Russian soil and to create an authoritative parliament. But it was clear to him that he needed to master modern technology that would be useful in warfare.

In Western Europe and some colonies, the experience of those developed countries with influential parliaments gave rise to doubts about the sense of a monarchical system. American philosopher and essayist Thomas Paine ridiculed the idea that the heir is the best ruler.[6] An ideological wave crested in continental Europe in the seventeenth and eighteenth centuries, washing away faith in absolute monarchy as a political system. A new paradigm grew in the public consciousness with elected parliaments as the necessary element in a rational political system; the belief grew that they should be responsible for setting taxes, as well as for determining how state financial resources were spent and how the executive power should be formed. Other methods of organizing society did not make sense. This new paradigm prepared the way for large-scale upheavals in political life, including the French Revolution and the acceptance of its ideas in Europe.

The spread, albeit slower, of these social concepts can be seen in Russia, far from the center of European development. The Decembrists, a group of liberal aristocrats who called for a constitutional monarchy in December 1825 and were exiled to Siberia by Nicholas I, were convinced that the retention of absolute monarchy was incompatible with becoming a civilized developed country.

Destruction of the legitimacy of the institutions of a traditional monarchy does not guarantee that democratic institutions will immediately take hold.[7] Even where parliaments had existed for centuries, they played a limited role: they were organs that met periodically and made decisions on issues related to taxation and budget expenditures. In that regard, they were a familiar, long-standing institution. Their transformation into higher organs of power was a break with tradition that led to disorder and confusion.

When the monarchic foundations are no longer legitimate and the democratic ones have not yet stabilized, the probability grows that a candidate who can use force will be able to impose his will on society without taking into account its preferences for political organization. That is the political basis of Europe's authoritarian regimes, like those of Oliver Cromwell and Napoleon Bonaparte in the seventeenth and eighteenth centuries.[8] The threat of such developments remained for a long time in countries that had embarked on the path of modern economic growth. In Western Europe, with its long parliamentary tradition, the last authoritarian regimes were dismantled and replaced with democratic ones only in the mid-1970s.[9] Eastern Europe was a decade and half behind.

One of the factors easing the rise of authoritarian regimes is the social disorganization that accompanies the early stages of modern economic growth. The difficulties of adapting to urban life among the first and second generations of migrants from the countryside and the loss of traditional forms of social support in the absence of adequate new services in an urbanized society create a basis for the political mobilization of the low-income population. As a rule, the property owners and taxpayers who had traditionally played key roles in the European political process were not prepared for this.[10]

Some countries have demonstrated the ability to solve these problems in developing democratic institutions. A flexible and adaptable British political system managed to include the entire population in the voting pool, step by step, without a great crisis. But that was not the situation everywhere. In the second half of the nineteenth and first half of the twentieth centuries, the fear that the political mobilization of workers and peasants would lead to socialist experimentation and a redistribution of property was an important factor in the support of the middle class of authoritarian regimes.[11]

In the non-European world, which has no extensive history of authoritative parliaments or Greco-Roman tradition, guaranteeing political stability in the early stages of modern economic growth is more complicated than in northwestern Europe. The contrast is striking between the weakness of traditional regimes and the power of the West, which had moved far ahead (military defeat and imposed treaties had turned non-European states into colonies or semi-colonies). Instability undermined the legitimacy of traditional monarchies. To the educated elite it was obvious that borrowing European models of political organization was necessary for development. However, authoritarian societies had no institutions or traditions that could be used to support their transformation; there was no medieval legacy of freedom for separate groups of the population and their right to defend themselves against the arbitrariness of the ruler; there was no deep conviction in the legality of resisting his whims, which was so important in the formation of the modern concept of a free society.[12]

These obstacles were the cause of a lengthy period of instability and institutional crisis. The legitimacy of traditional ways was undermined, but new methods of organizing political life were not yet in place. These are the conditions in which violence (victory in a civil war or a coup d'état) is the means to power.

In the early 1960s, when decolonialization led to the founding of dozens of new states, many scholars felt that authoritarian forms of rule were optimal. In 1959, De Schweinitz wrote that the public's participation in political affairs had to be checked in order to achieve economic growth.[13]

As noted earlier, authoritarian regimes usually come to power through force. There are exceptions. Sometimes future autocrats come to power through democratic procedures and then use their power to suppress rights and freedoms. They can turn to state structures for their own uses, or they can use force against opponents through a lack of resistance from the state. Hitler is an example of a politician who used both strategies.

Regardless of how an authoritarian regime formed, violence plays a prominent role. As long as society is convinced that the rulers will use force against the people in order to hold on to power and suppress the opposition, the authoritarian regime can have political stability. If the regime and the public believe this, repression can be used selectively and in a limited way. Otherwise, it must be applied on a large scale. Even then, the autocrat will not be able to hold on to power for long.

The Instability of Authoritarian Regimes

Regimes that come to power through force are not stable in the long run (over decades). Discussions of whether power alone is enough to make a regime have been going on since the days of Thucydides.[14] It was obvious to Machiavelli that a regime based only on violence was unstable.[15] Rousseau thought so as well.[16]

The absence of legitimacy—that is, a clear and acceptable explanation of how the leaders of an authoritarian regime are ruling the country—is the reason for its instability. The government has neither tradition nor clear procedures to validate the legality of the regime. These are the key issues that leaders of such political constructions face.[17]

A monarch has an heir; a president or prime minister in a democratic country comes to power through understandable and accepted rules. For the majority of authoritarian regimes, establishing rules of succession is impossible. An official heir is a threat to the autocrat. The leader's death or inability to rule puts the stability of the regime at risk.

History has shown that authoritarian regimes do not last for a long time.[18] However, the period of political instability that comes from the collapse of old institutions and the absence of new ones, when monarchies are replaced by young democracies, which in turn are replaced by authoritarian regimes, can extend for centuries.

As I have already noted, the leaders of authoritarian regimes often sincerely believe that they will rule forever. But transience is characteristic of this method of power. Even when such structures are formed with support from a public that is disillusioned by incompetent and corrupt politicians who came to power by democratic means, over time they begin to be perceived by society as illegitimate, and talk turns to ways and means of restoring democratic institutions.[19] When these discussions become significant, the leader and his entourage have difficulty developing an exit strategy that will guarantee their freedom, safety, and wealth after they leave.

These circumstances are illustrated by the rule of Augusto Pinochet, one of the most effective dictators of the twentieth century, who implemented a sound economic policy that laid the foundation for the Chilean "economic miracle." On his initiative, amendments were made to the constitution that were supposed to protect him after he retired. But those protections did not work.[20]

Pinochet was not the first dictator to ponder this problem. An awareness of its urgency stimulates corruption in circles close to the top of an authoritarian regime. The instability of the situation and the unreliability of power force the ruling elite to focus on the short term. History knows of no cases of authoritarian rulers respecting property rights. Statistics demonstrate a relationship between the stability of a democratic system and the reliability of contractual rights.[21]

Authoritarian regimes construct a simple mechanism of rule. As Edmund Burke noted, however, "The simple governments are fundamentally defective, to say no worse of them."[22] The lack of checks and balances and public discussion that informs people of the decisions made under the influence of corrupt interests undermines the already fragile belief of society—and of the regime itself—in its right to govern.

One of the attempted responses to the challenges of unstable authoritarian regimes is closed, or managed, democracy. These are political systems in which formally democratic institutions and procedures are retained, but the ruling elite decides on the succession of power and controls the electoral process, predetermining its outcome. I have written about this form of political organization in an earlier work.[23] Let me simply note here that strategically this choice is a dead end. Countries that chose closed democracy in the twentieth century were forced to reject it and begin forming functioning democratic institutions. This happened in Italy, Japan, and Mexico, all considered models of this form of government.

There is another response to the challenges of unstable authoritarian regimes—the formation of a totalitarian government, which is in essence a subtype of authoritarianism.[24] Totalitarian regimes are also formed without a tradition of hereditary succession and without competitive democratic procedures. The key role in their establishment is the authorities' readiness to use unlimited force. They also impose stricter controls over daily life than what leaders of authoritarian regimes deem reasonable and promote a messianic ideology intended to legitimize the regime. In an authoritarian regime, the authorities do not want people interfering in public policy, participating in demonstrations, writing petitions, or appealing to the foreign press with exposés of the criminal regime. What they say among themselves in their kitchens does not matter. In a totalitarian regime, even telling a joke at home about the leader can land the raconteur behind bars.

Messianic ideology is a distinguishing trait of totalitarian regimes. Authoritarianism explains its necessity with prosaic arguments: the imperfection of the democratic authorities, the imperatives of dynamic economic development, the need to oppose extremism. Totalitarianism appeals to religious and pseudo-religious symbols: the thousand-year Reich, world communism, the global caliphate.

The problem with this ideological construction is that it does not fit the realities of the modern world. In light of history, it is difficult to believe in. The idea of a thousand-year Reich led to world war, collapse, and capitulation. The desire to build a world communist system led to the creation of an inefficient and unstable economy. Time will show where attempts to create a global caliphate will lead and how many lives will be lost in the process.

In order to adapt to a changing world, we must help, or at the very least not hinder, global transformation and the concomitant socioeconomic changes:

urbanization, higher educational achievement, changes in employment structures. Authoritarian regimes justify their existence by concentrating on economic development and narrowing the gap between themselves and leading states. But we have seen that the achievement of these goals still does not guarantee political stability.

Mexico in the late nineteenth and early twentieth centuries provides a characteristic example of the influence of dynamic development on the political destabilization of an authoritarian regime. In the twenty years before the 1910s, the rate of GDP growth in Mexico was high. The production of mineral raw materials and sugar rose by 400 percent, the textile industry was created, oil production developed, and metallurgical plants and railroads were built. The national currency remained stable and there were favorable conditions for foreign loans. The volume of foreign trade and tax revenues grew tenfold. But none of this stopped the revolution.[25]

Development undermines the foundations of undemocratic political systems. An authoritarian regime can be enduring in an illiterate peasant country. The society makes no demands for freedom. Only an insignificant minority is interested in it, and sometimes it even understands that freedom could mean the escalation of social demands from the poor and a zeal for redistribution to which it would fall victim. The ruling regime is supported by the army that is recruited from the peasants, who are indifferent to the ideas of the urban intellectuals. As the country industrializes and education grows, the situation changes.

Taiwan is an example of an authoritarian regime that confronted the crisis of legitimacy as the society transformed with economic modernization. By the late 1970s, Taiwan had a highly industrialized economy and was a significant exporter of high-quality technology and information technology. At that point, traditional methods of political control stopped working. Repression undermined the regime's authority and increased the popularity of opponents. Corruption became a subject of public discourse. Shutting down disloyal mass media provoked rallies and clashes between protesters and police. The conviction grew among the intelligentsia that the political system was flawed and that mechanisms had to be put in place to permit competition among political parties. Opposition associations formed in universities. Deputies who did not belong to the ruling party walked out of parliamentary sessions in protest against its arbitrary rule. In the second half of the 1980s, the regime saw that it would be impossible to retain authoritarianism. In 1987 the ruling party, the Kuomintang, had to repeal martial law and permit the other political parties to operate.[26]

The leaders of the authoritarian regime in Spain believed that the swift economic growth of the 1960s would help form a conservative society uninterested in politics. In fact, it promoted cultural, social, and political changes that undermined the regime's stability.[27]

There are elements of prosperity and quality of life that cannot be measured by a GDP index. The right to travel, to choose one's residence, to participate in solving the country's problems, to read and listen to anything one wants, and to freedom of speech are intangible goods that cannot be valued in monetary terms. As prosperity grew, so did the demand for these rights and their meaning for society.

It is difficult to explain this to people who have lived all their lives in a stable democracy. They read about freedoms and democracy in textbooks, but those rights are as natural to them as breathing. It is not hard to understand that it is important, but people do not think about it every day. I often encounter left-wing intellectuals who try to convince me that Deng Xiaoping was right in separating economic and political reforms and starting with a functioning and growing market economy instead of setting goals of political liberalization. For some reason, they take umbrage and never answer my question: for how much would you sell your freedom of speech? They must feel that they, unlike other people, are guaranteed those rights by virtue of being born in a state with a stable democracy. People who have lived in authoritarian and totalitarian regimes have an easier time understanding the freedoms that they were denied.

In countries without democratic traditions and with autocrats in power, the demand for freedom rises with development. It can be stopped only by force—the main resource of such regimes. The problem is that the ability to use force is reduced in a modernizing society.

Even in agrarian China, the use of troops in Tiananmen Square in 1989 was not an easy issue for the leaders. The Beijing garrison was considered too unreliable. The troops that quelled the protest had been brought in from the Soviet border.[28]

The collapse of the authoritarian regime in South Korea is an example of the problems that arise when such regimes are guaranteed political permanence. The collapse came after decades of economic growth at high rates.

Socioeconomic transformation leads to political mobilization among broad strata of the population, particularly the youth. Such movements undercut the authorities' ability to use force to restrain political activity.[29] Socioeconomic development is formed by urban society. Educated people understand that they are dealing with an illegitimate, undemocratic, and corrupt regime. In this situation, the active minority, ready to give anything at all to overthrow the regime, including their lives, can be organized. It is difficult to find people ready to die for the regime.

The Batista government in Cuba in the late 1950s is a typical example. The Cuban economy in the 1950s was developing rather quickly by Latin American standards. Average GDP growth per capita in Cuba between 1950 and 1957 was 2.3 percent. The regime, dealing with the challenge of domestic armed protest, took measures for self-preservation, introducing harsh censorship and empowering the secret police. Feeling endangered, Batista increased the army. People considered disloyal were routinely tortured and murdered. The army and police leadership was made up of those close to Batista, who had an interest in maintaining the status quo.

After taking care of the rebels, Batista acted energetically: armed sentries were placed around government buildings; planes and boats patrolled the coast; government troops bombed villages harboring rebels; hundreds of people were jailed. Corpses of suspected sympathizers of the enemies of the regime littered the streets.[30]

This was not enough to stop the revolutionaries. In December 1956, there had been eighty-two; after the rout only twelve survived. In the spring of 1957, journalists argued about their number: fifty or a hundred. By fall of that year, the number was a thousand. In mid-1958, there were five to ten thousand rebels.[31] The fate of the Cuban Revolution was determined not by a formal correspondence between the number of government soldiers and number of rebels, but by the fact that society considered the Batista regime corrupt and unjust.[32] Corruption charges were central to Fidel Castro's propaganda.[33]

Mechanisms of the Collapse of Authoritarianism

It is difficult to predict when the crisis will begin in an authoritarian regime. Sometimes it is slow to start, but when it does, it unfolds much faster than imagined. The leaders of authoritarian regimes often have no idea why it happens. The last shah of Iran, Mohammed Reza Pahlavi, was stunned by events in 1978, according to former U.S. ambassador to Iran William Sullivan: "What bothered him, he said, was that this intrigue went beyond the capabilities of the Soviet KGB and must therefore also involve the British and the American CIA. . . . Why was the CIA suddenly turning against him?"[34]

The mechanisms of collapse vary. Often they are related to the dictator's personal life. The stability of the political structure depends on the life or health of the autocrat who is the center of the political elite. With his death, squabbles among the ruling class can break out. The death of Chiang Kai-shek in 1975 opened the way to democracy in Taiwan; the assassination of President Park Chung Hee in October 1979 accelerated democratization in South Korea.

Sometimes the mechanism of crisis is related to military defeat. Consider the development of events in Argentina after the Falkland Islands war.

Information globalization creates instability in authoritarian regimes. Most people in the early twentieth century had only a vague idea of what was happening outside their village or what other political structures existed. Over the course of the twentieth century the world became integrated. Knowledge about the political systems of developed nations is generally accessible. There is no way to explain to people, especially young and educated ones, that their peers in other countries have the right to freedom and can participate in solving the country's problems; they do not, for it is done for them by leaders who have force on their side.

Another cause of crises that lead to the collapse of authoritarian regimes is ethnic conflict. That is why such regimes are less stable in countries that are ethnically and religiously heterogeneous.[35]

There are other variants, as well. The collapse of the shah's regime in Iran was not precipitated by military defeat, the autocrat's death, or an ethnic conflict. It occurred in a favorable oil market and while prosperity was growing. But it is most common for the collapse of an authoritarian regime to be precipitated by an economic crisis.

The world of modern economic growth is dynamic and difficult to predict. Accurate predictions of prices for raw materials or currency are beyond the capabilities of economics. Life forces people to adapt to external challenges, which are hard to foresee. The twentieth century is filled with examples of crises that neither the national authorities nor the international community had expected. This is the reality with which we must deal. Neither the International Monetary Fund nor the U.S. Treasury had expected the Mexican crises of 1994. Just as unexpected was the financial crisis of 1997–98 in Southeast Asia, which then expanded into the post-Soviet territories and Latin America.[36]

In the late 1990s, a book was written on the problems that faced oil-producing countries when the oil prices fell in the 1980s. It presented Indonesia as an example of a successful adaptation to the changing conditions in world development.[37] But before the book came out, the Indonesian regime collapsed as a result of events in Southeast Asia.[38]

In an economic crisis, the government must reduce budget spending, raise taxes, devalue the national currency, limit imports, and reduce subsidies. These are all difficult and unpopular measures. The regime must be certain that the society will accept them or that it is capable of using force to stop possible riots. The weakness of authoritarian regimes facing economic crises is that they have neither resource. It is hard to persuade a society that considers the regime illegitimate or corrupt to tighten its belt. Corruption that in prosperous times was seen as an unpleasant but inevitable phenomenon becomes a challenge to the concept of a rational and just social structure in times of crisis.

The collapse of an authoritarian regime is preceded by a period of instability, a time when the regime loses the remnants of legitimacy. In retrospect, it is easy to pinpoint its start. In Iran, for instance, it was 1970–78, when the shah's regime increased control of its secret police over daily life and repression against opposition leaders. In 1970, not a single bomb was used for political purposes. In 1972, politically motivated explosions numbered thirteen. In 1974, there were student riots and unrest stemming from food shortages in Tehran. Radical fundamentalism became more attractive from the mid-1970s. In 1977–78 mass demonstrations, accompanied by the use of force, became a characteristic of life in Iran.[39]

If an autocrat retains control over the army and police, he can suppress social unrest with the usual authoritarian methods, showing that he will shed as much blood as necessary to stay in power. But in a crisis situation, the conviction that the regime is illegitimate often extends to soldiers, sergeants, and junior officers. At a time when the dictator particularly needs loyalty, the army and police stop working.

The problems of instability in authoritarian regimes do not end with their collapse. In the absence of a legal political process and a responsible parliament that influences the public, the opposition focuses on the simplest slogans. Their essence is standard-issue: "Death to the anti-people regime!" "Justice and Redistribution!" (which means, take away everything and share it); "No to the regime of national betrayal" (radical nationalism). These slogans work well against the regime. They were used, for example, by Castro's July 26 movement in Cuba in the 1950s. Trying to embody these slogans in real life is not the best guarantee for a stable democracy, however.[40]

An authoritarian regime, for all its illegitimacy, is a functioning one. There are police on the streets maintaining order; if the country is relatively developed, children go to school; and there are hospitals. The collapse of an authoritarian regime means the end to institutions that had preserved some kind of law and order.[41] In Iraq in the summer of 2003, the debaathification decision by American authorities, which included dismissing the police and army of the regime of Saddam Hussein, did not consider the consequent need to guarantee order in the streets, a reliable electricity supply, and the safety of the property of state institutions.

That a regime's monopoly on the use of force is a key element in a stable state structure has been known at least since the publication of Max Weber's classic work *Politik als Beruf* (*Politics as a Vocation*).[42] With the collapse of an authoritarian regime, the new regime is very limited in its ability to use force to impose order. Even when the army and police structures remain, they lose their taste for continuing their own work. They are not certain how long the new regime will last or whether the old regime will return, in which case they would be punished for collaborating with the new rulers. The natural strategy is to do nothing.

Political regimes that come to replace authoritarian ones do not have historical legitimacy and traditions to ensure their permanence. That is the fundamental problem after the collapse of authoritarian regimes: there is no guarantee that permanent democratic institutions will follow.[43]

External factors play an important role in the solution of this problem. In Eastern Europe, after the Soviet Union no longer had control, the influence of the European Union and the prospect of membership in that organization, which united the communities of highly developed countries, was an important factor in stabilizing democracy. In Latin America after the end of the Cold War, when the pragmatic principle "He may be a son of a bitch, but he's our son of a bitch" fell out of favor, the influence of the United States promoted the stabilization of democratic institutions. But external factors such as these do not work in all regions of the world.

Spain is a developed European country with a long parliamentary tradition, and its political elite implemented a peaceful transformation from authoritarian regime to democracy. In 1980 it joined the European Community. Nevertheless, for almost ten years after Franco's death, the country's leadership had to deal with the difficult issues of establishing civil control over the army. The country found itself on the brink of a military coup several times.[44] This is an example of how complex the transition from authoritarianism to democracy can be even under good circumstances.

It is axiomatic in the literature devoted to postauthoritarian transitions that a successful transformation depends on the separation of politics and economics. The people must be persuaded that attempts to combine radical changes in the political system and the economic structures are untenable.[45] Unlike in other authoritarian regimes, in socialist countries the political system is inextricably tied to the organization of everyday economic life. Political instability compounds the fact that the socialist system of economic management cannot work without a totalitarian political regime. It collapses when state control over all aspects of life weakens.

CHAPTER III

THE
OIL CURSE

Better we had found water!

—Sheikh Ahmed Zaki Yamani,
FORMER OIL MINISTER OF SAUDI ARABIA

In ten or twenty years you will see that oil will lead us to collapse.

—Juan Pablo Pérez Alfonzo,
FORMER OIL MINISTER OF VENEZUELA

IN 1985–86, WORLD OIL PRICES dropped precipitously. But the USSR collapsed for other reasons, not because of speculation that oil prices would fall. The bard Bulat Okudzhava put it well in his last public appearance in Paris on June 23, 1995. He read this brief poem:

> Universal experience tells us
> That kingdoms perish
> Not because the life is hard
> Or the suffering great
> They perish because—
> And the longer it takes, the more painful it is—
> People no longer respect
> Their kingdoms.

The crisis in the Soviet economy that led to the collapse of the USSR was closely connected to developments on the oil market. Why did it happen the way it did? Naturally, first came the conspiracy theories. But I saw with my own eyes what an incredible surprise the collapse was for the American administration. I saw how stunned they were, and I do not believe any theories that place the U.S. government at the center of a conspiracy to bring down the Soviet Union.

But even if we were to accept that the collapse was "intentional," it would only make things worse. Then we would have to talk about ignorance, irresponsibility, and betrayal of national interests on the part of several generations of Soviet leaders who placed the country's economy and fate in the hands of decisions made by the United States, which was considered our primary enemy.

The USSR was not the first or only resource-rich country to encounter a severe crisis resulting from hard-to-predict changes in prices for their raw materials exports. In order to understand what happened in the Soviet Union in the late 1980s and early 1990s, we must analyze the causes of price fluctuations and how they influence the economies of exporting countries. This is a rather long story. . . .

The Spanish Prologue

Spain in the sixteenth and seventeenth centuries, after the discovery of America, provides the classic example of how revenue windfall from natural resources can affect a nation's economy. Discoveries of gold and silver deposits and the introduction of technology to extract them efficiently by contemporary standards led to an unprecedented influx of precious metals into Europe.

Over 160 years, between 1503 and 1660, 16,000 tons of silver were delivered to Seville, tripling the silver reserves in Europe. In that same period the import of 185 tons of gold increased European resources by approximately 20 percent (see figure 3-1).[1]

The growth of the gold and silver supply in the still slow-growing European economy brought sharp price increases to a society used to price stability.[2] In Spain, where the precious metals went first, prices rose faster than elsewhere in Europe (see figure 3-2). This reduced the competitiveness of Spanish agriculture. For many decades, Castile had to import food products.[3] The crisis in the Spanish textile industry was also the result of anomalously high prices in Spain, caused by the influx of precious metals from America.

In the late sixteenth century, complaints about high prices in Spain were widespread. The Cortes Generales (the Spanish legislature) discussed it frequently. The parliamentarians proposed banning the export of Spanish textiles even to the Spanish colonies in America. The high price of food products and textiles prompted measures to limit price increases, which in turn led to shortages. The liberalization of food and textile imports in Spain was inevitable.

FIGURE 3-1. Total Imports of Precious Metals to Spain, 1503–1650

Millions of pesos in constant 1580 prices

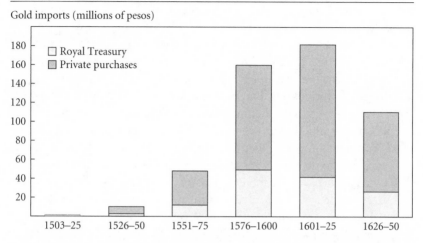

Gold imports (millions of pesos)

Source: Estimates from E.J. Hamilton, *American Treasure and the Price Revolution in Spain, 1501–1650* (Harvard University Press, 1934), p. 34. Price index from D.O. Flynn, "Fiscal Crisis and the Decline of Spain (Castile)," *Journal of Economic History* 42 (1982): 142.

FIGURE 3-2. Changing Price Levels in Spain (Castile-Leon), 1503–1650

Averages for five-year periods (1580 prices = 100 percent)

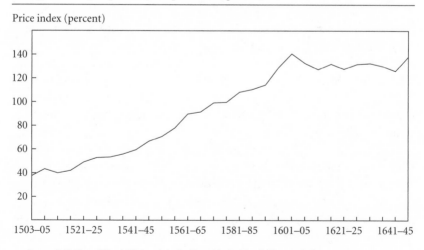

Price index (percent)

Source: D.O. Flynn, "Fiscal Crisis and the Decline of Spain (Castile)," *Journal of Economic History* 42 (1982): 142.

González de Cellorigo, in his analysis of Castile's economic problems, related them to the discovery of America. In 1600 he wrote that the influx of gold and silver had paralyzed investments, as well as the development of industry, agriculture, and trade, and maintained that the discovery of America was a misfortune for Spain.[4] The Flemish scholar Justus Lipsius wrote in 1603 to his Spanish friend, "The new world you conquered has conquered you, weakening and exhausting your former courage."[5]

The role of precious metal revenues in the budget of the Spanish crown in the middle of the sixteenth century, modest at first, increased gradually. This became obvious with the discovery and exploitation of silver in Potosi. The use of these revenues did not depend on decisions by the Cortes. The new income expanded the government's freedom of action. American gold and silver seemed a reliable guarantee for loans that international banks readily offered.

In accordance with the standards of the time, the crown spent more than half of its revenues on military needs. American gold and silver financed Spain's foreign policy activity to defend Catholicism and protect Spain's supremacy in Europe, and it paid for a number of expensive wars.

At the end of the sixteenth century, the flow of precious metals from America slowed down. By 1600, the richest silver deposits were exhausted.[6] And higher domestic prices had reduced government income and hence the Spanish budget in real terms. Besides that, the Spanish crown had taken on large debts. These circumstances led to a trail of bankruptcies, which defined Spanish finances in the second half of the sixteenth century. The state declared itself unable to pay its debts in 1557, 1575, 1598, 1607, 1636, 1647, and 1653.[7]

As often happens, the authorities responded inadequately and inappropriately to economic problems caused by fluctuations in resource income. Banning Spanish students from studying abroad, limiting trade monopolies, increasing taxes on wool exports, and imposing customs duties on the borders between parts of the kingdom were not effective ways to finance military campaigns.[8]

It had been easy to take on imperial obligations, but it was difficult to jettison them when necessary. In 1609, Spain was forced to conclude a peace agreement with Holland because of growing financial difficulties. Ten years later it became clear that this had done little to solve Spain's budget problems. Dutch operations at sea, their attacks on Spanish vessels and colonies, demanded as much spending on the armed forces as had been necessary during wartime.

The Duke of Olivares, prime minister of Spain from 1621 to 1643, a contemporary and a rival of Cardinal Richelieu, tried to implement liberal reforms (by regulating the tax system, reducing budget expenditures, and shrinking the state bureaucracy), to limit the power of the oligarchs who had access to state revenues,[9] and to restore the grandeur of the empire. He was competent, hard-working, and not corrupt. But his efforts were also insufficient to restore economic order and to finance the military action needed to preserve the empire. In 1631, realizing the impossibility of his goals, Olivares made the famous comment, "If the great conquests of this monarchy have brought it to this pitiful state, it can be said with some certainty that without the New World it would be much more powerful."[10]

By 1640 the Spanish crown had lost its European holdings outside the Pyrenean peninsula and was on the brink of losing control of Asturia, Catalonia, and Aragon. In September 1640, Olivares wrote, "This year may be considered the most disastrous for the monarchy in all its existence."[11] And yet the Spanish army did not lose a major land battle until 1643.

Spain in the sixteenth and seventeenth centuries is an example of a state that suffered no wartime defeats, but whose economy collapsed under the weight of its disproportionate ambitions, which were based on unreliable revenues from American gold and silver. The fate of twentieth-century states whose might depended on revenues from natural resources, including Russia, is well known.

Resource Wealth and Economic Development

The problems that confronted Spain in the sixteenth and seventeenth centuries were also known in the late eighteenth and early nineteenth centuries at the dawn of modern economic growth. And yet the persistent axiom was that having wealth in natural resources, supplies of minerals important for industrialization, and an abundance of arable land were positive factors in development. Twentieth-century experience showed that the correlation, alas, is more complex and dramatic.

Between 1965 and 1998, the per capita GDP in the resource-rich countries of Iran and Venezuela declined by an average of 1 percent a year, in Libya by 2 percent, in Kuwait by 3 percent, and in Qatar (1970–95) by 6 percent. Overall, between 1965 and 1998 the GDP in OPEC member states declined by 1.3 percent a year while the countries with low and medium per capita income saw an average increase of 2.2 percent a year.[12]

The past several decades have seen quite a few books on the influence of resource wealth on economic development. Defining resource wealth is not simple. Some authors define it as the percentage of raw material in export and volume of GDP, and others as the territory per resident of the country. The important point is that regardless of the definition the results of the studies are similar.[13] They demonstrate the statistically significant *negative correlation* between long-term rates of economic growth and resource wealth.[14] To put it simply, the presence of natural wealth not only does not guarantee future prosperity, but is more likely to complicate its achievement.

A typical example of many in this sad group is Nigeria. Large oil deposits were brought into production in 1965. Over the next thirty-five years, total revenue from oil, not counting payments to international oil corporations, was approximately $350 billion (in 1995 prices). In 1965 the per capita GDP was $245. In 2000, it was at the same level.[15] Scholars disagree about which factor in resource supply creates the greatest obstacle to dynamic economic growth.[16] However, the list of risks related to resource wealth is well described.[17]

Natural resources and the revenue they provide allow the authorities in a country "hanging on to God's beard" to increase their budgets *without needing to raise taxes* on the citizenry (see table 3-1).[18] That means that *there is no need* to embark on a long-term dialogue with the public—the taxpayers and their representatives. Historically, such a dialogue (which leads to compromises) is the only path to forming institutions that check the power of the authorities and guarantee rights and freedoms. That difficult dialogue establishes the rules of the game that allow the mechanism of modern economic growth to begin.[19] This is why the people of a resource-rich country have less chance than those in resource-poor nations to develop systems of checks and balances (extremely popular in Boris Yeltsin's time and now no longer in fashion) and reliable institutions to limit corruption and the arbitrariness of the authorities and bureaucracy.[20] The atmosphere is different, and so is the climate. Saltykov-Shchedrin gave a classic description of that atmosphere in one of his novels: "When the bureaucrats were dividing up the western provinces first and then the Ufa Province, we were witnesses to truly amazing phenomena. One would think, What more do you want? You've stolen your piece of the state pie. Now go away! But no, this is where we saw the full-blown squabbling, envy, hatred, and shamelessness, the main target of which—alas!—was that very affluent hand that had started the divvying up with the sole purpose of sating the gentlemen officials and, it goes without saying, laying the foundation of 'the corporation of the content.'"[21]

Assessments by international organizations of the quality of national institutions are subjective. But they all show that there is a powerful negative correlation between political freedoms, civil rights, quality of bureaucracy, and practical application of the law on one side and resource wealth on the other.[22]

TABLE 3-1. Share of Oil Income in the Total Budget Revenues of Venezuela,
Mexico, and Saudi Arabia, 1971–95

Averages for five-year periods (percent)

Country	1971–75	1976–80	1981–85	1986–90	1991–95
Venezuela	67.0	61.7	54.7	60.4	. . .
Mexico	14.9	19.0	42.7	32.6	. . .
Saudi Arabia	. . .	89.1	74.4	61.0	74.5

Source: Calculations for Mexico and Saudi Arabia are based on data from R. M. Auty, ed., *Resource Abundance and Economic Development* (Oxford University Press, 2004); for Venezuela from J. Salazar-Carrillo, *Oil and Development in Venezuela during the Twentieth Century* (Westport, Conn.: Praeger, 1994).

Decisions about the distribution of revenues generated in the economy of countries rich in resources are made by the government.[23] These decisions stimulate competition between companies, not to devise ways to improve quality and production at lower costs, but to bribe officials and increase what Anne Krueger in her classic work called "administrative rent."[24] And resource wealth increases the risk of political instability, which is related to the struggle over redistribution of revenues.[25]

Even in highly developed and democratic Norway the share of exports in GDP has remained unchanged since the discovery of oil deposits in the North Sea in 1969. The rise in oil exports in relation to GDP was offset by a decrease in other exports. Among OECD member states in that same period only one other resource-rich country showed similar development, Iceland, with fish making up half of its exports.[26]

This is a solvable problem. There are countries rich in resources that have developed taxpaying democracies that gradually transformed into democracies with universal suffrage with effective, relatively uncorrupt bureaucracies. The United States, Canada, Australia, and Norway are examples. But these are countries in which the democratic mechanism was formed over centuries and where the political institutions were efficient and strong enough to deal with the challenge of resource wealth.[27] There are states without long-standing democratic traditions that have managed to handle resource wealth effectively (Botswana, Chile, Malaysia, and Mauritius).[28] But experience shows that it is harder to create democratic institutions where the role of natural rent is large than in countries where that risk factor is absent.

The rent income from the resource sector complicates the development of other sectors of the economy. The topic is thoroughly examined in works about the decline of manufacturing after Holland's discovery of large natural gas deposits in the North Sea in the 1960s.[29] The problem came to be known as the "Dutch disease," though Holland dealt with it more successfully than most other resource-rich countries. But the term stuck. The disease could just as easily have been called Venezuelan, Nigerian, Indonesian, or (in the past few years) Russian.[30] And if we extend it to raw materials that are not fuel, the disease could be called Zambian and Zairian (copper) or Colombian (coffee).

The essence of the Dutch disease is that income from newly discovered natural resources raises the value of a nation's currency, making its manufactured goods less competitive with those of other nations.[31] When the sectors whose production and services face international competition become uncompetitive in both the domestic and foreign markets, they have to reduce production.[32] This is one source of risk in an economy that is largely dependent on fluctuations in raw materials prices.

A characteristic of resource-rich countries is insufficient attention to education. The reasons are not obvious, but many scholars relate this to the structure of employment demands made by extraction companies.[33] The problem may also be related to the psychological characteristics of the elites that develop in these countries, described by Saltykov-Shchedrin: transitory officials do not think about the future, and education is an investment in the future.

In the 1950s and early 1960s, there was a widespread perception that the most important problems for states whose economies depend on raw materials exports are connected to the long-term tendency of prices for the raw materials to fall in relation to the prices of manufactured goods. This view, based on the crisis in the world economy in the 1920s and 1930s, was widely disseminated in works published by the UN Economic Commission for Latin America and in books and articles by the famous Argentine economist Raul Prebisch.[34]

Events in the second half of the twentieth century showed that prices on the raw materials market in relation to prices for manufactured goods really do go down. But it is a slow process. The average rate of decline over a long period was approximately 1 percent per year. A more important problem is that prices for raw materials fluctuate in a wide and unpredictable range. And those fluctuations create serious problems for both exporters and importers.[35]

The well-known American economist and Nobel laureate Paul Samuelson wrote: "Economists can forecast (well, almost forecast) everything but prices." This assertion applied in particular to prices of raw materials in the second half of the twentieth century (see figures 3-3 and 3-4).

FIGURE 3-3. Change in the Real World Prices of Some Commodities,
1950–2004

Percentage change (2000 = 100 percent)

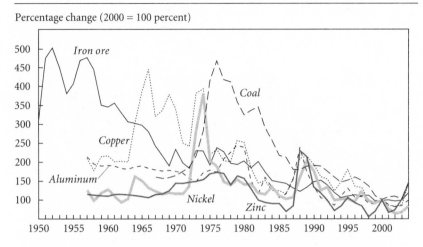

Source: International Monetary Fund, *International Financial Statistics 2005* (Washington: IMF).

FIGURE 3-4. Price Indexes in the Overall World Economy and for
Individual Commodities (1960–2004)
Ratio of nominal GDP to real GDP

Percentage change (2000 = 100 percent)

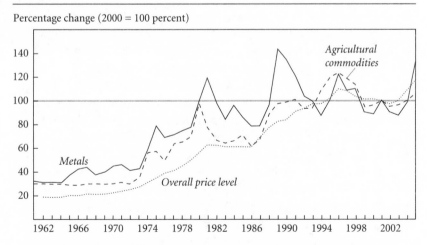

Source: Calculations based on data from International Monetary Fund, *International Financial Statistics
2005* (Washington: IMF), and from World Bank, *World Development Indicators*.

The factors that determine price fluctuations are known. Production in raw materials sectors requires a lot of capital investment, and that takes many years. Current expenses compared to capital ones are not great. Increasing production over a short period is difficult or impossible, and decreasing it is not easy from either a technological or a social viewpoint.

One factor that led to the price wars of the mid-1980s was that Saudi Arabia, having reduced oil production by almost 80 percent between 1981 and 1985, had difficulty delivering gas to its population. Lower oil production forced the state to reduce the production of natural gas, on which the communal services of the country depended. This is only one example of the myriad problems in raw materials–dependent economies.[36]

In the short term, the volumes of raw materials production are weakly linked to world prices. The demand for raw materials is tightly tied to the world economic situation. It rises with accelerating rates of world economic development and falls when they slow down.[37] Since raw materials sectors have very limited capacity for increasing and decreasing production, their prices fluctuate much more than those for manufactured goods. The data in figures 3-3 through 3-9 illustrate how powerful the influence is on the dynamics of raw materials prices of even an insignificant deceleration in the development of the world economy.

The equally hard-to-predict changes in the world's climate also influence the raw materials market.[38] What happens in the commodities markets affects global development. From the early 1970s, oil price changes had a greater influence on the world economy than exchange rate fluctuations.[39] Resource-rich countries have to solve problems caused by severe and unpredictable fluctuations in prices of the commodities they export and on which their financial situation depends. Increases in prices of raw materials affect the world economy more than decreases.[40] But that is small comfort to exporting countries.

Price volatility that is connected with world events affects the problems of raw materials sectors. Technical advances and new production methods change the volume of demand. Classic examples of this are the mass introduction of materials to replace copper in the second half of the twentieth century[41] and the increase in demand for palladium caused by the demand for cleaner emissions in the car industry.

Predicting the discovery of new deposits that are easier to work than those in existing sites is not simple. New mines may also lead to the risk of falling prices. But the world is not insured against the possibility that new deposits will not be found for decades, in which case shortages will lead to long-term price increases.

FIGURE 3-5. Changes in Average Annual Prices for Copper on the London Stock Exchange, 1965–75

Cents per pound in constant 1957 U.S. dollars

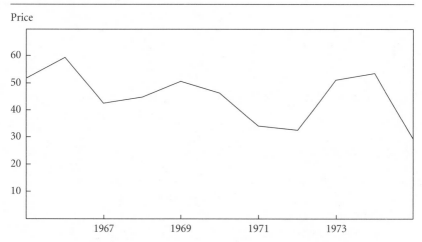

Source: R. F. Mikesell, *The World Copper Industry: Structure and Economic Analysis* (Johns Hopkins University Press, 1979).

Another factor in the instability of raw materials markets is their dependence on politics. An example is the copper market in the late 1940s and early 1950s. The outbreak of the Korean War and the growing needs of the military-industrial complex led to greater demand for that metal. Because it was impossible to increase copper production quickly, prices jumped in the early 1950s and fell again after the war (see figures 3-5, 3-6).

With the onset of the 1973 Arab-Israeli War, oil prices rose to unprecedented heights. The war was more an excuse for than a cause of this. The situation in the world oil industry had changed radically in the previous ten to twenty years. The international oil companies had lost their power to set the terms of work, and the real rights of the oil-producing countries had grown. The 1973 crisis was the trigger on a loaded rifle.

Within a few years after the events associated with the war, against the backdrop of growing unrest in Iran, oil production in that country dropped from 5.5 million barrels a day (mbd) in October 1978 to 2.4 mbd. In January, after the arrival of Ayatollah Khomeini in Iran and the overthrow of the shah, oil production declined to 0.5 mbd.[42] After the establishment of the new regime and the restoration of a semblance of order in April–July 1979, output leveled off at 3.9 mbd, significantly less than in the period of stability

FIGURE 3-6. Monthly Changes in Current Global Prices of Nonferrous Metals, 1978–84

January 1978 = 100 percent

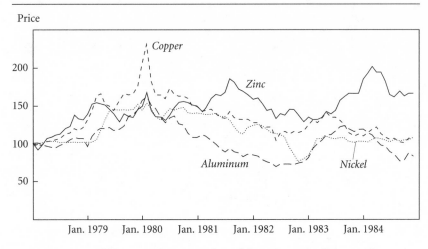

Source: International Monetary Fund, *International Financial Statistics 2004* (Washington: IMF).

FIGURE 3-7. Rate of Growth of the World Economy, 1978–84

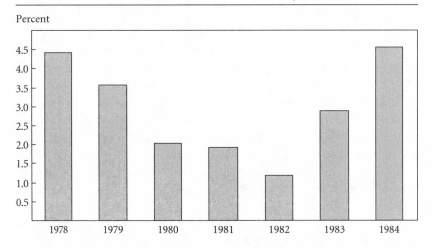

Source: Calculations based on A. Maddison, *The World Economy: Historical Statistics* (Paris: OECD, 2004).

FIGURE 3-8. Monthly Changes in Current Global Prices of Nonferrous
Metals, 1988–95
January 1988 = 100 percent

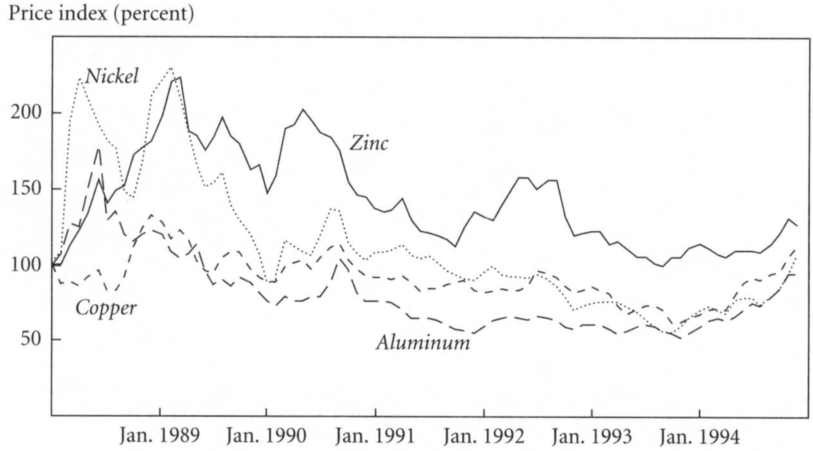

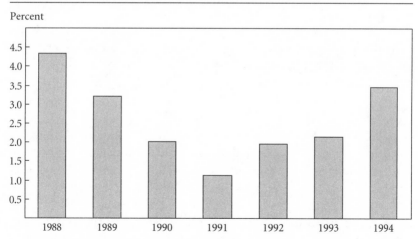

Source: International Monetary Fund, *International Financial Statistics 2004* (Washington: IMF).

FIGURE 3-9. Rate of Growth of the World Economy, 1988–94

Source: Calculations based on A. Maddison, *The World Economy: Historical Statistics* (Paris: OECD, 2004).

FIGURE 3-10. Monthly Changes in Current Global Prices of Oil, 1979–81

U.S. dollars per barrel[a]

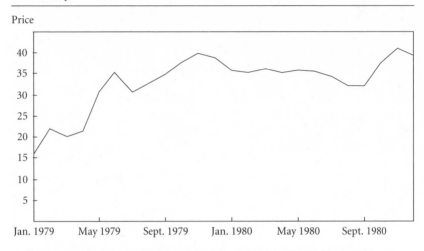

Source: International Monetary Fund, *International Financial Statistics 2004* (Washington: IMF).
a. Here and elsewhere the data are based on average weighted global prices of crude oil.

under the shah (5.7 million barrels a day in 1977).[43] When the Iran-Iraq War began in 1980, both countries had to reduce oil production. World prices multiplied.

Many observers assumed that prices had reached a new level and would remain there. This error was an expensive one for oil-producing countries, including the USSR. In the mid-1980s it became clear that the prices in 1979–81 were based on temporary circumstances. In 1985–86, they fell steeply (see figures 3-10 and 3-11). That would have been impossible to foresee in 1981.

In countries where the commodity accounts for a limited share of the country's economy, price fluctuations create problems for individual sectors. But there are quite a few states whose economies depend strongly on what happens in commodities markets (see table 3-2).

With quickly and unpredictably changing prices, even the fundamental index of the state of the economy, the per capita GDP, fluctuates within a very large range. The influence of the unstable commodities market on budget revenues is stronger.[44] We know that the state revenues derived from higher oil prices cannot be considered stable. Oil prices are volatile, and events not connected to the economy can radically change their level. Hence the extremely important task for oil-producing countries: to prevent situations where the

FIGURE 3-11. Monthly Changes in Current Global Prices of Oil, 1985–86
U.S. dollars per barrel

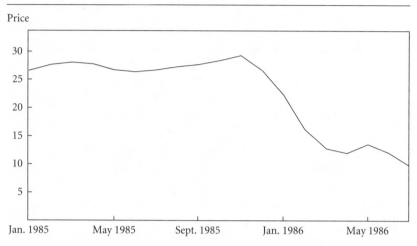

Source: International Monetary Fund, *International Financial Statistics 2004* (Washington: IMF).

discharge of budgetary obligations and the preservation of financial stability depends on the dynamics of a hard-to-predict parameter that no one can control. In a favorable market, it is easy to increase budget expenditures. When the market changes, it is not easy to reduce them.

In diversified market economies that face a financial crisis, stabilization programs are rarely designed to reduce expenditures by more than 10 percent in real terms. The implementation of such programs requires courage and a willingness to pay for the decisions needed to stabilize the national economy.

TABLE 3-2. Share of Oil Exports in the Total Exports of Selected
Oil Exporters, 1971–90
Averages for five-year periods (percent)

Country	1971–75	1976–80	1981–85	1986–90
Venezuela	90.9	85.4	81.3	80.9
Iran	77.5	85.0	85.0	92.5
Iraq	91.1	91.4	97.3	89.8
Nigeria	85.6	92.3	95.7	89.5
Mexico	3.7	21.9	55.7	20.5

Source: Calculations are based on data from J. Salazar-Carrillo, *Oil and Development in Venezuela during the Twentieth Century* (Westport, Conn.: Praeger, 1994); B. R. Mitchell, *International Historical Statistics: The Americas 1750–1993* (London: Macmillan Reference, 1998); World Bank, *World Development Indicators,* online data.

Governments in this position usually pay a high political price. But in countries that depend on the production and export of raw materials, when rent revenues fall by many times, problems on a different scale appear.[45]

When world market conditions are favorable, the producing countries have access to international financial markets. They often attract large-scale foreign loans, which they then try to use to force economic development and begin to launch large-scale investment projects. But when market conditions change, the credits that were formerly so easily available become prohibitively expensive and sometimes disappear entirely. It becomes impossible to take out new loans to refinance the old ones. The borrowed funds have to be repaid out of a budget whose revenues have shrunk as a result of falling commodity prices.

In an unfavorable world market, a resource-rich country risks a budget crisis, balance of payments problems, reductions in hard-currency reserves, and the inability to service and repay foreign debt. There are many examples of this turn of events in economic history. The change in public sentiment in these circumstances often leads to change in the political regime. It can happen in various ways: political liberalization in Mexico, a coup in Nigeria, civil war in Algeria, a crisis of democracy in Venezuela.

Oil in this regard is not unique. Copper, which is key for Chile, Papua New Guinea, Zaire, and Zambia, is the second-largest raw material commodity after oil on the world market, and its volatility offers quite a few surprises to the exporting countries. But oil has a greater significance for the world economy.

Specifics of the Oil Market

Oil is an unusual commodity. In the production of other mineral resources, the difference between the average cost of production in regions rich in deposits and the price on world markets—the economic rent—as a rule over a long period of time has not been as high and as persistent as it is in the oil sector.[46] Normally, price and output dynamics are determined by the behavior of the market's highest-cost producers. It is their decision to increase output when prices are high and decrease it when prices are low—when their activity becomes loss-making—that determines prices and levels of output. But it is different on the oil market. Countries with the lowest operating costs have in the past few decades been ready to reduce production in bad times and increase it in good.[47]

The most sensible thing I have had the occasion to hear on the subject of oil prices comes from Professor Anne Krueger, based on a wealth of experience and common sense. In her opinion, when the majority of market actors

FIGURE 3-12. Long-Term Historical Changes in Crude Oil Prices, 1880–2004

U.S. dollars per barrel in year 2000 constant dollars

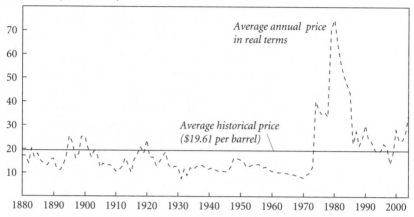

Source: Calculations based on International Monetary Fund, *International Financial Statistics 2004*, IMF; Energy Efficiency and Renewable Energy Website, U.S. Department of Energy (www.eere.energy.gov).
Note: Here and elsewhere (unless indicated otherwise) calculation of year 2000 prices is done using the U.S. GDP deflator.

believe that oil prices will remain high for only a short period, that is what happens. When the opinion predominates that prices have reached a new, stable level and will stay there for a long time, they fall. The prospect of a lengthy period of high prices stimulates consumers to reduce consumption. Producers can then profitably increase investments and production. When oil prices fall, the picture is reversed. The long-term dynamic in oil prices in real terms is shown in figure 3-12.

Regulating the Oil Market in the Twentieth Century

The oil market in the twentieth century was never fully free or strictly regulated. The 1928 agreement in Achnacarry, Scotland, divided the market among the seven largest international vertically integrated companies (Standard Oil Company of New Jersey, Texaco, Royal Dutch/Shell, Mobil Oil, Gulf Oil, British Petroleum, and Compagnie Française des Petroles), combining research, extraction, refining, and sales. It defined the rules of the game for decades.

The world then still lived by the laws typical of the early phases of modern economic growth. The right of the strong prevailed. "Cannon diplomacy" guaranteed access to raw material resources in less-developed and militarily poor countries and the ability to impose terms that benefited the international companies.[48] Vertically integrated companies do not care whether they profit from extraction, refining, or sales of oil products. They care about increasing their market share and do not worry excessively over the size of the royalty paid to the governments of oil-producing states. Their financial obligations to the countries with oil are not determined by their income from refining and sales of fuel. Hence the stimulus is to keep crude oil prices low because the greatest profit comes from refining and sales. The practice of transfer pricing, well known from the Russian scandals in the 1990s and early 2000s, is not the invention of red directors and oligarchs. It has all been seen before.

In the 1950s and 1960s, oil corporations competed to be first to lower prices on oil below the agreed price in order to attract consumers. The Soviet Union entered the world oil market during this period and tried to increase its share by dumping. In its contracts for barter supply of oil to Western Europe, particularly to Italy, Soviet oil prices were approximately half of international rates in the 1960s. It is hard to tell whether the low prices were intended to support the communist movement or outright dumping. But the backstory did not interest international oil companies. The practice itself lowered oil prices.[49]

After World War II, the era of empires, colonial and semi-colonial states, and cannon diplomacy receded into the past. Things that were acceptable a century earlier became untenable in the changed world. The return of Iran's oil resources to the control of British Petroleum, which was forced to share its ownership with the Americans, harked back to a vanishing era. After the failure of the Franco-British operation in the Suez in 1956, it became clear that the threat of force against oil-producing countries that wanted to increase their share in oil profits or to nationalize oil production was minimal. In the subsequent fifteen years the role of governments of oil-producing states grew in every aspect of that sector. After the 1950s, step by step, they improved the terms of their contracts with international corporations. A milestone on that path was Venezuela's agreement to share profits equally with oil companies. These terms became the norm over time.[50]

Countries with oil resources had to develop a common position in their dialogue with international corporations, sharing their experiences in order to evaluate the situation. The creation of OPEC, an organization that allowed that dialogue to expand, helped countries to institutionalize their interaction and coordinate their efforts. OPEC was created in September 1960 by representatives of Iran, Iraq, Kuwait, Saudi Arabia, and Venezuela. Qatar joined in 1961, Indonesia and Libya in 1962, the Arab Emirates in 1967, Algeria in 1969,

Nigeria in 1971, Ecuador in 1973, and Gabon in 1974. In its early years, OPEC was a consultative organization. It did not conduct negotiations with oil companies on its own behalf.

The agreements made by OPEC members were intended to improve contract terms and were predicated on coordinated changes in export prices, expanded oil refining, and the creation of national companies.[51] In 1968, OPEC developed its Oil Policy Guidelines. The organization demanded that the states have a share in the oil companies, the opportunity to perform geological studies and oil extraction, and the right to control declared prices. The measures passed in 1970–73 to implement these principles changed the balance of power in the oil sector.[52] By the end of the 1960s, OPEC had managed to keep companies from lowering oil prices below official prices.[53]

The level of prices in the early 1970s was historically low, reflecting the former relationships in the sector.[54] By then, oil reserves in the United States had fallen and the demand for imported oil was growing. America could no longer regulate the world oil market. In March 1971, America began producing at 100 percent of capacity.[55] Between 1967 and 1973, imported oil as a share of total consumption rose from 19 percent to 36 percent.[56] In April 1973, the U.S. government ended the system of quotas on imported oil.[57] The transformation of the United States into a net importer of oil strengthened the position of the oil producers.[58]

An extremely important factor in determining the development of the markets was the weakening of U.S. fiscal policy. In the 1960s, the United States had taken on massive obligations in social programs and at the same time had to finance the war in Vietnam. This changed the world state of affairs. Prices for raw materials began to grow before the oil price hike in 1973.[59]

On October 17, 1973, the Arab producers agreed to reduce their oil production and exports. Saudi Arabia, the largest producer in the Arab world, announced that it was reducing production by 10 percent and introducing an embargo on oil to the United States. On November 22, 1973, Saudi Arabia warned the United States that if it did not stop supporting Israel, Saudi Arabia was prepared to reduce production by 80 percent, and if the United States tried to use force, Saudi Arabia would blow up its oil wells.[60] With that, the price hike to adjust the anomalously low levels in the 1960s and early 1970s was a fait accompli.

Between 1970 and 1974 OPEC revenues jumped 1,100 percent. As one of the finance ministers of OPEC wrote, oil-producing countries made more money in those years than they ever dreamed possible. Iraq's oil export revenues rose from $1 billion in 1972 to an annual rate of $33 billion

FIGURE 3-13. Changes in Average Monthly Global Oil Prices, 1972–74[a]

U.S. dollars per barrel in year 2000 constant dollars

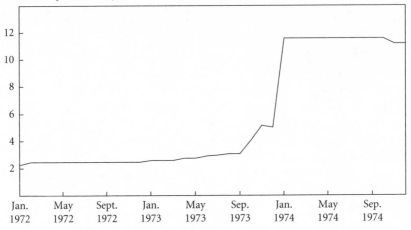

Source: International Monetary Fund, *International Financial Statistics 2004* (Washington: IMF, 2004).
a. In year 2000 dollars the price of oil in 1972 was $8.08.

in the month preceding the outbreak of the Iran-Iraq War.[61] The flow of petrodollars to producer countries gave rise to hopes for steady growth in prosperity and faith that their dreams of national grandeur could be realized. Their leaders assumed that they would be able to finance the development of other sectors with oil revenues (see figure 3-13).[62]

The peak of OPEC's influence was the period 1973–81. At that time, many analysts thought that the organization had unlimited power to regulate the volume of production and oil prices and that further cost increases were inevitable.[63] The oil-consuming countries instituted energy-conserving policies, having already dealt with a price hike in 1973 and the concomitant inflation and deceleration of economic growth (see table 3-3).

OPEC's share in the world oil trade grew smaller. Higher prices stimulated oil exploration in less accessible sites. OPEC did not have mechanisms to apply sanctions against members who were producing over the agreed limit.

The slowdown in world development in 1981–82 reduced oil demand (see table 3-4). This joined the instability of speculative price increases with the start of the Iran-Iraq War. OPEC faced a difficult choice for the first time since 1973. If its members continued increasing production, prices would crash. To maintain the price level, they had to reduce production. But that meant

TABLE 3-3. Changes in the Energy Intensity of GDP in Germany, Japan, Great Britain, France, and the United States, 1975–85
Percentage change from the previous year

Year	France	Germany	Japan	Great Britain	United States
1971	0.1	. . .	0.1	−0.2	−1.1
1972	1.2	−0.4	−1.4	−2.7	−0.6
1973	2.1	1.2	3.9	−3.2	−2.0
1974	−6.1	−2.3	1.7	−2.5	−1.8
1975	−5.1	−3.5	−8.0	−4.4	−2.0
1976	2.2	2.7	2.1	−0.7	1.3
1977	−4.9	−2.7	−2.5	−0.3	−1.2
1978	1.8	0.4	−4.3	−3.6	−2.7
1979	0.8	0.3	0.2	2.3	−3.3
1980	−1.8	−3.7	−5.0	−6.6	−3.5
1981	−3.4	−3.5	−5.3	−2.1	−5.2
1982	−4.9	−2.6	−2.5	−2.3	−2.2
1983	1.1	−1.5	−1.5	−3.6	−4.2
1984	1.9	1.0	4.3	−2.6	−2.7
1985	3.5	1.0	−4.7	2.1	−2.9

Source: Calculations based on data from World Bank, *World Development Indicators.*

lowering OPEC's share of the world market. Companies not involved with OPEC would use the cartel's problems to increase their share in the world oil trade (see tables 3-5 and 3-6). On February 17, 1983, the British National Oil Company lowered the price for oil from the North Sea by $3 a barrel. OPEC member Nigeria, whose oil competes with British and Norwegian oil, was forced to follow. The USSR also joined the race to lower oil prices.

TABLE 3-4. Oil Consumption per Unit of GDP in Germany, Japan, Great Britain, France, and the United States, 1970–85
Barrels per thousand dollars

Year	France	Germany	Japan	Great Britain	United States
1970	1.15	. . .	0.77	1.06	1.44
1975	1.13	1.03	0.75	0.87	1.39
1980	0.97	0.91	0.65	0.72	1.21
1985	0.69	0.74	0.50	0.61	0.96

Source: U.S. Energy Information Administration (www.eia.doe.gov/emeu/international/petroleu.html); World Bank, *World Development Indicators.*

TABLE 3-5. Oil Production in Great Britain, Norway, and Mexico, 1973–85
Thousands of barrels per day

Year	Great Britain	Norway	Mexico
1973	2	32	465
1974	2	35	571
1975	12	189	705
1976	245	279	831
1977	768	280	981
1978	1,082	356	1,209
1979	1,568	403	1,461
1980	1,622	528	1,936
1981	1,811	501	2,313
1982	2,065	520	2,748
1983	2,291	614	2,689
1984	2,480	697	2,780
1985	2,530	788	2,745

Source: U.S. Energy Information Administration (www.eia.doe.gov/emeu/international/petroleu.html).

The end of the war between Iran and Iraq and their desire to reestablish the share of the market they had in the mid-1970s were factors that led to the price war of 1985–86. Saudi Arabia had the largest oil reserves. Production costs were low. In 1981–85, when it became clear that the price level reached in 1979–81 was not stable, the Saudis became the main operators on the market: they were ready to reduce production to maintain prices, compensating for other OPEC nations that had exceeded their quotas, the reduced world demand, and increased production by non-OPEC members.

TABLE 3-6. Share of OPEC Members in Global Oil Production
and Trade, 1973–85
Percent

Year	Share of OPEC in global oil production	Share of OPEC in global oil exports
1973	55.4	86.1
1975	50.5	83.3
1980	44.4	75.6
1985	28.5	51.2

Source: OPEC, *Annual Statistical Bulletin 2004* (2005), pp. 22, 34.

Despite this, oil prices went down in the first quarter of 1981. At first this process was slow. The price was $31.76 in 1982, $28.67 in 1983. By 1984–85 it had reached $27 (in current prices).[64] By 1985, Saudi Arabia had reduced its production to 2.5 million barrels a day, almost one-quarter its 1981 levels.[65]

In March 1983, OPEC decided to lower the official price from $34 to $29 a barrel. An estimate of the real market price for oil in 1983–85 is complicated by currency fluctuations. In 1983 the oil price in dollars fell, but it was stable in European currencies.[66] In 1985, the dropping oil prices were an obvious factor in the development of the world economy.

On September 13, 1985, Oil Minister Yamani of Saudi Arabia announced that his country would not lower oil production any further and would begin increasing it.[67] The more than threefold production increase in Saudi Arabia in 1985–86 radically changed the market. Oil producers competed to lower prices in order to maintain their market share (see figure 3-14).

In 1986, prices fell to an unprecedented low for the previous decade—less than $10 a barrel in prices at that time.[68] Between 1980 and 1986, oil production revenues (in real terms) fell by 64.5 percent in Venezuela and by 76.1 percent in Indonesia. Oil-producing countries had to cut their state expenditures sharply.[69]

FIGURE 3-14. Quarterly Changes in Oil Prices, 1985–1986, in Comparison with the Average Historical Level

U.S. dollars per barrel in year 2000 constant dollars

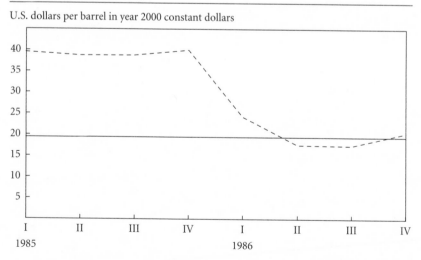

Source: International Monetary Fund, *International Financial Statistics 2004* (Washington: IMF, 2004).

By late 1986, OPEC members understood that an agreement on pricing discipline and production levels was needed; the alternative was an economic crash. A semblance of order was restored to the market. In December 1986, OPEC made an unprecedented decision to reduce oil production in order to restore prices. Production was reduced to 15.8 million barrels a day,[70] the lowest level in the organization's history. In the late 1980s, oil prices began returning to average levels. However, OPEC's peak of influence was behind it, as much in the past as the influence of international oil corporations. After this moment, there were no structures that could determine what would happen on the oil market. Prices fluctuated widely (see table 3-7).

Until 2000, the sharp declines and rises in prices caused by political events (the Persian Gulf War) or financial shocks (the crisis in Southeast Asia) led only to short-term deviations in the average prices over many years (see figures 3-15 and 3-16).

TABLE 3-7. Change in Global Oil Prices, 1986–2005

Dollars per barrel in year 2000 constant prices

Year	Average price
1986	19.9
1987	24.9
1988	19.5
1989	22.8
1990	28.2
1991	22.9
1992	22.0
1993	19.0
1994	17.7
1995	18.7
1996	21.7
1997	20.2
1998	13.6
1999	18.4
2000	28.2
2001	23.8
2002	24.0
2003	27.3
2004	34.6
2005, 1Q	41.6
2005, 2Q	45.5

Source: International Monetary Fund, *International Financial Statistics 2005* (Washington: IMF, 2005).

FIGURE 3-15. Quarterly Changes in Oil Prices in 1990–91 in Comparison
with the Average Historical Level

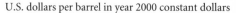

U.S. dollars per barrel in year 2000 constant dollars

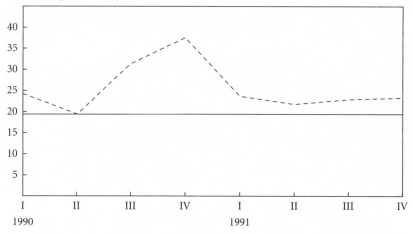

Source: International Monetary Fund, *International Financial Statistics 2004* (Washington: IMF, 2004).

FIGURE 3-16. Quarterly Changes in Oil Prices in 1997–99, in Comparison
with the Average Historical Level

U.S. dollars per barrel in year 2000 constant dollars

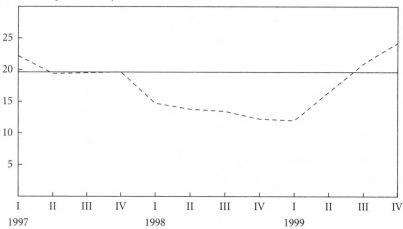

Source: International Monetary Fund, *International Financial Statistics 2004* (Washington: IMF, 2004).

Challenges Related to Price Fluctuations of Commodities: Mexico and Venezuela

Events in Mexico and Venezuela since the early 1970s illustrate the problems caused by fluctuating oil revenues in oil-producing countries. Venezuela and Mexico at that time were states with a per capita GDP comparable to that of the USSR (see table 3-8).

Oil, an important component in the structure of the economy in the early twentieth century, did not play a key role in the Mexican economy in 1970. Oil production was approximately 70 million barrels a day. The economic growth of the 1950s–70s was not related to oil. Venezuela in the early 1970s was one of the biggest oil producers in the world. Oil revenues were essential for balance of payments and budget revenues. But here, too, in the decades preceding the price jumps in 1973–81, production in non-oil sectors was growing fast.

For decades, Mexico had been a politically closed democracy. Venezuela until the early 1990s was one of the few stable democracies in Latin America. The Ministries of Finance in both countries had a good reputation. For many years they were led by people who understood the risks related to unpredictable commodity prices.

The jump in oil prices in 1973–74 coincided with the discovery of new large deposits in Mexico.[71] In the second half of the 1970s, oil production went up and so did budget revenues (see table 3-9). By 1970 the oil sector represented 2.5 percent of Mexico's GDP and produced 3.5 percent of the federal revenues. By 1983 the sector's share of GDP had risen to 14 percent.[72] In 1974 oil was approximately 0.5 percent of export revenues in Mexico, and in 1980 oil and gas made up 67.3 percent of the country's exports. The share of manufacturing exports fell to 16.5 percent.[73]

Greater revenues from oil exports combined with the crisis of industrialization that replaced imports and the slowdown in the Mexican economy in

TABLE 3-8. GDP per Capita in Mexico, Venezuela, and the USSR, 1970
International dollars in 1990 prices

Country	GDP per Capita
Venezuela	10,672
Mexico	4,320
USSR	5,575

Source: Calculations are based on A. Maddison, *The World Economy: Historical Statistics* (Paris: OECD, 2004).

TABLE 3-9. Changes in Oil Production and Its Share in Government Income in Mexico, 1975–85

Year	Average annual oil production (thousands of barrels per day)	Oil proceeds as a share of total budget revenues (percent)
1975	705	14
1976	831	14
1977	981	15
1978	1,209	17
1979	1,461	21
1980	1,936	27
1981	2,313	31
1982	2,748	40
1983	2,689	51
1984	2,780	48
1985	2,745	44

Source: *EIA International Petroleum Monthly* (www.eia.doe.gov/emeu/ipsr/supply.html); R. M. Auty, ed., *Resource Abundance and Economic Development* (Oxford University Press, 2004).

the first half of the 1970s. José López Portillo, who became president in 1976, decided to use the oil revenues to speed up the development of the national economy.[74] Mexico embarked on a series of large-scale investment projects. Because of the limited abilities to use the oil revenues and the inefficiency of the government apparatus, many of the projects were substandard or never completed.[75]

State expenditures as a share of GDP, which in the late 1960s was 20 percent, approached 50 percent by 1982. Investments financed by oil and foreign loans grew at a rate of approximately 20 percent in 1978–81, and the GDP growth rate was 8.4 percent.[76] If this economic policy had been sustainable, GDP would have doubled in ten years. But experience showed once again that attempts to speed up rates of growth, using means that are dangerous for long-term stable development, end up costing the economy and the society dearly.

The government increased its foreign debt. Creditors, certain that high oil prices were a guarantee for their investments, offered loans. In 1981 Mexico's foreign debt in the state sector was $40 billion and $20 billion in the private sector.[77]

By the early 1980s, Mexico's oil income was approximately 20 percent of GDP. The leadership was convinced that the rise in oil prices in 1979–81 reflected long-term tendencies and that they would not fall for many years.[78]

In 1981 the Mexican government adopted an even more aggressive financial policy based on the assumption that over the medium term oil revenues would grow 12 percent a year.[79] As so often happens, this decision was made at the worst possible time.

The situation changed in 1981–82. Prices stopped going up. U.S. efforts to control inflation and interest rate hikes made servicing foreign debt more expensive all over the world, including in Mexico. Uncertainty about its ability to pay back the national debt stimulated capital flight. In February 1982 the Mexican government was forced into a 70 percent devaluation of the peso. This move exacerbated the debt problem. The authorities took a series of dangerous steps: they introduced a system of dual currency exchange, refused to pay back loans, increased controls on currency movement, and nationalized the banks. These events took place against a background of falling oil prices.[80]

Starting in 1983, the government tried to stabilize its finances by halting uncompleted investment projects, raising taxes, and reducing budget obligations. Meanwhile, oil prices went even lower. Hence began the series of started and unfinished stabilization programs and the halt in economic growth. The average yearly growth rate of per capita GDP in Mexico in the 1980s was negative (−0.54 percent).[81]

On the eve of the discovery of new petroleum deposits, Mexico had been a country with a market economy integrated into the global financial world. The consequences of López Portillo's policies were felt quickly. The authorities managed to retain political stability, but the crisis of the 1980s made it impossible for Mexico to remain a closed democracy.

Venezuela, with decades of experience in the oil market, as one of the founding members of OPEC, and with a stabilization fund, was better prepared to deal with the challenges of managing revenues from higher oil prices. The government understood the role of oil in the country's economy (see table 3-10).

TABLE 3-10. Share of Oil Exports in the Total Exports of Venezuela, 1971–90
Averages for five-year periods (percent)

	1971–75	1976–80	1981–85	1986–90
Oil exports				
Share of oil exports in total exports	90.9	85.4	81.3	80.9

Source: Calculations are based on data from J. Salazar-Carrillo, *Oil and Development in Venezuela during the Twentieth Century* (Westport, Conn.: Praeger, 1994); B. R. Mitchell, *International Historical Statistics: The Americas 1750–1993* (London: Macmillan Reference, 1998).

Right after the jump in prices in 1973, Venezuela implemented a cautious budget policy and did not permit a swift strengthening of the national currency. However, it is even more difficult in a democracy than in an authoritarian regime to withstand the wave of populism that arises with greater budget revenues. A great number of ideas developed on how to use oil income. The colorful populist Carlos Andrés Pérez won the election in 1974 with such a platform. He began a large number of investment projects based on the idea of diversifying Venezuela's economy and improving the infrastructure. The state's social obligations increased and taxes on non-oil sectors were reduced. But changes in the world situation in the mid-1980s made this policy untenable.

Between 1950 and 1980 the per capita GDP in Venezuela grew by 234 percent. Between 1980 and 1989 it shrank by 18.1 percent. The national currency, which had been relatively stable for decades, fell tenfold in that period. By 1989 the annual inflation rate was 84 percent. The foreign debt, which was practically nonexistent in 1974, was 54 percent of the GDP in 1989, equaling the country's exports for three years. In the sixty years preceding 1980, the average growth of productivity in nonpetroleum sectors was 6.7 percent. Between 1920 and 1979 the average annual per capita growth in GDP was 6.4 percent. In the twenty years after 1980, productivity in nonpetroleum sectors fell. By the late 1990s it had reached 1950 levels. In 1978, Venezuela's credit rating was AAA. In 1983 it announced it would cease paying its foreign debt.[82]

After several years of belt-tightening policies, the voters returned Pérez to the presidency in 1989. They associated a period of prosperity with him, when oil prices were high. But the situation had changed. The president himself knew that the only option was a strict budgetary policy. He said that if the government expenditures were not sharply curtailed, the country would face a budget crisis.[83] This was not what people had expected from him. The attempted coup in 1992, led by Hugo Chavez, ended the period of stability in Venezuelan democracy. Like many other countries, Venezuela illustrates the difficulties resource-rich states have in dealing with the challenges created by commodity price fluctuations.

In Search of a Way Out: A Response to the Dangers of Unstable Commodity Pricing

That the supply of raw materials and their prices are unstable is not news. Many resource-rich countries have grappled with the issue. Hedging risks and signing forward/futures contracts is one possibility, rational from an economic point of view but politically dangerous. When the pricing dynamic is better than what was presumed in the futures contracts, it is hard to explain to the public why the budget has shortfalls. There will always be populist politicians who claim that the government entered into a contract with the intention of harming the national economy.[84]

This does not mean that these questions are insoluble. The most wide-spread measure for regulating the problems stemming from price instability is creating stabilization funds to which deposits are made in good times and which are used when prices fall.[85]

By the late 1970s the Chilean balance of payments and the state budget were strongly dependent on copper prices. In 1976 the revenues from copper exports covered more than 50 percent of government expenditures. In the 1980s this share was still high (approximately 40 percent). Before the start of the 1990s, payments from the state copper company represented 20 percent of the budget revenues. Nevertheless, the Chilean government rejected large-scale investment projects that would diversify the economy. Instead, it created institutional bases for developing competitive products in the non-copper sector, formed a well-managed stabilization fund, did not permit a sharp strengthening of the national currency, and ensured conditions for economic growth that were unprecedented in twentieth-century Latin America.

The management of the Norwegian stabilization fund is considered exem-plary and is emulated by other resource-rich countries. The fund in Alaska, the Kuwaiti Reserve Fund, the Fund for Future Generations, and the State Reserve Fund in Oman are similar institutions.[86] The motivation for creating such funds is obvious: the governments understand the scale and seriousness of risks related to unstable budgetary revenues in resource-rich states.

There are two types: funds to protect the country's economy from price fluctuations, and funds for future generations, created to support prosperity when the resources are depleted. Sometimes their functioning is legislated by a formula that establishes the scale of withdrawals in accordance with export prices. In other cases, the deposits are determined with each annual budget. A stabilization fund is an effective instrument for regulating the risks of price instability. But its utility should not be overestimated.[87]

Stabilization funds are limited when it comes to strengthening the real exchange rate of the national currency and the concomitant problems of developing other sectors. The growth of financial reserves invested in highly liquid and reliable international funds raises the investment attractiveness of national securities and stimulates an influx of short-term capital.

However, the political contradictions in the functioning of stabilization funds are very marked. In nondemocratic states (which many resource-rich countries are) there is a great risk that money will be invested in ineffective projects financed by the state. Much of it is embezzled. The history of the Nigerian stabilization fund is a classic example.[88]

In democratic countries the large financial resources of stabilization funds complicate the necessary limits on budget obligations required in view of price instability. The competent and responsible minister of finance in Venezuela said in October 1978: "The most important weapon of a minister of finance who gets numerous budget requests is his ability to say 'There is no money'; but how can I say that when there is so much money available?"[89] It is difficult but not impossible to say there is no money to heads of agencies that spend budget monies, political lobbies, and parliament members. It is much harder to prove that it should not be done because it will strengthen the real exchange of the national currency, which in turn will undermine the competitiveness of other sectors, which will create obligations that cannot be met if the commodity market goes down.

Norway is a country that uses its oil revenues wisely and responsibly. Twenty years after the discovery of its North Sea deposits in 1969, it maintained a lower share of state revenues in the GDP than Denmark, Finland, and Sweden.[90] The Norwegian stabilization fund is known to be transparent and well managed. However, since it was established, no ruling coalition has ever been reelected.

The rhetoric about the government sitting on pots of money and refusing to solve important social issues is a powerful weapon in politics. In early September 2005, the United Nations Organization called Norway the country with the highest standard of living. This did not help the ruling coalition get reelected. The opposition campaigned on the idea that it was important to spend money while oil prices were high and to fund various social programs.

Competing political parties in Norway have a long history and they are politically responsible. After winning an election and forming the government, they explain to the voters that they overestimated the potential for spending the stabilization fund without risk. The new opposition can charge them with breaking election promises and build its political platform around that. In a stable economy with an effective democracy this is not terrible. Unfortunately, not all resource-rich countries have such political systems.

Modern economic growth is without historical precedent and therefore difficult to predict. The changing conditions in world development create new problems that require adequate answers and can change social institutions and the forms of organizing public life. In countries where the economy depends on raw materials, their unpredictable pricing complicates decision-making. Inflation levels, people's incomes, and the ability to repay foreign debt depend on the dynamics of the commodity price. This is a serious challenge. Not all countries are capable of handling it. This is one of the reasons that economic growth is slower in countries with natural resource wealth than in countries without it. The experience of solving problems created by unstable commodities markets has not yielded any easy recipes for handling future problems. What it has shown is that the political elite must be prepared to respond to changes in the world and must understand that those changes can threaten their country's security.

In the second half of the twentieth century and the early twenty-first, wars have become more the exception than the rule. There have been no armed conflicts between major powers in the past sixty years. But the military tradition of the nineteenth century calls for having a "plan for the military application of armed forces," an elaborate program of actions to take in case of attack or threat of attack from a potential enemy. Twentieth-century experience has shown that resource-rich countries facing a downturn must be prepared and know what the government will do if prices fall, as well as what consequences this will have for the budget, the balance of payments, and the consumer market; they must have a plan for servicing foreign debt and for stabilizing the banking system; the plan must be detailed and realistic. The Soviet Union in the early 1980s did not have a plan. The consequences are well known.

CHAPTER IV

CRACKS IN THE FOUNDATION

THE SOVIET UNION IN THE EARLY 1980s

Something's rotten in the state of Denmark.
— Shakespeare, *Hamlet*

The Roman Empire in the time of the fall
Appeared to be completely in order
The caesar was in place and his entourage with him
Life was wonderful, if you believed the reports.
— Bulat Okudzhava

AT THE END OF THE LEONID BREZHNEV era, the great majority of Western observers who analyzed the unfolding situation in the USSR were certain that the Soviet economic and sociopolitical system had lost its dynamism and was inefficient but stable. Kremlinologists assumed that it would continue to exist for a long time. The ability of Soviet analysts to discuss these issues was limited, for obvious reasons. But they, who knew better than Westerners how the country's economy functioned, also agreed that it was inefficient but enduring.

The regime's power depended on an efficient secret police. Moreover, the hallmark of the Brezhnev era was social stability. Mass unrest that was forcefully suppressed by the authorities had dwindled since the mid-1960s. In the period 1963–67 only occasional outbursts had to be put down with force—in Chengen, Frunze, and Stepanakert in 1967, for example. In the flowering of the Brezhnev era the authorities learned how to minimize the risks of anti-government demonstrations. Seven of the nine mass demonstrations against the Brezhnev regime occurred early in his administration. During Khrushchev's administration, the government used weapons in eight of eleven riots, but in Brezhnev's it used them only three times. The regime learned how to manage without resorting to violence, putting down open expressions of dissatisfaction without gunfire.[1]

Of course, the mass construction of housing (the Khrushchevky) and land allotments for personal gardens quickly led to the loss of the government's total control over people's personal lives. The shift from communal life (as depicted in Andrei Platonov's novel *The Foundation Pit* and Alexei Guerman's films *My Friend Ivan Lapshin* and *Khrustalev, Get the Car!*) to a life, albeit Soviet, but separate from the state (Yuri Trifonov's phrase) was made in a decade. After much of the population had moved into private apartments, a new space for the expression of free thought appeared—the kitchen. And garden allotments that allowed people to grow their own produce removed the average person from reliance on communal, state-organized labor.

Between the early 1950s and the mid-1980s, the information situation changed radically. In 1950, only 2 percent of Soviet citizens had short-wave radios. By 1980, half the population had access to them. The Soviet leadership took measures to keep domestically manufactured radios from receiving Western stations, which they jammed.[2] But by the 1980s the world in which all information that reached the people was centrally controlled had become a thing of the past. Many Soviet citizens had access to sources of information about current events besides the state-controlled channels. In the mid-1970s, the KGB reported to the Central Committee of the CPSU that young people were developing revisionist, reformist ideas. This was most widespread among college students in the humanities, where the KGB had identified forty-three groups under the influence of the ideology of revisionism and reformism. The report stated:

> An analysis of statistical data shows that the majority of people who have demonstrated positions that would be politically harmful to the state are under direct ideological influence from abroad. Such factors as listening to Western radio programs, reading bourgeois newspapers, books, and other printed materials sent into the USSR, and personal communication and correspondence with hostile foreigners have influenced 47 percent (2,012 people). The main factor is the influence of foreign radio propaganda. . . . An analysis of the materials suggests that there is widespread interest among young people in foreign broadcasts. Thus, according to the research on "Audiences of Western Radio Stations in Moscow," done by the applied social

research department of the Institute of Informatics Systems of the Academy of Sciences USSR, 80 percent of university students and around 90 percent in the upper grades of vocational and technical schools listen more or less regularly. Most of the listeners to foreign radio do so habitually; 32 percent of university students and 59.2 percent of all students listen at least once or twice a week.[3]

And from a KGB memorandum to the Central Committee in December 1970:

> An analysis of so-called samizdat literature circulating among the intelligentsia and students shows that there have been qualitative changes in samizdat in the last few years. Five years ago, we noted that it was primarily ideologically flawed works of fiction that were being passed around; now documents of a programmatic political character are more widespread. Since 1965 more than 400 studies and articles on economic, political, and philosophical questions have appeared, all criticizing from various point of view the historical experience of socialist construction in the Soviet Union, reviewing the foreign and domestic policies of the CPSU, and proposing various kinds of programs for opposition activity. . . . Among the scientific, technological, and part of the creative intelligentsia documents are . . . those that promote various theories of "democratic socialism." . . . In late 1968 and early 1969, a political nucleus formed from the oppositionist elements known as the "democratic movement," which as they see it has three necessary signs of opposition: "it has leaders, activists, and the support of a significant number of sympathizers." . . . The centers of distribution of uncensored materials remain Moscow, Leningrad, Kiev, Gorky, Novosibirsk, and Kharkov.[4]

Samizdat (literally, *self-published*) and *tamizdat* (literally, *published over there*—that is, banned books smuggled into the Soviet Union) circulated widely. (In the days before photocopying, banned literature was retyped, and carbon copies were circulated among readers who would make more carbon copies and pass them along.) At least among the educated residents of major cities, it was considered downright indecent not to be familiar with the banned works of Andrei Sakharov or Aleksandr Solzhenitsyn. But the dissident movement, for all its moral authority among the intelligentsia, posed no serious threat to the regime. Closed borders and limited contacts with the outside world ensured political control and appeared to bar the organization of an opposition movement that would endanger the authorities.

Between 1958 and 1966, 3,448 people were found guilty of anti-Soviet agitation and propaganda. In the period 1967–75, there were 1,538. In 1971–74, to

use KGB terminology, 63,100 people had been given "prophylactic work"[5]—
meaning that Soviet citizens suspected of thinking differently had been handled by the secret police. Potential dissidents were made aware that their
activities were known and that the alternatives were to go to prison or to
express loyalty.

Ethnic conflicts were still potentially dangerous. The main hot spots were
considered Kazakhstan, Armenia, and Abkhazia. On April 24, 1965, somewhere between three thousand and eight thousand people staged stormy
demonstrations in Armenia. The demonstrators demanded the return of
Nagorno-Karabakh to Armenia and the release of their Armenian supporters. Abkhazia saw riots and turmoil that lasted for two weeks in 1967.[6] However, things did not progress to an armed standoff.

Growing Problems and Bad Decisions

The USSR's economic growth from the 1930s to the 1950s was due to the redistribution of resources from agriculture to industry. Huge numbers of laborers
from the countryside were called into service in the construction trades. Capital investment as a share of GDP was anomalously high. In the 1930s agricultural exports financed the purchase of imported equipment. In the late 1940s
and 1950s the newly created industrial base and the tense relationship with the
West stimulated greater use of domestic equipment in construction.

The development model the socialist system was trying to achieve was the
creation of major new enterprises. But such enterprises cannot be efficient if
there is no one to work in them. In the 1960s the supply of labor to industry
dried up. In a socialist system, it is not easy to replace labor with additional
investments. Subtle manipulation of investments to improve production
power is not its strong point. By the late 1960s, these problems were apparent
to the people who wrote the speeches of the high-placed party leaders.[7]

Recognition of looming problems related to the inefficiency of the Soviet
economy led in the mid-1960s to an attempt at economic reform. A resolution of the Central Committee and Council of Ministers dated October 4,
1965, announced an expansion of the rights of enterprises; greater discretion
for businesses in the use of funds for production and for worker incentives;
the introduction of a system in which wages would be based on individual
performance as well as the success of the enterprise; the development of direct
connections between manufacturers and consumers, based on the principle
of mutual financial responsibility; and a strengthening of the role of profit in
motivating workers.[8]

The announced program was more cautious than the measures implemented in Yugoslavia, planned in Hungary, and years later undertaken in China. Nevertheless, this was the last serious attempt to change the management of the Soviet economy and restore the market mechanisms that had been dismantled in the late 1920s and early 1930s before the socialist system spiraled downward. It is difficult to assess the degree to which the reform efforts helped, but the five-year period 1966–70 achieved the fastest rates of economic growth in the final three decades of the existence of the USSR.

Examples of the inefficiency of the Soviet economy are well known. The Soviet Union mined eight times as much iron ore as the United States. That ore yielded only three times as much pig iron, and the pig iron only twice as much steel as was produced in the United States. Finally, from that steel it was able to produce machines worth roughly the same as those produced in the United States.

The use of raw materials and energy in the production of each final product was, respectively, 1.6 and 2.1 times greater than in the United States. The average construction time for an industrial plant in the USSR was more than ten years, in the United States less than two years.[9] In manufacturing per unit, the USSR in 1980 used 1.8 times more steel than the United States, 2.3 times more cement, 7.6 times more fertilizer, and 1.5 times more timber.[10] The USSR produced 16 times the number of grain harvesters, but harvested less grain and became dependent on grain imports.[11]

Mikhail Gorbachev, in his report to the Plenum of the Central Committee of the CPSU on June 16, 1986, said: "Every unit of growth of the national income and industrial and agricultural production in the current situation demands more resources from us. . . . At the present time, in industry alone there are around 700,000 unfilled jobs. And this is with one-shift use of the equipment. At the coefficient of 1.7 shifts worked per day, the number of vacancies in industry will exceed 4 million. Tens of billions of rubles were spent to create them."[12]

Ideas for ambitious, large-scale projects, without consideration of their costs, occurred to Soviet leaders with regularity. In 1963, when the country had begun buying wheat abroad, Nikita Khrushchev returned to a project for building roads between Komsomolsk-na-Amure and Sakhalin.[13] Many of the projects in which significant resources were invested turned out to be either ineffective or pointless. A typical example comes from the land reclamation construction industry, where investments were greater than in light industry (see tables 4-1, 4-2).

TABLE 4-1. Capital Expenditures on Soil Amelioration and Light Industry as a Share of Capital Expenditures in the USSR Economy, 1971–85

Percent

Years	Light industry	Amelioration
1971–75	4.2	6.0
1976–80	4.3	5.6
1981–85	4.3	5.2

Source: Statistical Yearbooks *Narodnoe khoziaistvo SSSR* [USSR National Economy] and *Sel'skoe khoziaistvo SSSR* [USSR Agriculture] (Moscow: Finansy i statistika, various years).

Note: The data for the share of capital expenditures in light industry from 1976 are given for consumer goods.

In 1986–90, there was a plan to produce 35,000 excavators, 32,000 bull-dozers, 10,000 K-700 tractors, 4,400 tractors that could haul 10 tons or more, 22,000 scrapers, and 6,300 cranes to improve land reclamation capabilities. National and local newspapers, the State Radio and Television Committee, and the State Cinematography Committee were ordered to cover the achievements in construction as part of the Agricultural Program of the USSR.[14] The results of all this activity were modest. Over time, the acreage of failed irrigation and drainage projects grew to almost equal the amount of newly introduced acreage (see table 4-3).[15]

A textbook example of a large-scale project in the USSR in the last decade of its existence is the separation of the Kara-Bogaz-Gol Bay from the Caspian Sea. A dam was built to keep the level of the sea from falling. It soon became clear that the Caspian was rising and the dam was interfering with the work of the Kara-Bogazsulfat plant, which was important for the national economy. The dam was opened and water allowed to return to the bay.[16]

After the decision to stop trying to reverse the course of northern and Siberian rivers to flow south, the government had to pass a resolution writing

TABLE 4-2. USSR Investments in Soil Amelioration, 1971–85

Expenditures	1971–75	1976–80	1981–85
Capital expenditures for soil amelioration activities (billions of rubles)	29.6	40.0	43.9
Capital expenditures for soil amelioration activities (percent of GDP)	1.3	1.4	1.2

Source: Statistical Yearbook *Sel'skoe khoziaistvo SSSR* [USSR Agriculture] (Moscow: Finansy i statistika, 1988). GDP shares calculated using figures in S. G. Sinelnikov, *Budzhetnyi krizis v Rossii* [Budgetary Crisis in Russia] (Moscow: Eurasia, 1995).

TABLE 4-3. Increase in the Area of Drained and Irrigated Land in the USSR, Various Periods between 1971 and 1987 (difference between commissioning of land improvements and the end of the land's usefulness)
Millions of hectares

Type of land	1971–75	1976–80	1981–85	1986	1987
Drained land	4.4	3.6	3.5	0.70	0.63
Irrigated land	4.5	3.8	3.3	0.61	0.55

Source: Statistical Yearbook *Sel'skoe khoziaistvo SSSR* [USSR Agriculture] (Moscow: Finansy i statistika, 1988).

off the enormous expenses to develop the project.[17] Formally, all these expenses added to the official Soviet GDP.

Acute ecological problems were created, for example, by the long-term and large-scale use of DDT (dichlorodiphenyltrichloroethane) after it was banned in developed countries.[18] The widespread use of pesticides in Soviet agriculture is a typical reflection of the country's systemic problems. After signing a ban on chemical warfare, the state had excess chemical production facilities that had been created in the 1940s and 1950s, which it then used in other industries, including food production. Research in the 1980s revealed that tens of millions of people became victims of pesticide poisoning through contaminated food products produced in those plants.[19] This catastrophe affected the nation's health and influenced the demographic situation for decades. But these problems did not threaten the regime's stability in the short term.

The command system as it was constituted from the 1930s to the 1950s worked as long as it was based on mass fear, the threat of harsh sanctions, throughout society. After 1953, when Stalin's death reduced the public's fear of repression, the effectiveness of traditional socialist methods of governance declined. Labor discipline suffered as well. Khrushchev, after a visit to the Donbass region, described the situation at a meeting of the Presidium of the Central Committee with a curt and exhaustive comment: "They're stealing everything."[20]

Growing alcoholism, which from the early 1960s reduced the life expectancy of men, combined the worst aspects of alcohol abuse in the city and the country. Urban alcoholic behavior reached the villages: the typically episodic drinking pattern in country villages (usually on holidays) took on a daily aspect. In turn, the village traditions of lengthy eating and drinking parties punctuated by arguments and fights permeated city culture. The percentage of alcohol consumed in socially controlled places (cafes, restaurants, and bars) in the USSR in 1984 was 5.5 percent, as compared to 50–70 percent in developed countries. When the habit of street drinking took root, the probability of arrests for illegal conduct increased by 2.3 times, without a change in the amounts of alcohol consumed. In twenty years, the per capita consumption of spirits more than doubled; the number of crimes connected to alcohol abuse rose by 5.7 times; and the number of patients treated for alcoholism increased sevenfold.[21] Approximately 90 percent of missed workdays were due to drinking.[22] In 1986 there were 4 million officially registered alcoholics in the USSR. Close to 9 million people received alcohol treatment annually.[23]

Discipline in planned work continued to fall. When an industry or enterprise cannot fulfill a plan, it receives fewer commissions. The former chairman of Gosplan USSR, Nikolai Baibakov, wrote, "Returning from the Kremlin, I recalled the meetings with Stalin that I, as a people's commissar, had attended. Questions were put bluntly, members of the Politburo spoke their minds, and deadlines were set and people responsible for meeting them were appointed. We knew that if Stalin gave us an assignment, it was law for us. You would do it, no matter what. So why are the government's resolutions so poorly executed? Where does this irresponsibility come from?"[24] This should not have come as a surprise. If you remove the linchpin from an economic system that is built on fear of the regime, it will stop working well.[25]

Gradually, beginning in the late 1950s and early 1960s, the economic system was transformed into what Vitaly Naishul called "an economy of argument and reconciliation."[26] I called it a "system of hierarchical deals."[27] The benchmarks for production and the system of resource allocation were not dictated from above but were a product of internal negotiation among the organizational hierarchy. The more influential agencies could allocate resources and impose sanctions on subordinate managers. The knowledge they possessed about production problems and how to deal with them was only rarely shared with authorities.

Declassified documents show that even in the 1930s the system was not a purely command one and that some negotiations occurred within the hierarchy.[28] I am not talking about qualitative differences but about a gradual evolution, how over time the ability of the upper echelons of power to impose their will was reduced. But a stronger role for those in lower management could not improve the efficiency of the socialist system or solve the problems caused by a lack of market instruments.

Attempts to improve the efficiency of the Soviet economy through administrative methods failed. Planning discipline eroded. It was impossible to compensate for inadequate labor resources with increased capital investments. The deputy chairman of Gosplan, Lev Voronin, wrote to the Council of Ministers on February 23, 1984, that the labor shortage caused by a steady overcreation of jobs was reducing labor efficiency.[29] Economists Stanley Fisher and William Easterly believed that a system that did not allow for capital investments to compensate for reductions in the work force was the main factor in the crash of the Soviet economy.[30] These problems were real, but they extended over time, and the difficulties accumulated over decades. Extrapolating from these trends would allow us to predict economic decline and stagnation, but not a crash.

Economic growth was slowing down, but the slowdown did not threaten the economic and political structures. Calculations made in the USSR about the long-term economic development of the Soviet economy predicted that this trend would continue. Although it was risky to include predictions of fading growth in the final version of documents intended for the leaders of the country, that is how the professional economic community saw the picture. That was also close to the view of most Western specialists studying the Soviet economy in the late 1970s and early 1980s. According to that vision, economic growth in the USSR would stop in twenty to thirty years.[31]

Here is an evaluation of the Soviet economy by one Communist Party ideologue in the second half of the 1980s, Vadim Medvedev, secretary of the Central Committee and member of the Politburo:

> The eighth five-year plan (1966–71) was perhaps the last successful period in the country's socioeconomic development. Economic development influenced by reforms in the 1960s and more or less beneficial foreign economic factors turned out to be even greater than in previous years. . . . Subsequently, economic development worsened quickly and inexorably. The following two five-year plans, including their social programs, were ruined. From time to time, the economic state of affairs was sustained by high world prices for fuel, energy, and raw materials. Only one sector of the economy steadily flourished—the military industrial complex. The country was staggering under the burden of military expenditures.[32]

The effectiveness of the Communist ideology had been undermined by then. The country's leaders treated the ideological formulas and slogans as inherited rituals that had to be observed. The public either overlooked them completely or used them as the butt of jokes. The move to deintellectualize the Communist leadership, under way for years, had by the end of the 1970s produced an aging Politburo incapable of making rational decisions.[33] But when things run on momentum with the same old rules in effect, a high intellectual level is not needed to manage the country.

Food Supply Problems

Socialism, as was noted long ago, is the economy of deficit.[34] It is not easy to explain how it works to people who have not encountered it firsthand. Someone who has not lived in a socialist society will have trouble picturing the socialist hierarchy of access to deficit resources, or how important it is for a family to have a friend who works in a store, or even better, who is a department manager. After making a monthly trip of two or three hundred kilometers to a city with privileged food supplies and spending several hours in line, no normal person will limit himself to buying only 300 grams of sausage, but will buy as much as he can afford.

Research has shown that shortages of consumer goods and related problems intensified in the second half of the 1960s. The transition from the entrenched deficits of the late 1970s and early 1980s, coupled with the government's inability to meet its obligations to deliver resources even through rationing, led to a real crisis in the food supply in the late 1980s and was the most important economic reason for the public's loss of confidence in the regime and its collapse.

Getting food to large cities was a major economic and political problem that began with the tsarist regime during World War I. The regime's inability to solve it resulted in the revolution of 1917. Food supply issues were paramount during the Civil War of 1918–21. By introducing food reallocation and spilling rivers of blood, the Bolsheviks showed that they knew how to mobilize food resources.

At the end of 1928 and in early 1929, the crisis of food supply to cities again became the center of fierce economic and political debate. Stalin's choice—dekulakization, collectivization, and a return to food rationing—set the trajectory of the country's development for decades.

Contrary to Karl Marx's famous line about history repeating itself, first as tragedy and then as farce,[35] events in the USSR showed that history can repeat itself more than once and not necessarily as farce. In the second half of the 1980s, supplying food to large cities became a key issue in economic policy yet again. The fate of the country hung on its resolution. But before moving to an analysis of the crisis, we must understand its causes.

In countries where industrialization began in the late eighteenth and early nineteenth centuries, industrial growth was preceded by a process known as the "agrarian revolution." Europe in that period still used traditional tools, but new agricultural methods and techniques for handling soil and seeds spread quickly through books and articles. The efficiency of agricultural production

TABLE 4-4. Average Annual Grain Production in Russia, 1891–1913

Period	Yield (million tons)
1891–1900	47.7
1901–10	55.6
1911–13	74.6

Source: P. I. Liaschenko, *Istoriia russkogo narodnogo khoziaistva* [History of the Russian Economy] (Moscow: Gosudarstvennoe izdatelstvo, 1930).

leaped ahead and in turn brought advances in food production and delivery to the growing urban populace. The growth rate in agricultural production was slower than in industry. But for the time, both were high and sustained.[36]

The state had a limited role in financing industrialization in countries that had started on modern economic growth. There was no consideration of supporting it through taxation of the peasantry or mobilizing resources for government investments. The eldest son of a peasant continued to run the household while his younger brothers sought work in the city. The large immigration from Europe across the ocean was predicated in large part on people's desire to remain farmers rather than join the industrial workforce during the first decades of industrialization.

In countries where industrialization was catching up, events unfolded differently. There the role of the state was greater. State investments needed to be financed. If the majority of economic activity was concentrated in the countryside, then the peasantry was the natural object of taxation in order to realize state investment projects.

The degree to which overtaxing the peasantry held back agrarian development in Russia between 1870 and 1913 has long been a topic of discussion among economic historians. However, the connection is obvious between preserving the *obshchina*, or communal village structure, for decades after the repeal of serfdom and using the dues of the *obshchina* as a form of taxation to help pay for railroad construction.

The model of delayed industrialization created political risks. These were fully manifest in early twentieth-century Russia. However, the policy of the tsarist government did not lead to an agrarian crisis because industrial production grew as agricultural production diminished. The decades-long average grain harvest grew steadily. Russia remained the major exporter (see tables 4-4, 4-5).

The socialist model of industrialization that was formed in the USSR in the late 1920s and early 1930s at first appears to continue the government policy traditional in Russia of the late nineteenth and early twentieth centuries

TABLE 4-5. Average Annual Grain Exports, 1896–1913
Million tons

Exporting country	1896–1900	1901–05	1906–10	1911–13
Russia	5.21	6.81	7.54	6.76
United States	2.88	2.45	1.77	1.70
Canada	0.35	0.71	1.24	2.76
Argentina	0.98	1.68	2.19	2.58

Source: Data for Russia from P. Liaschenko, *Istoriia russkogo narodnogo khoziaistva* [History of the Russian Economy] (Moscow: Gosudarstvennoe izdatelstvo, 1930). Data for other countries from B. R. Mitchell, *International Historical Statistics* (London: Macmillan Reference, 1998).

of a delayed industrialization that was organized by the state and financed at the expense of the countryside. But the process of taking resources from the countryside grew and intensified, eventually leading to a different type of development.

Collectivization took away the peasants' freedom to choose where they lived and worked and forced them into unpaid labor. Growing their own food on private lots was the only way for them to feed their families, though they were heavily taxed in produce and money in the second half of the 1940s. The system became tantamount to a restoration of serfdom. The only difference was that the state was not one of many slave owners, but the only one. Modern methods of enforcement, the absence of moral scruples, and the authorities' conviction that whatever happened in the countryside was not nearly as important as investments in industry removed the usual limitations in agrarian societies on taking away resources from the peasantry; the resulting redistribution of wealth from the countryside to the cities was unprecedented in world history.

Once work in state agriculture became compulsory and turned into a form of *barshchina*—a system known to generations of Russian peasants that required them to perform a certain number of days of work for a landlord—the mores of pre-emancipation Russia, described in Russian literature, became the norm. Working for a landlord was a job to be avoided, and in the serf system, quite rationally so. In Eastern European countries that went through a second serf system in the fifteenth through nineteenth centuries peasants had shared a similar attitude. In Russia, it was reflected in such proverbs as "Work isn't a wolf; it won't run away into the woods" and "Work loves fools" and in the etymology of the words for slave, *rab*, and work, *rabota*, which have the same root. There are many examples of the wisdom of avoiding compulsory labor in Russian and East European folklore.

In the early 1930s, the work ethic that had developed in Russia from the 1860s to about 1920 began eroding. Strong peasants working for themselves and their families recognized that this labor was not the same as working for the landlord and that they could become prosperous even while being part of the *obshchina;* they understood that they had to work hard, teach their children, and master new technologies. The destruction of this stratum was an unprecedented blow to the fragile work ethic of the peasantry, which only began after their emancipation in 1861. The long-term consequences of the decision made in 1928–29 are obvious today to scholars of the socioeconomic issues of the Russian countryside.

In the decade between 1928 and 1938, the factor productivity of Soviet agriculture fell by approximately one-fourth in comparison with the "inertia scenario" of development (1 percent growth annually). Nothing like this had ever happened in the history of modern economic growth. The grain harvest did not reach 1925–29 levels again until 1950–54. Such a long period of stagnation was also unprecedented for countries that had begun the process of modern economic growth.[37]

The social position of peasants in that period was markedly on the wane, unlike that of industrial workers. *Kolkhoz* (collective farm) workers in the USSR, who from the 1930s to the 1950s made up the majority of the population, were discriminated against as a class. Their annual income was close to an industrial worker's monthly wage. In the 1940s, additional high taxes in money and in kind were imposed on individual allotments in order to force peasants to give more attention to their work in the *kolkhozes*. Peasants started giving up their cows and chopping down their fruit trees. By 1950, 40 percent of peasant families no longer kept dairy cattle.[38]

In countries that were leaders of modern economic growth, there were differences in lifestyle and work but not in the average incomes of peasants and industrial laborers; in the USSR the income gap was huge. The income disparity is the source of the difference between the USSR and other countries in migration to the city and the makeup of the participants in that process.

In the more advanced economies, the choice to work in agriculture was not predicated on a lack of ability or willingness to work hard and adapt to new circumstances. The eldest sons, who usually remained on the farm, were brought up in the same way as the younger ones who moved to the city. The "choice" was determined by birth order. The traditional work ethic in the countryside had not been undermined. Industry grew, but agriculture developed dynamically as well. Many of the leaders of modern economic growth remain large net exporters of food (see table 4-6).

TABLE 4-6. Balance of Trade for Food Products in the United States, Canada, Australia, and France, Annual Averages, 1961–90

Country	Millions of dollars in nominal terms			Millions of year 2000 dollars		
	1961–70	1971–80	1981–90	1961–70	1971–80	1981–90
United States	1,395	11,768	15,504	6,042	27,858	22,604
Canada	511	1,159	2,563	2,200	2,900	3,746
Australia	1,830	4,710	7,882	7,800	11,596	11,185
France	−730	923	5,625	−3,227	2,232	7,777

Source: UN Food and Agriculture Organization, FAOSTAT data, 2005.

In the Soviet Union, for all of its limitations, there were always ways of migrating to the cities. The people who remained in the villages and those who left were different from those in countries that had not gone through socialist industrialization. The socialist model prompted the most educated and energetic peasant children to find a way to get out of the villages at any cost.

The problems of agricultural development created by migration from the countryside existed in countries that had not been through socialist industrialization. But their scale was not comparable to those that had formed in the USSR by 1950. In the late 1940s, flight from the villages increased. A 1932 law forbidding peasants to leave without special permission was in force, but people knew how to get around it. Industry and construction needed a workforce. Only the countryside could provide it.

Food Shortages—A Strategic Challenge

By the time of Stalin's death in 1953, the weakness of Soviet agriculture was apparent. It was understood by the party leadership. This is how Nikita Khrushchev characterized it:

> Let me cite a few figures. In 1940, the grain yield was 2,225 million *poods,* and in 1953 it,was only 1,850 million *poods,* that is, 375 million *poods* less. At the same time, in connection with the general increase of the economy, the significant increase of the urban population, and the rise in real income, the demand for bread products has been growing yearly. . . . The demand for grain for export is increasing not only for food but also for animal feed, but because of the insufficiency of grain we could only earmark 190 million *poods* (3.12 million tons) for export in 1954, while the demand was determined to be 293 million *poods* (4.8 million tons).[39]

At that point the government was not discussing whether to increase aid to agriculture. Everyone agreed that doing so was necessary. But opinions differed about priorities. Two proposals were on the table: send additional resources to the traditional agrarian regions or start a large-scale program to use virgin and fallow lands. It was decided to do the latter.

The program to develop virgin lands as a method of solving grain problems and mobilizing the grain for state needs was first discussed in the late 1920s. Stalin supported it then. He liked the idea of applying industrial methods to agriculture: concentrating resources, organizing production on a large scale, and creating a privileged *sovkhoz* (state farm) sector in agriculture. He dismissed the doubts expressed by specialists, who were concerned that the use of virgin lands would make harvests even less reliable and hard to predict.

The sharp fluctuations in yield and state purchases of grain on virgin lands would later cost the Soviet Union dearly. But in the first stages of cultivation, the virgin lands increased the volume of grain in the hands of the state. By the end of the first five-year plan, the share of grain sold by *sovkhozes* was almost 10 percent of the total.[40]

Khrushchev's initiatives in the early 1950s corresponded to the tradition of economic development in the Soviet Union. In the logic of the socialist system, this made sense. Improving the lands that were not in the *chernozem* (black soil) belt and had been depleted by decades of Soviet agrarian policy required liberalizing agriculture, increasing the material incentives of the peasants, and probably breaking up the *kolkhozes.* The Chinese took a similar path in the late 1970s. The development of the Russian economy at the time they were cultivating virgin soil in the 1950s was higher than in China after the death of Mao Zedong. The development indicators for the USSR in the 1930s and for China in 1980 were the same. But in 1950, the USSR's were very different (see table 4-7). Per capita GDP in the USSR was twice that of China in 1980. And yet most of the population was still in the countryside.

The *kolkhoz* system had existed for one generation. The work ethic had been perverted by the new serfdom, but there were still tens of millions of people living in the villages who remembered individual farming and had not lost their skills. But in the USSR in the early 1950s, when decollectivization was outside the range of political discourse, only poor results could be expected from throwing resources at the non-*chernozem* lands. This was confirmed in the 1970s and early 1980s, when the USSR got very little for its huge expenditures.

TABLE 4-7. GDP per Capita among Those Employed in Agriculture and Urbanization in the USSR and China in the Years of Selecting a Development Strategy

Country	Year	GDP per capita (international dollars in 1990)	Urban population's share (percent)
USSR	1930	1,448	20.0
	1950	2,841	44.7
China	1980	1,462	19.6

Source: GDP per capita from A. Maddison, *Monitoring the World Economy 1820–1992* (Paris: OECD, 1995); A. Maddison, *The World Economy: Historical Statistics* (Paris: OECD, 2003).

Data for 1950, 1960, from United Nations, DESA, Population Division, Population Estimates and Projections, United Nations Statistics Division (http://unstats.un.org/unsd/cdb); Paul Bairoch, *Cities and Economic Development: From the Dawn of History to the Present* (University of Chicago Press, 1988).

By choosing to cultivate virgin lands, they could make large-scale capital investments in priority regions and grant those who did the work the same privileges that industrial laborers had, as opposed to *kolkhoz* workers. They could redistribute part of the flow of labor from the country to the city, born of the socioeconomic inequality of laborers and peasants, to work on this project.

These changes produced the hoped-for results. Grain yield went up. The new territories were large producers; the state could use their harvests to compensate for the falling production in traditional agrarian regions. These were the arguments Khrushchev used in 1958 to prove the correctness of the agricultural policy choices.[41]

Much of the virgin land was in risky agricultural zones. The weather was unreliable, but the harvests depended on favorable weather much more than in the traditional agricultural regions of Russia and Ukraine. The harvests stopped increasing on the virgin lands after 1958 and fell sharply in 1963. The per capita yield in 1963 was lower than in Russia in 1913: 483 kilograms and 540 kilograms respectively.[42] The unreliability of harvests increased the risk that the food supply to the major cities would be insufficient. The territories capable of cultivation were limited. But the growing demand of an urbanized society for agricultural products is a long-term process that does not end with the cultivation of virgin lands.

Despite all their efforts, state grain reserves continued to decrease from 1953 to 1960, as more was used each year than was purchased. The Soviet leadership was worried.

One might think that the natural response to such food supply difficulties would be to tap the state's industrial potential by increasing investment in the agricultural sector. This approach began to dominate in the late 1950s and

TABLE 4-8. Capital Expenditures in Agricultural Production Facilities
as a Share of the Capital Expenditures in the USSR Economy, 1946–90

Years	Share of capital expenditures in agriculture (percent)
1946–50	11.8
1951–55	14.3
1956–60	14.3
1961–65	15.5
1966–70	17.2
1971–75	20.1
1976–80	20.0
1981–85	18.5
1986–90	17.1

Source: Statistical Yearbook *Narodnoe khoziaistvo SSSR* [USSR National Economy] (Moscow: Finansy i statistika, various years).

early 1960s.[43] The share of capital investment for agriculture grew steadily from the early 1950s until the early 1980s (see table 4-8).

By increasing investment in the countryside, the state tried to make up for the damage its policies had caused from the late 1920s through the early 1950s. But it proved impossible to use the investments effectively. The country would be paying for many years for the destruction inflicted in the early stages of socialist industrialization. The deterioration of village social structures led to unsatisfactory results from the capital expenditures there. The decisions made in the late 1920s and early 1930s had consequences for decades to come.

Grain consumption continued to deplete the reserves. In 1960, the harvest, consumption, and state reserves of grain were respectively 46.7, 50.0, and 10.2 million tons, and in 1963, 44.8, 51.2, and 6.3 million tons.[44] In the 1960s, agricultural production grew approximately 3 percent a year; in the 1970s the growth rate was 1 percent.[45] Between 1971 and 1985, state capital investments in the agro-industrial complex were 579.6 billion rubles. Still, agricultural production was flat.[46] Average grain harvests in 1981–85 and in 1971–75 were the same (161.7 million tons).[47]

In his memoir, Georgy Shakhnazarov recounts a conversation he had with Yuri Andropov in the mid-1960s. I quote Andropov from the book: "You know, the Politburo is becoming convinced that our economic sphere needs a good shakeup. It's particularly bad in agriculture: we can't settle anymore for not being able to feed the country and every year having to buy more and more grain. If things continue this way, we're going to have to go on starvation rations soon."[48]

TABLE 4-9. Urban Population in the USSR, 1956–90

Year	USSR urban population (in millions)	Share of urban population in the USSR (percent)
1956	88.2	45.0
1970	136.0	56.0
1975	151.9	60.0
1980	167.3	63.0
1985	180.1	65.2
1990	190.6	66.0

Source: Statistical Yearbook *Narodnoe khoziaistvo SSSR* [USSR National Economy] (Moscow: Finansy i statistika, various years).

By the mid-1960s meat was no longer readily available in most of the country. Except in the capital and other privileged cities, it could only be bought in co-operatives or at a *kolkhoz* market at much higher than state prices.[49]

The growth of demand for animal feed on farms reduced the ability of the state to take grain from the *kolkhozes* and *sovkhozes*. This was one of the great socioeconomic issues of the late 1960s. In 1969, Leonid Brezhnev said, "So, in 1966, of the harvested 171 million tons we left more than 95 million tons in the *kolkhozes* and *sovkhozes;* in 1967, the harvest was only 147.9 million tons and still close to 90 million tons were left; in 1968 around 100 million tons were left in the villages out of 169.5 million tons; and in 1969 over 100 million tons were left out of 160.5 million tons."[50] As urbanization continued, the share of the population that could feed itself from private sources shrank even more (see tables 4-9 and 4-10).

Supply for the urban populace in a socialist economy depends on state agricultural reserves. The role of market mechanisms—the *kolkhoz* market, demand cooperation—was limited in major cities. State supplies stopped growing, and their instability became an acute problem for the country's

TABLE 4-10. Urban Population in the Russian Federation, 1956–90

Year	Urban population in the Russian Federation (in millions)	Share of urban population in the Russian Federation (percent)
1956	54.6	48
1970	81.0	62
1979	95.4	69
1990	109.8	74

Source: Statistical Yearbook *Narodnoe khoziaistvo SSSR* [USSR National Economy] (Moscow: Finansy i statistika, various years).

leadership.[51] Supplying food to the cities became a key topic of economic and political discourse in subsequent decades.

The USSR as the Largest Importer of Food

The crisis in agricultural production and its inefficiency would have created problems even in a market economy. Disproportionate demand and supply led to price increases on food products and to slower growth in the rate of consumption, and in the worst circumstances to a disappearance of food on the market. While not pleasant for the public and the regime, in industrial countries this rarely leads to an unmanageable crisis. Starvation in highly developed societies is not the result of crop failure. If it does occur, it is related to a failed system of delivery, civil or external war, a lack of money circulation that leads to paralysis in trade between village and city, or a deficit in the balance of payments. A lack of sufficient food by itself does not lead to mass starvation.

The socialist system does not use market mechanisms to regulate inequalities between food supply and demand. The inefficiency of Soviet agriculture is a result of the socialist model of industrialization, which also leads to a greater demand for food by the growing urban population. If the USSR had been isolated from the world economy in the early 1960s, the government could have done nothing but watch the food shortage unfold, observing the growing gap between the state's performance and the public's expectations: the greater number of hours average citizens spent in lines, the growing number of cities with consumer goods rationing, and the longer list of goods the state could not produce according to the planned norms. It would have watched all this and waited for the sociopolitical situation to become unmanageable.[52]

It was unthinkable for the USSR to even consider the natural response in a market economy to such a structural problem—a change in retail pricing. From the 1930s to the early 1950s the basis of the Communist regime's stability had been public fear of the authorities. It had been created by mass repression that paralyzed people and kept them from expressing their dissatisfaction even at home, much less through protest actions. Also, in those years, the Communist ideology still appealed to many people. In the 1960s, the fear of mass repression was a thing of the past. By rejecting state terror, which would have been in its own interest, the political elite tried to avoid the fate of its predecessors, who were its victims from the 1930s through the early 1950s. This eventually had an influence on public attitudes. The regime was seen as a necessary evil, but it no longer instilled blind horror. It could be discussed in the kitchen without fear of harm to the family. Its messianic ideology seemed less convincing.

The myth of the rule of the workers, the dictatorship of the proletariat, as the basis of the regime's legitimacy was one of the sacred myths still believed by Soviet leaders in the late 1950s. It was evident in discussions by the Presidium of the Central Committee of the Hungarian revolution of 1956. Until the very last moment, the Central Committee was sure that the situation could be saved without using Soviet armed forces by calling on the support of Hungarian workers. Only when they realized that this strategy would not work did they decide to use the army to put down the rebellion.[53]

How to use the peasant army to force peasants to give their grain to the state at below-market prices was a key topic, not always expressed publicly but understood in the economic and political discourse of 1928–29.[54] Stalin, certain that the troops were reliable and that they would shoot when ordered, had been right. The regime, using the loyalty of the peasant army, had enslaved the serfs once again, taking as much grain as it deemed necessary and continuing to export it even when there was famine in the country. But industrialization, changes in the social structure, and a higher level of development prevented the regime from using force against its own people.

A new contract between rulers and society took the place of the legitimacy the regime had once enjoyed. No one signed it, but the deal was understood: you, the regime, promise us, the people, that you will not repeal existing social programs even when they cost more, and you guarantee the stability of retail prices on the most important consumer goods. For this we are prepared to tolerate you and accept you as a necessary evil. What happened when the contract was violated can be seen in the events of 1962 in Novocherkassk that followed the decision to raise prices, moderate considering the scale of the disparity between wholesale and retail prices. Prices of meat and meat products went up an average of 30 percent and butter an average of 25 percent on June 1, 1962. The head of the budget statistics department reported to the Central Committee:

> The reduction in meat and meat product purchases, as reported above, is explained primarily by the increase in retail prices for these products. . . . Price increases on meat and butter had the greatest effect in families with a relatively low per capita income, which is evident in the following data grouping the budgets of industrial workers by income for May and June 1962. . . . In families of industrial workers with an income below 35 rubles per family member a month, the use of meat and meat products in June 1962 went down by 15 percent compared with May, while in families with income of 50–75 rubles per family member the decrease in meat consumption was 8 percent.[55]

Riots involving thousands of people broke out in Novocherkassk. Here is a description of the events on June 1 in Novocherkassk based on eyewitness accounts: "By the end of the workday the first units from the Novocherkassk garrison appeared on the square in front of the factory. They were unarmed. As they approached, the columns of soldiers were instantly swallowed up by the mass of people. Strikers and soldiers embraced and kissed. Yes, yes, they kissed. The officers managed to extricate the soldiers from the crowds, collect them, and lead them away from the strikers." The army troops were deemed unreliable, and troops from the Ministry of the Interior were sent from Rostov-na-Donu. Only after they received direct orders from Moscow did these troops fire to kill.[56]

The official Soviet press did not carry a single word about these events. But the leaders knew about it and understood that if it could happen in Novocherkassk, it could happen elsewhere. Chairman of the KGB Vladimir Semichastny reported on 1962:

> In the first six months of the current year, 7,705 anti-Soviet leaflets and anonymous letters were distributed . . . twice as many as in the same period in 1961. . . . After the promulgation of the decision of the CC CPSU and the Council of Ministers USSR on raising prices on meat products, the influx of anonymous letters increased. In June alone, 83 instances were recorded of distribution of anti-Soviet leaflets and signs. At the same time, 300 anti-Soviet anonymous letters were handed to the KGB from Party and Soviet institutions, from newspapers and magazines, which expressed dissatisfaction with the living standards in our country and called for the organization of mass protests, strikes, demonstrations, rallies, and boycotts demanding a reduction in food prices and increases in wages. The distribution of such documents is noted primarily in the country's industrial centers.[57]

After Novocherkassk, the fear of the Soviet rulers that soldiers would refuse orders to fire at protesters and would join them, as happened in February 1917, became the most important factor in their deliberations. The mass unrest that followed price increases in Poland in 1970, 1976, and 1980 convinced the Soviet leadership that they could not risk this occurrence under any circumstances.[58]

Problems increased in the monetary system.[59] Experts on the state of the consumer market of the USSR argued over when the overhang of financial demand over total supply of goods became evident.[60] in its analysis of unmet demand, Goskomstat (the State Committee for Statistics), assumed that the problem appeared in 1965 and that before then supply and demand

TABLE 4-11. Involuntary Savings by the Population (Unmet Demand)

Year	Unmet demand (billions of current rubles)	Rate of annual increase in unmet demand (percent)	Unmet demand (percent of GDP)
1970	17.5	. . .	4.6
1980	29	5.2	4.7
1985	60.9	16.0	7.8

Source: Russian Federation State Archive, F. 5446, Inv. 163, S. 185, P. 100; GDP shares calculated using data in S. G. Sinelnikov, *Budzhetnyi krizis v Rossii* [Budgetary Crisis in Russia] (Moscow: Eurasia, 1995).

for consumer goods had been balanced. See table 4-11 for that agency's calculations of unmet consumer demand. It is clear to everyone that the problem grew more acute after the mid-1960s.[61]

The shortages were increasing, but so were prices. In 1981–85, the average retail price of bread rose by 6.6 percent, potatoes 7.9 percent, vegetables 4.4 percent, and baked goods 11.6 percent. Prices of nongrocery items also rose over the same period: cotton textiles 17.9 percent, television sets 10 percent.

On July 1, 1979, the Secretariat of the Central Committee passed a resolution to raise prices for gold jewelry 50 percent, silver 95 percent, natural fur garments 50 percent, carpets and rugs 50 percent, cars 18 percent, and imported furniture 30 percent. The Ministry of Trade and the ministries and agencies supervising public eating establishments were instructed to increase prices in restaurants and cafes by 100 percent in the evenings. A note from the Secretariat of the Central Committee to the first secretaries of the party in the Union republics, regions, and oblasts read: "The Central Committee and the Council of Ministers were forced to take these measures in view of the difficulties of balancing the rise in the population's monetary income with the volume of production of consumer goods and services, and also in order to regulate trade in deficit items and to increase the war on speculation and bribery. As is known, despite the previous price increases on items of gold and silver, carpets, furs, cars, and imported furniture, the demand for them is not being met. These items are sold in conditions of long queues and often in violation of trade regulations."[62] But for nonluxury items the state tried to avoid unpopular decisions that would have political repercussions.

A survey in the 1980s revealed the different conditions of access to food in the USSR. At that time, 97 percent of purchasers in Moscow and Leningrad used state stores, where the prices were lower, and 79 percent did so in the republic capitals. There 17 percent shopped in co-operative stores and 10 percent bought food in *kolkhoz* markets (people could list several sources, so the numbers do not add up to 100 percent). In oblast centers, only 36 percent said they could buy meat and sausages in state stores, 37 percent used cooperative stores, and 35 percent shopped in markets. The higher the average family income, the more meat it bought in state stores (most often in those open only to employees of government agencies, military enterprises, and the like) at subsidized prices.[63] The system was outrageously unfair. Politburo member Konstantin Chernenko told the Secretariat of the Central Committee (February 1981):

> Letters from citizens report, often in sharp terms, temporary disruptions in the delivery of bread and baked goods, a smaller selection and lower quality of baked goods. . . . Reports have been confirmed about failure of delivery of bread to workers and its low quality in the past year from the cities of Irkutsk, Uralsk, Chelyabinsk, Artem (Primorksi Krai), Minusinsk (Krasnoyarsk Krai), Umani (Cherkassk Oblast), Roslavl (Smolensk Oblast), Uryupinsk (Volgograd Oblast), Belogorsk (Amur Oblast), Kirov (Kaluga Oblast), Kulebaka (Gorky Oblast), the village of Yurino (Mariisk ASSR), and many others.[64]

The USSR's political leadership was trapped, with no way out. It was impossible to speed up agricultural production sufficiently to meet the growing demand. Bringing demand in line with supply without raising prices, and also a decision to raise prices, would violate the unwritten contract between the regime and the people. As the gap between the wholesale prices of agricultural products and their retail prices kept growing, budget problems grew as well. The forced increase in agricultural expenditures as a share of capital investments limited the development of high-tech sectors.

The traditional Soviet responses to unrest in the satellite states of Eastern Europe had included using force and increasing economic aid.[65] In the 1950s, the Soviet Union supported the Eastern European socialist countries by providing grain. As the crisis in Soviet agriculture increased, it was able to supply less and less, but continued providing some assistance until the early 1960s (see table 4-12).

These deliveries were politically motivated, part of the payment for stability in the Eastern European empire. Characteristically, after the events in Poland in 1956, grain shipments to that country remained at former levels despite the general cutback in exports to Eastern Europe. It was only in 1963 that the USSR, faced with a major crisis in its food supply, ceased exporting food and grain to all of the Eastern European countries.

TABLE 4-12. Soviet Grain Exported to the Socialist Countries
of Eastern Europe, 1955–63
Thousand tons

Year	Exports
1955	1,624
1956	995
1957	4,677
1958	2,926
1959	4,439
1960	4,162
1961	2,743
1962	2,793
1963	2,602

Source: *USSR Agricultural Trade* (Washington: U.S. Department of Agriculture, 1991).

At a meeting of the Presidium of the Central Committee on November 10, 1963, Khrushchev spoke about a letter that had to be sent to the leaders of the European socialist bloc:

I think it should be written this way. Dear comrades, as you know this year was a very difficult one for agriculture in the Soviet Union (present arguments: such-and-such a winter, a summer drought), and your countries also suffered. . . . We are left without reserves, and when such poor conditions developed for agriculture in the Soviet Union, it became evident to you as well. Your agriculture in Rumania has been unable to meet your needs for many years, so in the past you turned to us and we always agreed to satisfy your request—when you came to us in accordance with our agreements and above and beyond them—and that caused our reserves to melt away. This year, when we used some of our last reserves in order to satisfy your request, we had hoped that good conditions would enable us to replenish our reserves, but now the situation is such that we do not have enough for ourselves and therefore have had to buy around 12 million tons on the world market. This created excitement on the international grain market. But we have difficulties not only in buying up grain but also in transporting it. It is clear to all that we cannot continue treating this situation in this manner; therefore we want to tell you our thoughts, not only in the interest of our own country but in your interest as well. (Do the math.) Perhaps for three or four years, and please understand us, we will not be able to take on any obligations in supplying grain and cotton. We will start by satisfying our own demand and setting aside a reserve, and that will be a reserve not only for the Soviet Union but for you as well. In the process of building up the reserve we will be able to ensure that the countries that cannot feed themselves buy grain on the world market right away, so that there will be no repetition of the situation we face today. So now, at the expense of other industries, we are adding capital investment to raise the production of mineral fertilizers in order to raise yields and guarantee a wholesale harvest that will meet the demand and create conditions for setting up a reserve. Without that we can no longer live.[66]

In 1963 another bad harvest and the depleted state grain reserves forced the Soviet government to buy abroad, using 372.2 tons of gold—more than one-third of the USSR's gold reserves.[67] The leaders considered the move humiliating, but no more than an accident caused by the whims of nature. At the same meeting of the Presidium, Khrushchev said, "We must have a year's supply of grain in seven years. The Soviet regime cannot bear such shame again."[68]

In subsequent years, buying grain abroad was the natural result of the choices made in handling the economic crisis in agriculture. In 1965 the Soviet government had to spend another 335.3 tons of gold to finance food purchases.[69] In the early 1970s agricultural exports and imports in the USSR were still more or less balanced. By the start of the 1980s, imports exceeded exports by more than $15 billion.

Imports of grain and other agricultural products fluctuated annually because of weather conditions, but grew steadily in the long term (see table 4-13 and figure 4-1). Soviet purchases of grain, 2.2 million tons in 1970, had grown to 29.4 million tons in 1982 and reached their highest point in 1984, 46 million tons. Russia had been the largest exporter of grain at the beginning of the century and by the mid-1980s had become the world's largest importer (see table 4-14).

In the 1980s, the Soviet Union bought more than 15 percent of the world's imported grain. In wheat purchases, the country was far ahead of other major importers (see table 4-15). By the mid-1980s, every third ton of baked goods was made from imported grain. Cattle production was based on grain imports. The USSR was forced to make long-term contracts on grain deliveries, guaranteeing the annual purchase of no less than 9 million tons from the United States, 5 million from Canada, 4 million from Argentina, and 1.5 million tons from China.[70]

Unlike many other commodities that could have been obtained through barter with Comecon countries, grain had to be paid for in convertible currency. The combination of large costs of importing grain (which could not be

TABLE 4-13. USSR Balance of Trade for Grain and Agricultural Products, 1961–90

Year	Grain (millions of dollars)	Agricultural products (millions of dollars)	Grain (millions of year 2000 dollars)	Agricultural products (millions of year 2000 dollars)
1961	445	−114	2,091	−536
1962	505	88	2,341	408
1963	188	−144	862	−661
1964	−353	−1,027	−1,595	−4,641
1965	−160	−1,061	−710	−4,707
1966	−303	−829	−1,307	−3,576
1967	252	−247	1,055	−1,034
1968	255	−213	1,024	−855
1969	443	−284	1,694	−1,086
1970	285	−1,006	1,035	−3,654
1971	391	−798	1,352	−2,760
1972	−571	−1,969	−1,892	−6,524
1973	−1,038	−3,236	−3,259	−10,160
1974	162	−2,602	466	−7,492
1975	−2,228	−6,791	−5,863	−17,871
1976	−2,808	−7,450	−6,985	−18,532
1977	−982	−6,725	−2,297	−15,731
1978	−2,313	−8,116	−5,055	−17,736
1979	−3,107	−10,824	−6,270	−21,845
1980	−5,183	−14,923	−9,591	−27,615
1981	−7,712	−18,199	−13,045	−30,783
1982	−6,255	−16,970	−9,971	−27,052
1983	−5,038	−16,182	−7,726	−24,815
1984	−6,602	−16,941	−9,759	−25,042
1985	−5,750	−15,695	−8,248	−22,515
1986	−2,776	−12,914	−3,896	−18,125
1987	−2,445	−13,352	−3,340	−18,240
1988	−3,838	−14,556	−5,071	−19,231
1989	−5,043	−17,052	−6,419	−21,706
1990	−4,606	−17,117	−5,645	−20,979

Source: UN Food and Agriculture Organization, FAOSTAT data, 2005.

reduced because they were the result of long-term problems in domestic agriculture and weather conditions), an uncompetitive manufacturing sector, and the unpredictability of raw materials prices (which could have been used to offset the food imports) became the Achilles' heel of the Soviet economy by the mid-1980s. In the period 1981–85, under the influence of increasing difficulties in supplying food, the share of machinery and equipment imported

FIGURE 4-1. Balance of Trade for Grain in the USSR and Member
Countries of the Organization for Economic Cooperation and
Development (OECD), 1961–90

Billions of year 2000 dollars

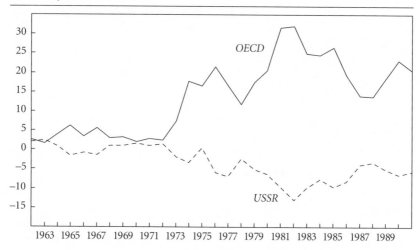

Source: UN Food and Agricultural Organization, FAOSTAT data, 2005.

from the capitalist countries was reduced from 26 percent to 20 percent, and
the share of imported food and consumer goods rose to 44 percent.

The sale of gold was the most immediate way of solving the problems that
arose from bad harvests. Its sale abroad increased sharply in 1973, 1976, 1978,
and 1981. After the collapse of the Bretton Woods accords in the early 1970s,

TABLE 4-14. Grain Exported by Russia in the Early Twentieth Century
and Grain Imports by the USSR in the Late Twentieth Century[a]

Exports/Imports	Share (percent)	Global ranking
Global grain exports, 1907–13	45.0	1
Global grain imports, 1980–90	16.4	1

Source: Calculations based on data in B. R. Mitchell, *International Historical Statistics: Europe 1750–1993*
(London: Macmillan Reference, 1998); B. R. Mitchell, *International Historical Statistics: The Americas 1750–1993*
(London: Macmillan Reference, 1998); B. R. Mitchell, *International Historical Statistics: Africa, Asia & Oceania
1750–1993* (London: Macmillan Reference, 1998); UN Food and Agriculture Organization, FAOSTAT data, 2004.

a. The share of Russia's exports in global exports has been calculated as an average for the period, using data
on grain exports by Russia, Denmark, France, Hungary, and Romania, and data on wheat exports by Canada,
the United States, Argentina, India, and Australia (net exports). The set of countries corresponds to the largest
grain exporters in early twentieth century (1907–13). Data for this period are for all grain exports by European
countries. For the countries of Asia and the Americas data are available only for wheat exports, the mainstay of
their grain exports.

TABLE 4-15. Grain Imported by the USSR, Japan, Italy, West Germany, Egypt, and China

Million tons

Year	USSR	Japan	Italy	West Germany	Egypt	China
1970	2.2	15.8	6.7	8.1	1.3	5.4
1975	15.9	19.0	7.2	6.8	3.8	3.7
1980	29.4	24.7	7.8	5.2	6.1	13.4
1983	33.9	25.5	6.4	4.5	8.0	13.4
1984	46.0	27.2	7.3	4.8	8.7	10.4
1985	45.6	26.9	7.5	7.0	8.9	6.0

Source: Statistical Yearbook *Sotsialisticheskie strany i strany kapitalizma v 1986 godu* [Socialist Countries and the Countries of Capitalism in 1986] (Moscow: Finansy i statistika, 1987).

higher gold prices helped the Soviet Union to finance its grain purchases. But even with higher gold prices in 1974–75, the USSR became a debtor on the international financial markets. A high percentage of its loans were short term, up to a year. In 1975, when the bad harvest forced the USSR to increase its imports of grain, it was forced to take on large international loans and to use its own hard currency reserves.[71]

Neither gold mining in the USSR, nor the country's gold reserves, nor foreign loans could serve as stable sources of funding for agricultural imports. From the late 1960s to the early 1980s, the Soviet Union sold gold only in years of bad harvest, when the demand for imported grain increased. It would have been impossible to use gold for regular purchases of millions and then tens of millions of tons of grain.

From the 1930s to the early 1950s the resources appropriated from the countryside helped to form the industrial base of the USSR. Large amounts of money were invested, particularly in the construction of manufacturing facilities. Manufactured goods are the foundation of international trade. When the USSR needed to finance the import of food in the early 1960s, the leadership might have hoped to pay for the imports by exporting manufactured goods. But that was not even considered. They knew that the production of machinery and heavy equipment was not competitive on the world market (see table 4-16). They could supply military technology to other Eastern bloc countries, but there was no hope of being paid in hard currency.

The USSR, like Russia before it, had throughout its history been a major supplier of traditional raw materials. Before the mass import of grains, these commodities along with agricultural production had guaranteed enough money to buy machinery and equipment for hard currency.

TABLE 4-16. USSR Trade in Machinery and Equipment with Developed Capitalist Countries, 1961–85[a]

Year	Export of machinery and equipment				Import of machinery and equipment				Net balance of export of machinery and equipment			
	Million rubles	Million dollars	Million year 2000 dollars	Share of machinery and equipment in gross exports (percent)	Million rubles	Million dollars	Million year 2000 dollars	Share of machinery and equipment in gross imports (percent)	Million rubles	Million dollars	Million year 2000 dollars	Surplus of imports over exports (times)
1961	17	19	87	1.9	417	464	2,180	26.7	-401	-445	-2,092	25.0
1965	37	41	181	2.5	450	500	2,220	18.6	-414	-460	-2,039	12.3
1970	84	93	339	3.3	1,003	1,114	4,048	26.5	-919	-1,021	-3,709	11.9
1975	262	364	958	5.2	3,627	5,042	13,267	39.6	-3,365	-4,677	-1,2309	13.8
1980	294	453	838	3.5	4,661	7,178	13,283	30.7	-4,367	-6,725	-1,2445	15.9
1985	354	425	609	3.5	5,437	6,524	9,359	21.0	-5,083	-6,100	-8,750	15.4

Source: Calculations based on Statistical Yearbook *Vneshniaia torgovlia SSSR* [USSR Foreign Trade] (Moscow: Finansy i statistika, various years).

a. Recalculation into dollars based on the official rate of the USSR Gosbank. The largest portion (30 percent in 1985) of machinery and equipment exports was to Finland, with which the trade was barter-based, rather than in exchange for convertible currency.

The USSR sold metals to capitalist markets but at the same time imported high-quality metallurgical products. This was also the case in many other industrial sectors. These mutual ties were built into the structure of Soviet foreign trade and the economy. It was difficult to create a sharp increase in the volume of non–raw materials exports. Refusing to buy imported equipment only increased the technology gap with the countries that were leaders of modern economic growth.

The USSR's transition in the 1960s to become the largest net importer of food created enormous problems. They were compounded by the fact that the Soviet Union had never maintained large hard currency reserves, instead choosing to maintain them at a level to service current trade.

The Soviet leaders realized the threat inherent in depending on countries that were potential enemies for their food supply.[72] But the agricultural crisis and the noncompetitiveness in heavy equipment manufacturing were givens. The government could do very little to solve problems that had accrued over decades.

Oil in Western Siberia: The Illusion of Salvation

The Soviet Union had started exporting oil in significant amounts in the 1950s. Between 1950 and 1960 oil production in the Volga Oil Basin grew sharply. However, at that time, the USSR was supplying the socialist countries and selling only limited amounts for hard currency. The discovery of oil deposits in Western Siberia in the 1960s seemed to be the answer to the food supply issue: oil exports would pay for food imports.

The first oil well in Western Siberia was opened in September 1953.[73] Large-scale geological discoveries came in the period 1961–65: in 1961, the Megionskoe and Ust-Balykskoe deposits; in 1963, Fedorovskoe; and in 1965, Mamontovskoe and Samotlor. They were characterized by high production levels, as a rule, exceeding 100 tons a day per well, at accessible depths of 1.8–2.5 kilometers.[74] From 1972 to 1981, oil production in the Western-Siberian Oil and Gas Province (ZSNGP) grew from 62.7 million tons to 334.3 million tons, more than 500 percent (see table 4-17). The increases in oil production in the USSR in those years were unusually high (see figure 4-2). Many of the deposits were unique by international standards, producing extraordinarily high yields.

The Soviet Union quickly developed a market for its oil in capitalist countries. Its need for hard currency prompted the use of methods that gave quick results but risked creating much lower yields in the following years. At the end

TABLE 4-17. Oil Production in Western Siberia, 1965–84

Million tons

Year	Glavtyumenneftegaz	Tomskneft	Total
1965	1.0	...	1.0
1966	2.8	0.05	2.8
1967	5.6	0.2	5.8
1968	11.7	0.5	12.2
1969	19.8	1.5	21.3
1970	28.0	3.4	31.4
1971	40.0	4.7	44.7
1972	56.8	5.9	62.7
1973	81.0	6.7	87.7
1974	109.8	6.6	116.4
1975	141.4	6.6	148.0
1976	175.0	6.7	181.7
1977	211.2	7.1	218.3
1978	245.7	8.4	254.1
1979	274.4	9.1	283.5
1980	302.8	9.8	312.6
1981	323.5	10.8	334.3
1982	341.5	11.4	352.9
1983	358.2	11.9	370.1
1984	365.4	12.5	377.9

Source: M. V. Slavkina, *Triumf i tragedia: razvitie neftegazovogo kompleksa SSSR v 1960–1980-e gody*
[Triumph and Tragedy: The Development of the USSR Oil and Gas Industry, 1960–1980], p. 69.

FIGURE 4-2. Oil Production in the USSR, 1960–84

Millions of tons

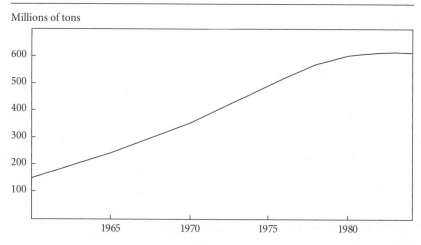

Source: Statistical Yearbook *Narodnoe khoziaistvo SSSR* (Moscow: Finansy i statistika, various years).

of the 1970s and in the early 1980s, Soviet officials responsible for the economy and those involved in developing the ZSNGP discussed how quickly production could be increased without causing irreversible damage to the long-term prospects for the deposits. Sometimes the discussions grew heated. Valentin Shashin, oil minister, told Gosplan and party officials repeatedly, according to his colleagues, that they were overstraining the production capabilities and not considering the consequences.[75]

However, continuing food supply difficulties pushed the Soviet leadership toward a strategy of forced exploitation of deposits. Chairman of the Council of Ministers Alexei Kosygin repeatedly appealed to Viktor Muravlenko, head of Glavtyumenneftegaz, the agency overseeing oil and gas production in Tyumen, in approximately this form: "Things are bad with bread, give me 3 million tons over the plan."[76] Over the period 1974–84, expenditures to extract an additional ton of oil increased by 70 percent. Expenditures for extracting fuel doubled from the early 1970s to the early 1980s.[77]

The need to increase oil production led to a concentration of efforts on the largest projects. Using methods that allowed for a quick increase in production but created unpredictable risks meant focusing on a few unique sites.[78] The foreign trade balance, the balance of payments, the food supply, and the preservation of political stability all depended on the weather on the virgin land and the situation at the oil wells. As the basis for economic and political stability of a superpower, that's not much.

Along with the discovery of large petroleum deposits, the unprecedented rise in world oil prices in 1973–74 and the jump in prices in 1979–81 provided significant boosts to the Soviet economy. As oil exports increased, the influx of hard currency was greater than ever beginning in 1973 (see figure 4-3). The hard currency from oil exports stopped the growing food supply crisis,[79] increased the import of equipment and consumer goods, ensured a financial base for the arms race and the achievement of nuclear parity with the United States, and permitted the realization of such risky foreign policy actions as the war in Afghanistan.[80]

Typically, in this period of great oil production, exports, and high prices from the mid-1970s to the 1980s, the Soviet government still did not create hard currency reserves or invest the income in liquid financial instruments that could be used in case of trouble on the oil market. The USSR had only enough hard currency on hand to meet its trade needs. Moreover, the Soviet Union increased its borrowing, despite the huge rise in oil revenues.[81] The only rational explanation for this policy is that the authorities were counting

FIGURE 4-3. Exports of Oil and Oil Products from the USSR to OECD Countries, 1972–85

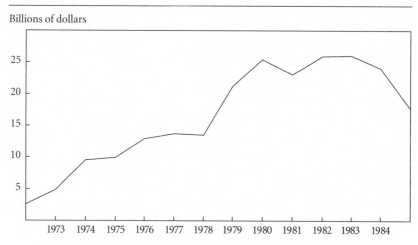

Billions of dollars

Source: Statistical Yearbook *Vneshniaia torgovlia SSSR* (Moscow: Finansy i statistika, various years).
Note: Data for OECD countries do not include Portugal and the territory of West Berlin.

on oil prices to remain high. The Soviet leadership clearly did not think about what would happen if prices fell.[82]

For all the high oil prices, the USSR had to deal with the problem of financing the deficit in the balance of payments. The cause was, as usual, agricultural: three years of bad harvests and a concomitant need to increase grain imports.

By 1980, oil and gas made up 67 percent of USSR exports to OECD countries. At the same time, prices remained high but stopped rising. The shortage of consumer goods increased, more money was printed, and prices in the *kolkhoz* markets went up. Budget expenses were financed primarily by the savings and investments of the population. The increase in financial imbalance in the economy, the growth of financial disparities, and the consumer goods shortages stimulated attempts to compensate for the lack of production by lowering product quality (for example, by increasing the amount of water and starch in sausage). Beginning in the mid-1970s, approximately half the increase in commodity circulation came from a reduction in quality and an increase in prices. Gosplan's report on this issue was distributed to the deputy chairmen of the Council of Ministers. The next day the copies were appropriated and destroyed.[83] This all took place against a background of increasing economic crime and corruption.[84]

The Soviet government always regarded foreign trade and paying out hard currency as a political instrument. Maintaining economic relations with like-minded people abroad, supporting their political goals, and stabilizing satellite regimes in Eastern Europe were closely intertwined. The USSR used its political influence actively and not unsuccessfully to manipulate decisionmaking on key political issues in developed democratic countries. The authorities were prepared to exploit foreign trade contracts in order to turn over the revenues to friends.[85] For example, the decision of the Secretariat of the Central Committee dated August 26, 1980, ordered the Ministry of Foreign Trade to work with Gosplan and other ministries to develop and implement measures to expand trade and economic ties with companies belonging to French friends.[86] On December 12, 1980, the deputy head of the International Department of the Central Committee, Anatoly Chernyaev, wrote to the leadership of the Central Committee:

> The firm Magra GmbH belongs to the French Communist Party and for the last fifteen years has been buying bearings from V/O Stankoimport for sale in the FRG. There is an outstanding debt of 2.8 million rubles in connection with the company investing that sum to expand its plant and the reduced demand in the FRG for bearings. In the opinion of the Ministry of Foreign Trade, if Magra GmbH is given an extension on its loan, it will be able to increase the sales of Soviet bearings in the FRG very quickly to levels that will allow it not only to repay the debt but also to guarantee future revenues in hard currency. At the same time, insistence on payment of the debt will lead to the firm's bankruptcy, to hard currency losses for us, and to other unwanted consequences. The leadership of our French friends supports the firm's request to extend the deadline for repaying its debt (telegram from Paris, No. 3922, 9 December 1980).[87]

Likewise, a Politburo resolution on January 18, 1983, ordered the Ministry of Foreign Trade (minister, Comrade Patolichev) to sell to Interexpo (president, Comrade L. Remiggio) 600,000 tons of oil and 150,000 tons of diesel fuel at a price discounted approximately 1 percent and to extend payment for three or four months so that the friends could make some $4 million on this deal.[88] The CPSU leadership heard about the ineffectiveness of such politically motivated contracts at a Politburo meeting on November 30, 1987:

> Many firms controlled by Communist Parties are economically weak, with limited ties and capabilities for trade, and some are even losing money. Companies of only a few fraternal parties—French, Greek, Cypriot, and Portuguese—are capable of developing cooperation with a tangible benefit

for themselves with Soviet foreign trade organizations. The percentage of their profits that the companies turn over to the party budgets is usually quite small—from 1 percent to 5 percent of profits or signed contracts.[89]

On March 1–2, 1982, a Polish party and state delegation visited Moscow. During a meeting with the Soviet leaders, Wojciech Jaruzelski, first secretary of the Polish Communist Party, spoke about the difficult situation in the Polish economy: it was using only 60 percent of its industrial potential, and there was a real threat of unemployment for 400,000 industrial workers and 200,000 construction workers. The Polish comrades thanked the Soviet Union for its emergency economic aid, which in 1980–81 was approximately 4 billion convertible rubles, including around $3 billion in hard currency. They agreed to a Soviet loan of 2.7 billion rubles for 1982–83. The Polish delegation asked about additional wide-ranging economic aid. On October 4, 1980, the Secretariat of the Central Committee examined the question of the influence of Polish events on domestic political developments in the USSR. Materials prepared by the *apparat* of the Central Committee read:

> Analysis of bourgeois propaganda, particularly radio broadcasts to the Soviet Union, relating to the Polish events shows that they are actively being used in attempts to compromise the principles of socialism, primarily to question the leading role of the party in socialist and Communist construction. . . . Some negative processes in Poland's mass media evince the possibility of an ideological disarray that will create additional difficulties for our informational-propaganda influence on the Polish populace. A weakening of control by the Central Committee of the Polish party over newspapers, radio, and television is evident. The press publishes with greater frequency controversial or simply dubious materials that in no way help the efforts of the Polish party to stabilize the situation.

In December 1980, the Secretariat took measures to limit the spread of information in the USSR about the events in Poland. The Chief Directorate on State Secrets in the Press, under the Council of Ministers of the USSR, was instructed to confiscate from stores such periodicals and other publications and send them to special warehouses.[90] As time passed, the costs of foreign policy activity and preserving the empire continued to rise.

A Drop in Oil Prices: The Final Blow

In the period 1981–84, the government of the USSR had only one instrument to handle the growing difficulties in foreign trade—increasing oil production.

Production rose from 93.1 million tons in 1975 to 119 million tons in 1980 and 130 million tons in 1983.[91] But the rate of growth in oil production went down in the late 1970s.

One would have expected the Soviet Union to know that the oil market is affected not only by economic factors, but also by political ones. It had taken an active part in manipulating the market. Chairman of the KGB Yuri Andropov wrote to Leonid Brezhnev on April 23, 1974:

> The KGB has maintained secret working contact with Wadia Haddad, Politburo member of the People's Liberation Front of Palestine (PLFP), head of the PLFP's external operations section. In a confidential conversation at a meeting with the KGB resident in Lebanon in April of this year, Wadia Haddad outlined a prospective program of sabotage and terrorism by the PLFP, which can be defined as follows. The main aim of special activity by PLFP is to increase the effectiveness of the struggle of the Palestinian movement against Israel, Zionism, and American imperialism. Arising from this, the main thrusts of the planned sabotage and terrorist operations are: employing special means to prolong the "oil war" of Arab countries against the imperialist forces supporting Israel; carrying out operations against American and Israeli personnel in third countries with the aim of securing reliable information about the plans and intentions of the USA and Israel; carrying out acts of sabotage and terrorism on the territory of Israel; organizing acts of sabotage against the Diamond Center [in Tel Aviv], whose basic capital derives from Israeli, British, Belgian, and West German companies. In order to implement the above measures, the PLFP is currently preparing a number of special operations, including strikes against large oil-storage installations in various countries (Saudi Arabia, the Persian Gulf, Hong Kong, and others), the destruction of oil tankers and supertankers, actions against American and Israeli representatives in Iran, Greece, Ethiopia, Kenya, an attack on the Diamond Center in Tel Aviv, etc. W. Haddad asks that we help his organization with the procurement of several kinds of special technology necessary for carrying out certain sabotage operations. . . .
> In view of the above, we feel it would be feasible, at the next meeting, to give a generally favorable response to Wadia Haddad's request for special assistance to the PLFP.[92]

The invasion of Afghanistan was perceived as a threat by the Gulf states, particularly Saudi Arabia, and was one of the factors in its radical change in attitude toward the United States, for its potential military support. America

TABLE 4-18. Oil Exported from the USSR, 1980–86
Million tons

Oil exports	1980	1983	1984	1985	1986
To socialist countries	84.8	80.0	80.6	77.9	85.3
To developed capitalist countries	30.7	44.8	44.0	33.3	37.6

Source: Statistical Yearbook *Sotsialisticheskie strany i strany kapitalizma v 1986 g.* [Socialist Countries and the Countries of Capitalism in 1986] (Moscow: Finansy i statistika, 1987).

needed lower oil prices. The two countries' mutual interest was first discussed on a high level in April 1981 during CIA chief William Casey's visit to Saudi Arabia.[93]

In the fall of 1981, prompted by serious balance-of-payments problems, the Soviet Union had to inform the socialist countries of Eastern Europe of a 10 percent decrease in the annual deliveries of oil and its intention to use the difference to increase exports to OECD countries. But even then, it was impossible to ignore political considerations. The critical situation in Poland kept the USSR from substantially reducing oil deliveries to its largest Eastern European satellite. The aid obligations had to be kept in mind if preservation of the Eastern European part of the empire was the goal.[94] In 1985, when oil production began to fall for the first time in Soviet economic history, supplies to the capitalist countries went down for the first time (see table 4-18). The Soviet Union was unwilling to decrease supplies to the Comecon countries.

Richard Pipes wrote a note to the American authorities in the early 1980s recommending using the dependence of the Soviet economy on oil prices to destabilize the Communist regime. William Casey, appointed CIA director by Ronald Reagan, had experience analyzing and using the enemy's economic weaknesses. He worked on this during World War II, trying to maximize the economic damage to Nazi Germany by the Allies. On March 26, 1981, there is an entry in Reagan's personal diary about a briefing on the state of the Soviet economy and its problems related to dependence on Western loans. In November 1982, President Reagan signed a directive on national security (NSDT-66), which set damage to the Soviet economy as a goal.[95] Naturally, the idea was to weaken the USSR in an economic and political sense. No one in the American leadership in those years even dreamed of using its economic vulnerability to destroy the USSR.

If this version of events is accurate, it is very telling about the intellectual level of the Soviet leadership in the early 1980s. It would take a long time to recruit leaders who were so incompetent as to make the economy and policy of a superpower dependent on the decisions of their potential enemy (the United States) and their main rival in the oil market (Saudi Arabia, where Wahhabism, the branch of Islam that regards the holy war against infidels as an unassailable requirement for an orthodox Muslim, is the official religion), and wait for them to come to terms.

The financial situation of the Eastern European countries was becoming more dire. Here is a letter from the Currency-Economic Directorate of Gosbank USSR:

> The socialist countries began widely using loans from Western banks in the early 1970s in political détente, the significant expansion of trade between East and West, the growth of the world economy, and the rise in prices for energy resources and raw materials. However, the growth of the world economy began to slow in 1981, and the general level of unpaid debt of the socialist countries reached a record for the time of $127 billion, and the ability of some of them to pay is very low. In 1982–83, the syndicated loans of socialist countries, with the exception of Hungary, were not addressed. In these conditions, the socialist countries were forced to reduce imports for hard currency, leaving exports at the previous level or increasing them slightly.[96]

In early 1984, the Academy of Sciences informed the Council of Ministers about the instability of the oil market:

> After a brief stabilization of the oil market in the third quarter, the situation in the fourth quarter has once again become complicated for exporting countries. The slow and erratic development of the capitalist economy, the effect of measures on energy saving, the unspoken violation of production quotas by a number of OPEC members, and the warm winter led to a surplus of oil reserves. The demand for oil on the capitalist market in the fourth quarter has fallen by 1 percent, and even though most official prices have not changed, the prices of one-time deals on the free market have fallen and by the middle of December broke away from the official ones for North Sea oil, like Brent at $9.70 a ton. . . . This course of events has increased disputes within OPEC, which was apparent at the last conference in Geneva in December. Nigeria, Iran, Iraq, and Venezuela demanded an official increase in their production quotas and also amendments in their favor in the existing structure of discounts and surcharges for various oils. And even though the conference decided to retain the existing previous

prices, the individual quotas, and the general volume of oil production in OPEC, it could not impose sanctions or preventive measures against violators of these agreements.

At that time, official documents showed the unpredictability of prices on the most important raw materials. Thus the next report of the Academy of Sciences spoke of stabilization on the oil market:

> Specialists believe that at this time the possibility of further decreases in the absolute volume of oil consumption, especially in Western Europe, has been exhausted and that the demand for oil in 1984 will grow by 1.5–2 percent, which will keep OPEC's official prices at the same level throughout 1984. Prices on the free market for the first quarter have almost reached the level of official prices. Consultations between OPEC and other oil-exporting nations continued on questions of maintaining existing prices. The strengthening of the market was also related to the increased conflict between Iran and Iraq and worries about the shutdown of the Strait of Hormuz.

Subsequent memos from the Academy of Sciences to the government reflected concerns about a sharp fall in oil prices and a sober recognition of the impossibility of accurately predicting that parameter's dynamics.[97]

In 1985, expenditures to develop new wells and to support yields on active wells, combined with a lack of resources, led to a fall in production of 12 million tons in the USSR. At the same time, the slow decrease in the real cost of oil, which began in 1981–84 after the decision of Saudi Arabia to more than triple production (see chapter 2), met with an unprecedented collapse in prices. In 1985–86, prices on resources that supported the Soviet budget, its foreign trade balance, the stability of its consumer market, as well as its ability to buy tens of millions of tons of grain a year, to service its foreign debt, and to finance the army and military-industrial complex, fell severalfold.

These problems did not cause the collapse of the socialist system. That had been preordained by the fundamental characteristics of the Soviet economic and political system: the institutions formed in the late 1920s and early 1930s were too rigid and did not permit the country to adapt to the challenges of world development in the late twentieth century. The legacy of socialist industrialization, the anomalous defense load, the extreme crisis in agriculture, and the noncompetitive manufacturing sector made the fall of the regime inevitable. In the 1970s and early 1980s these problems could have been managed if oil prices had been high. But that was not a dependable foundation for preserving the last empire.

The Collapse of the USSR: The Unexpected Becomes the Rule

In 1982, summing up the results of CIA reports on the state of the Soviet economy, Senator William Proxmire said, "It is worth highlighting the three principal findings of the study: First, Soviet economic growth has been steadily slowing down. However, there will be continued positive growth for the foreseeable future. Second, economic performance has been poor, and there have been many departures from standards of economic efficiency. But this does not mean the Soviet economy is losing its viability or its dynamism. And third, while there has been a gap between Soviet performance and plans, an economic collapse in the USSR is not considered even a remote possibility."[98]

Most observers had overlooked the radical change in the relationship between the USSR and the world that took place in the 1960s and 1970s. At that time, the Soviet economy, formally still closed, had in fact become deeply integrated into the system of international trade and dependent on world markets (see table 4-19). This change, as a rule, was noticed only by researchers concerned with grain and oil markets. The majority of analysts studying the socialist system considered its foundation to be solid.[99]

Some publications spoke of risk factors that could undermine the stability of the Soviet regime. But they were exceptions, and their influence on the future image of the USSR was limited.[100] In 1985 almost no one imagined that six years later there would be no Soviet Union, no ruling Communist Party, no Soviet economic system.

The unexpected collapse of the political and economic construction that had existed for many decades was a bombshell that cast a shadow on the reputation of specialists in Soviet economics and politics.[101] The fact that the CIA did not see signs of the looming crisis and collapse was considered one of its great failures. Many Sovietologists reacted defensively to criticisms of their work—if we were mistaken, they seemed to say, it was because it was impossible to predict the economic crisis in the USSR. This group shared a widespread idea of the subjective nature of the causes of this event and the errors of the Soviet leadership since 1985.[102]

This point of view is close to that of those who consider the collapse the result of international intrigue. In Russia, it is presented by those who believe in a world conspiracy against Russia. Accepting that position, it is not difficult to explain what happened in Russia in the late 1980s and early 1990s. We must take into account a long-standing tradition of blaming outsiders for Russia's woes.

The widespread image of the CIA's demonic powers in Russia is the mirror image of Washington's conviction that the CIA showed total ineptitude

TABLE 4-19. USSR Foreign Trade with OECD Countries, 1950–89[a]

| | Millions of rubles in nominal terms | | Millions of dollars | | Millions of year 2000 dollars | |
Year	Exports	Imports	Exports	Imports	Exports	Imports
1950	236	204	262	227	1,586	1,371
1960	913	1,004	1,014	1,116	4,822	5,302
1965	1,347	1,469	1,497	1,632	6,640	7,241
1970	2,154	2,540	2,393	2,822	8,694	10,251
1975	6,140	9,704	8,535	13,489	22,459	35,496
1976	7,834	10,824	10,419	14,396	25,918	35,811
1977	8,817	9,925	11,815	13,300	27,637	31,110
1978	8,701	10,979	12,703	16,029	27,761	35,029
1979	12,506	13,248	19,009	20,137	38,364	40,640
1980	15,862	15,721	24,427	24,210	45,203	44,801
1981	17,247	18,112	23,973	25,176	40,550	42,584
1982	18,849	18,892	26,012	26,071	41,466	41,561
1983	19,653	18,719	26,532	25,271	40,686	38,753
1984	21,349	19,574	26,259	24,076	38,816	35,589
1985	18,581	19,294	22,297	23,153	31,986	33,213
1986	13,109	15,853	18,615	22,511	26,126	31,595
1987	14,186	13,873	22,414	21,919	30,620	29,944
1988	14,666	16,321	24,199	26,930	31,971	35,579
1989	16,392	20,497	25,899	32,385	32,968	41,224

Source: Statistical Yearbook *Vneshniaia torgovlia SSSR* [USSR Foreign Trade] (Moscow: Finansy i statistika, various years).

a. Calculation into dollars based on the official rate of the USSR Gosbank.

about the events of the late 1980s and early 1990s in the USSR and then in Russia.

There is one more theory about the nature of the collapse of the Soviet economy. It is related to the intensification of the arms race that came with the Reagan administration, when the USSR could not handle the burden of increased military spending.[103] In order to judge the accuracy of that view, we must understand the mechanism of decisionmaking on military spending and arms purchases in the USSR in the late 1970s and early 1980s.

Along with helping foreign socialist countries, military spending was an important priority.[104] Its share of the GDP was not known to the leaders of the country and the armed forces. This is clear from the contradictory data cited by the last president of the USSR, Mikhail Gorbachev, and the head of the General Staff, General Vladimir Lobov.[105] The data cannot be compared because they went through different budget lines. It is not clear to what extent

Soviet prices for military technology reflected economic reality. But obviously, by any international standard, military expenditures made up a large share of the GDP. If a country with an economy about one-fourth the size that of the United States manages to support military parity with the United States and its allies and at the same time can finance forty divisions on the Chinese border, common sense tells us that the military was expensive. The scale of military expenditures was held back by the development of the civilian sector of the Soviet economy.[106] But even without the military burden, investments in the economy in the 1980s were not effective.

There is little convincing evidence that when the Soviet Union faced more intense military competition with the United States in the early 1980s it increased military spending significantly.[107] Inertia was the primary characteristic of the Soviet military-industrial complex. The production of weapons was not determined by military needs but by production capabilities. If technologically there was a possibility of increasing production, a justification for doing so was always found. When Georgy Shakhnazarov, an aide to General Secretary Mikhail Gorbachev, asked, "Why do we need to make so many weapons?" Chief of the General Staff Sergei Akhromeyev replied, "Because through enormous sacrifice we have created first-class plants that are no worse than what the Americans have. What, are you going to tell them to stop working and make pots and pans instead? That's simply Utopian."[108]

An example of decisionmaking about the volume of arms production in the USSR is provided by the history of Soviet tanks. In the 1970s, the USSR made twenty times more tanks than the United States. After the Arab-Israeli War, when the Israeli army needed large numbers of new tanks, the United States increased production over a few years to approximately a quarter of what the USSR produced. The Soviet army had more than 60,000 tanks, many times more than the United States and its allies.

An attempt to analyze military construction in the 1970s and early 1980s from a military strategy point of view would lead Western experts observing the speed at which tank armadas were being created to the natural conclusion that the USSR was preparing for an invasion in Western Europe toward the Bay of Biscay. In fact, that was not the case at all. We now know that the main argument for continuing the production of tanks in unprecedented numbers during peacetime was the conviction that the United States had a greater capability to increase tank production in wartime. The General Staff analysts maintained that losses of Soviet troops in tanks could be extremely high in the first months of war. Hence the conclusion: we must produce as many tanks as possible in peacetime.[109]

They did not accept the reasoning that in the decades since World War II the equipment had become so complex that it would be impossible for the United States and its allies to quickly speed up production of tanks. The main factor in discussions of this issue was not military strategy, but the fact that the tank factories were already built and people worked there. Those people had to produce tanks. The same reasoning applied to other forms of military technology.

The placement of medium-range SS-20 missiles is a case in point. A good missile was created and it could be mass produced. The Soviet Union decided to develop a new system of nuclear weapons. It did not take into account that doing so would provoke NATO to set up medium-range missiles in Western Europe and thereby increase the risks for the USSR since the enemy missiles would take less time to reach the country. When that became obvious, the USSR had to agree to the removal of medium-range missiles in Europe. But this happened only after great expenditures were made to build them.

In the early 1980s, the U.S. Congress voted to create a special commission to check the CIA estimates of Soviet military construction. The commission concluded that the volume of weapons production could not be explained by military or political logic unless the USSR were preparing to attack.[110] But documents show that no one in the Soviet leadership during those years was eager to get into mortal combat over world imperialism. In fact, the production of weapons and their supplies to the army and navy were determined by the production capacity of plants and factories. The military-industrial complex of the USSR in the early 1980s was not capable of using additional resources on a large scale and had to work within its capacities. This was a heavy burden on the Soviet economy, but a habitual one.

Yes, the military-industrial complex sucked up colossal resources from the country's economy and mobilized the best specialists. These expenditures held back the development of civilian branches of manufacturing. The military overload of the economy was one of the factors that made the Soviet economy so vulnerable. Military spending predetermined many of the difficulties in its development that the USSR faced in the 1960s through the early 1980s, but it does not explain the economic crash of 1985–91.

The twentieth century has shown that the laws of history are much less rigid than Karl Marx and Friedrich Engels had thought. The choice of a development strategy for decades ahead depends on factors that cannot be predicted. The role of the individual in history is much greater than Marxism's founders believed.

Decisions by the Soviet leadership played a large role in the development of the economic and political crisis in the late 1980s and early 1990s. Much depended on the leadership, but not everything. Or to put it another way: not everything, but a lot. Analysis of the situation in which the Soviet Union found itself in the mid-1980s leads to this conclusion: against the background of new realities (primarily the sharp drop in world oil prices), it would have been pointless to continue the policies of previous decades, which boiled down to conserving the economic and political system and changing nothing. Doing so would have made it impossible to avoid further serious economic and political shocks.

By 1985 the foundation had been laid for the profound economic crisis in the USSR, which required harsh, precise, and responsible decisions, an understanding of its nature and the measures that could and should be taken to mitigate the damage and at the very least prevent a crash. However, Soviet officials responsible for foreign economic relations were confident then in the stability of the USSR's hard currency situation.[111]

And in these circumstances, a new political leader appeared, representing a different generation of the political elite. His election demonstrated a rejection of the gerontocracy that had characterized the Soviet regime in previous decades.[112] He did not have a good idea of the real state of affairs in the country or understand how critical the hard currency situation was. There is no way of knowing whether it would have been possible to save the USSR in those conditions, acting energetically and precisely, without making a single mistake. But in order to have a fighting chance, the new leaders had to understand the scale and nature of the problems facing the country. It took them more than three years to get even a superficial idea of what was happening to the Soviet economy. That was too long in a crisis.

CHAPTER V

THE POLITICAL ECONOMY OF EXTERNAL SHOCKS

Things were going badly at the kolkhoz.

That is, not really very badly; you could even say they were going well,

But they got worse with every year.

—Vladimir Voinovich

MUCH HAS BEEN WRITTEN ABOUT the economic and political development of the USSR on the eve of the crash—that is, in the years 1985 to 1991. People at the center of the decisionmaking process have described a policy of accelerating all reforms and the strategy of *perestroika*, the unfolding of the anti-alcohol campaign, the development of civilian machine-building capabilities, the expansion of economic independence for enterprises, and the legalization of a private sector in the form of co-operatives; they have also discussed the ties between the development of market relations and political liberalization. The debate over what was done correctly and what mistakes were made, and who was right and who was wrong, will continue for a long time. In this chapter I address something else: the effect of an external shock, the sharp change in the oil market that the Soviet Union had to face in the second half of the 1980s.

Deteriorating Conditions for Foreign Trade: Political Alternatives

The concept of "external shock," a sharp change in the correlation of export and import prices, has been elaborated by economists living in developed and

FIGURE 5-1. Trends in World Economic Development (Rate of Growth), 1976–91

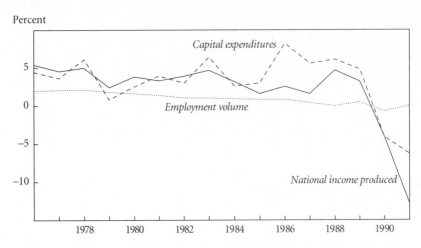

Source: *Rossiyskaia ekonomika v 1991 godu. Tendentsii i perspektivy* [The Russian Economy in 1991: Tendencies and Perspectives] (Moscow: Institute for Economic Policy, 1992), p. 24.

diversified economies. The data in figure 5-1 show that in such economies changes of more than 10 percent annually in trade conditions are the exception, not the rule. In the world's largest economy, the United States, this has happened only once in the past four decades, in 1974.

Export revenues in economies with a broad and varied range of exports that has no dominant component change little in the event of price fluctuations. Dealing with fluctuations requires a strict budget policy and sometimes a weakening in the exchange rate of the national currency. Importing countries experience similar difficulties when faced with higher prices on goods they import. The price shocks of 1973–74, 1979–81, 2004–05 (large hikes in oil prices) had a significant effect on the economies of importers of fuel and energy resources (see, for example, the figures for Japan in table 5-1). Nevertheless, fuel in most cases did not dominate imports even in the anomalously high prices of 1980. Even in such an energy-dependent country as Japan, the import share of fuel is only a small percentage of GDP (see tables 5-2, 5-3).

Countries whose export income depends on the market for raw materials are in a different position. When prices fall, the same production and export levels do not bring in as much hard currency as the national economy has

TABLE 5-1. Terms of Trade of Selected OECD Countries, 1960–2003[a]

2000 = 100 percent

Year	Canada	Germany	Italy	Great Britain	United States	Japan
1960	96	90	110	94	128	185
1961	94	94	109	97	132	176
1962	92	100	108	99	134	176
1963	90	108	107	111	133	175
1964	90	105	108	110	131	175
1965	91	104	105	113	134	178
1966	94	107	103	115	134	174
1967	95	111	103	115	136	177
1968	95	110	102	111	136	176
1969	95	110	105	112	136	177
1970	96	112	106	116	135	179
1971	95	115	105	116	132	176
1972	96	118	106	117	127	179
1973	102	115	96	104	125	162
1974	109	105	79	90	107	130
1975	105	110	84	97	110	116
1976	107	105	81	95	111	109
1977	101	104	83	97	106	109
1978	98	108	85	103	105	123
1979	103	102	83	107	100	106
1980	107	96	78	107	91	80
1981	101	89	74	107	94	79
1982	97	93	76	105	96	77
1983	98	94	78	104	102	78
1984	96	92	77	102	101	81
1985	94	93	78	103	103	82
1986	93	107	90	97	108	109
1987	96	111	92	97	102	112
1988	98	111	93	99	104	115
1989	100	108	92	100	104	112
1990	97	110	94	101	101	105
1991	95	107	98	101	102	108
1992	93	110	99	102	102	111
1993	93	111	99	104	102	114
1994	93	108	99	103	103	117
1995	97	107	96	100	103	115
1996	98	107	100	101	103	110
1997	97	105	102	103	104	104
1998	103	107	107	104	107	111
1999	110	107	108	102	105	110

(*continued*)

TABLE 5-1. (*Continued*)

Year	Canada	Germany	Italy	Great Britain	United States	Japan
2000	100	100	100	100	100	100
2001	99	102	101	99	103	101
2002	97	104	103	102	104	101
2003	104	107	104	104	103	98

Source: World Bank, *World Development Indicators, 2005.*

a. Terms of trade: the ratio of an index of export prices to index of import prices at a fixed structure of exports and imports of a country in 2000. The table includes those OECD countries for which data have been available in the World Bank database since 1906.

TABLE 5-2. Fuel Imports as a Share of GDP in the United States, Japan, France, Germany, and Italy

Percent

Country	1980	1990	2000	2003
U.S.	3.1	1.2	1.4	1.5
Germany	5.2	1.8	2.3	2.2
France	5.3	1.9	2.6	2.2
Italy	6.3	1.8	2.2	1.9
Japan	6.7	1.9	1.6	1.9

Source: Calculations based on World Bank, *World Development Indicators, 2005.*

TABLE 5-3. Fuel as a Share of Total Imports in the United States, Japan, France, Germany, and Italy, 1980–2003

Percent

Country	1980	1990	2000	2003
U.S.	28.7	10.9	9.5	...
Germany	20.6	7.0	6.9	6.8
France	23.0	8.3	9.4	8.9
Italy	25.5	8.9	8.0	7.5
Japan	45.8	20.1	17.4	18.4

Source: Calculations based on World Bank, *World Development Indicators, 2005.*

grown accustomed to having. They are forced to reduce imports and the manufacture of goods that depend on imported parts and materials. They must also reduce the volume of economic activity and ignore their customary consumer demand. The alternative is to increase production and exports of goods that do not rely on raw materials. The first path is difficult for political reasons. The second, at least in the short term, is difficult because of economic limits.

Quite often governments facing this problem try to solve it through foreign loans. They hope that the situation will improve, prices will rise again, and that the debt will be manageable. This is a dangerous strategy given the unpredictability of commodity markets. It has led many countries into bankruptcy and severe economic crisis.

If commodity prices remain low in the long term, which often happens, it becomes clear over time that servicing state debt is more expensive, and confidence in the borrower country falls. In two or three years, the country will find it impossible to get loans under any conditions, its hard currency reserves will be depleted, and the country will be forced to stop payments on foreign debt and reduce imports. Production and the standard of living fall. The problems that arose when the government faced the external shock do not go away. They are inherited by the next government, which will have even more trouble resolving them because of the greater foreign debt.

A symmetrical situation can develop if a country depends heavily on imports of one product and the price of that product rises. For a long period such a product for the USSR was grain.

In order to stimulate the agriculture sector, the state repeatedly raised subsidies to producers in the form of differentiated price increases, favorable tariffs on agricultural technology, lower interest rates on loans and periodic write-offs of loans, direct budget transfers (investments), and so on. The total share of subsidies in agricultural revenues kept growing.

In its final decades, the USSR, including Russia, had fallen sharply below the indexes characteristic of developed countries in agricultural production—that is, behind the rest of the world's technological progress in the field (see table 5-4).

These sectoral problems were exacerbated by the state's policy on supplying food to the population. Its main feature, attractive in the social sense, was the economically impractical principle of providing inexpensive food to the Soviet people. For many years, while incomes grew but agricultural production remained largely unchanged, prices for basic foods remained low.

In order to ensure enough meat for the growing demand, breeding complexes were built in the 1970s, which in turn sharply increased the need for grain as animal feed. Domestic farms could not meet the demand. After spending significant funds on the construction of these gigantic breeding complexes, starting in 1973, the state was forced to spend increasing amounts of hard currency to import feed grain and legumes.

Despite all of the expenditures to improve agricultural production, it remained inadequate. Difficulties providing sufficient meat and dairy products

TABLE 5-4. Agricultural Productivity Indicators in the USSR, Russia, Western Europe, the United States, and Canada, 1970 and 1989
Centner per hectare

Yield of grain crops	Western Europe	United States	Canada	USSR	Russian Federation
1970	27.9	31.6	21.1	15.7	13.7[a]
1989	45.8	44.8	21.2	18.9	16.1
1989 (1970 = 1.0)	1.64	1.42	1.00	1.20	1.18
Milk yield per cow (kilograms per year)					
1970	3,269	4,423	3,256	2,110	2,328[b]
1989	4,059	6,533	5,806	2,555	2,773[b]
1989 (1970 = 1.0)	1.24	1.48	1.78	1.21	1.19

Source: *Narodnoe khoziaistvo SSSR in 1985* (Moscow: Finansy i statistika, 1986); *Narodnoe khoziaistvo SSSR in 1990* (Moscow: Finansy i statistika, 1991); *World Agriculture: Trends and Indicators, 1970–1989* (Washington: USDA, 1990).
a. Average for 1971–75.
b. Not including private farming.

led to rationing, lines, and other signs of an acute food shortage. The state, maintaining its policy of supporting stable low prices on food, continued subsidizing the domestic consumer. In 1989, subsidies for food production made up approximately one-third of the budget, and the price of some foods was subsidized up to 80 percent (see table 5-5).

TABLE 5-5. USSR Government Subsidies as a Share of the Retail Price for Staple Food Products, 1989
Percent

Product	Share of subsidies in the retail price
Bread	20
Beef	74
Pork	60
Lamb	79
Poultry	36
Milk	61
Butter	72
Cheese	48
Sugar	14

Source: *Strategy of Reforms in Food and Agriculture Sectors of the Economy in the Former USSR* (Washington: World Bank, 1993), p. 253.

The government was subsidizing both the producer and the consumer. This type of subsidizing tends to be progressive: the more is given at time *t*, the more it will cost at time *t + 1* to support the same policy. A national budget can handle this situation in only two cases: when there is a monetary reserve that can be spent to increase food production, or when there is a growing source of state income that can cover the subsidies. The money spent on agriculture did not provide a commensurate return. Electricity use in agriculture between 1980 and 1990 went up 61 percent, fertilizer use rose 22 percent, and investments went up 40 percent. Gross annual production in the sector went up only 12 percent.[1] The budget revenues in the 1970s came primarily from oil and gas exports. When world prices for the country's main exports fell at the start of the 1980s, the national budget suffered.

In market economies, the authorities know what to do when faced with falling prices for their dominant export. They reduce subsidies for consumer goods, food, and fuel, lower state investments, raise prices for products and services for which they have a natural monopoly, increase taxes that are not related to income from raw materials, devalue the national currency, and sometimes introduce direct quantitative limits on imports. These decisions can cause problems for enterprises that depend on imports of materials, such as a lower standard of living, stagnation or a reduction in production, and higher unemployment. These are difficult but necessary measures. If the change in the foreign economic situation is long term, the measures will have to be implemented sooner or later. But governments that understand the political price of the question would like to believe that they are dealing with temporary difficulties that can be mitigated by borrowing abroad.

The public is not required to understand the nature of the threats related to external shocks or that the authorities are taking measures to respond to the challenges facing the country. This creates political risk for the government. Often a government that tries to introduce stabilizing measures is forced out. Sometimes the result of such a crisis is the collapse of the regime.

The nature of the challenges from external shock is essentially no different in socialist countries than in those with market economies. Socialist countries are also tied to the world market and depend on its fluctuations. A drop in prices changes the trade and payment balances. The authorities are expected to take measures that will help the economy adapt to new conditions in foreign trade. Attempts to maintain import volumes and structures through foreign loans increase the risk of state bankruptcy. In a difficult crisis of the economic and political system, the implementation of stabilization measures can threaten the state's very existence.

Unlike in countries with market systems, in socialist countries where prices are regulated by the state, the financial problems caused by economic decline appear first in the consumer market, as shortages. The government monopoly on foreign trade forces the authorities to take responsibility for decisions related to limitations on imports and leaves no room for market methods of adaptation. The state, trying to manage everything, is forced to answer for everything. This makes stabilization measures particularly difficult politically. In addition, if the basis for the decades-long socialist regime's legitimacy is the thesis that the ruling party knows better than the society how to guarantee the country's forward development, then telling the people "We were wrong and we will have to implement measures that are inevitable but will lower the standard of living" is political suicide.

The USSR and the Drop in Oil Prices: The Essence of the Choice

At the time that the Soviet Union faced a foreign economic shock in the mid-1980s, it was tightly integrated into the world market as an exporter of fuel resources as well as the world's largest importer of grain and one of the large importers of food products (see table 5-6). From a sociopolitical point of view, reducing food consumption from the usual level is dangerous for the authorities in any society. Nevertheless, if there is no opportunity to increase exports of nonpetroleum products on a significant scale or to reduce the import of products bought for hard currency—which by then had determined the working conditions in many branches of the Russian economy (see table 5-7), including those not related to food—the decision has to be made. Otherwise, it will take place automatically after gold reserves and foreign credits are exhausted.

Here is what Nikolai Ryzhkov, then head of the Council of Ministers of the USSR, wrote about the Soviet economy in the mid-1980s:

> In 1986, there was a sharp decrease in oil and gas prices on the world market, but energy resources traditionally were important exports. What was to be done? The most logical thing was to change the structure of exports. Alas, only the most economically developed countries could do that with sufficient speed. Our industrial products were not competitive on the world market. Take machine building, for instance. Its production volume has not changed since 1986, but it went almost exclusively to Comecon countries. The "capitalists" took barely 6 percent of all our machine-building exports! That is why we exported such large amounts of raw materials.[2]

TABLE 5-6. Volume of USSR Foreign Trade, by Groups of Countries, 1980–89[a]

Billions of rubles or dollars

Indicator	1980	1984	1985	1986	1987	1988	1989
				Total			
Exports (rubles)	49.6	74.4	72.5	68.3	68.2	67.1	68.7
Imports (rubles)	44.5	65.3	69.1	62.6	60.7	65	72.1
Exports (dollars)	76.4	91.5	87.0	97.0	107.8	110.7	108.5
Imports (dollars)	68.5	80.3	82.9	88.9	95.9	107.3	113.9
Exports (year 2000 dollars)	141.3	135.3	124.8	136.1	147.2	146.3	138.2
Imports (year 2000 dollars)	126.8	118.7	118.9	124.8	131.0	141.7	145.0
				Socialist countries			
Exports (rubles)	26.9	42.1	44.3	45.6	44.2	42.9	42.2
Imports (rubles)	23.6	38.2	42.2	41.8	42.1	43.4	44.7
Exports (dollars)	41.4	51.8	53.2	64.8	69.8	70.8	66.7
Imports (dollars)	36.3	47.0	50.6	59.4	66.5	71.6	70.6
Exports (year 2000 dollars)	76.7	76.5	76.3	90.9	95.4	93.5	84.9
Imports (year 2000 dollars)	67.3	69.5	72.6	83.3	90.9	94.6	89.9
				Developed capitalist countries			
Exports (rubles)	15.9	21.3	18.6	13.1	14.2	14.6	14.4
Imports (rubles)	15.7	19.6	19.3	15.9	13.9	16.3	20.5
Exports (dollars)	24.5	26.2	22.3	18.6	22.4	24.1	22.8
Imports (dollars)	24.2	24.1	23.2	22.6	22.0	26.9	32.4
Exports (year 2000 dollars)	45.3	38.7	32.0	26.1	30.7	31.8	29.0
Imports (year 2000 dollars)	44.7	35.6	33.2	31.7	30.0	35.5	41.2
				Developing countries			
Exports (rubles)	6.9	10.9	9.6	9.6	9.8	9.6	10.1
Imports (rubles)	5.1	7.5	7.6	4.9	4.7	5.3	7.0
Exports (dollars)	10.6	13.4	11.5	13.6	15.5	15.8	16.0
Imports (dollars)	7.9	9.2	9.1	7.0	7.4	8.7	11.1
Exports (year 2000 dollars)	19.7	19.8	16.5	19.1	21.2	20.9	20.3
Imports (year 2000 dollars)	14.5	13.6	13.1	9.8	10.1	11.6	14.1

Source: Statistical Yearbook *Vneshniaia torgovlia SSSR* for 1979 through 1987, 1989 (Moscow: Finansy i statistika, 1980–1990).

a. Recalculation into dollars based on the official rate of the USSR Gosbank.

The greatest obstacle to increasing exports of Soviet machinery for hard currency was the low technical level and quality of the products. They did not meet the requirements of the external market. Analysis by Soviet agencies showed that only 12 percent of domestic machinery was competitive. And that was only with the additional work done abroad before it was offered for

TABLE 5-7. USSR Imports of Equipment for Selected Industries, 1980–85[a]

Industry	Imports (millions of rubles)		Imports (millions of dollars in nominal terms)		Imports (millions of year 2000 dollars)	
	1980	1985	1980	1985	1980	1985
Food	455	830	701	996	1,297	1,429
Textiles	392	712	604	854	1,117	1,225
Chemical	1,244	1,043	1,916	1,251	3,545	1,795
Oil	141	121	218	145	403	208

Source: Statistical Yearbook *Vneshniaia torgovlia SSSR* for 1979 through 1987, 1989 (Moscow: Finansy i statistika, 1980–1990).

a. Recalculation into dollars based on the official rate of the USSR Gosbank.

sale. Soviet specialists believed that 62 percent of the products sent to foreign markets were obsolete. In the first half of 1988, there were more than 194,000 returns from abroad on exported machinery.[3]

The contradiction between the economic inevitability and the political impossibility of implementing a stabilization program was the essence of what was occurring in the USSR in the late 1980s. The development of events within a strict scenario of adaptation to external shock caused by a sharp fall in oil prices can be illustrated by data from a single sector—poultry breeding (see table 5-8). This industry had been almost totally dependent on mass purchases of feed from abroad since the early 1970s. As the number of birds bred rose in the period of high oil prices, so did it go down when prices fell. This process should have started in 1986, but it was postponed to 1990 thanks to the substantial increase in foreign debt. After the hard currency reserves and

TABLE 5-8. Poultry Population in the Russian Federation/Russia, 1971–2000

Year	Number (in millions)
1971	358
1976	394
1981	564
1986	628
1990	660
1996	423
2000	339

Source: Statistical Yearbook *Narodnoe khoziaistvo SSSR* for various years; *Russian Statistical Yearbook 2004* (Moscow: Finansy i statistika, 2004).

TABLE 5-9. State Procurement of Main Agricultural Products from Soviet Producers

Thousand tons

Product	1981–85 (average for the period)	1986	1987	1988	1988 (percent of average for the period 1981–85)	1986–88 (average for the period)	Average for 1986–88 (percent of average for 1981–85)
Wheat	33,684	43,823	35,195	34,840	103	37,953	113
Total grain crops	66,643	78,787	73,347	61,375	92	71,170	107

Source: Main Administration for Planning Social and Economic Development of Agroindustry, "Social and Economic Development of the USSR Gosagroprom in 1988 and the first three years of the twelfth five-year period," January 20, 1989 (RGAE, F. 650, Inv. 1, S. 3848, P. 27).

possibilities of foreign loans were exhausted, the number of birds went back down to the levels before mass grain imports.

When oil prices fall, it is impossible to sharply reduce the import of major food products, including grain. But it is equally impossible to maintain previous levels. Good harvests due to favorable weather in 1986 and 1987 allowed the Soviet leadership to soften the consequences of the drop in oil prices, increase grain reserves within the country, and temporarily reduce hard currency purchases of grain. Import expenditures went down by $2–$3 billion. But 1988 showed that this was just a brief respite (see table 5-9).

The uncertainty of weather-dependent harvests, particularly after the 1950s decision to exploit virgin lands, and the continuing low oil prices made the foreign trade balance catastrophic. This, not Mikhail Gorbachev's personal qualities or the errors made by his team, was the first cause of the crisis in the Soviet political and economic structure.[4] Taking the measures necessary to handle that crisis threatened not only the leadership in power but the entire Communist regime. Rejecting them, if the changes in the world market were long-lasting, would make the crash of the socialist economy and the Soviet Empire inevitable.

When oil prices fell in 1985–86, the government still had strategies that made managing the crisis seem possible. They could have done a number of things: raise retail prices on a scale comparable to their increase in the mid-1930s; impose food rationing; reduce production in manufacturing, which would have helped increase the supply of raw materials to sell on the world market; lower the amount of fuel and raw materials delivered to Comecon countries, which brought no hard currency; reduce their capital investments; and sharply reduce the purchase of technology in the West. The financial crisis related to the external shock could have been regulated by increasing the share of imported industrial consumer goods and thereby increasing budget revenues. These would have been difficult, politically risky, but economically responsible decisions. Increasing retail prices would have violated the fundamental social contract formulated in the late 1950s and early 1960s, the importance of which was seen in the 1962 tragedy in Novocherkassk.

But as a social policy, retaining fixed prices on food in radically changed circumstances was absurd. Most food subsidies were given to one-tenth of the population, who were also the most well-off. According to budget research (1989), families with a per capita income below 50 rubles a month paid one and a half times as much for a kilogram of meat as families with a per capita income of 200 rubles a month.[5] But this was not about socioeconomic expediency. Keeping prices steady was one of the most important components of the social contract that guaranteed the regime's survival in exchange for stable living conditions.

In the mid-1980s the Soviet leadership was not prepared for a serious discussion of uncompensated price hikes. This is not hard to understand. The demand for basic food products is not very price-elastic. Even with a sharp increase in prices, the substantial reduction in grain purchases from abroad could have led to a shortage of bread and feed needed for cattle breeding. There was a large ruble overhang by this time. Soviet citizens, unable to buy popular goods, had accumulated cash savings. Even if the government did increase prices on a large scale, it would still face the risk of continuing shortages of basic food products. The threat to the regime from this policy seemed insurmountable in the mid-1980s.

Food rationing was in keeping with the spirit of early messianic socialism. By the mid-1980s this system of distribution of consumer goods was the norm for most of the country's regions. In early 1986, Minister of Trade of the USSR Grigory Vashchenko wrote to the Council of Ministers: "The sale of meat products . . . in the majority of regions in the past year, as previously, was accomplished using various forms of rationing. The demand for many forms of nonfood items was not satisfied. . . . The supply of retail and wholesale products on January 1, 1986, as compared to the same date last year, was adequate for three fewer days of trade. . . . The supplies are below the norm for almost all basic food products, clothing, knitwear, hosiery, and all forms of footwear."[6]

However, after sixty years of Soviet rule, introducing ration cards for the entire country, including the privileged cities, was politically difficult. If this decision were to be made, it would have to apply to all categories of the population. And that would contradict the logic of the entrenched system of differentiated consumption—that is, access to deficit resources depending on social status.

The idea of national rationing was popular. According to polls done by VTsIOM at the height of the crisis (early 1991), it was supported by 60 percent of those surveyed (16 percent supported increasing prices to get products into the stores).[7] However, the state did not have the resources to ensure smooth functioning of a rationed supply system even in major cities, much less throughout the Soviet Union. This version was frequently considered at the highest levels in the mid-1980s and always rejected as being unrealizable.[8]

It was possible to decrease production in manufacturing and use part of the freed raw materials to increase exports. A sharp reduction in military spending and arms production would have also freed up raw materials that could be sold on international markets for hard currency. However, just as in civilian manufacturing, a greater supply of such military-industrial materials as nickel, titanium, and steel might destabilize world markets and lead to a drop in their prices. In addition, a move in this direction would mean direct conflict with the armed forces and the military-industrial complex.

The sociopolitical threats tied to reduced production in manufacturing and the jobs associated with it were also obvious. Many military-industrial enterprises are located in towns with only one major industry, where there is little or no alternative employment. When fluctuations in the business cycle make employment cutbacks necessary in market economies, unrest is often a result. But the authorities can at least claim that circumstances are beyond their control. Leaders in a socialist country who tell the workers that the factory that had once been so necessary to the homeland must now be shut down should be prepared for serious sociopolitical repercussions.

Reducing oil and petroleum products to the socialist countries and redistributing the exports to importers who paid in hard currency became a regular practice in the mid-1980s. Meanwhile, the debts of the socialist camp continued to grow. By 1988 the hard currency foreign debt of the socialist countries to the West was $206 billion. The total debt increased to $154.1 billion (see table 5-10).[9]

To preserve the empire, the USSR had to resort more and more frequently to "the final argument of kings"—force. At the end of the twentieth century, this was not a reliable method for maintaining control over its "vassal" states. By early 1987, the government began appreciating the extent of the financial

TABLE 5-10. Foreign Debt of Socialist Countries to Western Creditors
Billions of dollars in nominal terms

Debtor	1981	1984	1986	1987	1988
Poland—Total	25.9	26.9	33.6	39.3	38.9
Of which, net debt	25.1	25.4	31.9	36.3	36.9
USSR—Total	26.5	22.5	33.1	40.1	41.5
Of which net	18.1	11.2	18.3	26.0	27.2
CMEA countries as a group—Total	99.2	87.6	120.5	142.7	140.5
Of which net	83.2	63.3	90.9	111.2	109.8
All socialist countries—Total	127.8	115.7	163.9	191.2	205.7
Of which net	105.0	71.7	119.7	143.4	154.1

Source: July 13, 1989 (GARF, F. 5446, Inv. 150, S. 73, P. 70, 71).

disproportions. In a speech to the Plenum of the Central Committee of January 27–28, 1987, Chairman of the Government Nikolai Ryzhkov said:

Take finances. Here is the most critical situation. The country has reached the twelfth five-year plan with a heavy financial burden. We have been unable to make ends meet for a long time and are living in debt. The lack of balance is becoming chronic and has led to the brink of a breakdown in the financial and credit system. None of this was scrutinized fully. Finances were the prerogative of a certain narrow circle of people and agencies. Moreover, the true state of affairs in this sphere was hidden by the appearance of prosperity and was not the object of profound, multifaceted analysis or discussion. . . . An extremely difficult situation formed in monetary circulation, about which Mikhail Sergeyevich [Gorbachev] spoke today. In the 1970s and early 1980s this discord occurred. We have reached the point of inflationary processes beginning. . . . Things are no better in the country's hard currency situation. . . . Foreign trade has become vulnerable to various sanctions.[10]

A decrease in capital investments and a halt in large-scale purchases of technology from abroad is the natural economic response to the crisis stemming from a worsening trade balance and a drop in commodity prices. It creates the least conflict in the relationship between authorities and society. But the leaders had to think about their relations with the economic and political elite, which is part of the Central Committee of the Communist Party. For them, these measures were as unacceptable to the public as raising retail prices.

The question of how much money will be invested in an industrial region and what construction must be undertaken there was the most important one in Soviet political and economic life since the 1920s. It would have been a vio-

TABLE 5-11. New Construction in the USSR, 1986–1988

Year	Total estimated cost of new construction (billions of rubles)	New construction as a share of investments in the economy (percent)	New construction as a share of GDP (percent)
1986	48.5	25.0	6.1
1987	38.3	18.6	4.6
1988	59.1	27.1	6.8

Source: Data on the estimated cost of new construction are from the personal archive of Ye. T. Gaidar.
Figures for new construction as a share of investments in the economy and new construction as a share of GDP are based on data from the Statistical Yearbook *Narodnoe khoziaistvo SSSR v 1990 g.* (Moscow: Finansy i statistika, 2000).

lation of the rules of the game to tell the first secretaries of regional Party committees and ministers that the investment in their region or industry was being reduced and that the technology they requested will not be imported. If Gorbachev had tried moving in this direction, the only difference between his fate and Khrushchev's would have been the speed with which he was forced out. No one who understands Soviet life in the 1980s can doubt it. And there was no certainty that this measure would have been enough to avert the crisis or would merely have postponed it. Political suicide was guaranteed, and the chance of success was minimal. Despite the looming financial difficulties, the pace of new construction picked up (see table 5-11).

Even in view of the catastrophic financial situation in 1989–90, the government did not reduce investments in agriculture. In a report on the state budget for 1990, Finance Minister Valentin Pavlov said:

The financial situation in foreign economic activity continues to decline, which dilutes the revenue base of the budget and seriously weakens our efforts to liquidate the deficit. . . . The share of this income is reaching the lowest point in recent years, making up only 14 percent of the budget revenues. Foreign debt is growing. The size of foreign debt has reached the level where it continues to grow without new loans, but simply through the increasing expenses of servicing it. In order to pay the debt and interest in 1990 we will have to use almost the entire income from oil and gas exports. . . . In the social reorientation of the budget, the key point is increasing centralized financing of the agricultural-industrial complex. We propose providing 116.5 billion rubles in 1990, which is 8 billion rubles more than in the current year and 10.4 billion rubles more than projections for the five-year plan. This creates additional strain on the country's budget and finances, but we must make these expenditures in order to accelerate the solution of the food problem.[11]

Gosbank informed the Soviet government that, according to the experts at OECD, there was a sharp decrease in 1985 and 1986 in the payments balance of European socialist countries, that a significant portion of their foreign debt was for short-term loans with due dates in less than a year, and that their currency and financial position was unstable.[12]

In the first half of 1988, the OECD observed continuing growth in the hard currency foreign debt of socialist countries. However, by September 1988 credit raters considered the USSR to be the most reliable financial partner among the socialist countries, ahead of China. One factor that eased the USSR's access to international credit resources in 1985–88 was an overestimation of its gold reserves by Western experts. They believed that the country held reserves of approximately $36 billion, but by that time, because of the huge spending on food, reserves had been reduced to approximately $7.6 billion.[13]

Western observers did note that in the previous three years Soviet debt had grown by $17.6 billion, of which $10 billion was in short-term loans. Nevertheless bankers and capitalist countries continued to give the USSR new loans at fairly good rates.[14] This allowed the country to continue its economic and political course and put off finding solutions. In 1989, uncompleted construction projects ate up four-fifths of the increase in national revenues.[15]

Large-scale purchasing of imported equipment continued. Much of it was not used. In a letter to the Council of Ministers, Valery Serov, the chairman of Gosstroi (the State Committee on Construction and Architecture) wrote:

On the whole, in 1989 the stock of unused imported equipment has grown by 1 billion rubles. . . . The usefulness of this equipment in terms of its completeness and obsolescence has not been determined by either the ministries of the USSR or the Councils of Ministers of the Union republics. . . . An analysis of the course of construction using imported equipment shows that the failure to meet deadlines in a number of projects came about primarily because the ministries who commissioned the building did not give the construction sites domestic technology and because of the continual changes they made in the targets for the projects.[16]

This is a demonstration of the authorities' inability to take responsibility even in the face of escalating financial problems. Cognizant of the risks of getting into conflicts with the administrative and economic elite, the Soviet leadership continued discussing enormous projects to be financed by new foreign loans. The state-owned Vneshekonombank (State Foreign Economic Bank) wrote to the government: "According to data at Vneshekonombank USSR, at the present time work is completed or being completed on Technical-Economic

Bases (TEO) of at least nine major oil and gas and chemical complexes (NGKhK), the cost in hard currency for each exceeding 200 million rubles, and the realization of which is planned on the basis of joint enterprises."

The projects were to be financed by loans from foreign banks and export agencies on Soviet guarantees. The foreign partners refused to guarantee the loans, even in proportion to their participation. This relieved the foreign companies of financial responsibility for completing the projects. For most of the projects, all the risks were taken by the Soviet side, and the hard currency expenditures would be included in the USSR debt.[17]

The situation—having to choose between imposing higher retail prices and reducing investments and military spending—created a dilemma for the government: deciding between conflict with the public or with the Party economic elite. But not making a decision heightened the risk that, as the crisis developed, there would be conflict with both the public and the elite.[18]

The new generation of leaders clearly did not understand this. The traditional management of the economy was oriented on natural, rather than abstract, parameters. The development of cattle breeding was discussed at the highest level more frequently than the country's budget. Industry and business leaders regarded finances as necessary but dreary bookkeeping.[19] In addition, information on the real state of the budget, hard currency reserves, foreign debt, and balance of payments was available only to an extremely narrow circle of people, many of whom understood nothing about it anyway.

In his memoir Gorbachev wrote, "Andropov asked Ryzhkov and me to evaluate everything one more time and tell him our conclusions. Trying to get to the heart of matters, we asked for an opportunity to examine the budget. Andropov just laughed: 'Look what you're asking for. I'm not letting you into the budget.'"[20] And Vladimir Kryuchkov, one of Andropov's closest comrades in arms, wrote that Andropov admitted that he was an ignoramus when it came to economics.[21]

The deintellectualization of the leadership was promoted consistently by the Communist authorities. The Party's personnel policies are well illustrated by a note in the transcripts of the Presidium of the Central Committee: "On Comrade Zasyadko. They say he's stopped drinking. Then shall we make him minister to Ukraine?"[22] The proportion of people from the capitals and major university centers in leadership positions fell consistently, and the proportion of people from the villages with only a basic education continued to grow right up until perestroika.[23] The new generation that came to power in 1985 were better educated than their predecessors.[24] But neither they nor their close associates in charge of economic issues had a good economics education.

They did not understand how the world market operated or the connections between the foreign trade balance, the budget, and the food supply, and they could not appreciate the strategic threats the country was facing. They attributed the main problems—a slowing of economic growth, low efficiency, and lagging behind the West—to the previous leadership's errors.

Gorbachev's words in the summer of 1990 at the Plenum of the Central Committee could be interpreted as self-justification. Nevertheless, he spoke the truth: "We have been given a highly difficult inheritance. Our economy and entire social organism are exhausted by chronic diseases. The dilapidation of the village, agriculture, and manufacturing, the woeful state of our ecology, the obsolete structure of production and lagging behind in science and technology—is not all this the consequence of the economic and technical policy implemented for decades?"[25] It is another matter that in 1985 he was unlikely to have understood the acuteness of the problems he and his colleagues would have to handle.

The future chairman of the government of the USSR, Nikolai Ryzhkov, had this to say about the economic situation at the end of the Brezhnev era: "And so, we have begun. The situation was, I repeat, really complex. In 1982, for the first time since the war, the growth of real income of the population stopped: statistics showed zero percent. . . . The state of the economy could easily be described by the proverb: wherever you throw, it's another blow. Metallurgy was full of problems, and oil extraction, and electronics needed more juice, and chemicals—whatever you name, you wouldn't be wrong."[26]

Nevertheless, the new leaders made clear in their speeches in 1985–86 that they were sure they could return the lost dynamism to the Soviet economy, raise the rate of economic growth, and catch up to the more developed countries.

A Series of Mistakes

History may never know exactly what Mikhail Gorbachev and Eduard Shevardnadze had in mind when they talked about not being able to live this way any longer in December 1984 in Pitsunda. All the available archival materials indicate that they did not have a specific plan of action for the moment when they would take power.[27] And twenty-two months after taking office, speaking at the January Plenum of the Central Committee in 1987, Gorbachev admitted that the scale of problems facing the country was greater than he had imagined.[28] The consequences of the crisis required total concentration of efforts and readiness to make the hard decisions and accept responsibility for them, and the new leadership did not see or understand the nature and scope of the threat.

However, they did pay attention to a dangerous trend, the decrease in oil production since 1985, and tried to correct the situation. After Gorbachev's trip to Tyumen in September 1985, the firing of a number of directors, and the allocation of additional funds, the decrease in production in the region was stopped. But the industry's fundamental problems, related to the forced exploitation of the largest deposits in the 1970s and early 1980s and the worsening conditions for extraction, were not resolved. The Soviet leadership understood that a reduction in oil production would raise difficult issues. At a meeting of the Central Committee on August 23, 1986, Gorbachev said:

> Here is what I would like to say first, comrades. We must all, I want to say this frankly in this circle, see that in view of the situation with oil and gas condensate production our export resources, and consequently our ability to import, in 1986 have been reduced significantly. And this seriously complicates balancing not only our export-import plan but the economy in general. In these conditions the issue of hard currency economics becomes more acute than ever. We already spend a lot of hard currency on agricultural products—grain, meat, and other products. We buy more than 9 million tons of ready steel and steel pipes for 3 billion rubles. A large amount of raw materials and semi-processed products for chemicals, nonferrous metallurgy, light industry, and so on. In general, we need all of that. We have to buy it because we cannot live without it.[29]

Increasing oil production, even at much lower rates than those achieved in the 1980s after several unique deposits were exploited, was fundamentally important to the stability of the economy. But it would cost more. In the middle of 1988 the chairman of the board of Promstroibank (Industrial and Construction Bank) USSR reminded the government by letter that the fuel and energy complex in the period 1986–90 would require almost one-third more capital investment than in 1981–85, and three times what was spent in 1971–75. The fuel and energy complex's share of capital construction had grown from 14 percent in the ninth five-year plan to 23 percent in the twelfth. The rate of increase in investment outstripped the rate of increase in production.[30]

Gorbachev's speeches in 1986 reflect his concern with the problems created by lower oil prices. But his tone conveys a lack of understanding of the scale of the problem. Measures intended to handle the crisis in the balance of payments and the financial crisis were not discussed on the political level in 1985–86. Moreover, decisions contrary to the logic of an anti-crisis program were made.

The government, facing an unfavorable state of affairs for its main exports, caused three additional blows to the country's financial system.[31] First, the anti-alcohol campaign lowered revenues; second, the program for accelerating economic development assumed a significant increase in state capital invest-ments; and third, the government reduced spending on imported industrial consumer goods. Former chairman of Gosplan Nikolai Baibakov recalled:

> There was a meeting of the Secretariat of the Central Committee in April to discuss the decision to reduce alcohol production. In the 1985 plan, vodka rep-resented 24 percent of trade, and therefore at the meeting I cautiously warned them, "Comrades, don't rush this—we'll unbalance the budget. We're talking about 25 billion rubles here." "No," said Ligachev, "let's first sharply curtail production of alcoholic beverages and then introduce a dry law." . . . At the next meeting, in the fall, the Secretariat analyzed the implementation of this resolution. They noted that work in this direction was taking place, but at the same time they criticized the regional and oblast Party heads for reducing pro-duction so slowly. Then came the proposal to reduce vodka production by half, not by 1990 as had been planned, but by 1987, the 70th anniversary year of the Great October Socialist Revolution. After that meeting, the campaign against drunkenness and alcoholism became even more active. They reduced production and sale of alcoholic beverages, including wine and cognac.[32]

According to the plan for 1985, passed before the anti-alcohol resolutions, rev-enue from alcoholic beverage sales was estimated at 60 billion rubles. After the resolutions, revenue in 1986 was 38 billion; in 1987, 35 billion; and in 1988, because the anti-alcohol campaign was repealed, a bit over 40 billion rubles.[33]

The war on alcoholism presupposed an annual reduction in production and sales of vodka and other liquors by 10 percent, getting down to half over five years. Production of fruit-based alcoholic beverages was supposed to stop. By 1985–86 production had been reduced by more than half. At the start of the anti-alcohol campaign the Soviet government had hoped that increas-ing alcohol prices would compensate for approximately 80 percent of the budget losses and trade.[34] This did not happen.

At the Twenty-Seventh Congress of the Communist Party, the goal was set to double the USSR's economic potential by 2000. The program of acceleration called for the development of machine building to be 1.7 times faster than gen-eral industrial growth and for its quality to reach world levels by the early 1990s.

Manipulation of data by the statistical departments of the USSR showed that the Soviet economy was growing faster in 1985–86. By excluding alcohol revenues from the total national revenues, the pace of growth was almost dou-bled.[35] But statistical sophistry cannot halt a financial crisis. These decisions, along with the drop in oil prices, made it inevitable that the deficit would rise (see tables 5-12, 5-13, 5-14, 5-15).

TABLE 5-12. Implications of Falling Oil Prices for Revenues from the Sale of Oil and Oil Products, 1984–87

Item	1984	1985	1986	1987
Total revenue from the sale of oil and oil products (billions of hard-currency-equivalent rubles)	30.9	28.2	22.5	22.8
Of which, revenue from developed capitalist countries (billions of hard-currency-equivalent rubles)	13.6	10.6	5.5	7.1
Total revenue from the sale of oil and oil products (percent of GDP)	4.04	3.63	2.82	2.76
Of which, revenue to the developed capitalist countries (percent of GDP)	1.8[a]	1.4[a]	0.7	0.9

Source: Calculations of GDP shares based on data in S. G. Sinelnikov, *Budzhetnyi krizis v Rossii: 1985–1995* (Moscow: Eurasia, 1995).

a. Ye. T. Gaidar, "On Good Intentions," *Pravda,* July 24, 1990.

TABLE 5-13. Fiscal Implications of the Anti-Alcohol Campaign, 1985–87

Item	1984	1985	1986	1987
Tax revenues in the state budget from sales of alcohol products (billions of rubles)[a]	36.7	33.3	27.0	29.1
Tax revenues in the state budget from sales of alcohol products (percent of GDP)	4.8	4.3	3.4	3.5
Retail sales of alcoholic beverages (billions of rubles)[a]	52.8	47.7	37.0	36.6
Retail sales of alcoholic beverages (percent of GDP)	6.9	6.1	4.6	4.4

Source: Calculations of GDP shares based on data in S. G. Sinelnikov, *Budzhetnyi krizis v Rossii: 1985–1995* (Moscow: Eurasia, 1995).

a. From the personal archive of Ye. T. Gaidar.

TABLE 5-14. Sales of Alcohol Products in the USSR, 1985–88
Million decaliters

Beverage	1985	1986	1987	1988
Vodka	251.2	156.6	123.6	136.9
Wine	386.8	189.5	156.7	184.7
Cognac	8.5	8.8	9.4	11.3
Beer	667.8	496.9	514.6	564.8
Champagne	21.9	20.7	20.6	21.8

Source: S. G. Sinelnikov, *Budzhetnyi krizis v Rossii: 1985–1995* (Moscow: Eurasia, 1995).

TABLE 5-15. Supplies of Imported Manufactured Consumer Goods, 1984–88

Item	1984	1985	1986	1987	First six months of 1987	First six months of 1988
Import of manufactured consumer goods (billions of hard-currency-equivalent rubles)	7.6	8.7	8.4	7.9	3.8	4.2
Of which, imports from developed capitalist countries (billions of hard-currency-equivalent rubles)	1.2	1.5	1.1	0.8	0.4	0.4
Supplies of imported manufactured consumer goods for retail sale (billions of rubles)	27.1	33.0	30.2	24.8	10.4	11.5

Source: Yu. V. Ponomarev to the assistant of First Deputy Chairman of the RF Government V. B. Bogdanov, "Data on the foreign debt as of January 1, 1992," May 15, 1992 (personal archive of Ye. T. Gaidar).

The growing financial imbalance led to a sharpening of the deficit in consumer goods. Minister of Trade Kandrat Terekh informed the Council of Ministers in December 1987:

The Ministry of Trade USSR reports that at the present time there is a tense situation in supplying the populace with many consumer goods. One reason for the change in the trade situation and increased demand for certain items is the sharp reduction in the sale of alcoholic beverages. . . . Before 1985, the sale of sugar and preparations containing alcohol was universally level. A good selection of colognes, lotions, hair spray, toothpaste, and other products was on sale continuously. The jump in demand for sugar appeared in the second half of 1986. From July to December 1986 sugar sales grew by 22 percent, and in the first half of the current year, compared to the same period last year, by 16 percent. Sugar supplies in retail trade have diminished by 625,000 tons, and we expect another reduction in 1987 by 700,000 tons.[36]

Then the minister pointed out that in 1986 the sale of cologne in Moscow grew by 150 percent and that in all oblasts of the Russian Socialist Federal Soviet Republic (RSFSR) alcohol-containing products and toothpaste were now rationed, and sales of glue had gone up more then 30 percent and of window washing fluid by 15 percent.[37] The letter is imbued with an almost overt hatred for the initiators of the anti-alcohol campaign that destabilized the situation on the consumer market for which the minister was responsible.

In the first three years (1986–88) of the five-year plan, state revenues fell by 31 billion rubles and expenditures grew by 36 billion rubles. Money outlays in 1986 were 3.9 billion rubles; in 1987, 5.9 billion rubles; and in 1988, 11.8 billion rubles (the average annual expenditure for the years of the eleventh five-year plan was 3.6 billion rubles). In estimating the volume of unsatisfied demand, Gosbank used the relationship between money in circulation and trade volume in the period between 1959 and 1961. Using that methodology, on January 1, 1986, the ruble surplus in circulation was 29 billion rubles, and on January 1, 1988, 35 billion rubles. Over the period 1971–80, the surplus of money in circulation rose by 15 billion rubles and in 1981–87 by 16 billion rubles.[38]

The Ministry of Finance and Goskomstat estimated the deficit in the state budget for 1985 at 18 billion rubles. According to their figures, it reached 90.1 billion rubles in 1988. Preliminary data for 1989 showed that the deficit in the state budget would be 92.2 billion rubles. The state debt at the start of 1989 was 312.4 billion rubles.[39] In late 1989 it reached 400 billion rubles, or 44 percent of GDP.[40] To cover the budget expenditures, the state relied heavily on the resources of Gosbank and people's savings; 65 billion rubles from Gosbank's savings account deposits were used as loans for agriculture, with repayment not due until 2005.[41]

In the spring of 1986, the government considered measures intended to improve the financial health of agriculture and to strengthen currency circulation. By the start of the thirteenth five-year plan (1991), the financial balance was to be restored in all spheres of the economy. The plan was to mobilize additional financial resources, 37.8 billion rubles by the ministries and 58 billion rubles by the Union republics.[42] Chairman of the Council of Ministers Nikolai Ryzhkov, Chairman of Gosplan Yuri Maslyukov, and Chairman of Gossnab L. Voronin wrote to the Central Committee on July 17, 1988, about the serious financial imbalance in the economy. This had no practical effect on the situation. The budget deficit was expected to be higher in 1989 than in 1988 (10 percent of GDP).[43] Gosbank informed the government of the sharp decline in currency circulation:

> According to our specialists, the amount of money in circulation in the early 1970s corresponded to the demands of trade. In 1971–80, the amount of money in circulation increased by 2.3 times, while income increased only 1.8 times. . . . By the early 1980s, difficulties arose in satisfying the demand for goods and

services, creating an overhang of money in the amount of approximately 19 billion rubles. Over the period 1981–85 the amount of money in circulation grew by 34.1 percent with a 22.6 percent rise in income and 19.8 percent in retail trade. Tension on the consumer market has increased and, despite frequent increases in retail prices, the overhang by the beginning of 1986 was estimated at 29 billion rubles. The situation in the current five-year period has deteriorated rapidly. Based on the estimates, people's income in 1990 will be 52.6 percent higher than in 1985, while retail trade will grow less—42.5 percent, which will leave in circulation 90.5 percent more money by the end of 1990 than in 1985. The surplus of cash in circulation at the start of 1990 was estimated by Gosbank as 47 billion rubles, and the general amount of unsatisfied consumer demand for goods and services as 105 billion rubles.[44]

Table 5-16 illustrates developments in this sphere. The connection among the disintegration of the financial system, money circulation, and escalating shortages of consumer goods did not become clear to the Soviet leadership until the end of 1988.[45] By then, the county's finances and consumer market were destroyed.

In the fall of 1988, the government decided to stop the anti-alcohol campaign. By then, according to expert analysis of the rise in sugar sales since 1984, illicit production of alcohol had risen 600 percent, completely replacing the reduction in alcoholic beverage production by the state.[46] In early September 1988, Chairman of the Council of Ministers Ryzhkov sent a memo to the Politburo.

The analysis shows that in the last three years lines have grown almost half again as long because of the sharp decrease in the sale of alcoholic beverages. . . . In connection with the savings from not buying these beverages, a

TABLE 5-16. Issue of Currency, 1986–89

Period	Annual issue of currency (billions of rubles)	Annual rate of increase in the issue of currency (percent)
1986[a]	3.9	8.3
1987	5.9	51.3
1988	11.8	100.0
1989	18.3	55.1

Source: Calculations were made using data in RGAE, F. 2324, Op. 33, S. 741, L. 165, 166.

a. Rate of increase for 1986 indicated in relation to the average annual value of currency issued in the period 1981–85, totaling 3.6 billion rubles.

significant part of the population has switched its demand to food, clothing, shoes, socks, cultural, and domestic items. . . . Since the second half of 1986 there has been a great increase in the purchase of sugar, baked goods (caramel and gingerbread), fruit juices, tomato paste and some other grocery items that are used in making moonshine. The sale of sugar, for example, in 1987 was 9,280,000 tons and compared to 1985 had increased by 1,430,000 tons, or by 18 percent, and at the present time is handled by ration coupons. According to Goskomstat USSR, in 1987, 1.4 million tons of sugar was used for moonshine, which equals approximately 140–150 tons of moonshine and has compensated for the reduced sale of vodka and spirits.[47]

In 1989 the government's concern over the country's financial circumstances became public. In January 1989, Gorbachev announced a program to reduce military spending by 14.2 percent (compared to 1987) and arms manufacture by 19.2 percent. These measures were to be implemented over a two-year period.[48] At the Congress of People's Deputies on May 30, 1989, he said, "The state continues to live beyond its means. The expenditures of the budget in this five-year plan are growing faster than the national income. This leads to the increasing budget deficit. Economically this is simply unacceptable and cannot be seen as anything but a serious miscalculation in economic policy, for which the main responsibility lies with the Ministry of Finance and its staff. The frontline of uncompleted projects in capital construction has not been reduced, as planned by the decisions of the Twenty-Seventh Party Congress, but on the contrary has grown significantly by 30 billion rubles."[49]

On March 15, 1989, a resolution of the Central Committee and the Council of Ministers was passed intending a joint reduction of state expenditures and an increase in revenues by 29.3 billion rubles in 1989 and 33.7 billion rubles in 1990. It anticipated reducing capital investments on the construction of sites for production by 7.5 billion rubles. It assumed greater revenues to the budget through taxes on trade by 1.1 billion rubles, revenues from foreign economic activity by 4.1 billion rubles, and changes in the structure of import and export activities that would improve efficiency.[50]

Finally recognizing that mounting financial problems were a serious threat, the Soviet leaders decided that conflict with the administrative and political elite was the lesser evil. However, the measures were incommensurate with the problems. Even though they had begun to recognize the severity of the crisis, they were not prepared to discuss measures that would be strong enough to have a chance of averting catastrophe.

Mounting Problems in the Soviet Economy

The tone of the documents sent to the government by the ministry responsible for the oil industry was becoming more anxious. From V. A. Dinkov's letter dated June 30, 1989:

> The Ministry of the Oil Industry feels it imperative to report to the Council of Ministers on the difficulty of meeting the goals set for 1989 in delivering oil to the country's refineries and for export. In the six months of this year we are 2.5 million tons behind the state order, and bear in mind the additional centrally distributed deliveries—5 million tons. The expected insufficiency for the half-year will be 10 million tons. . . . As early as the second half of 1988 an alarming situation formed in meeting planned goals. . . . The orders from the Bureau of the Council of Ministers on machine building have not been followed by the Ministry of Chemical Machinery in making up for the undelivered drilling and other oil production equipment as well as equipment to complete the site that was put into exploitation in 1989 and 1990. The program of technical re-equipping of the oil industry with new forms of equipment and machinery has been ruined. . . . The situation is complicated also by the fact that Gosplan's resolution no. 33, dated June 16, 1989, has lowered the limits on material and technical resources for 1989 on budget lines that are decisive for oil production: seamless electro-welded pipelines by 30,000 tons, and welded pipes of large diameters by 18,000 tons. . . . On the whole, in connection with not promoting a balanced production program for 1989 through capital investments and material and technical resources, and also because of sharply deteriorating geological conditions in the exploitation of a number of sites, the minister of the Oil Industry estimates that it will be able to produce 591.6 million tons of oil, which is 10.8 million tons less than the established state order and 17.8 million tons below the goal, in view of the additional centrally stimulated distribution.[51]

From the end of 1988 onward, the economic situation plummeted. The critical factor was the latest drop in oil production. The Ministry of the Oil and Gas Industry wrote to the government in August 1989: "In the current year, the situation is becoming particularly tense and fraught with unpredictable consequences. In connection with the extremely difficult situation, the Ministry of the Oil and Gas Industry deems it necessary to reexamine the state order on oil production to the above-mentioned associations and lower it to an intense but realistic goal. Based on this, we ask that the state order for oil in 1989 as a whole be lowered by 15.5 million tons."[52] The mounting difficulties in oil production contributed to the general economic crisis. Secretary of the Central Committee Vadim Medvedev described the development of events in the Soviet economy in 1989 this way:

> In that sense 1988 turned out to be the last more-or-less successful year. Then came the most serious complications, a real economic crisis was brewing, striking the consumer market first. It was in such an unstable state that even a small, isolated malfunction incurred enormous consequences and waves of agitated demand. Unaccountably, sugar and baked goods, or soap and washing powder, or school notebooks, or batteries, or zippers, not to mention meat, shoes, and fur garments would vanish from the shore shelves. Economic reform got stuck in a bureaucratic morass. After the June Plenum . . . the program of economic reforms of 1987 was in fact buried and was remembered more and more rarely. The most important thing is that control was lost over privately held cash, the populace's income, and that gave a powerful push to the inflationary spiral, which became harder and harder to stop.[53]

A survey by the All-Union Scientific Research Institute on conditions and demand showed that, by the end of 1989, of 989 consumer items only 11 percent were readily available for purchase, and that stores no longer had televisions, refrigerators, washing machines, laundry soaps, most household chemical products, many kinds of furniture, electric irons, razor blades, or perfumes and cosmetics, and that items that as recently as 1987 were produced without any problems had become deficit goods, including soaps, school notebooks, pencils, and oilcloth.[54]

Gosbank reported on the mounting problems in money circulation:

> In 1989 problems continued to mount: the gap increased between income and spending, the printing of money has grown, the situation with satisfying demand for goods and services has grown acute, and the buying power of the ruble has diminished, which is creating negative social consequences. These difficulties are caused by the failure to meet the basic goals of the state plan and the resulting negative balance in the economy's development. In 1989 the goals were not met on national income, productivity of public works, volume of industrial and agricultural production, or production of consumer goods. In these conditions, the income of the population has significantly exceeded the plan: it has grown 12.9 percent since 1988, while the plan had foreseen an increase of 1.2 percent, and income was more than 57 billion rubles higher than the plan. The rate of growth of income was 1.4 times higher than the rate of growth of spending on goods and services. The remaining money in cash,

deposits, certificates, and domestic obligations and securities for 1989 has increased by 61.9 billion rubles, which is 11.1 percent of income. The amount of money that remains out of circulation, kept by the public, is growing annually: in 1988 it was 41.8 billion rubles or 8.5 percent of the total income; in 1987, 31.8 billion rubles, or 7 percent; in 1986, 27.7 billion rubles or 6.4 percent; in 1981–85 the population saved an average of 17.3 billion rubles or 4.4 percent of their annual income. The high growth of ruble overhang in the population is an index of the escalation in unsatisfied demand because of a lack of goods and services, which for the start of 1990 is estimated by Gosbank as being around 110 billion rubles, as opposed to 60 billion rubles at the start of 1986. . . . Gosbank is not using the printing of money as a resource for loans: the total sum of credits to the economy in four years of this current five-year period (1986–89) has gone down by 133.5 billion rubles, including 16.7 billion rubles in 1989. At the same time, the bank's resources continued to be directed at covering the state budget deficit. The state budget owed Gosbank 350.1 billion rubles at the end of 1989, compared to 243.4 billion rubles at the start of the five-year period (January 1, 1986), including 82.4 billion rubles in 1989. The state domestic debt at the end of 1989 was 400 billion rubles, having grown 358 billion rubles since January 1, 1986, including 88 billion rubles in 1989. The state's systematically exceeding spending over income is one of the main causes of the devaluation of the ruble.[55]

Because prices were fixed, the swelling wave of the financial crisis did not yet lead to high, open inflation. It was manifest in mounting discord in the consumer market and acute shortages of consumer goods. And the public did not understand what was happening or why.

Here are excerpts from workers' letters to the Central Committee in 1989: "What is going on with supplies to the populace? Where have consumer goods vanished? Things get worse every day. We would like an explanation of the reasons for lowering the sugar quota from 2 kg to 1.5 kg per person" (Pavlovsk). "In our town, the stores have no household or toilet soap or laundry powder. When a sugar shortage developed and coupons were introduced, we were understanding. But now that the local authorities have established such miserly quotas on soap and detergent we are outraged. Explain to us, please, whose fault it is that all cleaning materials have vanished?" (Alexandrov). "I have nothing to feed my five-month-old boy Yegor. There are no children's juices or pureed fruit or infant formula in the city" (Apatity).[56]

The authorities realized that the situation on the consumer market was more than alarming, but they had no recipe for stabilizing it. From a July 1989 memo from the Agrarian Department of the Central Committee to the Central Committee: "Recently the supply to Moscow of dairy products, sausages, and pastry has deteriorated. We observe blackouts of several days, a narrow assortment of goods, and violations of the delivery schedule. The shelves in many stores are empty most of the day."[57] After relatively stable harvests for twenty years, production of durum wheat was under goal by 43.7 million tons (see table 5-17).[58] The grain crisis grew even more acute from that point. The Ministry of Bread Products wrote to the government:

> As of January 1, 1989, the state reserves had 61.3 million tons of grain, when the plan called for 85.7 million tons. The state order has been under-fulfilled by 30 percent, specifically 40 percent for the RSFSR, 42 percent for Kazakh SSR, and 52 percent for the Estonian SSR. Compared to 1987 levels there is 11.9 million tons less, or 16 percent, of which there is 217,000 tons less of wheat, 860,000 tons of rye, 179,000 tons of buckwheat, 551,000 tons of millet, 458,000 tons of legumes, 7,186,000 tons of barley, and 928,000 tons of oats. . . . In a number of regions where farms had significant amounts of ground grain, there were instances of holding it back from sale to the state.[59]

In 1989–90 the growing crisis in the USSR trade balance had an additional parameter—low grain harvests in the world, which raised world demand over supply and created a seller's market. Wheat prices went up in particular (see table 5-18). The situation in grain supply is well illustrated by two letters to the government:

> In connection with the acute situation in grain for forage, we are presenting a preliminary account of harvest for these cultures in 1989. The account shows that we are lacking 30.7 million tons of forage crops. . . . Bearing that in mind, the need to decide on buying forage abroad is more urgent.[60]

> The Ministry of Trade reports that Gosplan (resolution December 31, 1988, No. 105), on the basis of the decision of the Council of Ministers, has reduced market funds for 1989 in general, and in particular for the first half-year, for flour by 1,266,000 tons and grain by 519,000 tons. As a result of the reduction, market funds in the first half of this year are 15,084,000 tons of flour, or 395,000 tons less (2.6 percent) than the first half of 1988, and 1,881,000 tons of grain, which is 314,000 tons (14.3 percent) less, and not counting Moscow, Leningrad, and other centralized receivers, this is significantly less than last year (556,000 tons less in flour and 337,000 tons in grain). In conditions of insufficiency of vegetables and shortages of some other foods, there is a greater

TABLE 5-17. State Procurement of Grain from the 1988 Harvest for Republics of the Union

Republic	State procurement in 1988 (thousand tons)	Total stocks, including the loan, as of January 1, 1989 (thousand tons)	Plan performance without the loan (percent)	Procured			1988 as a percentage of 1987	1986–88 as a percentage of 1981–85
				1987 (thousand tons)	1986–88 annual average (thousand tons)	1981–85 annual average (thousand tons)		
USSR	85,721	61,375	70	73,089	71,084	66,643	84	107
Russian Federation	47,000	29,165	60	34,909	35,385	35,002	84	101
Ukraine	17,500	17,321	98	18,057	16,866	13,367	96	126
Kazakhstan	16,400	9,749	58	14,601	13,678	12,625	67	108

Source: M. G. Sheludko, "Performance Results of the Social and Economic Development Plan of the USSR Ministry of Grain Products in 1988 and the first three years of the 12th five-year period," January 26, 1989 (RGAE, F. 8040, Inv. 19, S. 4393, P. 269).

TABLE 5-18. Global Wheat Prices, 1987–90[a]

Year	1987	1988	1989	1990
Average annual prices (in year 2000 dollars per ton)	133	176	207	178

Source: Calculations based on *International Financial Statistics 2005* (Washington: IMF, 2005).
a. Global prices obtained as the average price of supplies from the United States, Australia, and Argentina.

demand for bread products, and in the fourth quarter of 1988, compared to the same period in 1987, the growth in demand for flour in Ukrainian, Georgian, Latvian, Kirgiz, Tadzhik, and Armenian Union republics, Dagestan, North-Ossetian, Chechen-Ingush, and Udmurt ASSR, Moscow, Kalinin, and Kaliningrad Oblasts of the RSFSR was from 1.5 percent to 8 percent, and for flour in the USSR as a whole it was 3.6 percent, and in numerous Union republics, autonomous republics, and oblasts of the Russian Federation, up to 35 percent.[61]

The grain crisis unfolded during a continued decline in the supply of consumer goods. The chairman of Goskomstat informed the Council of Ministers in October 1989 that in the third quarter the reserves of goods in wholesale and retail trade had dropped by 5 percent: "As of October 1 of this year they are 17 percent lower than established norms. Despite the fact that my ministry authorized 5.5 times more imports of soap and detergents, only 29 percent more than last year reached the stores, and in most regions soap must be bought with ration coupons. The deficit of synthetic detergents is acute. The problems supplying the public with tobacco products are greater now, and there are gaps in sales everywhere."[62]

In this situation, the leadership had trouble setting priorities and deciding what was more important: to spend rapidly dwindling hard currency to import grain or to use it to try to stabilize the supply of nongrocery consumer goods. That dilemma explains the appearance of the documents cited below. The Presidium of the Council of Ministers wrote (October 1989): "Significant difficulties are experienced as before by consumers in purchasing meat, animal and vegetable fats, baked goods, sugar, and tea. Delivery has deteriorated for top grade and first-grade flour, grain, vegetables and fruit, fish and fish products, and tobacco products. The situation has grown much more acute in the production and delivery to market of a large group of nongrocery items, including fabric, shoes, children's tights, school notebooks, lumber and construction materials, and matches."[63]

By the end of 1989, the problems related to the financial crisis and the concomitant threat were well understood by the country's leader and were the subject of public discussion. Here is a citation from the government's report of the Second Congress of People's Deputies in November 1989:

> This has all turned into a profound discord in state finances, money circulation, and the consumer market. The growth of resources in the budget for three years of the current five-year period is primarily due to loans. With the general increase in expenditures for the 1988 budget of 73 billion rubles over 1985, revenues are almost stable. The deficit in the state budget for 1989 will be 92 billion rubles and will reach 10 percent of the gross domestic product. The amount of money being issued has increased sharply. In the current year it is 18 billion rubles, as compared to 4 billion rubles in 1985. The circle of deficit products is expanding. The ruble is losing value and failing to perform its role in the development of the socialist market. Inflationary processes are strengthening. Foreign debt is mounting, particularly in hard currency. In the current five-year period, it will grow by almost 18 billion rubles.[64]

It is clear from these citations that at last the authorities realized the acuteness of the situation in the consumer market and in state finances. But it is also clear that the authors of these documents do not know what to do to keep the crisis from continuing to worsen. By mid-1989 the USSR credit rating had dropped, but was still high. However, by this time Western analysts were worried by the swift growth of Soviet debt and the large proportion of short-term credits in it ($11.4 billion). They estimated the payments of the Soviet Union to service foreign debt in 1988 at $8.3 billion and in 1989 at $8.8 billion.[65]

Beginning in mid-1989, the problems with paying off contracts signed by Soviet foreign trade organizations and delays in payments for goods became obvious to the major Western companies that had trade relations with the USSR.[66] It would have seemed reasonable to reactivate efforts to get satellite countries to repay their loans on easy terms. In fact, it was impossible. The transcript of the Politburo meeting of August 23, 1989, records:

> The basic interests of the USSR as creditor are tied to the loans of developing countries . . . on state credits (official debts). On January 1, 1989, it was more than 61 billion rubles (or approximately 85 percent of the entire "third world" debt to the USSR), including more than 32 billion rubles to socialist developing countries—Vietnam, Cuba, China, and Mongolia. . . . Bearing in mind the real creditworthiness of our partners, the USSR periodically is forced to ease their debt burden. In the most recent period, payments by Algeria,

Angola, Vietnam, Iraq, Cuba, China, Libya, Mongolia, and Nicaragua were postponed from 1989–90, for a total of more than 7 billion rubles. We have observed a tendency of our friends in the "third world" to make their payments to the West a priority on the assumption that they will be able to come to terms with us. This in no small degree was aided by our readiness in the past to refinance their debt out of ideological considerations without due consideration of interest in developing mutually beneficial economic cooperation.[67]

In late 1989 and early 1990, Soviet foreign trade organizations, influenced by the looming currency crisis, continually missed their contract payments. Deputy Chairman of the Council of Ministers of the USSR Stepan Sitarian received this communication from Deputy Chairman of the State Commission on Food and Supplies Yuri Borisov:

> The recent systematic delays in payments by the Soviet side for shipped imported goods have led to a halt of further contracted shipments to the USSR of 211,600 tons of vegetable oil in the amount of 74.4 million rubles, 177,100 tons of meat and meat products for 160.0 million rubles, 66,500 tons of cocoa beans for 78.7 million rubles, 45,500 tons of butter for 39.4 million rubles, 30,000 tons of soy paste for 7.1 million rubles, 20,400 tons of beef for 14.3 million rubles, 19,900 tons of tea for 26.9 million rubles, various infant foods for 69.3 million rubles, 3 billion acetate filters for the tobacco industry for 7.3 million rubles, for a total of 478.3 million rubles. . . . The undelivered food products on signed contracts for a total of 478.3 million rubles can be shipped only on condition of payment of the food products already delivered to the USSR in the amount of 237 million rubles. Thus the total payment for imported food required is 715.6 million rubles.[68]

Domestic production satisfied only 40–45 percent of the need for pharmaceutical products in the Soviet Union. The effect of the hard currency crisis on medicine was considered the potentially most dangerous problem by both Soviet and foreign experts. The purchase of medicine was made the priority, but the growing deficit of hard currency made it impossible to pay the bills. Minister of the Medical Industry Valery Bykov wrote to Deputy Chairman of the Council of Ministers Sitarian:

> In accordance with the decision of the Council of Ministers dated March 10, 1990, on setting the priority in paying accounts to foreign firms by foreign trade organizations, the Ministry of the Medical Industry reports that Vneshekonombank has still not allocated funds to pay for medicines and substances purchased from countries that require payment in hard currency. The

past-due bill of Medesport to foreign firms as of April 1, 1990, is 43,418,300 rubles in hard currency (note attached). Because of the lateness in payment, foreign firms are adding penalties and at the present time, many have announced that they will stop delivering medications that have already been contracted for. Moreover, in signing contracts to purchase medicines of which there is an extreme shortage for 1990, as ordered by the Ministry of Health, the foreign firms are demanding advance payment or bank guarantees, but Vneshekonombank is refusing these forms of payment.[69]

The breakdown in import contracts exacerbated the problems in the consumer market, including food supply issues. The deputy chief of Glavsnab of Moscow Yuri Luzhkov wrote to Deputy Chairman of the Council of Ministers Sitarian:

> At the present time, because the plan set by the Moscow City Executive Committee for 1990 for importing unprocessed food is not being met, it has become extremely difficult to fulfill the state order and contractual obligations to supply bread, baked goods, and lacquer and paint products to trade organizations in Moscow and to enterprises. . . . In order to meet the goals set by the plan, the Moscow executive committee asks for a positive decision to purchase these products abroad or to give orders to the State Commission of the Council of Ministers on Food and Purchasing to put the Moscow Committee in touch with domestic suppliers.[70]

By the start of 1990, the catastrophic economic situation was apparent (see figures 5-1, 5-2, 5-3). At the same time, Sberbank USSR (the State Savings Bank) reported to the government on record deposits in savings accounts:

> In the fiscal year the institutions of Sberbank attracted into deposits, certificates, state loan obligations, and lottery tickets 45.6 billion rubles, or 23.5 billion rubles more than planned for in the income and expenditure balance for the population for the year. The main factor in attracting greater savings to the bank was the faster rate of income growth (it grew by 64 billion rubles, or 12.9 percent) than of expenditures for goods and services (by 9.1 percent). On the whole for the four years of the current five-year period, the money in savings accounts has increased by 117.1 billion rubles, or 53 percent. Savings grew so rapidly because income grew by 32.7 percent while spending on goods and services grew only 23.9 percent. The average rate of growth in income for 1986–89 was 7.3 percent, expenditures on goods and services 5.5 percent, and savings 22.2 percent.

FIGURE 5-2. Rate of Growth of Agricultural Output, 1976–91

Percent

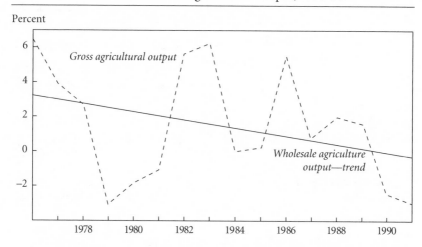

Source: *Rossiyskaia ekonomika v 1991 godu. Tendentsii i perspektivy* [The Russian Economy in 1991: Tendencies and Perspectives] (Moscow: Institute for Economic Policy, 1992), p. 26.

FIGURE 5-3. Rates of Growth of Population Income and Retail Sales, 1976–91

Percent

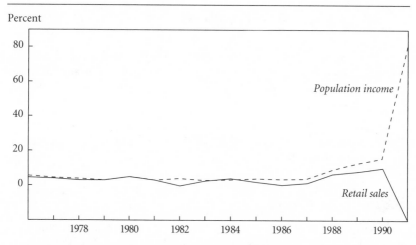

Source: *Rossiyskaia ekonomika v 1991 godu. Tendentsii i perspektivy* [The Russian Economy in 1991: Tendencies and Perspectives] (Moscow: Institute for Economic Policy, 1992), p. 28.

TABLE 5-19. Performance of the Credit Plan of the USSR Sberbank in 1989
Billions of rubles

| Item | As of January 1, 1989 | As of January 1, 1990 | | Deviation from the plan | |
		Plan with changes	Actual	Amount	Percent
Resources					
Bank's expense fund	0.87	0.75	0.93	+0.18	23.7
Deposits by the public in individual accounts	297.84	331.09	341.17	+10.08	3.0
Funds in current accounts of institutions and organizations and other funds	3.16	2.46	7.12	+4.66	190.1
Total	301.87	334.30	349.22	+14.92	4.5
Use of resources					
Short-term credit investments	0.26	0.30	0.28	−0.02	−4.7
Long-term credit investments	4.73	6.11	6.07	−0.04	−0.7
Fixed and other assets of the bank	2.30	1.00	4.37	+3.37	337
Corresponding account at the Gosbank	294.58	326.89	338.50	+11.61	3.6
Total	301.87	334.30	349.22	+14.92	4.5

Source: Report on the Performance of the USSR Savings Bank (Sberbank) in 1989 (RGAE, F. 2324, Inv. 33, S. 721, P. 3).

As can be seen in table 5-19, Sberbank overfulfilled the plan to increase people's savings and to use the money through Gosbank for goals set by the Council of Ministers.[71]

By early 1990, the close relationship between the state of the budget, money circulation, and the consumer market, so little understood by the leaders of the country in the mid-1980s, was evident to all.

The Hard Currency Crisis

In the spring of 1989, Chairman of the Board of Vneshekonombank Yuri Moskovsky informed Chairman of the Council of Ministers Nikolai Ryzhkov that the Soviet Union's growing indebtedness was becoming a frequent object of intense scrutiny in the Western press, and the actions of the Vneshekonombank were being thoroughly analyzed in business and banking circles. As a result, parties considering new loans to the USSR were growing more cautious.[72] The chairman of the board of Vneshekonombank wrote to the government in August 1989:

> Recently, representatives of a number of banks and financial companies in conversations at Vneshekonombank expressed their thoughts about becoming more cautious in offering hard currency loans to the Soviet Union. . . . Moreover, some banks in the FRG (DG-Bank, Bestdeutsche Landesbank, Norddeutsche Landesbank, and others) have begun refusing new credits for importing goods for investment purposes, alleging that the limits at Vneshekonombank for these operations have been exhausted. They have also suggested that the credit risk for the USSR may be raised.[73]

In early 1990 the fact that Vneshekonombank was slowing down the planned payments on imports still caused sincere amazement on the part of high-ranking Soviet officials:

> Vneshekonombank as of January 18 of this year has ceased paying foreign companies in hard currency for deliveries to the USSR of goods used in non-ferrous and ferrous metallurgy. As of February 16 of this year there is an overdue debt of 223.3 million rubles (66.3 for nonferrous and 157.0 for ferrous). In addition, another 313.7 million rubles is due at the end of the quarter (80.7 for nonferrous and 233.0 for ferrous). Thus payments for the first quarter of this year for delivered production, besides those already made, will be 537 million rubles.[74]

That same year, the Ministry of Foreign Economic Relations introduced operative accounting for the debts of its associations on signed and executed contracts. By late May 1990 it reached 767.1 million rubles in hard currency.[75] By fall 1990, the total in overdue payments to the ministry's foreign economic associations was more than 1.1 billion rubles.[76]

The agencies became more persistent in demanding hard currency to meet their payments and for Vneshekonombank to give them letters of credit. Facing an acute hard currency crisis, the management of Vneshekonombank was forced to inform the government of the situation:

> Work on attracting medium-term financial resources took place in conditions of a steadily increasing negative attitude from foreign creditors, especially ones that were not tied to the Soviet Union; and some withdrew previously offered credits. These difficulties had been reported to the Council of Ministers. . . . The problems with attracting financial credits arose in the middle of last year when the Banc National de Paris was organizing an international

consortium to arrange a medium-term bond issue in the amount of $150 million for Vneshekonombank. Of the 300 foreign banks asked to participate in the consortium, only five agreed, for a total of $29 million. . . . Thus at the end of 1989 negotiations broke off with the major British bank National Westminster on credits for $300 million. Attempts to renew negotiations were not successful. We had negotiations with the British Midland Bank in 1989 for a bond issue in the amount of 300 million British pounds sterling. . . . The issue was intended for November 20, 1989, but a day before the signing it was postponed indefinitely. . . . From the summer of 1989 there had been intensive negotiations with Deutsche Bank, Frankfurt-am-Main, about an issue of bonds for $300–$500 million. . . . Morgan Grenfell, one of the largest creditors of the Soviet Union in Great Britain, at our request looked at the possibility of issuing medium-term bonds for Vneshekonombank in the amount of $500 million. Despite the elaborate documentation and conditions, in the course of lengthy negotiations in Moscow in November of last year, the bank's representatives rejected the deal, citing the "sharp fall of confidence in the USSR on the part of Western banks." The bank refuses further negotiations. In late 1989 and early 1990 there were negotiations with a number of American and other financial companies that specialize in issuing bonds of varying amounts (for a total of approximately 2 billion rubles); however, they eventually declined. These are companies that have a high professional reputation in capital markets: Credit Suisse First Boston, Goldman Sachs, Shearson Lehman Hutton, UBS Phillips and Drew, and others. Now some of them indicate that attracting finances to the Soviet Union at present can be done only if they are backed by concrete assets (gold, oil). . . . Given the great reduction of medium-term credits in 1989, we had to increase resources on a short-term basis (in the form of interbank deposits). As a result the bank is dangerously dependent on this form, which is used in attracting 50 percent of foreign loans. . . . The real possibility of a sudden outflow of short-term financing in large amounts was reported to the Council of Ministers in our note no. 2231 of August 15, 1990. From the end of January to the present time, more than 1.5 billion rubles has not been renewed, and according to our calculations, approximately 85 counteragent banks have stopped offering short-term loans to Vneshekonombank. There is a real danger of a further recall of monies; even by the end of May of this year we do not rule out the nonrenewal of up to 2–3 billion rubles.[77]

Western banks repeatedly suggested to their Soviet counterparts that they turn directly to the governments of Western countries for financial aid, explaining that getting additional commercial credit was unlikely or completely impossible. Deputy Chairman of the USSR Council of Ministers Sitarian, who was aware of the critical situation in hard currency reserves and the payments balance, wrote to Chairman of the Council of Ministers Ryzhkov in May 1990:

> In accordance with your order by telegram from Bonn, and with the participation of Comrades Katushev, Gerashchenko, Moskovsky, Khomenko, and Sitin, we analyzed the possible steps on our side for getting financial credits from the governments of the EU countries, particularly the FRG, France, Italy, and perhaps England. The heads of Deutsche Bank recommend asking the governments of the listed countries directly for loans. This appeal may yield results if it is done on your level, in the opinion of Deutsche Bank. Bearing in mind Deutsche Bank's recommendation, which can be trusted, you should use Comrade Shevardnadze's trip to Bonn to raise this question in his meeting with Helmut Kohl and the ministers of England and France and learn how Kohl and his colleagues from the EU feel about your request for credits.[78]

At a conference in San Francisco in June 1990, the representatives of the world's largest commercial banks expressed the opinion that further credits to the Soviet Union should be given only with the participation of the governments of the West's leading countries and no longer by private banks.[79] The chairman of the board of Vneshekonombank informed the government of the Soviet Union of this on June 14, 1990.[80] Deputy Minister of Foreign Economic Relations Kachanov wrote to First Deputy Chairman of the Council of Ministers Voronin in October 1990:

> The giving of credits from most Western countries is contingent, according to our ambassadors, on the quickest passage in the Soviet Union of a real program of transition to a market economy and the signing of a Union agreement with clear division of the competencies of the central government and the Union republics. In the absence of these measures the West, apparently, will show restraint in giving the USSR new loans. Now the Western side is pressing the question of payments from Soviet organizations for goods supplied by Western firms on contracts.[81]

On July 16, 1990, speaking in Zheleznovodsk, Gorbachev made a careless remark about the need to extend the payment of Soviet loans. As was to be expected, financial markets thought this revealed the intention of the USSR to stop payments on foreign debt. The Soviet leader's remark caused a panic on the financial markets. Right after that statement the Bank of England put the USSR on its list of unreliable borrowers.[82] At that time, Gosbank warned the government of the consequences of an official question about restructuring debt and suggested backing loans with the country's gold reserves. Chairman of the Board of Gosbank Gerashchenko wrote to Deputy Chairman of the Council of Ministers Sitarian:

> As the experience of the countries that were forced to take this path in the 1980s shows (Mexico, Brazil, a number of other countries in Latin America, and also Poland and Yugoslavia), the official request of the debtor nation for an extension on paying foreign debts brings unfortunate economic and political consequences and is perceived as an admission of its total lack of creditworthiness. Therefore the "restructuring" of the Soviet Union's foreign debt is in our opinion an unacceptable measure that can do damage to the country economically and politically on an unpredictable scale.[83]

And from a memorandum prepared for the meeting of Shevardnadze and Kohl in May 1990:

> At the present time, in connection with insufficient reserves of hard currency in the Soviet Union, the country is experiencing an acute shortage of means for securing undisrupted payments on state debt and also on contracts for imports to the USSR. In connection with this, there are already significant sums of missed payments to foreign firms and companies (for your information, approximately 2 billion rubles). This circumstance, despite the timely debt and interest payments by Vneshekonombank, has created a swift outflow of money from its accounts and has given our Western partners reason to raise the issue of the country's inability to pay. This in turn has deprived us of the ability to attract money from foreign banks in amounts that would meet the needs of the plan for 1990. . . . In the course of the meeting on April 27 of this year between Vneshekonombank and Deutsche Bank, the latter's management feels it wise to have meetings in the nearest future between the Soviet government and the governments of EU countries, first and foremost the FRG, France, Italy, and perhaps England, on getting state guarantees for banks of these countries to make financial loans to cover the deficit of the balance of payments of the USSR and to finance further restructuring of the economy. . . . We could be talking about a total sum of 20 billion marks (7 billion rubles) for 5–7 years.[84]

Economic and Political Liberalization against the Background of Hard Currency and Financial Problems

Economic and political liberalization and management of the currency and financial crisis were crucial for the future of the USSR, but they were different problems. Liberalization in an educated and urbanized country is inevitable. The question that should have been discussed was how long and what form it would take.

The first known official document to raise doubts about the need to retain not only the economic but also the political system of the USSR is a letter from Alexander Yakovlev to Gorbachev in December 1985. In it he wrote:

> Today the question is not only economic—that is the material basis of the process. The key is the political system. . . . Hence the need . . . for a consistent and complete (in accordance with the historical possibilities at every stage) democratization. . . . Democracy is first of all freedom of choice. We have a lack of alternatives, we have centralization. . . . Now we do not understand completely the essence of the ongoing and historically inevitable transition from a time when there was no choice, or when it was historically impossible, to a time when it is impossible to develop successfully without democratic choice in which every single person participates.[85]

At a Politburo meeting on September 25, 1986, Chairman of the KGB Viktor Chebrikov raised the question of the wisdom of freeing first one-third and then half of the political prisoners.[86] The first signs that the political situation was changing appeared even before the government signaled that it was ready for such changes. On May 13, 1986, the Union of Cinematographers, contrary to tradition, elected leaders who were not approved by the Communist Party. The Union of Theater Workers followed suit. Then came personnel changes, this time sanctioned by the authorities, in the literary journals, which opened the way in the summer and fall of 1986 to the publication of previously banned literature. At the Plenum of the Central Committee on January 27–28, 1987, Gorbachev said:

> Yet we see that changes for the better are taking place slowly and the work of perestroika is more difficult than we had thought; the reason is that the problems that have accumulated in our society are deeper than we had first imagined. The deeper we get into the work of perestroika the clearer its scale and significance become, the more we find unsolved problems that we inherited from the past. . . . In general, comrades, there is a pressing need to once again

return to an analysis of the problems that the party and Soviet society encountered in recent years, preceding the April Plenum of the Central Committee.[87]

Ryzhkov made the position even more clear at the Plenum: "The more than eighteen months since the April Plenum have shown that the situation in our society, especially in the economy, is much more complex and dangerous than it had seemed then."[88] Medvedev writes about the key role of 1987 in determining the strategy for the country's socioeconomic changes:

It is a widespread and generally acknowledged idea that perestroika began in April 1985. That is true, if you mean the announcement of ideas and declaration of intentions. But the real start of perestroika came later, in 1987. The watershed character of 1987 is determined by three major milestones in the life of the Party and the country. The January Plenum of the Central Committee gave the initial impetus for reform of the political system. It was the June Plenum of the Central Committee that elaborated the complex program of economic transformations. And finally, it was the 70th anniversary of the October Revolution, in connection with which came a reevaluation of the most important stages of Soviet history, which defined to a significant degree the ideological mood of the country.[89]

The inefficiency of the socialist economic system made its dismantling strategically inevitable. However, this had no direct bearing on the short-term and acute problems created by the drop in oil prices. Regulation of the balance of payments crisis did not obviate the need for profound economic and political reforms. The government could try to combine the economic and political solutions for these problems, but it could not hope that liberalization on its own would deal with the currency and financial crisis. The choice made in 1987 by the Soviet leadership for economic and political liberalization, in the middle of an acute currency and financial crisis that it was not prepared to manage, had a major impact on development tactics and on how the Soviet economy collapsed.

Politically, it is not difficult to understand the logic of the decisions that were made then. If the measures necessary for stabilizing the economy are extremely unpopular, creating discontent among both the public and the elite, if dissatisfaction with the leadership grows along with disruptions in the consumer market, popular measures must be introduced demonstrating that the authorities have a vision for the future and an understanding of where the country must go. This was the basis of the economic and political liberalization formulated in 1987–88, which was intended to replace the difficult and unpopular measures and to create a new source of legitimacy for the regime.

The discussion of how to perfect the socialist economic system began in the early 1960s. There was a ban, out of political considerations, on steps to change it radically until the mid-1980s. The term "market economy," even a socialist one, could not be used in the open press about the USSR. The word "reform" was used for the first time since the early 1970s in an open document in 1986 in Gorbachev's speech at the Twenty-Seventh Congress, and it was used extremely cautiously. When ideological blinders are removed, the ideas that used to be discussed only off-stage suddenly become part of the open discourse. Most of the discussants know what needs to be done: expand the independence of enterprises, increase labor incentives, increase the role of profit, and switch from directive planning to a system of state orders. This range of ideas had wide support among the influential factory and plant directors. The problem was that serious movement toward the market, even a socialist one, with the retention of the power of the Communist Party presumed a transition to prices that balanced supply and demand.[90] Without these prices, market mechanisms at best work poorly or not at all. This was shown in Poland in the 1970s and 1980s, which attempted unsuccessfully to combine price stability with greater independence for enterprises. Events in the largest country in the Eastern European empire demonstrated that if there are no market prices, there are no incentives to improve efficiency. In that case, the expansion of enterprise rights leads merely to a weaker fiscal policy and less control over income, and to an increase in cheap merchandise; it allows manufacturers to exploit shortages and force consumers to buy shoddy goods.

The first sign that the authorities wanted to move toward liberalization of economic activity, to follow the path that China began in the late 1970s and early 1980s, was the law "On Individual Labor Activity," passed on November 19, 1986.[91] The legalization of individual farming, which took effect on May 1, 1987, was another step in the same direction. It too reflected the influence of the Chinese experience. But these decisions had no noticeable effect on the economy. That was the difference between three generations of Soviet citizens living without a market economy and a country with only one such generation—China. People's knowledge about how to run their own businesses without state control had almost disappeared. In China in 1979, the first signs of readiness on the part of the authorities to permit limited independent farming and disband the communes were supported by a mass popular movement. But nothing of the sort occurred in the USSR.

In 1988, the announced changes in the system of managing the economy had only a limited influence on the realities of economic life. Inertia and the conviction that the reforms were only for show, as had happened before in the USSR, took its toll. Directors of enterprises confidentially maintained that the rights they had been given were only formalities. The obvious signs of weakening of the central authority that became evident in 1989 changed the situation. Management and labor collectives began to realize that Moscow was not prepared to employ harsh measures if they did not follow orders from the center.

Unsystematic measures that were not intended to stabilize finances or liberalize prices, such as expanding the independence of enterprises and the rights of ministries in foreign economic activity, and the swift increase in the number of co-operative banks, merely exacerbated the problems related to the changes on the oil market. Deputy Chairman of the Government Leonid Abalkin described the situation this way:

> On one hand, everyone who spoke demanded independence, the repeal of the dictate of ministries and agencies, and a reduction in the share of the state commission. And at the same time they insisted, in unison, on guaranteed supplies of materials. After my election as deputy chairman of the Council of Ministers, I often sat next to Nikolai Ivanovich Ryzhkov, and I saw the situation he was in. He was approached by dozens of deputies with written and oral requests to ensure supplies, guarantee material and technical support, and so on and so forth. Everyone should have understood that if you've taken away the state commission from the government, with which it gathers its resources, then you do not have the right to expect it to supply you. There's a direct connection.[92]

The idea of bringing workers into management had been discussed before the Bolsheviks came to power in Russia. It had always been part of the discourse among the Soviet political elite. When Tito brought Yugoslavia out from under Soviet political control, he juxtaposed that idea with the Soviet economic model. On November 5, 1962, at a meeting of the Presidium of the Central Committee, Khrushchev said, "We must have, apparently, some kind of council on enterprise; develop a resolution requiring the director to make a monthly or quarterly report. There should be a workers' commission as well that could study the bookkeeping, the finances, materials, and so on. What's wrong with that? . . . I can see a time when the director of a plant or chief of a factory shop will run for the office and the council will vote on which candidate it prefers."[93]

Passed in 1986 and enacted in 1987–88, the decision to create councils of labor collectives, from the point of view of Communist ideology, was not as exotic as it might seem today. Since the Soviet regime came to power with the slogan "Factories to the workers!" why shouldn't it try to bring that to life when it faced a serious crisis?

The newly independent enterprises quickly raised wages. In 1988, salaries rose 8 percent; in 1989, 13 percent. In December 1989, the head of the Chief Directorate of Information of the Council of Ministers, Vladimir Kossov, wrote to First Deputy Chairman of the Council of Ministers Voronin that the growth in income might increase to 15 percent during the following year.[94] Electing directors had a bad effect on labor discipline and weakened the ability of the central agencies to regulate the economy through administrative methods. In the absence of market pricing and strict financial limits, this led to even more acute problems.

In May 1988 the law "On Cooperation in the USSR" was passed, de facto opening the way for the expansion of the private sector in the Soviet economy. Most of the cooperatives were formed within state enterprises. They bought goods at state prices, processed them, and sold them (and often simply resold them without any improvements) at market prices. With the shortages of goods and financial imbalance, enterprise management and the people controlling the co-operatives were able to make good profits.[95] The wealth of many Russians in the list of dollar billionaires came from this period.

By mid-1989 the number of workers in co-operatives grew to 4.9 million people. Four-fifths of the active co-operatives were created within state enterprises. The wages of co-operative workers in 1989 were double the average salary of laborers and white-collar workers. In early 1991, 6 million people were working in co-operatives.[96]

In accordance with the law "On Rent" passed on November 23, 1989, an enterprise had the right to fully or partially purchase property it was renting.[97] This law opened the way for greater privatization for the benefit of the management of enterprises and persons affiliated with them.

Resolution of the Central Committee and the Council of Ministers no. 721, dated July 6, 1988, "On expanding foreign economic activity of the Komsomol," and the resolution of the Council of Ministers no. 956 of August 4, 1988, "On assistance to the economic activity of the Komsomol," gave access to scientific and technical creative youth centers—organizations controlled by the Komsomol elite—to commercial and foreign economic activity.[98]

The creation in a short period of more than a thousand commercial banks, for which there were no qualified personnel or tradition of banking regulation, made them instruments for moving money from enterprises out of the state's control (the number of banks grew from 43 in January 1989 to 1,357 in January 1991).[99] The management at Gosbank understood these problems. A letter from the Directorate of Commercial Co-operative Banks to the Board of Gosbank dated May 7, 1991, read in part:

> An analysis of the balances of individual commercial and co-operative banks for the recent year shows that a significant number of banks have not managed to find the required amount for their statutory funds, since they were founded in the last five months. However, some of them have already started active credit operations. This is a clear violation of the rules of Gosbank and the charters of the banks. . . . We are particularly concerned by some commercial and co-operative banks' violation of the credit limit for a single borrower.[100]

Minister of Internal Affairs Vadim Bakatin wrote about the same issue to Yuri Maslyukov on July 13, 1990. In his memo, he said that the limits on state control of the credit and finance mechanism promote the growth of bribery and manipulation of financial resources.[101]

However, Ryzhkov was certain that things were going well in that sphere. With his deputies Maslyukov and Voronin, in a letter to the Central Committee on July 17, 1988, he expressed his categorical disagreement with the premise that the number of commercial banks was growing too quickly: "World experience shows that we have few banks and their network cannot satisfy the needs of the economy."[102] Subsequently, Ryzhkov wrote in his memoirs about Gosbank's resistance to the development of a network of commercial banks in the late 1980s.[103] However, it was not surprising that after several decades of a nonmarket economy, the country's leaders had trouble understanding that the banking sector is one of the last and not at all the first sector of the economy that should be liberalized. If we remember that for decades the country had no commercial banks, no trained personnel, and no apparatus for bank supervision, this debate is very telling about the level of understanding of the problems involved in the formation of a market economy.

The inconsistent liberalization measures did not help to solve the key problems facing the country: a swift reduction in hard currency reserves, a financial crisis, and disintegration of the consumer market. But the administrative turmoil, combined with the deterioration of everyday life, made the attitude toward the regime more critical. In 1985 the new leader, representing a different generation, had developed a reserve of confidence from the people, but by mid-1988 it was melting away.

On April 5, 1989, the Kemerovo Oblast Party Committee passed the Resolution "On the facts of workers refusing work in a number of enterprises." It also decreed on July 11, 1989, that the situation in the coal mines of Mezhdurechensk had become urgent. On July 17–18, 1989, the protocol "On coordinated measures between the regional strike committee of Kuzbass and the Commission of the Central Committee, the Council of Ministers, and the All-Union Central Council of Trade Unions" was signed. It held that in order to improve food and consumer good supplies Kemerovo Oblast would receive, in the second half of 1989: 6.5 thousand tons of meat, 5 thousand tons of animal fats, 5 million units of canned milk, 10 thousand tons of sugar, 3 thousand tons of soap, and 3 thousand tons of detergents.[104]

The problem for the Union authorities was that such promises are easier to make than to keep in a collapsing economy. Soon both the government and the miners saw that only the salary payments would be made. But there was almost nothing to buy with the money. This incited a new wave of strikes. The political and economic disintegration of the regime that led to its collapse was set in motion.

CHAPTER VI

DEVELOPMENT
OF THE CRISIS IN THE
SOCIALIST SYSTEM

"Hey! No hysterics! We're going to hit shore!" the
commander said.

—Vladimir Vysotsky

THE SITUATION IN THE OIL INDUSTRY described in the previous chapter was one of the determining factors that pushed the economic crisis into a catastrophe (see table 6-1). Archival documents allow us to examine it more closely.

At a meeting on September 17, 1990, Chairman of the Council of Ministers Nikolai Ryzhkov said that oil production in the period from 1975 to 1990 fluctuated within the range of 500–600 million tons, while capital investments grew from 3.8 billion rubles to 17 billion rubles in 1991 [this was in a discussion of the plan for 1991—author]. The number of wells required to produce 1 million tons grew from 16 in 1975 to 165 in 1990. The number of meters drilled grew tenfold. And oil production was beginning to fall, despite all that.[1] From the transcript of the meeting:

Comrade Ryzhkov: What will we do with 547 tons, how will the country live?

Comrade Ryabyev: For domestic consumption, there will be 467 million tons. . . . Exports are falling.

Comrade Ryzhkov: But still, what needs to be done to get 580, as we had discussed at first?

Comrade Ryabyev: Those are very difficult numbers. We need to increase drilling and introduce 25–26 thousand new wells. There has to be a sharp

TABLE 6-1. Oil Production in the USSR and the Russian Federation, 1988–91

Million tons

Item	1988	1989	1990	1991
USSR	624.3	607.2	570.0	515.8
Increase or decrease from the previous year	+0.1	−17.1	−37.2	−54.2
Russian Federation	568.8	552.3	515.9	461.9
Increase or decrease from the previous year	−0.6	−16.5	−36.4	−54.0

Source: *Toplivno-energetichesky kompleks SSSR 1990 g.* [USSR Fuel and Power Sector 1990] (Moscow: VNIIKTEP, 1991), pp. 108–09; *Toplivo i energetika Rossii* [Fuel and Power in Russia] (Moscow: RF Ministry of Fuel and Power, 1999), pp. 158, 408–09; Goskomstat of Russia.

increase. And capital investments are growing substantially, and the whole-sale price per ton is 155 rubles. . . .

Comrade Sitarian: How much money is needed for these two things?

Comrade Ryabyev: Approximately 800 million rubles in convertible currency.

Comrade Sitarian: And how much will you give?

Comrade Ryabyev: Now it is important not to fall from the level. We are losing yield every day. In January we will start the count at 25 million tons. . . .

Comrade Ryzhkov: Your task is to find a way to get out of the situation.

Comrade Ryabyev: We have looked into all of this. The first variant was presented to you in July—to redistribute resources in the country. There simply are no other resources. I hold meetings of the government commission twice a month, and I have constant shorter meetings too. There are no resources. None. . . .

Comrade Ryzhkov: Leonid Ivanovich, please . . .

Comrade . . . : Today we must have guarantees from the Ministry of Foreign Economic Relations. If we do that now, then the firms are prepared to work with us. Then the money must be transferred. Six million goes on our account, but there is also the all-Union account. This is a complex situation; I will deal with it personally. This is the proposal. Today Vneshekonombank must reassure the firms and give them the ministry guarantee. As soon as the guarantee appears, we start purchasing, because we have prepared contracts with our foreign partners.

Comrade Sitarian: The general situation is such that if export is 60 million, then we put the relationships with other countries in an extremely difficult position. That is, if today 34 million tons goes to hard currency, that leaves 26 million for all the Eastern European countries plus Finland, India, Cuba, and so on. . . . If we are losing 20 million now, that means that our hard currency resources for next year will be 14 billion. I feel that signing for 60 million in exports should not be done. . . . The point is that we cannot fail to deliver oil to certain countries. If we stop at this number, it means a complete collapse inside the country and with many countries. If we give Poland zero, then Poland will not sell us anything. . . .

Comrade . . . : Let me start with the most painful thing, that's 580 or 547, the understanding of the situation. Nikolai Ivanovich, there is no returning to 580. When it was put in the budget, it was based on the expectation that with the planned drilling of 41.3 million meters we would get 39, when in fact we got 35.5.

Comrade Maslyukov: We understand that the only source of hard currency is of course oil, so I will make this proposal. I feel that we must approach those proposals made by the geologists and take the most determined measures to achieve additional oil production, whatever the conditions may be for the riggers. Second. I would think that all the necessary resources that were named should definitely be purchased from foreign firms. . . . I have the presentiment that if we do not make all of the necessary decisions now, then we may spend next year in a way that we haven't even dreamed of. . . . Things can end most critically in the socialist countries. This will lead us to a real crash, and not just for us, but for our entire system. . . .

Comrade Voronin: I can only say that the oil industry has never been in this situation, not even in 1985. It has reached the point that we may even fear not getting 500 million tons of oil, if things continue this way. . . . I understand that if we can't get at least 560–570 million tons, we will let down everything, the socialist countries, and our food production and machine-building. . . . The really hurtful thing is that oil is at a good price and it will keep rising, while we will be producing less and less. Therefore we must give the socialist countries the minimum for hard currency, and reduce the domestic demand as much as possible. . . . The most important task is to immediately cover all expenses with financial resources.

N. Ryzhkov: We need guarantees from Vneshekonombank, and it can't give them. . . . We have to make the decision to go for 547 million tons, and of that there will be only 60 million tons for export, both to socialist countries and to capitalist countries, which will ruin everything. . . . If we don't find the formula now to save the oil and gas industry, we won't get even 547. There has to be a definite system; either we force them to reach the goal, or we will stay on the downward slide. I am concerned that we have already met several times this year and we can't handle the situation. We have to stay at 560 million tons and we have to devote all of our material resources to it, and not just make a list but write everything precisely and create a system of control. . . . I see that if there is no oil, there is no economy. . . . At the start of the year we talked about 625 million, and today we're expecting 547—that's the result of our conversations. What are we waiting for?[2]

A memo from the socioeconomic department of the Central Committee dated September 19, 1990, stated:

In seven months of 1990 relative to last year the production of oil and gas condensate decreased by 16.5 million tons, and of coal by 22 million tons. . . . Over seven months of 1990 of the planned 13.4 million kW of new energy resources only 3.1 million kW were introduced . . . (*even in an anomalously warm winter*). From January to July 1990, as compared to last year, the number of blackouts increased by 2.3 times. The balance of electric power for the coming winter is at a deficit of approximately 8 million kW.[3]

With falling oil production and oil exports, the problems with hard currency increased. The minister of foreign economic relations, Konstantin Katushev, wrote to Ryzhkov: "The Ministry of Foreign Economic Relations is reporting on the catastrophic situation in trying to meet the deadline for delivery of oil and petroleum products for export in the fourth quarter of this year. . . . If this situation does not change, in October and November we will be behind by more than 4 million tons of oil and petroleum products and will not receive more than 400 million hard currency rubles."[4]

Supplying agriculture with fuel grew more complicated with each passing year. From a letter to the government:

The fuel and energy sector came out of last winter with unusually low potential. In connection with the reduction in oil and coal production and the creation of fuel oil, the resources of boiler and heating fuel in the first quarter of 1991 has fallen from the first quarter of 1990 by 11 million tons. At the same time the use of boiler and heating fuel inside the country, despite the reduction of manufacturing of industrial products in the period January–March of this year, surpassed the expenditures in the first quarter of 1990 by 10.9 million tons of equivalent fuel, which is partially due to weather that was colder than the unusually warm first quarter of 1990. The reserves of fuel consumers are down from 68.9 million tons (16.8 days of heating) on April 1, 1990, to 59 million tons (14 days) on April 1, 1991. . . . On the whole in 1991, resources for heating and boiler fuel for consumption within the country, in view of the expected exports, is expected to be 1,497 million tons of equivalent fuel against 1,509.1 million tons for 1990, while the demand for equivalent fuel is 18–20 million tons more, which will lead to a reduction of reserves of consumer fuel at the end of the year to 43 million tons from 69–73 million tons in the past three years. This must not be allowed, since such low reserves will disrupt the work of agriculture in the coming winter.[5]

In 1991, the situation in the oil sector deteriorated. From a letter of the deputy chairman of the Cabinet of Ministers Lev Ryabyev to the chairman of the Cabinet Valentin Pavlov, dated May 31, 1991:

Because of the lag in development of the machine-building base, the disruption of established ties, and the failure of enterprises and suppliers to meet contractual obligations, the demands of the sector are only 50–60 percent equipped and supplied with materials. Deliveries of imported equipment and pipelines have decreased by almost half because of a lack of hard currency. . . . At the present time, 22,000 oil wells are not functioning. . . . In the period January–May of this year, the average daily production of oil was at a level guaranteeing the production of 530 million tons a year, supplying refineries with 452 million tons and 61 million tons for export. . . . In recent years, with the increasing deterioration of mining and geological conditions and the exhaustion of reserves from the most productive deposits, the sector loses almost 100 million tons of oil a year and the economic indicators of the enterprises' work are falling sharply. In the past five years the debits of the wells have doubled, the amount of water in the production has grown by 80 percent, and the specific expenses for creating new wells have doubled.[6]

To a great degree the drop in oil production was due to geological factors. The most productive deposits had been overused. By the second half of the 1980s, productivity of the wells had decreased significantly (see table 6-2), and the number of exhausted wells had increased. The new deposits were more difficult to extract, requiring greater expenses per ton of oil.

The technical structure of the oil industry could not compensate for the more difficult production conditions. Soviet technology was significantly below world levels, and any improvement in output was labor intensive. With the increase in the relative capital costs in 1986–90 up 80 percent from the

TABLE 6-2. Oil Well Production in the USSR and the Russian Federation, 1975–90

Average tons per month

Oil production	1975	1980	1985	1988	1989	1990
USSR						
All wells	652.2	621.1	447.8	368.4	338.7	314.4
New wells	1,755.8	1,167.3	808.4	609.5	549.9	518.1
Russian Federation						
All wells	882.7	828.8	555.0	429.1	394.5	354.2
New wells	1,873.6	1,214.7	851.9	627.7	566.3	522.1

Source: *Toplivno-energetichesky kompleks SSSR 1988 g* [USSR Fuel Energy Complex for 1988] (Moscow: VNIIKTEP, 1989), p. 127; *Toplivno-energetichesky kompleks SSSR 1990 g* [USSR Fuel Energy Complex for 1990] (Moscow: VNIIKTEP, 1991), pp. 140–41.

previous five-year period, the real growth in investment in the sector was only 28 percent.[7]

The drop in oil production and its export exacerbated the problems in the balance of payments. The lack of hard currency, in turn, made work in the industry that much harder. Minister of the Oil and Gas Industry Leonid Churilov wrote this to the government:

> At the present time, our foreign trade associations have signed contracts for the delivery of material and technical resources for the Ministry of the Oil and Gas Industry for an amount close to 800 million rubles. Contracts are ready to be signed for another 1.3 billion rubles in convertible currency according to the official rates at Gosbank. However, further signing of contracts, which has been postponed several times already, is held up because the ministry lacks hard currency. . . . Vneshekonombank has reported to the Cabinet of Ministers of the USSR on the impossibility of executing the order, which puts the oil sector in a critical situation in terms of fulfilling its production goals.[8]

Political Credits

For many decades the Soviet Union conducted a cautious credit policy, not wanting to be dependent on Western banks. After its refusal to pay tsarist debts, the USSR always paid its foreign debt on time. In the mid-1980s, the

USSR had a deserved reputation as a first-class borrower with almost un-limited access to credit. However, with the growing financial disruptions, it was difficult to maintain lenders' confidence. As was shown in previous chapters, by 1988 Western banks began to doubt the stability of the USSR's fiscal situation. The opportunity to get commercial loans became more limited and the terms grew stricter, both rates and deadlines.

Yet the need for additional loans grew in order to finance the deficit in the balance of payments with developed capitalist countries. This was due to the pressures caused by the drop in oil prices, the continued need to pay for imported food, and the impossibility of either reducing spending or increasing exports of non-oil products. In 1988–89 it became clear that financing previous loans with new ones would be difficult. The payments had to be covered by current income from exports. And the deficit in the current accounts of the balance of payments made it more difficult to finance capital operations.

The leadership decided to use hard currency reserves and increase the sale of gold. The gold reserves of the USSR, which since the early 1960s had financed urgent purchases of grain after crop failures, had dwindled by the mid-1980s. Soviet hard currency reserves had never been significant. Gold and currency are quickly exhausted resources, and they cannot be used to finance a long-term deficit in the balance of payments.

In 1988–89, the Soviets found themselves with the same choice they had faced in 1985–86, but in worsened conditions. The absence of hard currency resources forced them to adjust the volume and structure of production and consumption to the new realities. This could have provoked an economic and even a political crisis. Because it would be risky to impose harsh stabilization measures, particularly in view of the nascent political liberalization, it seemed to the leadership that the only possible step was to attract large Western state credits that would compensate for the reduced access to commercial loans. But these credits always have a political character. If you are running a super-power, it is useful to know that.

In 1985, no one in the world seriously discussed the possibility that the USSR might have to turn to the West for credits and make political compromises in order to get them. It took only three years for this idea, once considered absurd, to become central to Soviet foreign policy. Without politically motivated loans, the country would not be able to ensure even minimal stability in agriculture. The miners' strike in the summer of 1989, caused by lack of food in the mining regions, showed the government that further deterioration in the consumer market would be explosive.

In Poland in the early 1980s, the country became hostage to the large Western debts it had incurred over the previous decade. The resulting fiscal crisis that forced the Polish authorities to take the politically risky measure of raising retail prices was a prelude to the events in the USSR in the late 1980s and early 1990s.[9] In Poland in the early 1980s and the USSR in the early 1990s, fiscal and currency issues were the root of the problems. The Soviets understood that when Poland invoked martial law and suppressed Solidarity, it could not expect help from the West in solving its fiscal problems and that the USSR would have to pay. But in those years, the USSR still had resources to support the satellite regime. In the late 1980s and early 1990s, there was no socialist country prepared to cough up money to save the political structure of the USSR.

When getting large state loans is of paramount importance, then you must adjust your policies to suit the lenders. Using perestroika and the new thinking to improve relations with the West seemed the only way out. Gorbachev knew that long-term problems were creating unusually high military expenses for the USSR, and he tried to stem their growth. This decision led to a new tone in negotiations over limiting strategic arms, obvious in the summit meeting in Reykjavík (October 1986) between Gorbachev and U.S. president Ronald Reagan. However, until 1988, arms limitation was tied to a strategic choice: the long-term future of economic growth and military security. With the start of the foreign debt crisis, the situation changed. Now there was no choice—the risk of the collapse of the Soviet economic and political system forced the Soviet authorities to negotiate with the West for financial aid to the ruined Soviet economy.

Only President Gorbachev's awareness of the acuteness of the economic problems in the Soviet Union in 1988 explains his initiative to reduce arms, which he formulated in December 1988 at the United Nations, the Soviet agreement to an asymmetrical troop reduction in Europe, and the agreement on medium-range missiles that was practically identical to what NATO had proposed.[10]

The new tactics were evident in the negotiations between Gorbachev and President George H. W. Bush in Malta (November 1989). Gorbachev's amiability and willingness to make arms concessions was not related so much to a desire to lower the burden of military expenditures. That was strategically important but politically difficult. It would take time for the reduction in military spending to influence the economic situation in the USSR. Something else was of critical significance for the Soviets: the willingness of the United States and its allies to support government loans to the USSR, loans from the

IMF and World Bank. For the Soviets, this was fundamental. In order to improve their chances of getting the money, they provided informal assurances that the USSR would not use force to maintain its political control in Eastern Europe.[11]

Gorbachev is the best judge of how much these promises reflected his own convictions. However, even if the Soviet leader had been a consistent foe of the West who was not prepared to commit political suicide by implementing a serious anti-crisis program, he would have been forced to follow a similar line with the West. It was determined not by personal preference but by the country's economic and political situation.

The Price of Compromise

The Western partners in the negotiations understood the situation in which the Soviet Union found itself and how dependent it was on politically motivated loans. This lent the dialogue a different tone. As long as the main problem had been regulation of the arms race and the two sides had military and political parity, they were prepared to continue lengthy and tortuous negotiations, negotiations as equals. Now, with the Soviet leadership asking for economic aid, there was no trace of equality left.[12] That is the way of the world. Crude errors in economic policy, including those made decades earlier, and the unwillingness to pay the political price domestically to fix them, led to foreign policy concessions. Now the Soviet leadership had to play by the rules imposed on them when dealing with important political issues.

They had to forget about using force to maintain political control in the Eastern European part of the empire. Any steps in that direction would end their hope of getting large-scale economic aid. There had long been an unspoken mutual understanding that Eastern Europe was in the Soviet sphere of interest and that no matter how outraged Europeans and Americans were by military intervention in that region NATO member countries were not prepared to interfere. This mutual understanding was an important factor in the USSR's continued control there. After the events of 1968 in Czechoslovakia, force was no longer used. But everyone knew that the Soviets were prepared to use it again if necessary.

The unrest of 1980–81 in Poland, when the Soviet Party leaders pondered whether to send troops to suppress the workers' movement there, while continuing the war in Afghanistan, was the first time that they confronted the issue of how far they would go to preserve the empire.[13] The question was not raised publicly, only discussed in confidence. The Polish regime was encouraged to solve the problem itself by introducing martial law. The Soviet decision to withdraw troops from Afghanistan, the inevitability of which was obvious to the political and military leaders by the fall of 1985, could have raised doubts about the Soviet willingness to use troops to save the Eastern European part of the empire. But no clear answer to that question emerged.

The unilateral reduction of Soviet armed forces, including the withdrawal of 50,000 Soviet soldiers from Eastern Europe, was a clear signal to the Eastern European societies that this meant the end of the Brezhnev doctrine, the doctrine of limited sovereignty with the Soviet Union prepared to use force to maintain control over its satellite states.

From late 1988 and early 1989, when the society and the political elite of the Eastern European countries saw that the USSR would not use force because of its economic dependence on the West, the fall of the Eastern European part of the empire was merely a question of form and time. In April 1989, negotiations began between the Polish government and Solidarity on the conditions for free parliamentary elections. Two months later, Solidarity dealt a crushing blow to the pro-Soviet regime and won full control of the lower and upper chambers of the parliament.

Without the support of Soviet military power, even President Ceausescu's unconditional willingness to use force against his own people in Rumania did not save his regime. It was only two months from the Malta summit (November 1989), when Gorbachev unofficially assured Bush that Soviet forces would not take part in military actions in Eastern Europe, until the collapse of the rest of the Eastern European empire.

As usually happens, once an empire starts to crumble, the process goes faster than expected. In September 1989, the Central Committee was certain that the Polish government would not be raising the question of leaving the Warsaw Treaty Organization.[14] Soon after that, there was no point in even raising the question since the Warsaw Pact no longer existed.

The economic price paid by the West for the USSR to give up control over Eastern Europe was not high: credits and grants to the FRG for an agreement to unite Germany, Italian tied credits, American grain credits—not a lot for the result. The USSR was in no position to impose conditions. The main thing was to get large credits and stabilize the economy.

The Western nations had more in mind for the USSR than controlling its behavior in Eastern Europe. They kept telling the Soviets that if they wanted economic aid they had to observe human rights and not abuse power. But what did such recommendations mean for a political and economic system based on the unlimited use of force against its own people for stability?[15] They were tantamount to a demand for its liquidation.

Baltic politicians who had called for a restoration of independence after the Molotov-Ribbentrop Pact of 1939 got a clear signal from the United States: if you proclaim independence, America can do nothing to protect your sovereignty and will not recognize the new governments. But the United States also informed the Soviets that forcefully suppressing independence movements in the Baltic states would do irreparable damage to relations with the West.[16] In simple language it meant, if you use repression, forget about money from the West.

Revelations about the past showed that the USSR had even more complex problems than other disintegrating empires. The latter had the rights of the conqueror as their source of legitimacy. To maintain its power, the USSR would have to appeal to Communist ideology and historical tradition. Glasnost, which provided public access to information about the treacherous regime and how it was formed, undermined what remained of the Soviet Union's legitimacy. As soon as the Soviet leadership allowed the truth to be told about its own history, the Soviet empire was doomed.

The Crisis of the Empire and the Nationality Question

As usually happens in authoritarian multinational states, the liberalization of the regime and the introduction of democracy led to the political mobilization of forces prepared to exploit nationalist feelings. In the USSR, the groups who suffered repression based on their ethnicity included the Korean, Kurd, Nenets, Karachaev, Kalmyk, Chechen, Ingush, Balkar, Crimean Tatar, Greek, and Meskhetian Turk peoples.[17] We can imagine the ethnic tensions and long-term problems (hidden until then) that were created by their repression.[18] In the absence of democratic traditions, slogans appealing to national history and interests and desires for revenge were an effective tool in political struggle. The events in the USSR in the late 1980s and early 1990s were no exception.

In the early years of his administration Gorbachev did not appreciate the explosive nature of interethnic relations and believed that the nationality question in the USSR had been resolved. His own words reveal the degree to which he had no understanding of the issues and the problems that could arise with liberalization: "If the nationality question were not already settled in principle in our country, then there would not be the Soviet Union as it now exists in social, cultural, economic, and defense relations. Our state would not have survived if there had not been a true equalization of the republics, if there had not been a community based on fraternity and cooperation, on respect and mutual aid."[19] This political error is an example of a leader believing official propaganda and ignoring the reality. He might have recalled that the mass protests in Georgia on March 4–9, 1956, the first postwar open manifestation of political protest in the USSR, came almost immediately after Khrushchev's liberalization of the regime. Approximately 30,000 people took part. On March 9 troops fired on them, killing thirteen people, and another eight of the sixty-three wounded died subsequently. That same day there were other clashes between protesters and troops that left wounded and dead victims.[20]

The risks of interethnic conflict in a multiethnic state with a totalitarian regime at the first sign of liberalization were demonstrated by the events of 1986 in Alma-Ata. Students rioted with nationalistic slogans. Approximately 10,000 people took part. They were protesting the appointment of a Russian, Gennady Kolbin, as first secretary of the Central Committee of Kazakhstan. The Soviet leadership, feeling no compunctions yet about the use of force, quickly put down the riots.[21] Almost 8,500 people were detained, and approximately 1,700 were wounded.[22] Despite the harsh treatment of the student rioters, Moscow showed the first signs of weakness afterward: the decision to appoint Kolbin was repealed and a Kazakh was appointed instead—Nursultan Nazarbayev.

With glasnost, the newspapers and magazines were filled with articles about national oppression, economic exploitation, and destruction of the environment in their regions. As had happened in Yugoslavia, these topics were actively discussed in the mass media of the republics that were the linchpins of the empire, respectively the Russian Socialist Federated Soviet Republic (RSFSR) and Serbia. The topic of the oppression of Russians in the USSR in 1988–89 was as vocally presented as the theme of discrimination against Serbs in Yugoslavia in those years.

In trade with other republics only Russia, Belorussia, Azerbaijan, and Georgia had a positive trade balance. The data on the balances of inter-republic trade and foreign trade in world prices for 1989–91, calculated by Alexander Granberg and Viktor Suslov, were no secret either (see table 6-3).

Naturally it would be wrong to conclude that Russia and Turkmenistan were the only donors in the Soviet Union to the other republics and that the dissolution of the USSR and a transition to trade at world prices would improve their economic situation. But these topics were useful tools in

TABLE 6-3. Balance of Inter-Republic and Foreign Trade Volume
in World Prices, 1988
Billions of rubles

Republic	Inter-republic trade	Foreign trade	Total
Russia	+23.88	+6.96	+30.84
Ukraine	−1.57	−1.32	−2.89
Kazakhstan	−5.94	−0.64	−6.58
Belorussia	−1.59	−0.46	−2.05
Uzbekistan	−2.63	+0.09	−2.54
Azerbaijan	−0.24	−0.21	−0.45
Lithuania	−3.33	−0.36	−3.69
Georgia	−1.61	−0.30	−1.91
Moldavia	−2.22	−0.41	−2.63
Latvia	−0.99	−0.32	−1.31
Armenia	−1.06	−0.31	−1.37
Kirgizia	−0.54	−0.52	−1.06
Estonia	−1.06	−0.24	−1.30
Tajikistan	−1.20	+0.08	−1.12
Turkmenia	+0.1	−0.06	+0.04

Source: A. G. Granberg, "Ekonomicheskii mekhanism mezhrespublikanskikh i mezhregional'nykh otnoshenii" [The Economic Mechanism of Inter-Republic and Interregional Relations], *Ekonomika i organizatsiia promyshlennogo proizvodstva*, no. 9 (1989); V. I. Suslov, *Izmerenie effektov mezhregional'nykh vzaimodeistvii: modeli, metody, rezul'taty* (Novosibirsk: Nauka, 1991); A. Granberg, and V. I. Suslov, "Mezhrespublikanskie ekonomicheskie otnosheniia nakanune raspada SSSR" [Inter-Republic Economic Relations on the Eve of the Collapse of the USSR], *Regional'noe razvitie i sotrudnichestvo*, no. 0 (1997): 17–25.

the hands of people who exploited the theme of oppressed Russians in the USSR.

By the summer of 1988 there were strong nationalist movements in the Baltics, Armenia, and Georgia. This wave quickly spread throughout the Soviet Union. As usual, the energetic leaders of national movements found outside enemies. The leaders of the national movements in Armenia and Azerbaijan did not have to look hard to find the enemy in each other. The same held for the leaders of national movements in Georgia, Abkhazia, and Ossetia. The list could be continued.

A sequence of ever more bloody clashes and pogroms unfolded. Some turned into military action, revealing the contradictory position of the Soviet leaders, particularly Gorbachev. Having started the process of democratization, he opened the way to the development of national movements, many of which wanted independence from the USSR. At the very least, in the Baltics and Georgia victory in democratic elections of forces for independence was a given. The Sajudis Association, which wanted independence for Lithuania, won election to the Supreme Soviet of the republic on February 25, 1990. This cleared the way for independence movements in other republics. From a memorandum to the Central Committee on the problems of inter-ethnic conflict:

> The acuteness of interethnic relations in the country has led to widespread forced migration. More than 600,000 people have left their homes. In a num-ber of regions this process has become irreversible. On the whole, the prob-lem of refugees is affecting eight Union republics and half the regions of the RSFSR, where they moved on their own or were brought in an organized way. More than 60 million people, including 25 million Russians, live outside the borders of their national regions. However, the problem of forced migration will affect not only the Russian population; its political and socioeconomic ramifications will touch the fate of millions of people of all nationalities who live in our country. . . . Work has been done, and more than 400,000 people have been given temporary housing, more than 100,000 have new jobs, and the needy have been helped with clothing and shoes. However, these measures are incommensurate with the scale and urgency of the problem.[23]

Gorbachev could have stopped the process only by employing force and repression. Instead, the wave of national liberation movements continued into other regions, including Ukraine. By September 1989, Ukraine, the sec-ond largest republic in the Soviet Union, was experiencing an overt national-ist movement. The firing of First Secretary of the Ukrainian Communist Party Vladimir Shcherbitsky, mass rallies by Ukrainian Catholics, and the First Congress of Ruh, a political movement wanting independence for Ukraine, made it a political reality.[24] That development was unacceptable to the major-ity of the Soviet administrative and political elite. However, the use of force would not only have undermined Gorbachev's authority as a democrat and liberator and the base of his political support that allowed him to stand up to the resistance to the new reforms; it would also have reduced his image in the eyes of the West.

Preserving the empire without using force was impossible; holding on to power without preserving it was impossible as well. Using mass repression would obviate the possibility of getting large, long-term, politically motivated credits that would at least postpone the looming state bankruptcy. The eco-nomic catastrophe that would follow the revelation that the path to Western money was blocked guaranteed the loss of power for the entire Communist leadership. This combination of circumstances is the basis for what might otherwise first seem to be odd behavior on the part of the Soviet regime in 1989–91.

In the 1980s, demographic changes, including an increase in the number of non-Slavic young people, aggravated the problems in the army. Other territorially integrated empires had faced similar problems. The officer corps remained primarily Slavic. But the rank-and-file was made up more and more of young men from non-Slavic groups, mostly from the Central Asian republics. While the elite units (strategic missile launch, paratroopers, air force, part of the navy, and the KGB troops) were mostly Slavic at the serviceman and sergeant levels, the land troops (tank, motorized infantry, and artillery) became less Slavic. In these conditions, it would be difficult to hope that multiethnic units would effectively suppress riots, particularly in regions that the soldiers considered close ethnically and culturally. The authorities would have to rely on the elite corps. But their number was limited. In addition, the use of force inevitably deepens the conflict between the ethnic populace and the metropolis.[25]

The military did use force during the unrest in Tbilisi in April 1989, though at the time the political leadership denied that it had ordered the move.[26] Such statements created even greater hostility and mistrust, and the army, which was blamed, became more reluctant to be the scapegoat time after time. This was seen in Fergana in May–June 1989, where there was a wave of pogroms against the Meskhetian Turks. The army command would not act until given direct and unambiguous orders to stop the riots. The political leadership hesitated. Thousands of people became victims of the paralysis of will and the absence of urgent action to restore peace and protect the citizenry.[27]

Loss of Control over the Economic and Political Situation

In 1989–90, the Union leadership lost even more control over the country's fate. The mounting economic difficulties, the shortages in the consumer market, and the expanding list of items that were available only through rationing undermined the legitimacy of the regime and ensured mass support for anti-Communist agitation. This sentiment was particularly evident in the capitals, Moscow and Leningrad, and in the large cities. Secretary of the Central Committee Vadim Medvedev described the political results of the first semi-free elections, which took place in the spring of 1989: "In the course of the elections to the Congress of People's Deputies of the USSR, 32 of the 160 first secretaries of regional party committees lost. . . . In Leningrad, not a single Party or Soviet leader of the city and region was elected, not a single member of the bureau of the regional committee, including the first secretary and even the commander of the military okrug (district). In Moscow, most Party workers lost, and 90 percent of Muscovites voted for Yeltsin."[28] Party leaders lost in the Volga region, in the Urals, Siberia, the Far East, southeastern Ukraine, the Baltics, Armenia, and Georgia.

Crime was increasing. In the first half of 1990, 1,514,000 crimes were reported in the Soviet Union, 251,000 more than in the same period a year earlier. Crimes involving guns had gone up by almost a third. The number of robberies was growing rapidly.[29] The state was losing its ability to ensure law and order.

The formality of electing directors and switching from the state plan to state commissions while keeping strict political control would merely have perpetuated the system of administrative control of the economy. Instead, the weakening of the regime made it possible for enterprises to exercise greater independence. Managers could ignore directives from the authorities. But the retention of fixed prices for products of state enterprises and free products produced by co-operative enterprises created the conditions for a massive semilegal redistribution of resources into private hands.

Contradictory decisions by Union, republic, oblast, and local authorities gave the enterprises freedom to maneuver. The fundamental trait of the socialist economy was manifest yet again: it can work only under a harsh political regime, and without this, it falls apart.

The resolution of the Congress of People's Deputies of June 9, 1989, demonstrates the unique nature of a society that did not have the experience of democracy but was no longer ruled by an authoritarian regime. It notes the problems related to the disarray of the financial system, the unbalanced market, and the shortages of consumer goods and services. After stating this, the authors nevertheless propose an immediate rise in minimal pensions for the elderly, an increase in pensions for the most severely disabled, an end to the limits on pensions for all pensioners and invalids working in agriculture, no matter their wages, and so on.[30]

The weakening of power and loss of political control gave rise to competition among Union and republican administrations to see who could do more to destroy the fiscal system of the USSR. In January 1991, the Supreme Soviet of the USSR decided to centralize payments for social welfare services at the expense of the Union budget and other sources in the amount of 47.6 billion rubles, including 2.5 billion rubles to increase aid in child care to the level of the minimum wage; 8.2 billion rubles for payments of monthly aid at 50 percent of the minimum wage for every child between the age of 18 months and 6 years; 0.7 billion rubles for a one-time payment of triple the minimum wage for the birth of a child; 19.7 billion rubles to implement the new pension legislation; an additional 2.1 billion rubles for medicine and other health needs; 2.6 billion rubles for additional measures to improve health care and to improve the material well-being of people living in areas of fallout from the Chernobyl disaster; 1.6 billion rubles for stipends for all honor students; 2.2 billion rubles to increase income in connection with the repeal and decrease of the income tax; 2.5 billion rubles to raise wages for people working in culture, health, social services, and education; and 1.7 billion rubles to set new tariffs and a wage structure for workers in nonmanufacturing branches where they had not yet been introduced.[31]

Where that money was going to come from in view of the budget crisis did not worry the Soviet Union any more than it did the Russian Federation leadership. The Congress of People's Deputies of the RSFSR decided to use no less than 15 percent of its revenues to support the rural economy and social development in the villages—the apotheosis of the popular but absolutely impossible decisions typical of the times.[32]

In the summer of 1988, the government sent a letter to the Central Committee about the need to complete pricing reform no later than the first half of 1989.[33] By fall it was clear that there was no will to do that. In February 1990, speaking at the Plenum of the Central Committee, Gorbachev said that the absence of transformation in the pricing system was the main missing link holding up economic reform. But his tone revealed his uncertainty about taking that step. He went on: "It is necessary to accelerate the decision on this problem. The Party retains its fundamental position. The pricing reform must be done in a way that will not affect the living standards of the public, especially the poor."[34] In July 1990, calling the consumer goods supply difficult and the consumer market intolerable, he nevertheless categorically refused to start a transition to a market economy by raising prices, calling the idea absurd. He wanted to start economic transformation with painless or popular measures.[35] Here is an excerpt from his speech:

> As a result, the question of prices has become seemingly the most important, as if it were the only measure for starting the transition to the market. We must indicate the priority measures in the transition to the market. No one is keeping us from starting auctions today of state enterprises, creating real freedom of entrepreneurship; turning small enterprises and stores over to be rented, including housing; putting shares and other securities and

some of the methods of production into the sphere of buying and selling. We must accelerate the formation of commodity and stock markets, reform the banking system, bring in a banking rates policy, and create conditions that allow competition among manufacturers, trade associations, and small and medium-sized enterprises, especially in the production of consumer goods.[36]

Nikolai Ryzhkov, chairman of the Council of Ministers of the USSR, responsible for the economy of the country, responded frankly to this: "I must say that no matter what form of pricing is chosen, we cannot form a market without pricing reform. The greatest mistake was yet again, as it was in 1988, showing indecision, postponing this incredibly complex but objectively necessary task 'for later.'"[37] Later, he still considered the rejection of pricing reform the greatest mistake made in the period when he headed the government. From his memoir:

> I am certain: our main error was breaking the chain of reform right there, at its main link. . . . But the most difficult were the problems relating to pricing reform. Here the interests of the manufacturers, and trade, and every family were tightly intertwined. The distortions in that sphere had become unprecedented by 1990! In the past thirty-five years the GDP had increased by 6.5 times, and the state price subsidies had grown by more than 30 times! In 1990 the subsidy for grocery items was close to 100 billion rubles, and with the introduction of new wholesale prices without a review of retail prices, it would have increased by another 30 percent and constituted one-fifth of all expenditures in the state budget.[38]

When a decision on pricing reform was crucial for the country, Vyacheslav Senchagov, chairman of Goskomtsen (the State Committee on Pricing) wrote to Ryzhkov in December 1990: "In connection with the new wholesale and purchasing prices introduced on January 1, 1991, the need for immediate reforms of retail prices is even more acute. The situation is such that state spending on the production and sale of all consumer products, including wine and vodka production and imports, is 20–30 percent higher than the revenue from selling them. This means that the difference between costs and income has to be covered by issuing money. The country's economy cannot tolerate these distortions in pricing much longer."[39]

From a speech by Deputy Chairman of the Council of Ministers Leonid Abalkin at the Fourth Session of the Supreme Soviet in September 1990: "The transition to new wholesale prices and tariffs while keeping retail prices has led to a negative balance of 110 billion rubles for the budget. Besides that, the revenue base of the budget required additional funds in the sum of 37 billion rubles, in accordance with decisions on the standard of living and the socio-cultural sphere. Thus, in addition to the 58 billion ruble deficit in the current year, another 190 billion rubles must be added."[40]

The draft of the government program for forming a regulated market economy, prepared in September 1990, characterized the state of the economy this way: "The crisis in material production is exacerbated by the disorder in the state's finances and currency circulation, the increasing trade and currency imbalance, and the increase in inflationary processes. 'Flight' from money, agitated demand, the total shortage of goods, and the strict rationing of purchases in many regions with high growth in commodity turnover all demonstrate that the present system of distribution relations is close to total collapse."[41]

The acuteness of the situation and the realization by the party leadership that a financial catastrophe was looming is reflected in the words of Central Committee Secretary Nikolai Slyunkov, who was responsible for the economy, at the February Plenum of the Central Committee in 1990: "In four years, revenues have exceeded expenses on goods, services, payments, and deposits by almost 160 billion rubles. . . . As a result, the savings in bank accounts have grown by one-and-a-half times and cash on hand by one-third. This inflow of money has disrupted the consumer market, washing all goods off the shelves, creating a certain social tension, and even sowing doubts about perestroika. Of the 1,200 types of goods, some 1,150 are on the deficit list. The measures taken by the government were inadequate, ineffective, and untimely."[42]

The Currency Crisis

The parallel growth of Russian grain purchases and grain prices on the world market led to a speedy increase in hard currency expenditures. By 1988, grain purchases grew to $4.1 billion (from $2.7 billion in 1987).[43]

The minister of Foreign Economic Relations of the USSR wrote to the chairman of the State Foreign Economic Commission of the Council of Ministers of the USSR, Stepan Sitarian, in April 1990: "Today a number of foreign firms . . . have already stopped shipping goods to the USSR, and ships loaded with grain and forage have been lying idle in ports awaiting solution of the issue."[44]

One would expect this catastrophic situation to rouse the Soviet leaders to consider a general reduction in hard currency spending. Not in the least. Even in these conditions, they could not refrain from financing large-scale foreign policy activity. In December 1989, Valentin Falin, head of the International Department, wrote to the Central Committee:

> The International Fund to Aid Left Workers' Organizations has for many years been supported by voluntary contributions from the CPSU and other Communist parties of socialist countries. However, since the late 1980s the Polish and Rumanian comrades, and in 1987 the Hungarians too, have stopped participating, citing financial difficulties. In 1988 and 1989 the Socialist United Party of Germany, the Communist Party of Czechoslovakia, and the Communist Party of Bulgaria refused to pay the expected dues, without explanation, and the fund was formed wholly on contributions from the CPSU. In 1987 the three named parties together contributed $2.3 million, approximately 13 percent of the total contributions. The CPSU share in 1989 was set . . . at 13.5 million hard currency rubles, which at the official exchange rate equals $22,044,673. In 1989 the fund helped seventy-three Communist, worker, and revolutionary-democratic parties and organizations. The total sum was $21.2 million, of which $20.5 million has been given to the parties. The parties, which for a lengthy period have received regular support from the fund, appreciate this form of international solidarity very highly, feeling that it cannot be replaced by any other form of aid. Most of these parties have already submitted requests for aid in 1990, and some are asking for substantially more. We believe it worthwhile to maintain the CPSU contribution to the International Fund to Aid Left Workers' Organizations for 1990 at approximately the level of this year, $22 million.[45]

In August 1990, under pressure from currency problems, the Soviet government decided to reduce payments from the Union budget in the second half of 1990 for unreimbursed aid to foreign states of more than 600 million rubles.[46] But even this was not enough anymore to manage the situation with hard currency reserves.

As the crisis unfolded, the tone of intergovernmental correspondence became more irritable: "The defaulted debt of the Union foreign economic associations that are part of the ministry's system as of October 1, 1990, to West German companies is 243.9 million rubles, including for rolled and sheet metal, and pipes of ferrous metal—50 million rubles; machinery and equipment—31.4 million; licensing and auxiliary equipment—25.9 million; nonferrous metals and concentrates—10.4 million rubles."[47]

And from another letter:

> Because of the delays by Vneshekonombank in opening letters of credit, the tankers *K. Fedko* and *E. Titov* are lying idle in the ports of Rotterdam (25,000 tons of rapeseed oil) and Surabaya, Indonesia (15,000 tons of palm stearin). . . . Contracts for the full amount have been signed with foreign firms. They are prepared to unload, however they will not confirm this until the payments for previous deliveries are made in the amount of 97.8 million rubles and the letters of credit for the new contracts have been received. . . . Vneshekonombank (Comrade Alibegov, T. I.) is not reacting to our repeated requests to open letters of credit.[48]

Given the situation of Vneshekonombank itself in the currency crisis, Alibegov's failure to respond is not hard to understand. Viktor Gerashchenko, chairman of Gosbank, and Yuri Moskovsky, chairman of Vneshekonombank, wrote to Ryzhkov:

> At the present time, the unpaid debt of Soviet foreign trade organizations for imports implemented according to the government's plan is approximately 3 billion rubles. Given the debt of numerous foreign trade associations, this commercial failure to pay formally does not cast doubt on the country's creditworthiness. Yet this could be the direct consequence of Vneshekonombank's failure to fulfill its obligations on the guarantees given in its name at the request of the government of the USSR. It must also be borne in mind that the total sum of these obligations is at present more than 5 billion rubles.[49]

The realization that Vneshekonombank could not pay outstanding debts did not make the leadership feel any better. It continued to receive more worrisome reports of the effect of the currency crisis on the economy. Various agencies sent urgent telegrams:

> Despite instructions, Vneshekonombank still has not covered the outstanding debt of 33.8 million rubles, including 5.6 million rubles for vegetable oil delivered in April–May of this year, 6.9 million rubles in late fees, 21.3 million rubles for vegetable oils delivered in October–early November of 272,000 tons. In addition, letters of credit in the amount of 71.5 million rubles have still not been opened. . . . In order to avoid ships lying idle and refusals from the firms to complete the contractual obligations, I ask for your directive to Vneshekonombank to obey PP-44341 dated November 13, 1990, and an immediate resumption of payments.[50]

Despairing of ever getting a reply from Vneshekonombank, the directors of the associations of the Ministry of Foreign Economic Relations appealed directly to the government. The chairman of Prodintorg wrote to Ryzhkov:

> The collective of the All-Union Association Prodintorg is forced to address you personally with an urgent request to resolve the question of payment for imported products. The association has repeatedly appealed to the government on this issue. As of August 15 of this year the association owes foreign firms 234 million rubles in hard currency. . . . Despite the decision made on priority payment for imported foodstuffs, Vneshekonombank is not making these payments, even though the deadlines are here. . . . Because of the payment delays, suppliers in the FRG, France, New Zealand, and Norway have announced that they will cease deliveries of animal fats, meat, meat products, and dry milk. Signed contracts for deliveries of meat and meat products from Brazil, vegetable oils from Malaysia and Cyprus, dry milk from Holland, and butter from Sweden have been canceled. Other consignments of food products are under threat of cancellation. . . . The noncompliance with government decision and plans on food imports for 1990 may have unintended consequences domestically. These products were to be sent to Moscow and Leningrad, to the coal mining areas of Kuzbass and Vorkuta, to the gas fields of Tyumen, the republics of the Transcaucasus, and other major industrial centers. Stopping deliveries to these regions will inevitably cause a sharp increase in social and political conflicts.[51]

As the import debt grew, the problems became more acute. Vorontsov wrote to Sitarian again: "In accordance with the request of March 10, 1990, the Ministry of Foreign Economic Relations reports that as of April 5, according to our data, Vneshekonombank has held up payments abroad on behalf of the foreign economic associations in the amount of 656 million rubles in hard currency. . . . Companies from the FRG (Mannesmann and others) participating in the Ruhrgas Concern are threatening to block our income from gas deliveries."[52] Given the circumstances, such letters could not solve the problems.

By the fall of 1990, the Soviet government was speaking openly about the catastrophic international economic situation. Yuri Maslyukov spoke at the Fourth Session of the Supreme Soviet of the USSR on November 26, 1990: "The situation in the foreign economic complex is close to an emergency: on one hand, we must fulfill our obligations on the country's debt (this has grown to a huge amount, 9 billion rubles); on the other hand, the situation

TABLE 6-4. Coal Production in the USSR, 1988–90

Million tons

Year	1988	1989	1990	1991
Coal production	772	740	703	629

Source: For data before 1991 see *Narodnoe khoziaistvo SSSR v 1990 g.* [USSR National Economy in 1990] (Moscow: Finansy i statistika, 1991); for 1991 USSR data see *Ekonomika SSSR v ianvare-sentiabre 1991 g.* [USSR Economy in January–September 1991] (Moscow: Information and Publishing Center, 1991); for 1991 Russian Federation data see *Kratky statistichesky biulleten za 1991 g.* [Concise Statistical Bulletin for 1991] (Moscow, 1992).

has been complicated by a drop in oil production, lumber production, and cotton harvest—these products have been our main source of hard currency for a long time."[53]

From Crisis to Catastrophe

In 1989 industrial production stopped growing. It began falling in 1990. Coal production fell as a result of the miners' strike (see tables 6-4 and 6-5). The fall of coal production, including coke, led to a reduction in metallurgical production. This was one factor in the drop of industrial production as a whole. Yet the demand for consumer products continued to grow. The chairman of Gosbank wrote to the Supreme Soviet in September 1990:

> In a number of regions food products are available only by coupons—rationing for sugar, meat, butter and oil, tea, buckwheat, and pasta. . . . The situation on the domestic market in 1990 has grown worse not only because of the high rate of income growth, but also as a result of changes in the behavior of consumers who, in expectation of higher retail prices and in response to suggestions by some economists that there is a need for money reform or "freezing" assets on deposit, are trying to use up their cash—stockpiling at home and buying excessive amounts (rather than their usual). This increases the pressure on the consumer market. We apparently will not be able to overcome this before year's end. In the nine months of 1990, savings in organized forms and cash on hand has increased by 47.3 billion rubles over the 38.4 billion rubles in the corresponding period of 1989, and on the whole for 1990 by 72.8 billion rubles from 61.9 billion rubles in 1989. . . . After approval by the Supreme Soviet of the plan for balancing the income and spending of the population, a number of measures were passed, whose realization is leading to an inevitable increase in income against the planned calculations: measures to stimulate state purchases of grain, which will lead to higher wages in agricul-

TABLE 6-5. Coal Production in the Russian Federation, 1988–90
Million tons

Year	1988	1989	1990	1991
Coal production	425	410	395	353

Source: For data before 1991 see *Narodnoe khoziaistvo Rossiyskoi Federatsii v 1990 g.* [National Economy of the Russian Federation in 1990] (Moscow: Republican Information and Publishing Center, 1991); for 1991 data see *Kratky statistichesky biulleten za 1991 g.* [Concise Statistical Bulletin for 1991] (Moscow, 1992).

ture; an income tax and a gradual decrease in taxes on bachelors, singles, and small families (from June 1, 1990); increasing stipends (from September 1, 1990), introducing additional benefits in pensions (from October 1, 1990) and social security for families with children (from December 1, 1990). These measures alone will increase income in the second half of 1990 by 9 billion rubles.[54]

That all these measures would have to be financed using the printing press is clear to anyone who makes such decisions.

The first deputy chairman of Goskomstat, Igor Pogosov, wrote to the Council of Ministers in November 1990 that the deficits in the marketplace were becoming more serious and that near-riot demands were taking place. The increase in purchasing was a reaction to the devaluation of the ruble. He focused attention on the fact that the reduction in imports in the second half of 1990 was having an impact. Imports had increased in the first half of 1990 by 11 percent but had fallen by 17 percent in the third quarter, and were down 25 percent by October; Pogosov noted that reserves of foodstuffs had dwindled by 29 percent over ten months, and almost all forms of food had joined the list of deficit items from August to October. The public was having difficulty buying meat and meat products even at the higher prices charged in cooperative stores. Price increases continued in *kolkhoz* markets. In June, as compared to the same period the year before, they were up 27 percent and in October, 38 percent. Only 73 percent of the plan to supply meat to Leningrad was met in nine months, and only 60 percent for Moscow. In mid-1990, of 160 items for domestic consumers, not a single one was freely available.[55]

"Extraordinary Efforts" instead of Reforms

In the spring of 1990, during yet another round of discussions about a program of economic reforms, Gorbachev was unable to decide between the more radical program proposed by Nikolai Petrakov and the more moderate one written under the direction of Leonid Abalkin. He put off his decision. Nevertheless, the situation demanded action. The fact that no more delay was possible was the dominant theme of public discourse in April and May of 1990. The government's proposal to overcome the economic crises, intended to reduce the budget deficit and balance the consumer market, was presented for discussion at the Presidential Council and Federation Council on April 17–18, 1990.[56] In May 1990, the Ryzhkov government presented a five-year program for transition to a regulated market economy. Its first step was to be a tripling of bread prices beginning July 1, 1990. Higher prices for other foods were to begin on January 1, 1991.

VTsIOM informed the chairman of the Council of Ministers that its poll in May 1990 showed that 56 percent supported a move to the market, but 60 percent felt that it would not bring positive results in the short term and might even provoke a political crisis.[57] A later poll in December showed that 56 percent of the population considered the economic situation critical and 37 percent not good. The majority of respondents saw 1990 as a harder year than the previous one. When asked what the Soviet Union could expect in the next few months, 70 percent responded that they thought things would get worse. More than half (54 percent) thought an economic catastrophe possible in 1991, 49 percent thought there would be mass unemployment, 42 percent predicted hunger, and 51 percent disruptions in water and electricity supplies. Seventy percent thought that their material situation had worsened over the previous two or three years. The main issues worrying people were survival, getting food and daily necessities for the family, higher prices, and the devaluation of money. Most of all, the citizens of the USSR were worried by the sharp decline in food supplies and the disappearance of soap, clothing, fabrics, shoes, and other everyday items from the stores.[58] Asked in early 1991 when the Soviet Union would emerge from the crisis, 45.8 percent replied that it would not be before 2000, and 12 percent thought never. The main problems of the Soviet economy according to 60 percent of the respondents were deficits, lines, and poverty. At the end of 1989, 52 percent had fully approved of what Mikhail Gorbachev was doing. His approval rating fell to 21 percent by the end of 1990. In 1988, 55 percent had responded that they thought he was the "man of the year." In 1990, only 12 percent thought so.[59]

The acts of the First Congress of People's Deputies undermined fear of the authorities and started to erode the regime's ideological base. This was a serious blow to the linchpin of the socialist economic system—faith that the regime could mobilize grain for centralized redistribution using state force if necessary, a faith that should have been firmly entrenched after 1928–29. The

1989 decision to pay hard currency to *kolkhozes* and *sovkhozes* for grain yields that exceeded the planned harvest was a sign that the regime had lost its ability to get what it needed by coercion.

In the outline for Gorbachev's speech of October 8, 1990, at the Plenum of the Central Committee, the situation was characterized in this way: "The extremely difficult situation on the consumer market, the serious disruption in economic ties, the destruction of transport communications, the sharp decline in state discipline, the sometimes very strident political clashes over property, sovereignty, separation of competency, and the continuing rise in crime—all this is evidence that for now the crisis is growing more profound."[60]

In an interview at that time, Grigory Yavlinsky, then deputy chairman of the Council of Ministers of Russia, said: "Now we have to learn how to live in conditions of strong inflation. This is also independent work that requires high professionalism, where great responsibility and courage are needed. We must remember: this work does not allow populism or hysteria or political dependence on anyone."[61]

At a meeting of the Politburo of the Central Committee on November 16, 1990, Gorbachev spoke about the food supply: "I tried to get a complete picture of the situation in the country in preparation for this session. But there is no full clarity. I got all the information I could, and I must tell you: extraordinary efforts are needed to create a stable food supply." First Secretary of the Leningrad Oblast Committee of the CPSU Boris Gidaspov spoke at that same session of the Politburo: "The situation is of course very hard. As I drive to work in the morning I see lines of a hundred, a thousand people. And I think—someone's going to smash a store window and the counterrevolution will begin in Leningrad. And we won't be able to save the country."[62]

But even the extraordinary efforts the president of the USSR demanded were not enough. The country's fundamental fiscal problems could not be solved with words alone. Action and political will were required. There was none. The situation on the consumer market continued to deteriorate. Trade Minister Terekh wrote to Ryzhkov in December 1990:

> In eleven months, according to Goskomstat, 21.7 billion rubles' worth of consumer items did not get to the market, including: food, 4.3 billion rubles, . . . products of light industry, 6.1 billion rubles, and other nonfood products, 12 billion rubles. . . . We are particularly worried by the supply of animal food products for residents of Moscow and Leningrad. . . . However, because invoices for the current year have not been paid and because there is a lack

of hard currency for purchases in the first quarter of 1991, the Ministry of Foreign Economic Relations cannot guarantee deliveries of food products in January, which will lead to a disruption in supplies to Moscow, Leningrad, and other centralized consumer markets. . . . In view of the extremely tense situation in trade of nonfood items, the Ministry of Trade appealed to the Council of Ministers for funding to import them in 1991, starting with an advance purchase in the fourth quarter of this year. The Council of Ministers gave the corresponding order to Gosplan.[63]

By mid-1990 prices in co-operatives were twice as high as state retail prices, and *kolkhoz* prices were three times as high.[64]

According to Goskomstat, the composite index of consumer prices, including the black market, was 105.3 percent. The growth of unsatisfied demand was estimated at 55 billion rubles.[65]

The privileged supply to the capital cities, Moscow in particular, was also considered a most important factor in maintaining control over the country's political situation. For all the deintellectualization of the Soviet leadership, they did know that the Bolsheviks' path to power began with food riots in the capital. By early 1991 the situation in the consumer market was catastrophic even in Moscow. Chairman of the Executive Committee of the Moscow Council Yuri Luzhkov wrote to Prime Minister Valentin Pavlov in February 1991:

All of the nonfood items available for sale in Moscow are worth 5.1 billion rubles, or 42 percent of last year. Moscow's share of imported goods in fabric, clothing, and shoes was 55 percent annually; this year imports will be reduced by 75 percent. But even this has not yet been confirmed. . . . In this situation we cannot even organize a quota supply for the populace. In view of the above, the Moscow Executive Committee asks you to consider and reply positively to the request to supply Moscow with nonfood goods and to buy imported goods, particularly everyday items, especially for the capital.[66]

In large cities other than the two capitals, the situation was even more dire. The Presidium of the Nizhny Novgorod City Council of People's Deputies wrote to Gorbachev in December 1990: "Esteemed Mikhail Sergeyevich! The situation with food supplies for the populace in Nizhny Novgorod has reached a nadir. The funds we are allotted are not enough to supply necessary products at the most basic levels for residents such as children, pregnant women, and nursing mothers. In the state stores, besides items sold by quota, there are almost no groceries. Thus the city is heavily indebted to its residents for the coupons they present expecting meat, granulated sugar, animal and vegetable fats, and so on."[67]

The example of the miners, who at least got lip-service redistribution of consumer goods in their favor, affected workers in other vital sectors, particularly oil and gas. A letter from Nikolai Trifonov, head of the labor union in Tyumen, to Ryzhkov and Stepan Shalaev, chairman of the All-Union Central Council of Trade Unions, printed on March 10, 1990, in the newspaper *Tyumenskaya Pravda*, warned: "If the numerous unanswered appeals of the oil and gas collectives to the Central Committee and government are not responded to by April 1, the collectives are prepared to stop the work of the oil and gas enterprises."[68] The result of the ultimatum was a decision to give part of the production to the enterprises to sell domestically and abroad. This reduced the already low amount of hard currency income the state had at its disposal.

From an address of the Supreme Soviet USSR to the Soviet people about raising retail prices: "There is a critical situation in supplying the people with bread and bread products. . . . In 1989, around 40 percent of the country's demand for grain was covered by income from exports. This means that for every kilogram of bread consumed one-third of its cost requires spending hard currency."[69]

The currency crisis also affected industry. The directors of the Kuibyshev Metallurgical Association VILS, the Stupin Metallurgical Combine, the Belokalitvinsky Metallurgical Plant, the Kamensk-Ural Metallurgical Plant, the Krasnoyarsk Metallurgical Plant, and the plant for light alloys of the Ministry of Aviation Industry wrote to Gorbachev in October 1990:

> The inadequate supply of primary aluminum has led to a stoppage in a number of rolling shops at metallurgical plants. In the nine months of 1990 we are short 35,000 tons of primary and 15,000 tons of secondary aluminum. In October 1990 as part of the state order for rolled aluminum, in his telegram LV-10-172 dated September 9, 1990, Comrade Voronin, L. A., requires the aluminum plants of the Ministry of Metallurgy to yield 20,000 tons of primary aluminum for export. This will lead to a stoppage of our rolling facilities and leave workers' families without means of support. Eighty thousand customers, metal-working enterprises in various industries, will not get 150,000 tons of rolled aluminum and will not fulfill their plans for consumer goods in the amount of more than 12 billion rubles. The consequences that will ensue with the stoppage of the plants cannot be compensated for by products that can be bought with the revenue from selling the aluminum. In view

TABLE 6-6. Main Economic Development Indicators of the CIS
and Russia, 1991

Rate of annual decrease, in percent

Indicator	CIS	Russia
National income produced	15.0	13.0
National income used for consumption and savings of which:	16.0	12–13
Accumulation fund	25.0	24–25
Consumption fund	13.0	11–12
Gross national product	17.0	13–14
Volume of industrial production	7.8	3.0
Retail sales	18.3	7.7

Source: *Rossiyskaia ekonomika v 1991 godu. Tendentsii i perspektivy* [The Russian Economy in 1991: Trends and Prospects] (Moscow: Institute for Economic Policy, 1992), p. 31.

of these circumstances, we must appeal to you to give the metallurgical plants of the Ministry of the Aviation Industry primary aluminum for the 1990 state order, work to the workers, and subsistence to workers' families. Our appeal to Chairman of the Council of Ministers Ryzhkov did not yield positive results.[70]

The words "crisis" and then "acute crisis" were commonly used in 1989, but by 1991 another word was prevalent: "catastrophe." From the program of the RSFSR government on stabilizing the economy and moving to market relations: "The republic's economy is moving closer to the line beyond which we can no longer speak of an economic crisis but of a catastrophe. . . . The degree of unmanageability is catastrophic."[71] Another word that often appeared in documents of the period was "extraordinary." The Resolution of the Presidium of the Supreme Soviet of the RSFSR of January 25, 1991, was titled: "On Confirming the Statute on an Extraordinary Commission of the Congress of People's Deputies RSFSR on Food." The analogies with the circumstances of 1918 are obvious. The title of Presidential Decree of January 26, 1991, no. UP-1380, "On measures to fight economic sabotage and other economic crimes," is very telling for people who are familiar with the economic realities of 1917–21. Production continued to fall (see table 6-6), most rapidly in fuel sectors. The reduction of fuel production from 1990 to 1991 was 6 percent, including oil at 10 percent (in Russia, 11 percent), and coal at 10 percent (in Russia, 11 percent).

Oil production was down sharply: in 1988 it was 568 million tons in Russia, and in 1991, 461 million tons were expected. Thus, in just three years, oil production went down almost 20 percent. And the rate increased with each year (in 1991 it was 55 million tons for Russia). The level of oil production in the CIS (Commonwealth of Independent States) and Russia in 1991 corresponds to that in the mid-1970s. The primary reasons for the drop in production were exhaustion of numerous old deposits and delays in introducing new production methods because of a sharp reduction in financial and material and technical resources for the development of the sector.[72]

The development of the oil-extraction industry was characterized by a high degree of exhaustion of highly productive deposits, a deterioration of the structure of the raw materials base, and a reduction of debits of new and active oil wells, a rise in water present in the oil, growing lack of equipment and materials, significant wear and tear, and destruction of the ecology.

The proportion of inefficient oil wells grew. At the start of the twelfth five-year period it was 34 percent, and in the main oil region, Tyumen oblast, 44 percent, but by the start of 1991 it was, respectively, 45 percent and 57 percent. This was due to the reduction in the proportion of high-yield deposits (down from 88 percent at the early stages of exploitation to 25 percent) and the near exhaustion (more than 60 percent) of the high-yield wells.

Domestic consumption of oil and petroleum products in Russia and the CIS in 1991 did not change significantly, because exports were reduced by half. In 1991 the drop in coal production that had begun in 1989 accelerated. In 1991 coal production in Russia was 352 million tons, 11 percent below 1990.[73]

The growing deficit of consumer goods and decline in production occurred against the backdrop of the government's obvious inability to manage the economy. Alexander Vlasov and Ivan Skiba, department heads in the Central Committee, wrote to the Central Committee in March 1991: "Even as the Central Committee and the government get repeated requests from Sverdlovsk, Perm, Chelyabinsk, Kemerovo, Irkutsk, and Chita oblasts and many other regions of the RSFSR, the Caucasus and Central Asian republics for help with food, the warehouses of sea ports because of an absence of train cars are filled with 9,000 tons of rapidly spoiling food, 10,000 tons of grains, coffee, tea, bakery products, and pasta, 179,000 tons of sugar. . . . At the same time, Azerbaijan SSR, Ivanovo, Novgorod, Nizhny Novgorod, and numerous other oblasts of the RSFSR have introduced bread rationing."[74] The fiscal crisis, the collapse of the consumer market, and the government's inability to handle freight flow, even its transport, developed in synergy.

In January 1991, President Gorbachev gave the Union-Republic Hard Currency Committee until February 1, 1991, to find the hard currency necessary to import the food and raw materials needed to produce food products.[75] The correspondence on the questions of oil production and accounts holding convertible currency leave no doubt that this order was impossible to fulfill. The deputy chairman of Gossnab wrote to the government in January 1991:

> Already in January of this year the Ministry of the Oil and Gas Industry has reduced planned production by 3 million tons, and this has brought about serious disruptions of gasoline and heating fuel deliveries. . . . There is a crisis in production of oils this year. Every year we imported additives for the production of motor oil. Because Vneshekonombank did not pay the debt to foreign companies for additives in 1990 and did not give credits for the third quarter of 1991, production of motor oils for APK, naval, railroad, and aviation transport and other important users has stopped. In addition, the question is still not resolved on the imports of oils, including transformer oil for the electrotechnical industry, for refrigerators, for medical uses, and for rolling equipment and paraffins that we do not produce in adequate amounts. To satisfy even minimally the consumer demand and defense needs in gasoline and oils will require: (1) increasing crude oil for refining in the first quarter by 4 million tons, that is, up to 116 million tons, by reducing the amount of oil available for export. If it is impossible to guarantee refined oil in the first and second quarters in the needed amounts, then the government must make a resolution limiting supplies (except for agriculture) of automobile gasoline by 70 percent and diesel fuel by 85 percent of their levels in 1990. . . . (5) [ordering] Vneshekonombank to immediately cover the 1990 debts for additives; [allotting] credits from centralized sources in the amount of 174.3 million hard currency rubles for advance payment on the purchase of additives, reagents, raw materials, and lubricants for the first half of 1991 with subsequent compensation from revenues from oil exports.[76]

In the summer of 1991 the numbers were much lower than the ones that had seemed catastrophic just a year earlier: "The balance accounts for the draft resolution use oil and gas condensate production levels adjusted by the ministries for 1991 of 518.4 million tons as compared to the previously expected 528.8 million tons, and the supply for refining as 448 million tons as opposed to 451.1 million tons, and coal production as 633 instead of 641 million tons, including 161.5 instead of 186.9 million tons of coke."[77]

The critical currency situation complicated operations in other economic sectors. Rem Vyakhirev, acting chairman of the board of Gazprom, wrote to Deputy Chairman Sitarian of the Council of Ministers on June 12, 1990:

> In accordance with the export-import plan for 1990, Gazprom is allotted 186,024 million rubles for material and technical support. At the present time,

there are contracts for foreign firms in the sum of 97,251 million rubles. However, in view of the lack of hard currency, the debt to foreign firms as of the end of May is 72.1 million rubles, of which the enterprises of Gazprom had debt in the amount of 11.8 million rubles. There are still unpaid invoices and unsigned contracts within the limits for pipes, equipment, spare parts, and chemical reagents. In connection with this, as the foreign trade organizations report, deliveries have stopped, halting work and further contracts for equipment and material for the Karachaganaksky and Orenburg gas deposits, the Astrakhan gas complex, and other gas sites.[78]

By spring of 1991, the Soviet leadership saw that the currency crisis was beyond them. Speaking at the Fifth Session of the Supreme Soviet, Chairman of the Cabinet of Ministers Valentin Pavlov said on April 22:

The country remains dependent on imports, particularly in food, light industry, materials for automobile transport and tractor building. The country is in fact dependent on foreign creditors. As a result of trade last year we are debtors of almost every country, even in Eastern Europe—Czechoslovakia, Hungary, and Yugoslavia. Today they also must be paid in hard currency. The life of a loan is not endless, naturally. The time has come to pay up. In 1981 we needed 3,800 million rubles in convertible currency to pay our debt and interest, this year we need to pay 12 billion rubles. Bearing in mind our level of domestic prices, this is the equivalent of a loss of almost 60 billion rubles.[79]

From materials of the Central Committee in spring 1991:

Low rates of development of pharmaceuticals, . . . the orientation for a lengthy period to mass purchase of medications from Comecon countries, [and] the sharp increase in recent years in demand for pharmaceuticals have led to an extremely acute situation in supplying our population.

Of the three thousand medications generally used in medical practice, a third are not manufactured domestically, and the rest require purchases abroad for almost 40 percent of their demand. In view of the extreme obsolescence of our manufacturing capabilities, the quality of domestic pharmaceuticals is low.

Purchases abroad of items we lack costs 1.5–2 billion rubles annually. Because of the current currency difficulties, there is a permanent deficit of almost every medicine, including the simplest items for first aid. The absence of Vneshekonombank bank guarantees for payment for 1991 and the unpaid debt of around 180 billion rubles for last year mean that there are almost no contracts for future imports.

Affecting the interests of the entire country, this problem has grown from a socioeconomic one to a political problem, felt by the state of the society and leaving a negative imprint on the evaluation of the work of the party and the government.[80]

The supply of medicines was just one of many problems that could not be solved without hard currency. The crisis expanded to other sectors of the economy as well. In his April 22, 1991, speech Pavlov also said: "This will have a serious effect on the villages and the social sector: we will not build housing, hospitals, schools, and roads. The level of consumption of material goods, and this must be said openly, will go down by at least 15–20 percent per person."[81]

Food supply was the key issue. However, keeping minimally satisfactory work levels in the agro-industrial complex required resources, including large-scale supplies of mineral fertilizers. Once again, the lack of hard currency was the stumbling block. Nikolai Olshansky, chairman of Agrokhim, wrote to Sitarian: "The State Agrochemical Association (Agrokhim) is obliged by the state plan and requests of the government to supply goods in the sum of 486.4 million rubles. As of October 29 of this year, of the chemical products worth 261.7 million rubles supplied thus far, only 117.2 million has been paid, and the delays in accounting with the foreign firms are six to nine months."[82]

The delivery of agricultural technology was in a similar situation: "The production of tractors and agricultural technology in the current period is held up for the lack of material and technical resources. . . . The decision to provide supplies for the first quarter 1991 at the levels of first quarter 1990 did not meet the requirements of enterprises since more than 156 million hard currency rubles' worth of imported metallurgical, chemical, and other materials were not purchased for lack of hard currency. . . . The situation is deleterious for production, leading to unrest in the labor collectives and the spread of strike talk."[83]

In April 1991 the authors of the action program for the Cabinet of Ministers of the USSR to bring the economy out of crisis described the situation thus:

> The main goal for 1991 is to prevent chaos and the collapse of the economy, to create conditions for stabilization of production processes and the normalization of economic ties. For this it is necessary together with the republics to liquidate administrative and economic barriers artificially created on the path to moving goods in a number of regions and republics; to normalize economic relations among enterprises and regions; to guarantee deliveries of the

most important resources, first of all for the needs of the agro-industrial complex and to strengthen its processing sectors for the production of primary goods to support the export potential. . . . For this, the Cabinet of Ministers of the USSR in cooperation with legislative and executive agencies will implement a strict anti-inflationary fiscal and credit policy while simultaneously liberalizing wholesale, purchasing, and retail prices and providing general incentives for business activity.[84]

On the Brink of Default

The currency crisis was becoming more threatening. Ever since mid-1989, the country had been on the brink of declaring itself insolvent, reported the head of the Socioeconomic Policy Department of the Central Committee in a memorandum to a member of the Politburo. The negative payments balance in 1990, according to documents, was $17.1 billion, and the current payment due on foreign debt for 1991 was $20.7 billion.[85]

Western leaders, or at least their economic advisers, were well aware that the structural problems of the Soviet economy could not be solved through grants or cheap long-term credits; without a serious program of fiscal stabilization and liberalization of the economy, that money would be used to patch holes in the budget and payments balance. Once it was used up, the country would find itself in the same situation.

Vadim Zagladin, an adviser to the Soviet president, wrote to the Central Committee in late July 1990: "In economics, the main theme of almost all our visitors can be formulated this way: the crisis is getting worse, but apparently there is no clear plan for getting out of it yet. And if it does exist, why isn't it being implemented?"[86]

In 1990, the leaders of the G-7 (Group of 7 largest industrialized countries) asked the IMF, the World Bank, the OECD (Organization for Economic Cooperation and Development), and the EBRD (European Bank for Reconstruction and Development) to analyze the state of the Soviet economy and recommend ways in which the country could create the conditions that would allow it to receive effective financial aid. It would not have been productive to explain to the experts from these organizations that the problems of the USSR could not be regulated without dealing with key macroeconomic issues. A long dialogue between the USSR and the West ensued. Its essence on the Soviet side was that we need money urgently or we will face catastrophe, and on the Western side, work out a clear action program that will bring the country out of crisis and then we can talk about financial support.[87]

The tone of the Soviet government was beseeching and anxious. From the diary of A. Chernyaev, an aide to Gorbachev: "In the evening I sat down to write Gorbachev's letter to Kohl. On the phone he did not bring up his request, but this is the SOS: starvation in some regions, the Kuzbass is on strike, calls of 'Down with the president!' The stores in big cities are absolutely empty, literally. M.S. is asking Kohl for urgent help—to force banks to extend credit and also to provide monetary advances, with the military property we left when our troops pulled out of Germany as collateral."[88] The following document provides a good example of how concerned the leadership was about getting Western aid. Sitarian wrote to Gorbachev:

> The FRG delegation was given our proposals for the implementation of primary measures to help the Soviet Union with deliveries of food, medicine, and consumer goods starting in 1991. We would also like to get from Germany and other European Community members: 1.1 billion rubles in food, 0.4 million rubles in medicine, 0.2 billion rubles in medical technology, and 0.5 billion rubles in consumer goods. From our side we would express the wish that part of these goods would be given as free aid, part on beneficial commercial terms with the use of subsidized trade credits to be paid back after 1995 through traditional Soviet exports. . . . At this meeting we agreed on deliveries of food aid and consumer goods in the sum of 415 million marks from the reserves of the federal government of the FRG and the Senate of West Berlin (for Moscow).[89]

The acute deficit paralyzed the work of the entire foreign economic and foreign policy apparatus of the USSR. Minister of Foreign Economic Relations Konstantin Katushev wrote to Prime Minister Pavlov in April 1991:

> The financial situation of the central apparatus of the ministry remains critical. . . . Aeroflot no longer sells tickets to ministry staff for short business trips abroad to solve intergovernmental issues; other organizations have been warned that telephone service, electricity, water, and heat will be turned off and that security services will be stopped. . . . The ministry is unable to pay off the debt of trade representatives of the USSR in the amount of 600,000 hard currency rubles (equivalent to 1,800,000 Soviet rubles) or to transfer funds for upcoming foreign business trips to negotiate intergovernmental agreements.[90]

In negotiations with George H. W. Bush and British prime minister John Major, Gorbachev repeated that the West, which had found $100 billion to solve the crisis in the Persian Gulf in late 1990 and early 1991, must understand how important it was to prevent a catastrophic event in the Soviet Union, and that it was absolutely necessary to find similar funds to help the USSR leaders deal with the country's fiscal problems. The amount $100 billion came up frequently in his conversations with Western leaders.[91]

Western leaders were prepared in principle to help Gorbachev. It was not a question of gratitude for what he had done to limit the Soviet military threat or for the liberation of Eastern Europe. Some of them, particularly Helmut Kohl, owed a lot to him. As documents published later reveal, the Germans were ready to pay much more than they actually did to get Soviet agreement on the unification of Germany.[92] But gratitude is not the most powerful argument when talking about tens of billions of dollars. It was something else. No one needs chaos and interethnic conflict on the territory of a disintegrating superpower filled with nuclear weapons. That Western leaders wanted to preserve the USSR is clear from Bush's speech in Kiev on August 1, 1991. He tried to persuade the Ukrainians not to leave the Union, saying, "Yet freedom is not the same as independence. Americans will not support those who seek independence in order to replace a far-off tyranny with a local depotism. They will not aid those who promote a suicidal nationalism based upon ethnic hatred."[93]

By late 1990, the Soviets openly appealed to the West not only for new credits and guarantees but for philanthropic aid as well. The European Parliament passed a resolution in December 1990 to send food and medicine to the Soviet Union.[94]

The armed forces of the USSR joined the requests for aid from a potential enemy. Deputy Defense Minister Vladimir Arkhipov wrote to Chairman of the Central Commission on Distributing Humanitarian Aid Lev Voronin in January 1991: "I ask you to deliver to the Ministry of Defense 8 million daily rations from the Bundeswehr (dry rations) that are coming from Germany as humanitarian aid addressed to Prodintorg in the ports of Leningrad, Tallinn, and Klaipeda, to be given to servicemen and their families." The ministry wrote to Voronin again three days later: "Please examine the possibility of delivering 7,000 tons of bread in cans to the Ministry of Defense."[95]

Grigory Yavlinsky, in an interview in April 1991:

Mikhail Leontyev: Now Gerashchenko and Orlov, minister of finance, "have realized" that a fiscal catastrophe is looming.

Yavlinsky: Dear comrades, beloved friends! You were informed of this at the beginning of August! And you responded that this was not so. Why are you so upset now? You took the huge budget deficit, about a fourth of a trillion, and spread it out over the republics, you put on all kinds of fig leaves to hide the shame of the real deficit. Did you seriously think that trick would work? . . .

Leontyev: We could end up in a situation when the fiscal system will completely fall apart.

Yavlinsky: We already have, actually.[96]

The collapse of the fiscal system went in tandem with the collapse of the consumer market. The looming catastrophe became ever clearer. Chairman of the Leningrad Soviet Anatoly Sobchak wrote to Pavlov in May 1991: "The supply of basic foodstuffs is continuing to worsen in Leningrad. Numerous appeals to the central government organs of the RSFSR and the USSR and direct contacts with the leadership of the Union republics are not producing the necessary results."[97]

A schoolboy wrote on February 14, 1991:

Last week I stood in a horrible line for meat. Do you know how long I stood in it? I'm afraid to tell you, but it was 5.5 hours. We used to have lines (as you know), but they weren't that long and we didn't stand in line for everything. But now we have lines for everything, starting with meat and shoes and ending with matches and salt. We stand for rice, for sugar, for butter. . . . It's an endless list . . . I never used to cry, I'm strong, but now I cry often. We're beginning to resemble animals. If you could see our crazed and hungry people in those horrible long lines, you would be shocked. Every country is helping us. We have asked for help openly and have taken it readily. We have forgotten one good word—pride. I am ashamed for my country.[98]

Such childhood traumas do not disappear without a trace. I would hate to think that the author of those lines is now dreaming of the restoration of the empire.

Things grew worse in oil production. From a letter to the Cabinet of Ministers:

In order to stabilize the work of the oil and gas industry the tax on export has been reduced to 10 percent for oil and 5 percent for gas, as compared to the established 40 percent, with money allocated to the sector's stabilization funds. . . . As a result, additional investments in oil and gas are estimated at 15 billion rubles (7.7 billion rubles into oil and 7.3 billion rubles into gas), including 2.1 billion rubles from lowering tax on profit and 12.9 billion rubles from lowering revenues from exports. Thus the deficit in the state's fiscal balance will increase by 65.3 billion rubles, including 19.6 billion rubles in the

Union budget. In addition, measures raising wages and solving other social questions for workers in the coal industry will require additional funding of 50 billion rubles in 1991 from the Union budget. . . . According to data for January–March of this year, revenues to the Union budget were 19.9 billion rubles rather than the planned 55 billion rubles. Expenses in the same period were 47 billion rubles rather than the planned 60.9 billion rubles. Expenditures exceeded revenues by 27.1 billion rubles. A serious gap is being formed in the execution of the planned revenues from foreign economic activity. In the first quarter we received 4.4 billion rubles, when the approved budget called for 17 billion rubles. In the first quarter, export prices of fuel have gone down (the price of oil at present is 60 rubles a ton, rather than the 105 called for in the plan), as a result of which the tax revenue on exports is reduced by 0.4 billion rubles. . . . The gap in the revenues from bank and commercial credits of 2.5 billion rubles is explained by Vneshekonombank using these sums to extinguish overdue hard currency debts for 1990 imports because foreign creditors were skeptical about being paid on time by Soviet purchasers.[99]

The government continued to look for a way out, to propose any set of measures that might stabilize the situation. Deputy Minister of the Economy Vladimir A. Durasov wrote to the Cabinet of Ministers on June 20, 1991:

> There is a need for additional measures in this extreme situation. Two variants for getting out of this state have been examined. The first is based on severe noneconomic ways of restricting money income. They include: (1) Reducing budget expenses for social programs. . . . To reduce the deficit of the budget system to the level forecast for this year (including changes in price scales—approximately 100 billion rubles) requires stopping social programs for 30–35 billion rubles. (2) Freezing wages in all spheres at the level of July 1 of this year. This would limit the growth of money income by approximately 100 billion rubles. It is also necessary to reduce expenditures of centralized monies to the maximum on capital construction, with all the consequences for economic growth of the economy. The essence of this version lies in a consistent liberalization of all prices, starting in July, so that by early 1992 there would be fixed and regulated prices on only a limited list of fuel and raw materials, tariffs on mass freight transport, and in retail prices on items that are the basis of the consumer budget.[100]

Political risks kept them from choosing the second path. A contemporary wrote about the miners' strikes in the spring of 1991: "There are picket lines and patrols on the streets: strong workers in white shirts. Perfect order, no crime in the city. The official authorities are not in their offices; they've voluntarily turned over their work to people they previously had turned away at the door. Kirovsk, Snezhnoe, Shakhtersk, Torez, Donetsk. . . . This wasn't a strike, it was a revolution."[101]

Some members of the Union government understood the moral risk in rejecting the necessary but unpopular measures. Vadim Bakatin said in a conversation with Mikhail Nenashev: "If I were to try to characterize the feeling our leaders experienced in the spring of 1990, I can't come up with a better word than cowardice. Gorbachev and Ryzhkov were afraid of the transition to a market economy; they were afraid out of ignorance, out of not understanding that it was inevitable, and that the delay, the shuffling of feet in place, was dangerous because it increased the destabilization of the economy and the juxtaposition of center and republics."[102]

The Soviet leadership once again faced the choice it had faced in 1985–86. But the situation was much worse now—the country had an unmanageable foreign debt, its hard currency reserves were melting away, the consumer market was in catastrophic shape, political stability was undermined, and a series of interethnic conflicts had taken place. Still unwilling to make the decisions needed to save the fiscal situation, the Soviet leaders discussed reform programs. The programs were unrealistic either economically or politically, and they would have no practical effect.

CHAPTER VII

ON THE PATH TO STATE BANKRUPTCY

But a half-hour of life . . .

—William Shakespeare

WHAT CANNOT BE PREVENTED eventually comes to pass. In the second half of 1990, the USSR, having exhausted its hard currency reserves and unable to obtain foreign loans, had to cut back sharply on imports. In 1991 the import volume fell from 82.1 to 44.7 billion convertible rubles. The dynamic of imports for two extremely important commodities in the first half of 1991 is shown in table 7-1. By then, the economic authorities understood the role the currency crisis was playing. Chairman of the Cabinet of Ministers Valentin Pavlov spoke at the Presidium of the Supreme Soviet on February 19, 1991:

> As for import purchases, the question was not solved for a long time because there was no hard currency. The decision on purchasing imported raw materials was made on January 30, 1991, by the Cabinet of Ministers. Therefore there were no advance purchases or deliveries. In connection with this, in January and early February there were clear signs of a slowdown in light industry. This is the decision we made on January 30: buy raw materials for a sum of no more and no less than 2.2 billion rubles in convertible currency. Judge for yourselves the dependence of our light industry on foreign suppliers. As you see, it does not earn the money itself and is in no condition to do so. Besides which, at present we are paying the debt for 1990 (since for now it appears that no one, despite our decision, had any intention of signing contracts or loading freight). As of February 15, our debt was 326 million rubles in hard currency. Shipments have begun, primarily of wool and components for the chemical industry. Basically, we are completing contracts for delivery of raw materials within the limits of this year. We have decided to pay for imported raw materials from the current revenues of more than

TABLE 7-1. Change in Volume of Key USSR Imports, 1990 to 1991
Percent

Commodity group	1st quarter, 1991	2nd quarter, 1991
Ferrous metals	−67.6	−68.3
Grain	−44.4	−10.4

Source: Statistical Yearbook *O rabote narodnogo khoziaistva strany* [On the Operation of the Country's Economy] (various months) (Moscow: Goskomstat, 1991).

400 million rubles. And in view of coming credits, we decided to spend another 250 million rubles. But bearing in mind that we have had disruptions, naturally, a gap remains. Obviously, we have to look at things realistically. The raw materials will reach enterprises sometime in mid-March. Individual deliveries will be made before that, but I am talking about when the situation will normalize.[1]

In fact, things were worse than the government thought in February. In April, Gosplan reported to the government that the hard currency situation was much more complicated than expected when they were forecasting the functioning of the economy in the State Plan for 1991 and the plans for the republics. Their calculation for 1991 projected revenues of 19 billion rubles to form the Union republics currency fund, including 9.9 billion rubles in convertible currency from capitalist countries. They also expected revenues to pay foreign debt of 9.7 billion rubles in accordance with the Presidential ukase of November 2, 1990. In the first quarter of 1991, payment for imports from the Union republics currency fund was only 1.7 billion rubles. The shortage of revenues in the fund was explained by "the extremely unsatisfactory situation with deliveries of Soviet goods abroad."[2]

Gosbank lost control of the money in circulation. The financial and monetary authorities in the republics ignored its directives. Gerashchenko, the bank's chairman, wrote to Gorbachev in April 1991:

Some republics—Lithuania, Latvia, and Estonia—attempted to print their "own" money. . . . Legislation and practical actions in a number of republics are blocking funds from the Union budget. The finance ministry is forced to use the extremely limited revenues and limited loans from Gosbank. Eventually there will be nothing left to pay the army and navy or to support Union administrative structures. Pensions are also threatened, since payments to the USSR Pension Fund are also blocked. This situation will lead to extremely uncontrollable credit and then to the printing of money, a spiral of hyperinflation with destructive consequences not only for the country's economy as a whole but also for each individual republic. Gosbank's attempts to develop relations with the central banks of the republics in order to have a single monetary and credit policy have not been received positively. . . . The authorities in the republics refuse to see the catastrophic consequences of monetary and credit separatism that both Soviet and foreign experts are warning us about. . . . We must bear in mind that the monetary and credit system can be dismantled fairly quickly.[3]

He also informed Chairman of the Supreme Soviet USSR Anatoly Lukyanov that the laws of the RSFSR, Belorussian SSR, Uzbek SSR, and other republics give their republic central banks the right to print their own money.[4] One more excerpt from his letter: "One of the reasons for the current state of the economy is the undermining of the single banking system, based on a common monetary unit—the ruble, the violation by the Union republics of the requirements of the USSR laws 'On the State Bank of the USSR' and 'On banks and banking activity.' If this process is not stopped, it will inevitably lead to higher inflation, the introduction of national currency, the explosion of economic ties on the Union market, and finally, to the collapse of the economy."[5]

From late summer to early spring, the message of the interdepartmental memos grew even more ominous. Deputy Chairman of the Cabinet of Ministers Stepan Sitarian and Minister of Foreign Economic Relations Konstantin Katushev wrote to Prime Minister Pavlov in May 1991:

We lack the necessary payment means for imports because of a lack of centralized export resources, which were reduced by half from 1990. Thus oil exports, which were the main source of payment, have been halved from 124 million tons in 1990 to 61 million tons in 1991. Oil delivery to Eastern European countries has been cut by almost 3 times (from 60 million tons in 1990 to 19 million tons in 1991). . . . Thus on January 1, 1990, the total debt of the USSR to Eastern European countries (including the former GDR, but not Poland, with which the question of regulating debt has not been agreed) was 6.1 billion rubles and at the start of 1991, 14.5 billion rubles. Our total debt to Poland as of January 1, 1990, was 5.2 billion rubles, and on January 1, 1991, the deficit was 1.3 billion rubles. At the end of the current year, the debt to all the countries listed above, if extraordinary measures are not taken, might increase to 18.6 billion rubles (including Poland). . . . In these conditions of ever-increasing debt, the Eastern European countries are insisting on being paid at least part in 1991 (no less than 1.2 billion rubles) and raise the question of an immediate balancing of exports and imports and a corresponding clarification of the lists of agreements. (The total deficit of centralized means for these countries is estimated at 3.5 billion rubles.) . . . Delayed payment for imported goods as well as chronic delays in opening letters of credit by Vneshekonombank have become a serious problem. For example, in this year, the Eastern European countries have not been paid for goods totaling 300 million rubles, and letters of credit in the amount of 600 million rubles have not been opened to pay for goods manufactured to our order and for goods in extreme deficit that were prepared for shipment (medicines and consumer goods, spare parts).[6]

The catastrophic drop in oil extraction along with low oil prices, the exhaustion of hard currency reserves, and the lack of commercial credits made a sharp drop in imports inevitable. Deputy Minister of the Economy Vladimir Durasov wrote to the Cabinet of Ministers in June 1991:

As a result of the fact that oil prices are much lower than predicted, the reduction in hard currency from exporting this product is close to 2.1 billion rubles. . . . In order to guarantee material and technical balance in production this year, production that is competitive on world markets has been taken off the market. The total value of resources removed from export and sent for domestic consumption is more than 2.9 billion rubles. . . . However, with the deficit of hard currency, the predicted level of purchases will not be reached and in the best case will be approximately 73 percent of the goal. And the delivery of imported goods even in that amount depends on no further reductions in exports, for barter operations will be under tight scrutiny and credits received through agreements with Western financial circles will be fully realized.[7]

After moving to accounting in convertible currency with Comecon countries, trade with Bulgaria was cut in half between the first quarter of 1990 and the same period in 1991, with Hungary it was down 1.7 times, with Poland 1.3, with Rumania 1.6, and with Czechoslovakia 1.3 times.[8]

The Soviets were reminded more frequently and more harshly about their debts to foreign partners. Deputy Chairman of Foreign Economic Relations Alexander Kachanov wrote to Sitarian: "The Ministry of Foreign Economic Relations received a letter from Secretary of Commerce Robert Mosbacher regarding the late payments by Soviet organizations on contracts with U.S. firms. The debt as of December 20, 1990, is around $117 million (the ministry's organizations are allotted $17.2 million—the list is attached)."[9] The president of the Association for Japanese-Soviet Trade, Tetsuo Sato, wrote to Chairman of the Scientific Industrial Union Arkady Volsky: "The Association for Japanese-Soviet Trade offers its profound respect and forwards for your information a detailed list of debts of Soviet foreign trade associations to the member firms of our Association."[10]

The Grain Problem

Council of Ministers' resolution no. 451 of May 7, 1990, introduced new purchasing prices for grain cultures. This demanded increasing state budget expenditures by 9 billion rubles annually. Gosplan proposed that the government increase retail prices for bread and rolls 300 percent and for grain 290 percent.[11] But political considerations prevented a decision to increase bread prices in 1990. In 1991 the grain problem was key for the Soviet authorities (as it had been in 1918 and 1928). Pavlov spoke at the Presidium of the Supreme Soviet on January 19, 1991:

> In 1990 we had one of our greatest harvests: 237 million tons in bunker weight and 218 million tons in granary weight. This truly is one of our highest yields. Yet the state received 66.8 million tons of grain last year, which is 18 million tons less than the state order and 28 million tons less than was stored in 1978, when we had the same harvest. That means that the answer to the question, where did the grain go, is clear: it remained with the producers, while the worry about supplying the population belongs to the government. The reason lies in "excesses of the transitional period," that is, in an undisciplined delivery system. Today grain has turned into hard currency; it is used as a lever and in trade. Now the government has decided to get the material and technical resources, including cars, that agriculture is requesting, wherever it can, including from the market funds. Many people are upset that they cannot get cars, that there are not enough of them, or other technology. . . . But even with this lack, we have decided to take these resources, allotted for 1991, and give agriculture everything it asks for (which is basically in three Union republics: Russia, Kazakhstan, and Ukraine), in order to get grain in exchange. We believe that on this basis we will be able to get approximately 3 million tons of grain. But we feel that in all conditions the question of discipline in delivery and fulfilling obligations remains open. Today we give and take, but what do we do in the future? The question will have to be solved in any case. The country cannot live like this, when some cities have bread for two or three days and the "thread" can break at any moment.[12]

Purchases of grain in the RSFSR from the 1990 harvest totaled 33.9 million tons. Only 72 percent of the plan was met. The state did not produce 13.1 million tons of grain it had counted on.[13] Viktor Akulinin, head of the department of agro-industrial sectors of the Council of Ministers, wrote to Prime Minister Pavlov in April 1991:

> The country is in danger of an extreme shortage of bread supplies for the population and concentrated feed for animal husbandry. Every month approximately 8 million tons of food-grade and forage grains are used for this. As of March 1, what is left in state reserves (not counting seeds) is estimated by specialists to be around 13 million tons, half of which is in the Kazakh SSR. This means that reserves of food-grade grain will be exhausted by the end of March (except in Kazakhstan, where it will last until the new harvest). Even today, the flour supply is critical. . . . There is only enough for ten days of flour for Moscow and the oblasts of Ivanovo, Tula, Nizhny Novgorod, Tyumen, Sverdlovsk, Chita, Kamchatsk, and some others. Imported grain is not solving the problem. In the period January–March, only 3.7 million tons were delivered of the 12.4 million tons planned. Numerous orders to increase deliveries of grain from the Kazakh SSR, as well as accelerated imports, have had no impact. . . . In view of the circumstances, we propose implementing these measures urgently. First: Send an authoritative group of responsible workers from the Center to Kazakhstan to settle the delivery issue. . . . Second: Demand that the foreign trade agencies and transport organizations ensure a monthly delivery to the country of no less than 5.5–6 million tons of imported grain. Third: Once more remind the republics of the need for additional purchases of overages from the 1990 harvest (so far approximately 100,000 tons were bought for the period February–March, but 3 million tons was the plan).[14]

The essence of a letter from Vitold Fokin, chairman of the Council of Ministers of Ukraine SSR, to Pavlov in February 1991 was a demand to return 1.2 million tons of wheat from the Union reserves for February and March and send 2.4 million tons of forage grain by the end of the year, and to increase by 1.2 million tons the republic's store of grain for making combined feeds and raw materials for the first half of the year.[15]

The leader of the Russian Communists, First Secretary of the Party RSFSR Ivan Polozkov, was more than worried by the grain situation in the spring of 1991. He wrote to President Gorbachev and Prime Minister Pavlov in March 1991:

In the Russian Federation, as in no other republic, there is extreme difficulty supplying flour, grain, and other bread products and feed for cattle. The heads of the Ministry of Bread Products RSFSR confirm the critical situation in getting milling grain and forage grains. For the first half-year Russia is short almost 18 million tons, or almost half its demand. Getting it now seems unlikely. The situation is catastrophic in twenty-seven regions; in a week mills may be shut down and no bread will be baked, and no feed will be delivered to poultry and cattle farms.[16]

Polozkov, a well-known opponent of Gorbachev's political and economic reforms, was not exaggerating, as interagency correspondence shows. First Deputy Minister of Bread Products Alexander Kudelia wrote to Deputy Prime Minister Fedor Senko in March 1991:

The point is that at the present time the Russian Federation has a critical shortage of grain supplies from government storage for making flour and for animal feed. This happened for the following reasons. One, because of the poor mechanism for purchasing grain for state storage, the high increase in prices for technology, the *kolkhozes* and *sovkhozes* sold the state 33.9 million tons when the state order was for 127 million tons. The rest remained on the farms or was sold directly, through co-operatives, bypassing the state. Second, the decision of the Council of Ministers on importing grain is not being implemented in a timely fashion. Last year, in the first quarter, 7.4 million tons were imported, and this year only 2.2 million tons is expected. As a result, as of April 1, state reserves, excluding seeds, consist of 4.4 million tons with a monthly demand of 5 million tons (last year at this time the reserves were 11.7 million tons). . . . The State Commission on Purchasing is planning to import 2 million tons of grain into the RSFSR (more than 50 percent of what comes into the USSR), and with deliveries from the Kazakh SSR of 0.2 million tons, and from Canada of 0.4 million tons, bought with guarantees from the Council of Ministers RSFSR, the bread enterprises in April will have 5.5 million tons of real supplies of grain. Bear in mind that with the need to create a minimal supply in its cities of Moscow, Leningrad, and other large industrial centers, the unchanging reserve that will guarantee no disruptions in bread production must be no less than 5.7 million tons, while as of May 1 of this year it was 0.5 million tons. These circumstances have led to disruptions in mills in Yaroslavl, Nizhny Novgorod, Ivanovo, and Vladimir oblasts, and in feed factories in the majority of regions.

With the unstable grain supply, central and republic leaders were continually revising the planned volume of bread and arbitrarily changing the delivery destinations. This caused further destabilization. Despite the shortage of wheat for flour, some of it was used for feed under pressure from local authorities. The author of the letter continued:

> In April the situation will be even worse and unless urgent efforts are made to accelerate delivery of grain from Kazakhstan and from abroad (at least 1 million tons in addition to the 2.6 million tons), there will be mass disruptions in bread deliveries and in feed deliveries. According to reports, the amount of imported grain in May will be much less than the April level and will not meet demand. The Ministry of Bread Products RSFSR, beginning in the fourth quarter 1990, has repeatedly reported to the government of the country and the republic about the critical situation. However, no exhaustive measures were taken. Esteemed Fedor Petrovich! We ask that you quickly resolve the questions of sources of payment for the planned purchases of imported grain and its delivery to the RSFSR for the period April–June of no less than 4 million tons monthly, and also from Kazakhstan (in accordance with intergovernmental agreements) of 800,000 tons of soft wheat in April and May.[17]

Wheat and grain supplies in the first half of 1991 are shown in table 7-2.

The shortages began to take a toll on daily life. Minister of Trade Kandrat Terekh wrote to Prime Minister Pavlov in March 1991: "At the present time, due to limited funds, the retail sale of flour in the RSFSR (except Moscow) and Ukraine SSR is almost halted, and in the other republics it is sold by ration cards. Grain is sold everywhere by ration cards (except Moscow) and in Ukraine with coupons, with disruptions."[18] The degree of urgency is made clear in this Central Committee document:

> In four months of this winter, milk production is down by 2.3 million tons from last year. It went down 10 percent in Russian and Belorussian SSR, 11–13 percent in Lithuania, Azerbaijan, and Moldova, 15 percent in Latvia and Estonia, and 21–24 percent in Georgia and Armenia. There is also a significant decrease in production and purchases of all forms of animal products in Komi ASSR, Bashkir, Mordovan, and Tuva Autonomous Republics, and Volgograd, Pskov, Ryazan, and Yaroslavl oblasts. . . . In January less than planned was sent to subsidized regions and large industrial centers, 53,000 tons less meat and 130,000 fewer tons of milk and dairy products. This had a negative effect on supplies of meat and dairy products in large industrial centers, and most of all in Moscow and Leningrad. This situation is explained in great part by the fact that there is less feed stored than last year in many regions, and it is of poorer quality. There are gaps in delivery of feed

TABLE 7-2. Grain Resources in the First Six Months of 1991
Million tons

Item	State Commission balance	Council of Ministers of the Russian Federation
Spending		
Flour production	12.3	12.3
Groats production	2.2	2.2
Industrial processing	2.1	2.1
For production of combined feed and for fodder:		
Under the funds of the Council of Ministers of the Russian Federation	5.3	9.2
For All-Union consumers	1.1	1.1
For exchange	5.5	5.5
For distribution of commercial seeds	0.5	0.5
For export	0.1	0.1
Write-off	0.6	0.6
Carryover as of January 7, 1991	4.5	4.5
Total spending with carryover	34.2	38.1
Resources		
Available as of January 1, 1991	18.9	18.9
Imports received:		
Pursuant to decisions of the Council of Ministers of the Russian Federation (January–March)	2.2	2.2
Pursuant to decisions of the Council of Ministers of the Russian Federation (from Canada in January–June)	—	4.0
From Kazakhstan (January–March)	0.7	0.7
Other inputs	0.5	0.5
Total resources	22.3	26.3
Required imports in April–June	11.9	11.8
Monthly average	4.0	4.0

Source: GARF, F. 5446, Inv. 163, S. 562, p. 60.

to poultry farms and large complexes producing pork and beef. The material and technical support for *kolkhozes* and *sovkhozes* has dropped. . . . Many *kolkhozes* and *sovkhozes* have reduced their numbers of cattle and poultry, which will undermine increases in meat resources for many years. . . . There are great difficulties in supporting the 1991 harvest and in increasing grain production. There are 5 million fewer unplanted hectares of winter wheat than last year, and this is the smallest planting in twenty years. . . . In a number of regions low seed supplies are holding up their preparation for planting. . . . The low speed and quality of technology maintenance is worrying. The country has 440,000 tractors, 254,000 trucks, 332,000 harvesters, and more than 250,000 tractor-sowers that are out of commission. Most of the enterprises of the Ministry of Agricultural Machinery are behind schedule in supplying the countryside with machinery, spare parts, and equipment.[19]

Chairman of the State Committee for Purchasing Mikhail Timoshishin wrote to the government in May 1991: "At present, the supplies of bread products are extremely limited. The remaining flour as of May 21 through the Union is 1.5 million tons, which will satisfy the demand for fifteen days."[20]

On the same day, Secretary of the Central Committee Oleg Shenin, subsequently one of the coup leaders in August, was concerned about something else. On May 21, 1991, he sent Gorbachev a note in which he demanded 81.5 million rubles in convertible currency to buy equipment and materials for the Party's printing presses and 17 million convertible rubles to purchase printing presses and other equipment for the Central Committee and local Party organs, and he wrote about the need to give the Central Committee and other Party organs 2,500 cars. He also asked for reimbursement from the Union budget for additional expenses for Party workers related to higher retail prices and tariffs. Another question worried the secretary of the Central Committee on the eve of economic catastrophe: "The question of free health care at institutions attached to the Cabinet of Ministers for workers and members of select Central Committee USSR and Central Committee RSFSR organs."[21] This is an amazing example of "common sense" and "social equality" from the reality of our socialist past. The economic difficulties that millions of people were experiencing were only now becoming evident to the leaders, who were least affected by them. I am referring to the clients of the closed stores and cafes. Here is an account from the diary of Anatoly Chernyaev, Gorbachev's aide, dated Sunday, March 31, 1991:

> Yesterday the Security Council met [on] the food issue. . . . More concretely, bread. It's 6 million tons below average. In Moscow and other cities there are lines like the ones two years ago for sausage. If we don't get it somewhere, there may be famine by June. Of the republics, only Kazakhstan and Ukraine can (barely) feed themselves. That there is bread in the country turns out to be a myth. We scraped the bottom of the barrel to find hard currency and credits to buy it abroad. But we are no longer creditworthy. No one will give us loans: our hopes are on Roh Tae Woo (M.S. agreed to stop at Lake Chuncheon on the way back from Japan to talk to the president of South Korea about 3 billion in credits). . . . And there is hope for Saudi Arabia.

Kuwait seems to be saying no, even though Faisal promised, expressed all kinds of gratitude to M.S. for support against Iraq. . . . Went to see N.N., she's still sick. She asked me to buy some bread for her. I drove around Moscow with Mikhail Mikhailovich, starting in Maryina Roshcha: the bakeries are padlocked or terrifyingly empty. I don't think Moscow has seen anything like this in all its history—even in the hungriest years.[22]

Prices Skyrocket

At this point, neither the political elite nor the public needed to be persuaded that urgent and decisive measures were needed.[23] At the end of winter 1990–91, the last Soviet government decided to implement what had been impossible even to mention a few years earlier—a large-scale price increase on the most important consumer items. It was formulated in a presidential decree on March 19, 1991. The new prices and tariffs were to be introduced April 2, 1991.[24] The government version of retail pricing reform called for price hikes of 60 percent. In fact, prices rose by an average of 90 percent, for meat and poultry 260 percent, sausages 310 percent, and baked goods 300 percent (see table 7-3).[25]

Despite apprehensions, this measure passed relatively quietly in most regions without creating mass disorder. The public saw that it was inevitable. But after prices went up, the public saw clearly what the experts had understood: harsh measures were not enough to correct the situation; more effective measures were needed. Compensation for the losses created by price increases, growing disproportions in the budget, and the unsolved currency issues led once again to shortages on the consumer market, even in areas

TABLE 7-3. Retail Prices for Selected Food Products
Rubles per kilogram

Food products	April 1990	March 1991	April 1991
Beef, 1st category (with bones)	1.97	3.35	7.90
Dressed chickens (chicks), gutted	3.03	3.52	5.85
Meat patties (per ten)	1.15	1.28	4.03
Meat pelmeni	1.38	1.53	4.40
Cooked sausage, premium grade	2.79	3.26	8.90
Link sausage, premium grade	2.40	2.82	7.34
Semismoked sausage, premium grade	6.23	8.43	19.12

Source: Letter from V. N. Kirichenko (Chairman of Goskomstat) to the Council of Ministers, on price dynamics, May 23, 1991 (GARF, F. 5446, Inv. 163, S. 185, p. 48).

where they had stopped briefly.[26] According to VTsIOM surveys in late April 1991, many people felt that it was not easier to buy goods and food after the prices had gone up. Almost no one believed that the pricing reform would do away with the deficits.[27]

The fact that the price increases had not brought improvements visible to the public created new and even more complex political problems for the regime. Igor Zaramensky, deputy head of the Department of Ties with Social and Political Organizations of the Central Committee, reported on April 15, 1991:

> In connection with price increases, sociopolitical unrest has grown more acute. Work collectives in other sectors and republics are joining the striking miners. A very difficult situation has formed in the Belorussian SSR. While just a month ago most of the labor collectives were reserved about the miners' strikes, in recent days their support has increased everywhere. The example of Belorussia shows that the economic demands the workers are making, under the influence of opposition forces, are turning political, expressing no confidence in the central organs of power and the CPSU.[28]

Compensatory payments to the population after prices went up destroyed any hope of correcting the financial situation. The problems of the Union budget grew worse. The total spent on compensation payments, higher wages in nonmanufacturing sectors, and support of state-financed institutions and organizations—240 billion rubles—corresponds almost exactly to the changes in prices and tariffs. The Union budget got no additional revenues from higher retail prices. The taxes went directly to the republic and local budgets. The budget savings were insignificant after the higher food prices were paid for. Most of the subsidies were financed from republic and local budgets. At the same time, the Union authorities had obligations to pay compensation to military personnel and other citizens and to Union institutions and organizations.[29]

By the middle of summer 1991 and with new, sharply higher prices, the food deficit was almost ubiquitous.

Kolkhoz market prices were almost six times state retail prices.[30] The share of the black market in trade of nonfood products was 30.9 percent, in food products 10.9 percent, and in services 25.7 percent.[31]

The public mood, and particularly the expectation of future problems, was reflected in an article printed in *Izvestiya* in May 1991: "The garden boom is ubiquitous today. People realize that they have to rely on themselves. So after work and on weekends they work their allotments with shovels and rakes.

Of course, this is not a complete solution to the food problem, but rather an aid in the event of disruption in the food supply."[32]

Money and the Fate of the Empire

The currency crisis, the drop in state revenues, and the growth of the budget deficit prompted an expansion of the money supply. The amount of money issued in 1991 reached a scale unprecedented in the last ten years of the USSR (see table 7-4).

The growing political crisis and the disintegration of Union authority made the possibility of attracting politically motivated credits very low. Even countries that had earlier spoken of signing agreements to restructure the debt owed to their firms as state obligations were more cautious by the summer of 1991. Minister of Foreign Economic Relations Katushev wrote to Prime Minister Pavlov on June 26, 1991, on Greek credit:

> In accordance with the assignment of the government (PP-17860 of June 5, 1991), we have been negotiating since June 24 with the Greeks on the terms of credit and goods. The Greek side on the whole is prepared to give us credit to buy various goods and to pay overdue debts; however it is concerned by the lack of any progress in reducing existing debt in the last half year, and this affected its position on credit questions. Thus, while at the end of last year the Greek side took the initiative in offering financial support, in June of this year, it was difficult to set up the schedule for official negotiations, and because of their unreadiness, negotiations were postponed from the beginning to the end of June.[33]

The Soviets even tried to get small political credits—$500 million from South Korea for restoring diplomatic relations, $200 million from Kuwait for

TABLE 7-4. Change in the Money Supply, 1988–91
Billions of rubles

Month	1988	1989	1990	1991
April	4.13	3.63	2.60	4.77
May	−0.93	−1.55	0.22	5.50
June	3.40	3.48	2.62	18.74
July	3.76	2.18	2.93	19.87
August	−2.06	−0.20	5.76	17.13

Source: GARF, F. 5446, Inv. 163, S. 41, p. 27.

the position they took during the Gulf conflict in 1989–90. Without the consent of its depositors, it withdrew $6 billion from accounts of Soviet organizations and citizens in Vneshekonombank.[34] Still, there was a catastrophic lack of hard currency. Vneshekonombank missed payment deadlines, Soviet ships were seized in foreign ports for nonpayment of cargo and port services. One of the main themes in interagency correspondence of the time was what to do with Soviet specialists abroad. There was no money to pay their salaries or to bring them back home.

At this point, the party leadership began to understand that the USSR could no longer give financial support to Communist parties abroad. On June 5, 1991, the second secretary of the Central Committee, Vladimir Ivashko, wrote to Prime Minister Pavlov: "The chairman of the Communist Party of Finland, Yrjo Hakanen, appealed to us because of their extremely difficult material situation. The chief reason for it is that Vneshekonombank is delaying payments of debts to the printing house Print-Jukhtiet, controlled by our friends. . . . If the debt is not paid in the next few days, the firm and the Party will be bankrupt, since the entire material base of our friends, including the personal property of the Party leaders, is mortgaged in banks that are demanding immediate payment and are not accepting any more guarantees."[35]

The last hope for stabilizing the situation was the meeting of the G-7 in the summer of 1991. Gorbachev asked to be invited. Yevgeny Primakov, who went to London in advance of Gorbachev's visit, spoke on British television about the threats inherent in the crash of the Soviet Union and the chaos that would result if the West did not provide economic aid.[36] The Western leaders could not refuse Gorbachev an invitation, but they were not prepared to promise funds.

The format of discussions at G-7 meetings is to elaborate approaches to an issue, rather than make decisions; therefore it is difficult to imagine that even if the Soviet leader had presented a realistic and tough program for emerging from the crisis he would have received financial aid on the scale and in a time frame that would have prevented the bankruptcy of the USSR. But the question did not come up. The Soviet leadership had not decided what to do to stabilize the economic situation even if got money. In those conditions, no substantive talks in London were possible.

By late 1990 and early 1991 the contradiction between the inability to retain the empire without using force and the fruitlessness of hope for financial aid from the West if they tried to save the empire with force became obvious. This is the explanation for the unexpected and sharp political turns made by the Soviet leadership.

Proponents of independence for the Baltic republics won in the elections to the Supreme Soviets of Lithuania on February 25 and of Latvia and Estonia on March 18, 1990. In a series of referendums on independence in February 1990, 90 percent of the population of Lithuania, 77 percent of Latvia, and 90 percent of Estonia voted yes. An unusual feature of the political process in the Baltic republics that distinguished it from that in other territorially integrated empires was the support for independence from a significant number of people originally from the metropolis.[37]

In the spring of 1990, Lithuania, Latvia, and Estonia proclaimed their sovereignty. This was a clearly formulated pretension against their status as dependent states. Their example was followed by Moldova, Ukraine, Belorussia, and Russia. By the end of the summer of 1990 most of the Union refused to obey the Union Constitution. The public clearly saw the constitutional crisis and the danger of circumstances in which the president of the USSR could neither recognize the new status of the republics nor change it.[38]

On April 13, 1990, Gorbachev and Ryzhkov sent an ultimatum to Lithuania. They demanded that the Supreme Soviet of Lithuania repeal some of the laws it had passed. They threatened economic sanctions if it did not. A partial energy blockade of Lithuania began on April 18.[39] The suspension of delivery of oil and oil products and appeals from Western leaders asking the Lithuanian authorities to seek compromise with Moscow forced the republic to start negotiations in the summer of 1990 on a temporary moratorium on decisions involving Lithuanian independence. The dialogue was not productive.

In the summer of 1990, Gorbachev concluded a political agreement with Boris Yeltsin. Its basis was a radical expansion of the rights of the Union republics and the coordination of an anti-crisis economic policy. The program that was proposed in August presupposed a transformation of the country into a soft confederation, without clearly defined mechanisms for making key decisions, as well as anti-inflation measures, primarily reductions in budget expenditures, especially on defense, and in capital investments. The 500-Day Program expected a reduction in fourth-quarter capital investments in 1990 by 20 percent, in military expenditures (purchase of technology) by 50–70 percent, in expenses on foreign economic activity (aid and credits to other countries were to be stopped), and in all unprotected lines in the budget by 10–15 percent.[40] Speaking only of economics, such a structural maneuver could have been attempted in 1985–86. In mid-1990, with the budget and currency problems, these measures were no longer enough. But that was not the only problem. Such a program was categorically unacceptable to the entire Union top leadership, the armed forces, and the KGB.

After long discussions within the leadership, including arguments over military exercises near Moscow, Gorbachev retreated and undertook a new attempt to come to terms with those who still believed in the possibility of solving problems by force. The president's new allies, who controlled the power structures, that is, the *siloviki,* tried to regain political control through force.[41]

Despite their tactical differences, all three Baltic republics wanted independence and to be reintegrated into Europe. A significant portion of the Russian-speaking population supported the independence movement. Gorbachev's attempts to persuade the Lithuanian elite of the need to preserve the USSR, which he began in 1990, were hopeless. The only argument left that could maintain the unity of the empire was harsh and determined use of force, which had allowed the Soviet Union to exist for decades.

This was discussed at the Politburo in spring of 1990. No decision was taken. Nevertheless in late 1990 and early 1991, when the attention of the West was on the war in the Persian Gulf, part of the Soviet political elite decided to demonstrate that a use of force could solve the Baltic issue. Commenting on the use of the armed forces in the Baltics, General Prosecutor Nikolai Trubin said in late January 1991: "As long as there is resistance in the Baltic region, as long as we have two police forces, two prosecutor's offices, we cannot guarantee the constitutional solution of problems."[42] A Soviet newspaper described what happened in Lithuania in January 1991 this way:

> On January 7 paratrooper units were sent into Lithuania. On January 8 they began to act. In the words of a commentator on the television program Vremya, they "took under guard" the House of Print and several other sites in the city. The House of Print was taken under guard with the use of firearms. There are wounded. All communications with Lithuania have ceased. The airport is not working, the trains are not running. . . . On January 7, Marshal Yazov also gave orders to use paratroopers to ensure the draft of young men into the army. Paratroopers were sent to Latvia and Estonia. There are reports of troop movements in other regions (Moldova, Georgia, Armenia, Central Asia). . . . On January 11, chairman of Gosteleradio Leonid Kravchenko gave the order

to turn off the information channels of the large independent news agency Interfax, whose service was used by many Western journalists in Moscow.[43]

Head of the Department of National Policy of the Central Committee Vyacheslav Mikhailov informed the leadership of the Central Committee on January 11, 1991, of events in Lithuania:

According to responsible workers of the Central Committee (Comrades Kazulin and Udovichenko) in Lithuania, on January 11 paratroopers took under control the House of Print and DOSAAF (which had the department of defense of the region) in Vilnius and the building of the officer corps in Kaunas. This operation went without major clashes. . . . At 17 hours local time there was a press conference at the headquarters of the Communist Party of Lithuania, where the head of the ideology department, Comrade Ermolavi-cius, announced that a Committee for the National Salvation of Lithuania has been formed. This committee is taking power. It is situated at a plant that produces radiation measuring devices (director, Comrade O. O. Burdenko). The committee sent an appeal to the people of Lithuania and also sent an ultimatum to the Supreme Soviet of the Lithuanian SSR, demanding an immediate response to the appeal of the president of the USSR.[44]

Anatoly Chernyaev (an aide to Soviet President Gorbachev) later told British ambassador Braithwaite that the decision was made on orders from the commander of land forces of the USSR, Army General Varennikov, without consultation with Gorbachev.[45]

The actions of the power structures of the USSR were met with energetic resistance. The parliaments of Russia, Ukraine, Belorussia, Kazakhstan, and Mossovet and Lensovet condemned the events in Lithuania. The strike committees in the Kuzbass demanded that Gorbachev resign and the Congress of People's Deputies be disbanded. The West, despite the Kuwait crisis, made harsh statements addressed to the Soviet leaders. Gorbachev defined the situation best at a session of the Union parliament: "It smells of kerosene."[46]

Western capitals took a frosty tone with Moscow. The currency and fiscal problems were still not resolved. Western credits were badly needed. The Soviets retreated. The ones who made the decision to use force pointed at one another, looking for someone to blame. In the end, responsibility was laid on the head of the Vilnius garrison. Yuri Shchekochikhin described the comments of the authorities on the Vilnius events:

Not-yet-confirmed minister of internal affairs B. K. Pugo could not explain to the deputies what the all-powerful "Committee of National Salvation" was and how it could bring tanks out onto the streets of Vilnius, and the explanations of defense minister Yazov brought nothing but disbelief. Saying that he did not know all the details (since he "was not on the scene") and had not given any orders for a tank and paratrooper attack, he offered his own version of the tragedy in Vilnius. He said that when the members of the "Committee of National Salvation" who had been beaten near the parliament came to the head of the Vilnius garrison, the sight of them so upset the general that he gave the order to take the television center, which was transmitting "anti-Soviet programs." That is, according to Marshal Yazov, the bloody tragedy at the television center was caused by the emotional outburst of one individual general! . . . And if the tragedy in Vilnius was caused by the actions of one general, they can be considered to be mutinous, for which, as in every civilized country, the military leader can be punished by law.[47]

Chernyaev, at the time one of the closest comrades-in-arms of the president, wrote to Gorbachev about how he saw the events (January 1991):

This time the choice is this: either you speak clearly and say that you will not tolerate the loss of an inch from the Soviet Union and will use all means, including tanks, to keep it from happening. Or you admit that there was a tragic event, uncontrolled from the center, that you condemn those who used force and killed people and hold them accountable. In the first case, it would mean that you are burying everything that you have said and done in the last five years. That you admit that you and the country were not prepared for a revolutionary turn onto a civilized path and that things will have to be done and people will have to be treated in the former way. In the second case, things can still be corrected in the name of continuing the course of perestroika. Even though something irreversible has happened.[48]

The anti-Union government forces in the Russian leadership and the workers' movements grew active. An important event in the spring of 1991, the miners' strikes, was dominated by political demands (the resignation of the Union leadership for a start). The losses from the strikes totaled 3.7 million man-days, and coke production fell by 15 million tons.[49]

Under pressure from the West, Gorbachev decided to distance himself from the violence in Lithuania in January 1991, which in essence was a signal that the independence of the Baltic states was a fait accompli. But this was not a personal choice. The freedom to maneuver was severely hampered by the currency and fiscal catastrophe on the horizon.

By spring of 1991 it was clear to Gorbachev that he could not preserve the Union by force. The political turn between March and July 1991, an agreement with the republic leaders to create a radical transformation of the government structure of the USSR, is evidence of that. During the negotiations in Novo-Ogarevo on July 30, 1991, Gorbachev made a key concession to the republic leaders, in essence ending the history of the USSR as a single state, and agreed to the idea of a single-channel system of taxation, in which the Union authorities would depend completely on the republic authorities for the financing of state expenditures. In essence, this was the decision to dissolve the empire, raising hopes that it could be transformed into a soft confederation.

CHAPTER VIII

THE
FALL

How I survived only you and I will know.
—Konstantin Simonov

ON JUNE 17, 1991, Mikhail Gorbachev signed the draft agreement "On the Union of Sovereign States" and sent it on to the Supreme Soviet of the USSR and the Supreme Soviets of the republics. After major changes, the final version was discussed in Novo-Ogarevo on June 23, 1991. Gorbachev, Russian president Boris Yeltsin, and Kazakh president Nursultan Nazarbayev decided in a meeting on June 29–30 that it would be signed by the heads of the Union republics on August 20.

On the eve of signing the agreement that outlined a peaceful and regulated dissolution of the empire, the vice president of the USSR, the prime minister, the minister of defense, the chairman of the KGB, and the commander of land forces, with the support of the chairman of the Supreme Soviet SSR, decided to do what they thought the president was too weak to do: use force, restore control, and preserve central authority. In three days it became clear that the issue was not Gorbachev but a changed country.

On August 19–21, 1991, what the authorities had feared for decades came to pass: the army shot at the people. It took only three days for the sociopolitical system of the superpower, which had always been prepared to use violence against its own people, to cease to exist.

The failed coup is remembered by many as being operetta-like. Yet its organizers had set themselves hard goals: in a developed, urbanized society, it is difficult to find officers prepared to order tanks to squash their fellow citizens or soldiers to execute those commands. The officers, who had learned in the 1980s that they, not the leaders of the coup, would be held responsible, did whatever they could to avoid taking action. The coup leaders had not come out of the revolution and civil war; they had lived through decades of stability. It was not surprising that they all tried to pass the buck. The GKChP (State Emergency Committee, as they called the group that took power) was not prepared to make decisions relating to bloodshed, hoping the Interior Ministry, KGB, or Defense Ministry would handle it; this is related in the memoirs of the late chairman of the KGB Vladimir Kryuchkov.[1]

The storming of the White House was supposed to start the night of August 20. The order to carry out the plan was given by Kryuchkov at 9:00 a.m. It was supposed to be a joint operation of the army, KGB, and Interior Ministry (MVD) troops under the code name "Grom," or "Thunder." The decision was discussed by the General Staff for most of the afternoon. The generals reported that from a military point of view taking the White House was not a problem. But mass civilian casualties would be inevitable. At first the operation was planned for 1:00 a.m., then postponed until 3:00 a.m., and in the end it did not take place. The main factor in rejecting it was the unwillingness of the coup leaders to take the responsibility for bloodshed. The army waited for the KGB to act, the KGB for the army, and the MVD for the other two. By night it was learned that the Alpha division of the KGB had refused to participate in the storming, the Tula and Dzerzhinsky MVD divisions had not left their positions, and the Teply Stan brigade was missing.[2]

Georgy Shakhnazarov wrote: "If the tanks brought into Moscow had opened fire on the barricades and had support from an air attack, it would have ended almost instantly. The republics would have given up, which is evident from their cautious reaction, hoping to gain time while they saw how things were developing in the capital. And if any bold fellows had called for resistance, they would have been strung up quickly."[3] But it was not that simple. In Petrograd in 1917 there were leaders who gave orders to shoot demonstrators.[4] In August 1917 the commander in chief of the Russian Army, General Kornilov, was also ready to give such an order. It did not save the regime. In such situations, the question is not only whether there are people to give these orders but whether there are troops to obey them and whether there are troops prepared to go over to the other side.

During those three days in August, Gorbachev did not use force to save the regime not only because he personally did not want to, but because doing so would have been impossible. The well-known political observer Maxim Sokolov described the consequences of the failed putsch:

> The last two days in Moscow have been funeral days: the idiotic regime died in an idiotic way. The putsch was stupid because the people had stopped being stupid. . . . A very important precedent was set—for the first time in seventy-three years the citizens forced the state, armed to its teeth, to capitulate. The

public began defining itself not through inertia caused by fear but through the momentum brought by fearlessness. . . . In other countries coups are usually the idea of a dozen villains who are then thrown in jail and life goes on, but our August coup was unprecedented. Almost the entire Union leadership has been charged under various articles of the criminal code: the power structures (army, MVD, and KGB), the executive branch (Cabinet of Ministers), the legislative branch (Lukyanov and the Union supporters), and the Party (the top of the CPSU). And when the entire top echelon of the state consists of either criminals or their accomplices and suffers a resounding defeat by the people, that government cannot remain. The entire leadership of the state falls into political oblivion, and a different state arises out of the political vacuum. It has, and not just one.[5]

The harsh economic situation in the USSR in August 1991 limited the possible variants of development. Even if the coup organizers could have held on to power, it would not have changed the economic picture.

The Political Economy of the Failed Coup

In early August, Gorbachev signed a decree on urgent measures to increase production of goods and services for the populace. It commissioned the Union-Republic Currency Committee, the Ministry of the Economy and Forecasting, the Ministry of Foreign Economic Relations, and the Bank of Foreign Economic Activity to ensure that priority hard currency funding went for imports of grain, medicines, raw materials, and components needed to produce consumer goods.[6] Comparing the stern directives in the decree with the interagency correspondence shows how far its tone was from reality. Chairman of the Board of Gosbank Victor Gerashchenko wrote to Chairman of the Cabinet of Ministers Pavlov in June 1991:

> Decisions made by the government at various times, beginning in 1959, have directed Gosbank to implement budget expenditures by compensating for the price differences between agricultural raw materials and other products by using special accounts to regulate differences in prices . . . through credit resources to be repaid from the budget. Because of systematic delays in repaying this debt, the sum has grown from year to year, with a negative impact on money circulation in the country. Starting in 1991, the Ministry of Finance has moved the reimbursement of the pricing gap to the budgets of the republics. . . . Yet with the transition to the market and the uncontrolled growth of prices, banks are forced to pay ever-increasing differentials for

agricultural and other products. Thus, in the first quarter this year credit resources of 29.2 billion rubles were needed to cover the gap, and in April 5.9 billion rubles. Including the sums paid last year, the debt of the budget to the banks over the period from the beginning of the year to May 1 has grown from 61.6 billion rubles to 96.7 billion rubles. For that reason, and also in connection with the growth of the total state debt, the centralized loan fund of Gosbank is directed completely to covering budget expenditures. If bank resources are automatically used to cover the reimbursement of price differences, then the only means of restoring resources is the expansion of credit and the printing of more money. If decisions are not made on this question the result will be ungovernable credit and cash emissions. We ask that you immediately do away with the above-mentioned manner of reimbursing price differences because it is destabilizing the economy and promoting uncontrolled inflationary processes.[7]

And First Deputy Chairman of the Cabinet of Ministers Vladimir Shcherbakov wrote to the Federation Council on August 16, 1991, three days before the putsch:

The country is rapidly falling into a deep financial crisis with the collapse of money circulation. These factors are determining the deterioration of the economic, social-psychological, and political situation. . . . For the most varied reasons, primarily related to the indecisiveness about taking unpopular measures, fear on the part of a number of leaders of a stronger Union government, a low level of coordinated organizational and economic work among various levels of the executive branch, and so on, the practical chances of implementing an anticrisis program decrease every day. The fundamental measures for stabilizing the country's financial situation should have been realized on July 1. However, the endless conciliations, discussions, and so on have cost us two months. In that period, albeit belatedly, we managed only to decide on stabilization work in the base economic sectors and partially in production of consumer goods. . . . We must realize that in two to four months we will need completely different measures to normalize the situation and the anticrisis program can be tossed into the garbage. A paradoxical situation is forming. On one hand, the budget system is going to throw its deficit into circulation in the amount of approximately 310–320 billion rubles, and on the other hand, enterprise will add another 250 billion rubles. . . . It follows that the budget system is becoming an important factor in generating powerful inflationary processes. . . . In our opinion, with the agreement of the republic, there could be a Presidential Decree to implement an immediate (as of September 1) freeze on all Union and republic programs of a social character unfunded as of August 1 and a continuation of this measure at least into the first half-year of 1992. . . . In the second stage (after December 1, 1991) there will be a transition to mostly free pricing, including a new mechanism for forming wage funds. . . . It must be stressed that these approaches will not solve the problem of fiscal balance as a whole but will simply move its solution beyond 1991. . . . Thus these measures will keep the situation from getting worse, but they will have no cardinal effect on the true causes of the fiscal imbalance.[8]

Currency reserves had been fully depleted by then.[9] Mere weeks separated the country from bankruptcy and nonpayment of foreign debt—and then only if it stopped all payments due for imports. There would be no large Western credits if the GKChP succeeded. The new authorities would have to make decisions about further reduction of food purchases, cutbacks in cattle, reduction of imports of other foods, and stoppages in factories for lack of components. One of the organizers of the GKChP, head of the Soviet military-industrial complex Oleg Baklanov, wrote to Gorbachev in January 1991:

> The economy at the present time is in crisis. . . . In addition, the country is becoming ever more dependent on the import of material-technical resources from capitalist countries. According to Gossnab, in 1991 the country physically lacks raw materials for the normal functioning of agriculture in the amount of approximately 9 billion rubles, which were mostly purchased abroad. . . . The inability to purchase resources is complicating the country's debts to foreign companies for raw materials, food, and industrial goods for 1990. By late 1990, the lack of raw materials slowed the production of many products, including consumer goods, and in the first quarter of this year we expect mass stoppages in factories, plants, and enterprises. In light industry alone, more than 400 factories, one-third of existing ones, may shut down, and approximately 1 million people will be without work. The situation is getting worse, with the possible closing in the near future of production at ZIL, Rostsel'mash, the Chernovtsy footwear plant, the Cheboksary Kontur plant, the Altai tractor factor, the Vostochny mineral combine in Dnepropetrovsk, the Moscow Stankolit plant, and many other enterprises.[10]

The organizers of the putsch knew all this. Otto Latsis quotes materials from a memo prepared by the KGB near the time of the coup:

The program of capital construction for 1991 is totally unbalanced. According to forecasts, the funds to be used in 1991 will be 30–35 percent less than last year, residential housing will be down 20–22 percent, and other objects in the social sphere down by 15 to 70 percent. To keep the aviation enterprises working without disruptions, 1,938,000 tons of aviation kerosene and 53,000 tons of aviation fuel are needed. As of August 1, the delivery has been only a bit more than half, 1,005,000 tons of aviation kerosene and 28,000 tons of aviation fuel. The reduction of herds on *kolkhoz*, *sovkhoz*, and mixed farms, which began in 1988, is increasing. . . . Moscow: Definite difficulties are noted in energy supply. Some power plants have equipment exhaustion of 70 percent. Supplies of heating oil are down to 50–80 percent of what is needed. The city energy system is functioning at the limit of its capacity. The consumer market is in difficult straits. Meat deliveries to the stores in the city are on average no more than 80 percent of last year's levels. Food deliveries are 60–70 percent, and supplies on hand will last only fifteen days. . . . The energy situation is difficult. All the power plants are working at capacity. The supply of coal and fuel oil is only at 50 percent of what is needed. Food distribution is disrupted. Thirty percent of the population was unable to use their coupons for June, July, and August for sugar, animal fats, and meat. Of particular concern is bread. The new norm is 250 grams per day per person. (N. A. Savenkov, head of administration KGB USSR, September 2, 1991)[11]

The man who signed the document headed the administration of the KGB, which included economic security.

The budget deficit in the third quarter of 1991 was quickly approaching 30 percent of GDP.[12] This meant that the situation on the consumer market would remain catastrophic. Without structural changes and a reduction in defense spending, agricultural subsidies, and capital investments, further price hikes would merely reproduce the deficit in consumer goods on a higher level. The unpopular and illegitimate regime would have to answer for all that. Considering what was happening in the Baltics, Georgia, Armenia, and Western Ukraine, its fate was easy to predict.

One of Gorbachev's close aides, Vadim Medvedev, told Valery Boldin, a participant in the conspiracy: "The Pinochet variant with generous foreign aid will not work; on the contrary, domestic disorders and the inevitable shutdown of channels for foreign economic aid will quickly bring the economy to catastrophe. The coup will not only weaken the centrifugal forces of the Union, it will lead to the inexorable collapse of the Union, because the republics will not want to live under that regime."[13]

Chairman of the Cabinet of Ministers Pavlov, who had a better understanding than the other members of the combined effects of the currency and fiscal situation, drank so heavily on the evening of August 18 that he was felled by a stroke. We will never learn what the head of the last Soviet government was thinking. But I do not rule out that he was thinking of the political and economic ramifications of the coup's certain failure.[14]

Political Death Throes

After the events of August 19–21, 1991, the death of the empire was no longer inevitable—it had taken place. The question was only how difficult the economic and political consequences of its collapse would be for the country's population.

Naturally, the Soviet authorities could have referred repeatedly to the March 17 referendum on maintaining the USSR and insisted that the December 1 referendum in Ukraine, which brought out 84 percent of the residents, 90 percent of whom voted for independence for the second-largest Union republic, was in contradiction to Union legislation.[15] None of that had any relation to the real political process. When empires fall, their fate is not determined by plebiscite. A few weeks before the March 17 vote, Maxim Sokolov noted accurately: "From the formally legal point of view, a flawed referendum cannot cause juridical consequences, and from the practical point of view, it does not give Gorbachev a single additional reliable division. . . . Gorbachev's readiness (or unreadiness) to take decisive action depends on less ephemeral factors than the meaningless reply of the citizens of the USSR to a meaningless question. There are more significant factors: anger of the population, reliability of the troops. . . ."[16] People knew that by December 1991, the time of the formal declaration of the collapse of the Union, the Union authorities would have no reliable troops at their command.

The first consequence of the failed coup was a demonstration of the regime's inability to use force to control its territory. By late August 1991 it was a given that not a single tank, not a single platoon, would move on orders from the Union government to protect them or impose public order.[17]

This is not new for collapsing empires. Austria-Hungary and Yugoslavia showed the difficulties encountered by state organs when the legitimacy of the central regime is undermined and the loyalty of the officers and soldiers is divided between the new national formations in the places they are from, the metropolis, and the authorities in the regions where they are based. As a rule, the result is that the military loses the capability to do anything.

Neither the Union nor the republican authorities could control the armed forces in the fall of 1991. Events in Chechnya in November demonstrated that. The attempts of the Russian authorities to bring in troops and maintain martial law failed, in part because the Union authorities were prepared to give the army an excuse to do nothing. When the state loses not only the monopoly on power but even the ability to employ it, it stops being a state in the usual meaning of the word.

After the August coup attempt, there came a string of declarations of independence from the republics. The Union had no power or authority to stop it. This showed the country and the world that the Soviet Union no longer controlled its territory and from the point of view of international law could no longer be considered subject to it. In the Baltics and Ukraine, the Union authorities lost control of customs and state borders. There were no organized borders between the republics.[18] The Soviet Union became a state without borders. On September 5, the Congress of People's Deputies dissolved itself, drawing a line under the seventy-plus years of the USSR's existence. This is how the mass media perceived this decision.[19]

The Treaty on the Economic Community prepared in early October by some of the Union republics was rather vague. Article 16 called for preserving the ruble as the sole monetary unit. It also mentioned the possibility of member states introducing their own national currency. For any state the money question is key. The treaty did not define how to resolve it; the republics intended to deal with it separately later. They established a banking union, working on the principle of a reserve system, but did not specify how it would work. The most important budget issue for any state and multistate formation was unresolved. The document read: "The budget of the Economic Community will be formed from the contributions of its members, determined in fixed sums. The amount and order of forming the fixed contributions will be determined by a special agreement among the members of the Economic Community." It is hard to tell what that means.

The leadership of the second largest republic after the RSFSR, Ukraine, had maintained a watchful position during the putsch. The chairman of the Supreme Soviet of the Ukrainian SSR refused to condemn the actions of the GKChP right up until August 21, when it was obvious that the coup had failed. That outcome made supporting the idea of independence for Ukraine a choice without an alternative for him and all the leaders of the Communist Party of Ukraine. Otherwise, he and the Party had no hope of political survival. On August 24, the Supreme Soviet of Ukraine passed the decision on independence almost unanimously.[20]

Chairman of the Supreme Soviet of Ukraine Leonid Kravchuk said on November 8, 1991: "The economic treaty can be seen only as general principles, nothing more. We will be against creating any central organs. We will not ratify the treaty if there are central organs of any kind behind it. There must not be any center anymore except for coordinating organs that will be created by the states participating in the treaty process."[21]

Political Disintegration: Economic Consequences

By the first half of 1991, before the August putsch, Russia got from the other republics only 22 percent of the planned deliveries of sugar, 30 percent of tea, 19 percent of cereals, and 22 percent of soap. All the republics, except Russia, introduced customs checks on their borders in order to limit the export of goods to neighbors, especially Russia. The customs restrictions worked only one way: bringing things into Russia was not allowed, bringing things in *from* Russia was. In early 1991, Ukraine and Estonia placed orders (in Canada and Sweden) to print their own money. As a preparatory measure, Ukraine planned to introduce coupons as temporary currency in November 1991.[22]

The former deputy chairman of the USSR government Leonid Abalkin wrote: "In early October, while in the United States, I met with Mr. Greenspan, head of the Federal Reserve system of the USA, one of the most experienced financial experts. We have known each other a long time and understand each other well, practically speaking the same language. He asked me: 'Do you understand that there are only a few weeks left to prevent a financial crash?' I told him our estimates were two months. Actually, the difference was only in the way of expressing the thought: a few weeks or two months is practically the same thing."[23] From Georgy Shakhnazarov's notes on a meeting of the state council on October 16, 1991: "At the meeting of the State Council, Grigory Yavlinsky spoke of the Economic Union. He gave figures: production fell 15 percent in 1991, in 1992 it is expected to fall 23–25 percent. . . . Stopping production and prices doubling or tripling will create a dead end."[24]

The very modest capabilities of the Union to collect taxes fell to zero in the fall of 1991. The government got a small amount of money from some of the republics. But now they were closer to gifts than to taxes. And the amounts were incompatible with the needs of the Union budget. Financing of state expenditures came almost completely from Gosbank credits.

In monetary policy, the Union lost its monopoly, could not stop the republics' central banks from creating currency, and became one of many competitors offering a supply of money. A letter from Gerashchenko to

Gorbachev dated August 9, 1991, reads: "In the conditions of using common currency, it is impossible to stop the destructive actions of those republics that are using their right to establish autonomous monetary and credit policies. The function of issuing money given to the Union in the treaty means only the technical function of releasing bank notes and coins into circulation. Real monetary emission that determines inflation processes will be carried out by the republics themselves through their central banks' credit operations."[25] The author of these lines saw the situation in fall 1991 this way:

By the time the Fifth Congress gave the president additional powers and opened the way to deeper economic reforms, there had already been six years of vacillation, indecisiveness, and compromises to create true socioeconomic chaos. . . . Everyone understood that the time had come to pay for the years of fiscal irresponsibility, for Vneshekonombank's insolvency, the nonworking ruble, the empty shelves, all those social demagogic promises that were given freely in recent years. . . . The autumn of 1991 saw a sharp fall in production and a halting of heavy metallurgy, which threatened to halt all machine building and construction. The fall of 1991 was a time of deep despair and pessimism, with the expectation of hunger and cold. In those difficult circumstances anyone who continued to waste time talking and waiting for a painless transition to the market, the stabilization of the economy, the creation of a competitive market environment, and the formation of effective private property rights would have waited until there was total paralysis in production, the death of Russian democracy, and of the state itself.[26]

The historical materials I had an opportunity to study show that this evaluation of the situation in Russia was correct. Let me quote a few documents:

Accounting practices define quantities of goods by their presence at the start of the workday. Since most goods are sold out immediately, we might as well accept that the ruble has no trade guarantees. . . . The trade and monetary imbalance in the economy is compounded by the huge unsatisfied demand of the population, which has been accruing for years and according to Goskomstat's estimates has reached 233 billion rubles. . . . The total budget deficit in the ruble zone is 300 billion rubles. A deficit of this size is catastrophic for finances and money circulation. At the same time it leaves no chance for a real correction of the situation before the end of the year. . . . The credits given by Gosbank to the Union and republic budgets for the period from 1986 to 1991 have grown from 141 billion rubles to 581 billion rubles, and if we include amounts borrowed in 1991, the sum is 644 billion rubles. . . . At the present time, people's savings accounts are distributed among the republics and are banking resources. Yet the entire sum of the population's savings, which with indexation is more than 600 billion rubles, is roughly equal to the domestic state debt.[27]

On the budget:

The execution of the Union budget has worsened the general economic picture and led especially to a reduction in income from foreign economic trade, which produces a substantial portion of the revenues of the Union budget. In just nine months of this year, because of the smaller production volume and price changes on the world market, taxes on exports are behind 15.1 billion rubles and income from imports, 9.2 billion rubles. Another 14.8 billion rubles were not collected from credit and other operations. In just nine months of this year the Union budget received 80.2 billion rubles in income, or 96.9 billion rubles less than expected in the revised budget for that period. The total deficit of financial resources for the Union budget and All-Union stabilization fund for 1991 is estimated at 204.6 billion rubles, of which 90.4 billion rubles falls to the fourth quarter.[28]

The state budget deficit for 1991, including the stabilization fund, was 156 billion rubles. The deficit of the consolidated budget of the states that were part of the USSR in 1991 was 197 billion rubles, including the deficit of the stabilization fund and 296 billion rubles to subsidize prices for agricultural products made using credit from the central bank.[29]

The budget crisis created more disruption in the circulation of money. The directors of Gosbank were horrified. From a letter of Gerashchenko to the State Council USSR in October 1991:

The income of the population is growing unchecked; in the nine months of 1991 it grew in comparison with the same period in 1990 by 63 percent. . . . In the third quarter of 1991 it almost doubled. In October the process is continuing. In the first half of October 1991, compared to the same period last year, income has grown by 2.2 times. . . . The consumer market is characterized by deficits in almost every possible good and item, the unsatisfied demand for goods and services is growing, speculation is increasing.[30]

Developments in monetary relations, the nominal income of the population, and the consumer market are illustrated in tables 8-1 and 8-2. The public was well aware of the critical situation. VTsIOM reported to the government:

TABLE 8-1. Relationship of Cash Savings to the Availability of Stocks
of Goods in the Retail System and Industry, by Population, 1970–91

Item	1970	1980	1985	1990	As of September 1, 1991
Funds held by population, deposits, cash, and securities (billions of rubles)	73	228	320	568	854
Funds held by population (percent of GDP)	19.3	36.8	41.2	55.4	69.5
Stocks of goods per one ruble of funds held by population (rubles)	0.62	0.29	0.30	0.13	0.14

Source: RF State Archive, F. 5446, Inv. 163, S. 41, P. 28. Calculations in GDP shares based on data for
1970–89: S. G. Sinelnikov, *Budzhetnyi krizis v Rossii* (Moscow: Eurasia, 1995); for 1990–91: GDP reconstruction
based on the data of the CIS Statistics Committee.

Consumer behavior in every stratum of the population, without exception,
is characterized by agitated demand, flight from money, the stockpiling of
goods (food, clothing, and so on). Judging from a survey conducted in August
of this year, almost one-third of the population, on average, want to buy up
deficit goods, whether they need them or not. Half the respondents expressed
a willingness to overpay for individual items. Distrust of money and the desire
to get rid of it is manifest not only in stockpiling (which is primarily determined by the shortages) but also in the formation of a savings strategy that is
typical in crisis economies. The most popular use of savings is buying jewelry

TABLE 8-2. Growth of Population Income, 1985–91

Year	Growth of population income (billions of rubles)	Growth of population income over the level of income in the previous year (percent)
1985	14.0	
1986	15.1	3.5
1987	17.3	3.8
1988	41.5	8.4
1989	64.5	11.6
1990	94.0	14.4
1991 (estimate)	570–90	517.0

Source: RF State Archive, F. 5446, Inv. 163, S. 41, P. 29. Calculations based on data from Statistical Yearbook *Narodnoe khoziaistvo* SSSR (Moscow: Finansy i statistika, various years).

(38 percent of respondents said that this is a good time for it); slightly less popular is purchasing hard currency (33 percent feel that this is good time to buy it). Lack of confidence in the government is seen in the low ratings of state forms of savings (savings banks, securities, and bonds).[31]

Stabilization was impossible without a radical budget reduction and normalization of state finances. However the crisis just continued to get worse. Chairman of the Control Chamber USSR Alexander Orlov wrote to Chairman of the Interstate Economic Committee Ivan Silayev in November 1991:

The budget deficit and the state debt for the nine months of 1991 has surpassed several times over the indexes ratified by the Supreme Soviet for the end of 1991. The limit for the deficit of the Union budget for 1991 was set at 26.5 billion rubles. In fact the deficit according to the Ministry of Finance on October 1, 1991, was 84.5 billion rubles, 3.2 times more than what was legally determined. The limit for state domestic debt for January 1, 1992, was ratified at 567.6 billion rubles. In fact the domestic debt has grown from 566.1 billion rubles as of January 1, 1991, to 890 billion rubles . . . as of October 1, 1991. The state debt will be higher than 1 trillion rubles by the end of the year. . . . The budget passed by the (last) Supreme Soviet, considered unrealistic by the executive branch, particularly in the revenue calculations, has become the main precondition of the fiscal-budgetary and credit crisis. . . . The main economic cause of the crisis of the Union budget is the manifold reduction of its revenue base from previous years and from the plan ratified for 1991. The Union budget does not get income tax revenue or tax from co-operative trade. Cutting off the Union budget from its direct ties to the income of the population and the new market structure and trade taxes was a grave strategic miscalculation and a blow to its stability and nondeficit standing. . . . Ukraine has not paid its share of common state programs. In the Baltic states, all revenues earned on their territories went into the republic budgets. . . . Sales tax turned out to be an unreliable source of revenue. In nine months only 6.5 billion rubles was paid into the budget, while the plan called for 26.8 billion rubles. . . . According to the Ministry of Finance, at best we can expect 34.8 billion rubles in income from foreign economic activity (20.6 billion rubles in nine months) instead of 86.3 billion rubles—that is, only 40 percent of the plan. . . . These great losses are due to the breakdown of contracts for our exports. Thus the annual quotas for coal, metallurgical coke, pig iron, rolled steel, ammonia, cement, lumber, cellulose, and trucks are only at 13–35 percent, for oil, iron ore, copper, salable wood, cardboard, tractors, and cars at 37–66 percent. Compared to the same period last year in the period January–September, coal exports fell by 18 million tons, crude oil by 48 million tons, natural gas by a billion cubic meters, cotton by 144,000 tons, and so on. The reduction in exports with the increase in payments on foreign debt forced the sharp decrease in imports from capitalist countries (by 36.6 percent). . . . Political factors affected the withholding of payments by foreign debtors (Iraq, Algeria, Libya, and Syria), keeping 9.1 billion rubles from the budget.[32]

Valentin Gerashchenko and Yuri Moskovsky reported to Ivan Silayev on a telegram from Riyadh Bank stating that the conditions in the USSR would force it to postpone delivering the second and third tranches of credit (a total of $500 million) for an indefinite period.[33] The scale of the concern in the international community over the USSR's economic situation is illustrated in a letter from Deputy Chairman of the Board of Vneshekonombank Yuri Poletaev to head of the Committee on Effective Management of the Economy Silayev:

> In connection with the decision of the president of the United States in late August of this year to accelerate guarantees to the USSR within the framework of the program of the U.S. Department of Agriculture, we report that Vneshekonombank through its representatives in New York has had negotiations with a number of American banks. However, none of these banks intends at present to participate in giving the USSR credits. The position of the American banks is explained by an unwillingness to take on any Soviet risk in view of the instability and lack of clarity of the economic and political situation in the USSR, since the conditions of the program guarantee only 98 percent of the principal and part of the interest payments. One possibility, proposed by the American banks and exporter firms, is to change the guarantee to 100 percent of the principal.[34]

The risk of losing even 2 percent in the event of unpredictable events in the USSR seemed excessive to American bankers then.

The last Soviet authorities understood how critical the situation was in the fall of 1991. Silayev wrote "On the Extraordinary Budget for the Fourth Quarter 1991" to Gorbachev in November:

> In order to characterize the extreme fiscal and monetary state I will cite just a few numbers. If you count the deficit in the stabilization fund as being 51.3 billion rubles, the total deficit is 204.6 billion rubles. The deficits of the republic budgets are also greater than planned. What are the fundamental causes of the growth of the deficit? The main one is that in the current year the revenue base of the Union budget has been severely reduced.

In nine months, compared to expectations, we are short 97 billion rubles, and for the year 147 billion rubles—that is, the budget received less than 47 percent of what had been planned. All of us—the executive and the legislative branches—have contributed to this. I mean the decisions to repeal the sales tax for all practical purposes, to lower the income tax from 45 to 35 percent, and to provide significant tax breaks. These decisions were made both at the center and in the republics. Ukraine's payment is short 8.8 billion rubles. That republic stopped transferring payments to the Union budget in July. Georgia and the Baltic republics are not paying what they owe. The Union budget also had to handle the expenses for a unified fund for social security. When the reform of retail prices was being prepared, it was supposed to be created from contributions by the republics. However, all the republics that were supposed to make payments have refused. And finally, with higher prices, defense expenses went up by 12 billion rubles. Thus the total deficit of the Union budget and the stabilization fund for only nine months is 114.2 billion rubles. In ten months, banknotes in the amount of 82.6 billion rubles have been issued, including 53.3 billion rubles for the RSFSR, 6.1 for Ukraine, 4.4 for Uzbekistan, and 5.6 billion rubles for Kazakhstan. Over the year the amount of cash in circulation will grow by 110–140 billion rubles.[35]

Orlov wrote to Silayev in late October:

The main sources for covering the huge deficit of the Union budget and the nonbudget funds are the loans received by Gosbank in the form of credits requested by the president and the Ministry of Finance (68 billion rubles) and the printing of money (40 billion rubles), which also has a credit character. Because none of these loans (except for 5 billion rubles) have been ratified by the Supreme Soviet, the president is put in a difficult situation. . . . According to our calculations the budget deficit can be reduced in the fourth quarter by 15–16 percent without a massive shutdown of defense plants or panic in the army. Accept the financing based on quarters I–III; take off the books wages for the servicemen (750,000 men) who are not serving; cancel planned training; reduce the central apparat of the Ministry of Defense, the types of troops, the military okrugs, the production of obsolete forms and types of military technology, and recruitment personnel; retire one-third of the generals and senior officers; dissolve military units that service dacha settlements and hunting farms, some of the marine and coast guard units, and some subunits of civilian defense. . . . In order to find additional sources of revenues for the Union budget it is necessary . . . to accelerate the transition to price liberalization.[36]

The rate of printing money was unprecedented (except during the hyperinflation of 1921–22): "In nine months 70.3 billion rubles were issued, which is greater than the amount in the previous five years combined (65.5 billion rubles)."[37] And from V. Kulikov of Gosbank:

> The growth of savings in organized forms (savings accounts, securities) in eight months is 58 billion rubles, an increase of 31.8 billion rubles over the period January–August of last year, or 2.2 times. The savings are in part forced, since citizens cannot spend their earnings on goods and services that don't exist on the domestic market. If urgent measures are not taken to increase production of consumer goods and the volume of paid services, and also to limit unjustified methods to pay labor at enterprises, the overhang of rubles in 1991 could increase by 250–280 billion rubles, including cash of 100–110 billion rubles. The amount of money in circulation could grow from 136 billion rubles as of January 1, 1991, to 240–250 billion rubles at the end of 1991. . . . Gosbank sees no possibility for further direct crediting of the deficit in the state budget through short-term credits—that is, by putting more cash into circulation. Even now, close to 60 percent of these resources are used to cover accounting of a budgetary nature, and continuing this practice will produce extremely negative consequences for the economy.[38]

On the state of the Union budget for 1991 in the view of the Ministry of Finance, see table 8-3.

Silayev wrote to Gorbachev: "At present, there is an extremely difficult situation in a number of sectors caused by the large indebtedness for completed work and services. It is necessary to solve the question of additional

TABLE 8-3. Expected Execution of the Union Budget in 1991
Billions of rubles

Item	Approved plan for 1991	Expected execution in 1991
Total revenues	250.1	112.1
Total expenditures	276.8	256.7
Deficit	26.7	144.6

Source: V. A. Raevsky (Deputy Minister of Finance) to the Committee for the Executive Planning of the USSR Economy, on the expected execution of the Union budget for 1991, September 12, 1991 (RF State Archive, F. 5446, Inv. 163, S. 41, P. 2, 3).

credits from Gosbank to the Union budget for October in the amount of 20 billion rubles, as well as to extend until December 31, 1991, the credit of 5 billion rubles given in accordance with the resolution of the Supreme Soviet of May 27, 1991."[39] Deputy Finance Minister Vladimir Raevsky wrote to the Committee on Effective Management of the Economy: "The total need for credits from Gosbank in October of this year for budget financing is 30 billion rubles."[40]

In the early days of December, Gosbank informed the Union authorities that it had stopped payments on expenditures financed through the Union budget throughout the country. This included salaries, stipends, certain pensions and subsidies, money to servicemen, and All-Union programs.[41]

Administrative controls over pricing allowed some control over inflation; prices rose, but much more slowly than the money supply. But the financial base for hyperinflation was already in place. The chairman of Gosbank wrote to the members of the Economic Community: "The issuing of banknotes over eleven months totaled 102.4 billion rubles . . . is over four times more than during the same period last year. . . . As a result, cash in the hands of the population and in organized forms of savings for January–November 1991 grew by 225 billion rubles, which is 167 billion rubles more than in the eleven months of 1990. The growth in ruble overhang for the period January–November 1991 was 98.6 billion rubles (as compared with 24.1 billion rubles for the same period in 1990)."[42]

By the end of 1991 one of the greatest problems was the inability of Goznak to print enough money to satisfy the needs of Gosbank. Gerashchenko wrote to Gorbachev in November 1991:

> The physical volume of retail trade in the period January–September 1991 was smaller than last year's volume by 12 percent, and retail prices for goods went up by 170 percent. The consumer market is characterized by deficits in almost every category, unsatisfied demand for goods and services is growing, and speculation is increasing. As a result, cash in the hands of the population and in organized forms of savings for the period January–October 1991 increased by 159.3 billion rubles. . . . The growth in the ruble overhang for January–October 1991 was 81.5 billion rubles (as compared with 20.3 billion rubles for the same period in 1990). Thus the gap between income and spending is increasing every month. . . . Goznak cannot satisfy Gosbank's augmented commissions for printing bank notes, since the paper supplies and printing presses of Goznak are overextended, work for 1991 has been

going on in three shifts. . . . The growth of the ruble overhang is expected to reach 250–280 billion rubles, which is 3.2–3.3 times greater than in 1990. The amount of cash in circulation by 1991 may reach 270 billion rubles; the increase over the year will be 110–140 billion rubles. . . . The total amount of money in circulation for nine months of this year will increase from 989 billion rubles to 1,661.2 billion rubles, that is, by 672.2 billion rubles, or 70.2 percent. . . . More than half of the money in circulation is used to cover the domestic state debt and budget expenses. The domestic state debt to banks as of October 1 was 843.7 billion rubles, and it has increased from January 1 by 325.1 billion rubles, or 62.7 percent. . . . One of the fundamental reasons for the worsening of the state of money circulation in 1991 is the growing deficit in republic and central budgets, which will total approximately 300 billion rubles in 1991. The efforts of Gosbank to regulate the massive amount of money in circulation are not yielding the desired results, since the banking system is now broken up and national banks in some republics are not obeying orders from Gosbank and are carrying out their own policies that run counter to the interests of a stable common monetary unit.[43]

Chernyaev recorded in his diary: "Gosbank has stopped all payments: to the army, officials, us sinners. We are without salaries now."[44] In a survey conducted by VTsIOM in November 1991, when asked the question, "Are we going through the most difficult times now, or are they over/ahead?" 69 percent replied that they were still ahead, 21 percent that they were going through them now. VTsIOM in the fall of 1991 had warned the authorities about the scale of a possible protest, the risks of losing control over the situation, and that the "latent panic" reigning in the public could turn into a real social explosion.[45]

The Ministry of Foreign Economic Relations informed Silayev on August 29, 1991, that Vneshekonombank had stopped providing guarantees on USSR credits for imported grain and that this could lead to a halt in its unloading and delivery to enterprises.[46]

In a conversation with the British ambassador in late August 1991, Gorbachev described the situation this way: payments on debt for the next four months of 1991 would total $17 billion. Exports for that period were estimated at $7.5 billion, and another $2 billion could be mobilized by coordinating credit lines. The gap between needs and abilities was $7.5 billion. He asked the West for $2 billion in new credits, which had to arrive within a few weeks, and for a restructuring of Soviet debt, and reminded the ambassador that the Soviet Union needed immediate aid in of the form of food and medicine. In the course of the conversation he once again repeated that the West had spent $100 billion on the Gulf War. Ambassador Braithwaite promised to report on this conversation to his government, but as he wrote, without great hope of success.[47]

The declared gold reserves of Gosbank in mid-1937 were 374.6 tons. No additions were made after that, and the reserves were turned over to the People's Commissariat of Finance. The size of the reserve had been kept secret since the late 1930s. Gerashchenko wrote to Gorbachev on November 15, 1991: "It was reported in October of this year that the official gold reserves of the country are only 240 tons. The declared level of official gold reserves, which is one of the most important indicators of a country's solvency, is not commensurate with the status of a superpower and leading gold producer, according to experts. Reports of the size of the USSR gold reserves created confusion among specialists on the gold market, who had previously estimated them to be 1,000–1,300 tons."[48]

Amid the growing currency difficulties of the Soviet Union, Soviet banks working abroad felt the crisis. Andrei Butin, acting financial director of Mosnarbank, wrote to the government of the Russian Federation: "Mosnarbank began having difficulty attracting money from the interbank market in mid-1990. The bank was forced to create large insurance reserves against the debts of former socialist countries (Bulgaria, Hungary, and Yugoslavia). In that same period it was taken under special control by the Bank of England. . . . In 1991 the bank's situation deteriorated rapidly. The outflow of deposits first reached 40 percent and then 75 percent. Selling shares could not solve the problem in sufficient amounts or time."[49] By late 1991, the bankruptcy of the Soviet foreign banking system was an almost irreversible threat. Representatives of USSR commercial banks abroad wrote to Boris Yeltsin in December 1991:

> The network of commercial banks abroad includes banks in Austria—Donau-bank; England—Moscow National Bank (Mosnarbank, founded in 1915); Germany—Ost-West Handelsbank; Luxembourg—East-West United Bank; and France—Commercial Bank for Northern Europe (Eurobank, founded in 1921). These commercial banks have branches in Singapore and Berlin, as well as a number of affiliated leasing, consulting, trade, and other specialized firms both in Russia and abroad. The total balance of all these banks is $9.7 billion. . . . There is a risk that creditors of Vneshekonombank will seize the funds it has deposited in foreign banks, including our banks

abroad. This and other factors, especially the acute shortage of resources in some of the banks abroad, worsened by the nonpayments of the USSR, make the official bankruptcy of these banks a real possibility. . . . Bankruptcy of these banks would bring about the bankruptcy of other commercial organizations abroad that are serviced by these banks and would complicate the work of shipping and Aeroflot and would lead to the loss of personal funds of our fellow citizens with accounts in them. The capital of the banks would be permanently lost.[50]

From the diary of Chernyaev, Gorbachev's aide: "Yavlinsky reports that on November 4, Vneshekonombank will declare bankruptcy: it cannot support our embassies, trade representatives, and other representatives abroad—and they won't have any funds to return. . . . M.S. asked me to write to [John] Major, coordinator of The Seven [G-7]: 'Dear John! Help!'[51]

Time changes our view of situations. Here is what Grigory Yavlinsky wrote about those days twelve years later: "Financial stabilization, which was basically achieved by the end of [the] 1990s through enormous social sacrifice and economic distortion, including a default on state obligations, truly was necessary—but before, not after, liberalization and privatization; and not at the expense of the population, which lost its confidence in the regime and in legal economic institutions, particularly the banking system, but at the expense of resources that had been accumulated in the hands of the state and its organs by the end of the Soviet period."[52]

On November 15, 1991, Mayor Anatoly Sobchak of St. Petersburg wrote to Silayev describing the food situation in the city: "With the sharp decrease in meat and dairy deliveries from the sovereign republics of the RSFSR, the food shortages for the general population of St. Petersburg, for the network of public care, and for other secure facilities and children's institutions are critical. The remaining meat supply in refrigeration is enough for three or four days for the city. Steady supplies for December and early 1992 are not expected. This could lead to a dangerous social and political situation in St. Petersburg."[53]

The shortage of grain was becoming more severe. First Deputy Chairman of the Committee for Food Purchasing Akulinin wrote to Silayev and his deputy, Luzhkov, on September 6, 1991: "In order to stimulate stocking grain and oil-seeds for the state, we have extended paying in hard currency to domestic farms. However, there are no funds planned for these purchases."[54] He wrote again to Silayev on September 27, 1991: "We have informed you of the critical situation with wheat at the flour mills. . . . At the present time, because of the unsatisfactory delivery of imported grain the supply of bread products may take a severe turn for the worse. . . . We ask that you order the Ministries of the Economy and of Foreign Economic Relations and Vneshekonombank to take measures to get credits for the country in September–October of no less than 1.2 million tons of wheat and immediately find hard currency sources to buy an additional 1 million tons of wheat by November 1, 1991."[55]

The Committee on Effective Management of the Economy passed a resolution on August 31, 1991, "On urgent measures for ensuring food for the populace." For those who know the economic history of Russia in the twentieth century, it sounds painfully like 1915–21. Here are a few actions called for in the document: "Declare it unacceptable that a number of places with enough grain resources are holding back its sale to the state. . . . Introduce temporary measures under which the orders of the Committee on Effective Management of the Economy on supplying grain and food to all-Union consumers, on inter-republic deliveries, and on deliveries of food to the Far North are mandatory and must be obeyed. Any questions of mutual accounting that come up are to be examined during the elaboration and signing of the Economic Agreement and confirmation of food balances for 1992." The people who signed this resolution were not capable of arresting and shooting hundreds of thousands of people as was done in 1918–21 during the food redistribution. Without the will to do that, resolutions like this do not work. Therefore the resolution also contained points like this: "The Ministry of Foreign Economic Relations and the State Committee on Purchasing Food in cooperation with Comrades Luzhkov and Kulik will take urgent measures to buy food products and raw materials abroad in the period September–December 1991, in accordance with the assignments for this year. Vneshekonombank will open letters of credit in a timely manner and ensure that these purchases receive priority payments, including transportation expenses. . . . Assign Comrades Luzhkov, Kulik, and Moskovsky, in participation with interested ministries and other state organs, to immediately hold negotiations with foreign banks about obtaining credits for advance purchases of grain, sugar, vegetable oils, and other foods."[56]

An explosive situation was brewing. Deputy Minister of the Interior Vitaly Turbin wrote to Silayev on November 8, 1991: "Reports coming to the ministry show that it remains difficult to ensure the presence of bread and other foodstuffs in a number of regions. . . . Long lines form outside stores, the citizens criticize the local and central authorities in strong language, and some of them call for protest actions."[57] A memo prepared for a meeting of the State Council with the president of the RSFSR in the fall of 1991 stated:

> The situation with bread may become critical. The low harvest and the inability to expand imports together with the refusal of farms to turn over their grain to the state may put the country and the republic on the brink of famine. The only way out of this situation is to allow the farms to sell grain freely at market prices with further liberalization of retail prices for bread. Without a transition to free pricing in conjunction with an accelerated reduction of state control in agriculture and trade, there will be no incentive for growth in production, which will make the situation even worse in 1992–93.[58]

But as VTsIOM informed the authorities, "The leadership of Russia is approaching price liberalization in an extremely tense social atmosphere, which is characterized by: a rejection of the idea of free prices by a significant proportion of the public; distrust of any measures for social security and supporting the standard of living; a weakened consumer market; an expectation of famine; a growth of dissatisfaction among the broadest strata of the population."[59]

In December the key problem was no longer mobilizing hard currency to buy food, but paying the shipping charges to transport goods to Russia. At the time Vneshekonombank received directives to use 80 percent of the weekly hard currency revenue to pay the freight of Soviet and foreign shippers:[60] "On the extreme situation in supplying the RSFSR with bread, bear in mind that Vneshekonombank has temporarily, as of December 19, stopped all forms of operations with hard currency to enterprises, organizations, and accounts of commercial banks that are not related to paying the freight for grain from the US and Canada, as well as payment in individual cases for food and medicine on letters of credit opened earlier under the guarantee of the government of the RSFSR to the account of the Republic Hard Currency Reserve of the RSFSR."[61]

One of the most important topics in negotiations between Western creditor-states and Union agencies and leaders of Union republics that had declared their independence in 1991 was who would be responsible for Soviet debts. Creditors had largely written off the USSR as incapable of meeting financial contracts. They needed to guarantee that the new de facto independent states would accept the obligations of the Soviet Union. Foreign and domestic hard currency debts of the USSR at the time it ceased to exist are shown in tables 8-4 and 8-5).

TABLE 8-4. External Debt of the Former USSR in Freely Convertible Currency as of January 1, 1992[a]

Billions of U.S. dollars[b]

External debt	Amount
Of which—	
1. Credits obtained or guaranteed by the USSR Government, USSR Gosbank, and USSR Vneshekonombank	70.5
Of which—	
a) Principal	57.1
b) Interest on all credits[c]	13.4
2. Liabilities on import letters of credit opened before December 31, 1991[d]	2.7
3. Open import letters of credit for medium-term bank credits	2.3
4. Confirmed letters of credit of third countries (principal and interest)	1.2
5. Import payments in arrears[d]	4.2
6. Credits obtained directly by various duly authorized enterprises and organizations (estimate)	2.4
7. Debt to foreign transportation companies for previous shipments of foreign trade cargo (estimate)	0.1
Total (1–7)	83.4
Additionally:	
Lend-lease[e]	0.8
Debt to former socialist countries (on balance)[f]	33.7
Debt under clearing barter accounts (not including open import letters of credit)[g]	5.9

Source: Yu. V. Ponomarev to the assistant to First Deputy Chairman of the RF Government V. B. Bogdanov, data on the foreign debt as of January 1, 1992, May 15, 1992 (personal archive of Ye. T. Gaidar).

a. Debt liabilities not included in the official Soviet foreign debt in convertible currency but included by the Vneshekonombank management in national debt liabilities totaled $40.4 billion, while the total Soviet foreign debt was estimated by the bank at $123.8 billion. Also not included are liabilities contracted by individual independent states without the participation of the Vneshekonombank. The original table included a large number of subsections, but they are not essential for understanding the Soviet foreign debt at this time.

b. Recalculated into U.S. dollars at ruble cross-rates for December 26, 1991.

c. Interest accrued for the remaining life of credits (estimate). The amount of interest will continue growing because of the accrual of additional interest on rescheduled credits (adjustments will be negotiated with creditors).

d. Based on documents on file at the USSR Vneshekonombank.

e. To be determined with the competent U.S. authorities.

f. Data cited only for current account balance in transferable rubles and for clearing (preliminary data subject to verification of the amounts and recalculation rate during negotiations with former socialist countries). Indicative rate: 1 transferable ruble = US$1.795).

g. Debt for clearing and barter accounts for the benefit of the USSR is US$0.7 billion (Afghanistan). Clearing currencies were recalculated into U.S. dollars at the international market rate.

A Civilized Divorce

The collapse of the USSR did not mean that it was immediately replaced by a regulated system of relations among the former republics. The borders of the newly independent states were not clear and were historically questionable,

TABLE 8-5. Domestic Currency Debt of the Vneshekonombank in Freely
Convertible Currency to Individuals and Corporations, as of January 1, 1992
Millions of U.S. dollars

Country	Corporate accounts		Individual accounts
	Total	Of which correspondent accounts of commercial banks and institutions of the Vneshekonombank	
Russia	8,856.3	2,036.6	433.8
Ukraine	462.1	421.1	45.8
Belarus	220.1	194.6	10.6
Uzbekistan	53.6	46.1	2.5
Kazakhstan	68.2	31.5	0.9
Georgia[a]	36.1	11.8	0.9
Azerbaijan	49.0	30.4	0.5
Lithuania	68.9	61.8	9.6
Moldova	16.0	15.3	. . .
Latvia	39.0	15.0	0.9
Kyrgyzstan	3.2	. . .	. . .
Tajikistan	3.8	1.0	. . .
Armenia	33.3	31.6	3.2
Turkmenistan	150.8	146.0	. . .
Estonia	19.6	. . .	. . .
Total	10,079.7	3,042.8	508.7

Source: Yu. V. Ponomarev to the assistant to First Deputy Chairman of the RF government V. B. Bogdanov, data on the foreign debt as of January 1, 1992, May 15, 1992 (personal archive of Ye. T. Gaidar).
a. Data as of December 1, 1991.

thus fraught with the potential for conflict and bloodshed. The lack of border clarity was the greatest obstacle to forming a stable democracy after the fall of the authoritarian empire.[62]

The new states encountered difficult relations with authorities below the federal level. They were particularly difficult in the national autonomous formations. No one knew which normative acts would apply to their territories. The authorities were incapable of guaranteeing even a minimal degree of law and order. In the fall of 1991 there was no more talk about preserving a united state, the question was how to get out of political and economic chaos while avoiding large-scale civil wars.[63] Considering the size of the Soviet nuclear potential now scattered across four states (Russia, Ukraine, Belorussia, and Kazakhstan), the fate of civilization was in question.

Before the collapse of the Soviet Union, three territorially integrated empires had collapsed in the twentieth century: the Austro-Hungarian,

Ottoman, and Russian. Yugoslavia collapsed almost simultaneously with the Soviet Union. In three out of four, the empire's collapse led to lengthy and bloody war. In one (Austria-Hungary), the armed conflicts establishing new borders were stopped by the armies of the Entente. Civil wars followed the collapse of the Ottoman and Russian Empires and of Yugoslavia. History did not suggest that the dismantling of the Soviet Union would pass without bloodshed.

If experts were asked in 1989 which of two socialist multiethnic countries would face the greatest risk of civil war if it were to collapse: the Soviet Union or Yugoslavia, which had come closer than any other country in Eastern Europe to joining the European Union and had a fairly liberal political system (by socialist standards) and an open market economy, most would have responded the USSR. History decided otherwise.

Left-wing intellectuals who live in stable, democratic societies have trouble understanding the dynamic of the processes that unfold during the crisis and collapse of an authoritarian regime. Their point of view is illustrated by Emmanuel Todd in *After the Empire,* a book popular in Russia for its anti-American views. For three pages he describes the harsh and pointless liberalization of the Russian economy in the period 1990–97 and how the Soviet and then Russian government liquidated the harshest totalitarian regime in human history, without resorting to violence, and agreed not only that their neighbors in Eastern Europe would become independent but also that freedom would be offered to the Baltic states, the republics of the Caucasus, Ukraine, Belorussia, and the republics of Central Asia; they agreed that the presence of enormous national minorities in the new states could not be obstacles to their independence.[64] The author does not seem to understand that the peaceful dissolution of the empire and economic liberalization were connected. The people who took part in elaborating the key political and economic decisions of the period know that the absence of mutual territorial demands, the unwillingness to use force as a way of getting food from the countryside, and the consequent need for immediate liberalization of the economy and the introduction of market mechanisms, do understand it.

Why did civil war break out in Yugoslavia and not in the former USSR? No one can answer precisely. That includes the participants who made key decisions. One can suggest hypotheses. Let me give you mine. It was a question of subjective factors: the differences in the personal priorities of Boris Yeltsin and Slobodan Milosevic and their political biographies. For Milosevic, the leader of the Serbian Communists, the way to retain power after the collapse of the former ideology was to play the radical Serbian nationalism card. Boris

Yeltsin, who in the public mind was a "fallen angel" who had suffered on behalf of the people, could bet on opposition to the Communist regime, which had lost its popularity and support.

I believe that the presence of nuclear weapons in the former USSR played a part as well. At the end of 1991, Ukraine had almost one-fifth of the ground-based warheads in the strategic triad. The total number of strategic weapons there was greater than the total in England and France combined. Data on the distribution of nuclear weapons on the territory of the former Soviet Union are not completely reliable. This is even more evidence of how dangerous the situation was for the country at the end of 1991. See tables 8-6 and 8-7 for (the sometimes conflicting) data provided by informed analysts who have studied the history of the USSR's nuclear endeavors.

The most serious problems were not with strategic nuclear weapons. They were controlled from Moscow. According to Soviet military experts asked by the Russian government, the newly independent states would need many years to develop similar capabilities. The situation with tactical nuclear weapons was much more complicated. The decision to use some of them could be taken by commanders of okrugs.[65] More precisely, they had the ability to use nuclear shells and mines. The use of tactical missiles was technically controlled by Moscow.[66] Even so, they were still a threat to civilization after the crash of a territorially integrated empire. The participants in the decision-making process understood the risks of armed conflict between post-Soviet nuclear states.

TABLE 8-6. Deployment of Soviet SNW Warheads in the Republics

| Republic | Type of SNW | Quantity | |
		Carriers	Warheads
Russian Federation	ICBM	1,064	4,278
	SSBN/SLBM	62/940	2,804
	HB	101	367
Ukraine	ICBM	176	1,240
	HB	21	168
Kazakhstan	ICBM	104	1,040
	HB	40	320
Belorussia	ICBM	54	54

Source: A. Pikaev and A. Saveliev, "Nuclear Might of the USSR: On Land, on Sea, and in the Air," *Nezavisi-maya Gazeta*, no. 137 (November 2, 1991).

Key: SNW = strategic nuclear weapon; ICBM = intercontinental ballistic missile; SSBN = nuclear-powered ballistic missile submarine; SLBM = submarine-launched ballistic missile; HB = heavy bomber.

TABLE 8-7. Distribution of Strategic Nuclear Weapons in the Territory of the CIS, 1992

Units/share in percent

| | Type of strategic nuclear weapons | | | | | | | |
| | Land-based ICBMs | | SLBMs | | Strategic bombers | | Total | |
Country	Carriers	Warheads	Carriers	Warheads	Carriers	Warheads	Carriers	Warheads
Russia	1,037/73	3,919/62	914/100	3,626/100	27/26	234/24	1,978/81	7,719/71
Ukraine	176/13	1,240/19	...	...	44/36	420/43	220/9	1,660/16
Kazakhstan	104/8	1,040/17	...	...	40/38	320/33	144/6	1,360/12
Belarus	81/6	81/2	...	...	...	...	81/4	81/1
Total	1,398/100	6,280/100	914/100	3,626/100	111/100	974/100	2,423/100	10,820/100

Source: Compiled using data from M. A. Pervov, *Raketnoe oruzhie raketnyx voisk strategicheskogo naznachenia* [Missile Weapons of the Strategic Missile Forces] (Moscow: Violanta, 1999), p. 213; *Strategicheskoe iadernoe vooruzhenie Rossii* [Russia's Strategic Nuclear Weapons] (Moscow: IzdAT, 1998), p. 12.

The threat that events would unfold in the post-Soviet space as they had in Yugoslavia was real. On August 26, 1991, Pavel Voshchanov, the press secretary to the Russian president, warned that the borders of Russia and the republics (excluding Lithuania, Latvia, and Estonia) could be "reevaluated" if they did not sign a Union agreement. The statement suggested Russian pretensions to territory in northern Kazakhstan, Crimea, and part of left-bank Ukraine. Voshchanov's words elicited an angry response from the leaders of Kazakhstan and Ukraine: they saw it as blackmail. Moscow mayor Gavriil Popov made even greater territorial claims on Ukraine on August 27 and 28, 1991. They extended beyond Crimea and part of the left bank to Odessa and the Transdniestr.[67]

In the fall of 1991 the Russian leadership did not discuss plans for using nuclear means against other republics in the event of territorial disputes. However, perceptions are as important as facts. From an article in *Nezavisimaya Gazeta* of October 24, 1991: "Even such a democratic newspaper (I used to think) as *Moskovskie Novosti* . . . published on the front page information from the corridors of the Russian government that there was a possibility of a preventive nuclear strike on Ukraine. When Ivan Plyushch and I were in Moscow, I asked Gorbachev and Yeltsin about it. Gorbachev replied, 'You know, Kostya, you'll do better if you read fewer newspapers.' And Yeltsin said that he had discussed the possibility with the military and that they don't have the technology. Neither reply satisfies me or the residents of Ukraine."[68]

U.S. authorities, with only a vague idea in 1991 of what was going on in the empire that had opposed them for decades, were perceptive in one regard. They had a sober estimation of the threat of uncontrolled use of tactical nuclear weapons on the territory of the dying superpower. That fall, George H. W. Bush addressed the problem. The U.S. administration presented a plan to destroy all land- and sea-based tactical nuclear arms. When realized, it would reduce the size of the USSR nuclear arsenal that the Russian republic could inherit. As often happens in history, even a strong and innovative proposal lagged behind reality. The Soviet Union no longer had the ability to put it into practice.

Internal correspondence between the Union and Russian governments at the end of 1991 focused on the problem of removing tactical nuclear weapons from the other republics. One key issue was how to store them. After they were removed from the Baltics and Transcaucasus, they would have to be warehoused. After discussing the risks of local resistance by organized groups opposed to their removal, the officials decided to remove the nuclear weapons, using the reasoning that they were complying with signed documents on disarmament.[69]

Nuclear weapons, which limited military activity during the cold war, were a restraining factor during the disintegration of the USSR as well. The leadership of the newly independent states was mature enough to understand that when talk is about borders, however notional or unfair they may be, talk is of war. The agreements reached in Belorussia on December 8 and ratified on December 21 in Alma-Ata opened the way for the signing of a strategic forces agreement (December 30, 1991). It obligated the member states to cooperate on the liquidation of nuclear weapons in Ukraine, Belorussia, and Kazakhstan; it established that by July 1, 1992, those republics would remove their tactical nuclear weapons to central bases for dismantling under joint control; and it spelled out that the parties saw no obstacles to moving nuclear weapons from the territories of Belarus, Kazakhstan, and Ukraine to the territory of the RSFSR.[70]

The tactical weapons in Ukraine were taken to Russia by May 6, 1991. Ukraine was prepared to hand over strategic nuclear weapons after receiving compensation and security guarantees from the United States and Russia. Such an agreement was signed on January 14, 1994, in Moscow and ratified by the parliament of Ukraine on February 3. The removal of nuclear missiles from Ukraine to Russia and the destruction of launch pads were completed by June 1, 1996.

On July 2, 1992, the Kazakhstan parliament adopted a decision to ratify Agreement SNV-1, and on December 13, 1993, the republic joined the Non-Proliferation Treaty as a non-nuclear state. Over that period nuclear warheads were removed to Russia and launch pads were destroyed in Kazakhstan.[71]

In the republic of Belarus, removal of nuclear weapons began in 1992, and by the end of the year the majority of weapons had been moved to Russia. On February 4, 1993, the Supreme Soviet of Belarus ratified the Agreement SNV-1. The official removal of nuclear warheads from Belarus to Russia was completed on November 23, 1996. Much in the history of post-Soviet space becomes clearer if one takes careful note of the date of the referendum in Belarus de facto legitimizing Aleksandr Lukashenko's monopoly on power (fall 1996), the Russian position on that question, and the date of the completion of the removal of nuclear weapons from Belarus (November 1996).[72]

On December 25, 1991, after Mikhail Gorbachev's resignation, the independence of the former republics of the Soviet Union became not only a political fact, but a juridical one as well.[73] This change offered a chance to overcome the mounting chaos, but nothing more. The problems facing the Soviet Union in early autumn 1991—an unmanageable army, the inability to maintain law and order, the absence of hard currency reserves, the friability and controversial nature of the borders, the paralysis of the administrative economic system in the absence of market mechanisms—were not solved by its dissolution.[74] Now the authorities of the new republics had to deal with them. Many have described how they chose new national political and economic institutions, decided how to address the problems of food supply and financial stability, fought against famine, and formed republic programs of market reforms.[75]

I do not want to repeat all of those stories here. But as a person who knows about these events not only from books and archival documents, I can say that the lesson learned from the last years of the USSR is that it is important when one is elaborating political decisions to remember that apparently solid, but inflexible, economic and political constructions that are incapable of adapting to the challenges of the contemporary world turn out to be fragile and collapse under the weight of circumstances that are hard to predict.

"For want of a nail, the shoe was lost; for want of a shoe the horse was lost; and for want of a horse the rider was lost, being overtaken and slain by the enemy, all for want of care about a horseshoe nail." The excuse for the profound economic crisis that provoked the collapse of a superpower was the fall of oil prices in the mid-1980s, which for all its significance is incommensurate with the consequences. Developments on the oil market were, for the Soviet economy, not the reason but the excuse for its collapse.

Joseph Stalin, in choosing a model for industrialization that was the opposite of Bukharin's, laid the foundation for an economic and political system that began to develop large cracks, creating the risk of its destruction under rather modest external influences. The development of events in the USSR in its last years demonstrates how important it is when one is elaborating an economic policy to consider the long-term risks, to evaluate decisions not only from the one-year or three-year perspective, but to look decades ahead. If that is not done, future generations of Russians will have to answer for the mistakes made today.

AFTERWORD

AS I HAVE DEMONSTRATED, in the mid-1980s the USSR faced a crisis in its balance of payments and accounting system that developed into a broader economic crisis and led to a steep decline in production and the standard of living, political destabilization, and finally the collapse of the political regime and the Soviet Empire.

By the end of the 1990s, Russia, the successor state of the USSR, had formed a fundamentally new and open economic system. It included a number of flawed but functioning market institutions: private property, convertible currency, a banking system, a system for regulating the stock market and natural monopolies as well as accumulated market knowledge and skills among the administrative elite and a critical mass of effective managers who could work in a market economy. This made it possible to move out of the transformational recession, begin economic growth, ensure sustainable improvements in living standards and positive structural changes in the economy, and stabilize the country's monetary system and foreign trade.

The structural changes undertaken in 1992–98 were similar to those the Soviet leadership should have made beginning in 1986–87. Capital investments, military spending, and grain imports were sharply curtailed, exports of raw materials and energy sources were expanded, and their domestic consumption was reduced. With fewer imports of materials and components from the West and the dismantling of the decades-old system of economic relations within the USSR and Comecon, production volumes fell as well; the forced adaptation to a new currency and the fiscal situation led to a significant decline in the standard of living. But the currency reserves that had been depleted by the end of 1991 were gradually replenished, and the deficit in the balance of payments in hard currency vanished. In late 1999 and early 2000 the country began restoring its reputation as a reliable borrower.

If these measures had been implemented by the Soviet regime, stabilization of production volumes and living standards might have been achieved in a shorter time. But the Soviet authorities were not capable of doing the most important thing—replacing the socialist system of central planning and management of the economy with the market system of a capitalist economy. So the results would have been ephemeral. Forced to deal with fiscal and currency stabilization and structural reforms simultaneously, Russia and other postsocialist countries had to travel an arduous path in order to form the shell of a market economy.

In the course of those years a young and imperfect democracy was created. It had elements of populism, political irresponsibility, and corruption. Nevertheless, the country had a system of checks and balances. This let us hope that once the most difficult consequences of the socialist experiment were overcome, the country would have in place the preconditions for sustainable development on market and democratic bases. Naturally, interethnic conflicts, especially in the Caucasus, remained a serious challenge to the country's security and political stability. Still, the system of federative relations gave reason to hope that the system was flexible enough to ensure stability in the organization of life and political processes in the huge and ethnically heterogeneous country.

Elements that could be moved and changed were built into the economic and political system, and this flexibility guaranteed its sustainability. In other words, if there were an unexpected challenge, the system could be anticipated to respond with appropriate changes instead of catastrophic collapse.

In 2000–2003, economic reforms, consistent and effective on the whole, improved the tax and fiscal system, made the financial basis of the federative relations more transparent and understandable, secured people's right to own land, passed labor legislation commensurate with a market economy, and implemented a series of other important and useful changes that expanded the basis for economic growth. Many people felt that the most serious problems on the path to a steady development of Russian democracy and market economy were solved. I must admit that I was among them.

However, as so often happens, history showed once again the danger of extrapolating from short-term tendencies. Since 2003–04, there have been worrying signs in the development of Russia's political system, federative relations, and economy.

In 2002–03 Russia had a parliament that was on the whole loyal to the president and government but still relatively independent, retaining its influence on decisionmaking. In order to get legislation through the Duma and Federation Council, the government had to conduct substantive discussions with deputies and seek compromises and possible solutions. Working with such a parliament was not easy. It was not a rubber stamp for government decisions. Its presence did, however, improve the quality of state government. A responsible and independent parliament does not allow decisions to be made in back rooms, without public discussion and advice from specialists who are not employed by the authorities.

When the parliament becomes an instrument of formal approval of the actions and intentions of the executive branch, the quality of the decisions suffers. Even an effective bureaucracy, if it does not respond to systematic professional criticism, makes mistakes, sometimes very crude ones.

In the early 2000s, there was a fairly independent press. It was not always moved by considerations of high morality or the public interest, and it often was the tool of information wars between oligarchic clans. But since the number of clans was greater than one, the public had an opportunity to get news from many sources and draw its own conclusions about what was happening in the country. When an ever-greater share of the press is under the direct or oblique but strict control of the authorities, one more instrument of public control is blocked.

A few years ago, Russia had influential entrepreneurial organizations, such as the Russian Union of Industrialists and Entrepreneurs (RUIE). Its voice was heard and taken into account in developing key economic and political decisions. This was beneficial for the country because the entrepreneurial community was objectively interested in raising Russia's attractiveness to investors. Investment from outside increases the capitalization of companies and expands their access to credit resources. Large Russian enterprises did a lot to improve legislation and economic policy. But in 2003, the RUIE began to evolve into an ornamental body.

Many (though not all) regional leaders in power at the turn of the new century were, to put it bluntly, not very competent or impeccably honest. Nevertheless, the residents of these regions were beginning to realize that when they elected a governor they were not selecting the person who would go to Moscow and yell louder than the rest about local problems, but were deciding who would determine the quality of their lives, their children's education, and their parents' health care, and ensure the delivery of heating oil and garbage pickup in their cities. This understanding comes only with experience. It took decades for it to form in developed democracies. Nevertheless, developments in Russia in the late 1990s and early 2000 were headed in that direction. The 2004 decision to return responsibility for the appointment of governors to Moscow permits the local authorities and regional elites to pass the buck to the center and say that they can do nothing about local problems.

Such decisions as the repeal of elections in single-mandate districts, which permitted outspoken political figures to have, if not influence, at least a voice in discussions of issues of state, and the introduction of the 7 percent barrier, which limits the ability of many political forces that reflect the views of millions of Russian citizens to be represented in parliament (a measure unusual in developed and stable democracies) are steps that, without being fatal, do create a higher risk for the survival of Russian democracy. Together they indicate a path toward the creation of a system that could be called closed (managed) democracy, or soft authoritarianism. Naturally, this system has little in common with the harsh totalitarian regime of the Soviet Union, but still the weaknesses and elements of instability that are characteristic of authoritarianism are beginning to show.

Such political constructions are stable only until they come up against a crisis, first and foremost an economic one that requires not only silent obedience but actual support from society. And then it becomes clear that getting that support will be difficult. This severely limits maneuverability at a time when it is most needed by the government and the country. The Soviet leadership of the second half of the 1980s learned that the hard way. Unfortunately, it was not alone in having to pay for that bitter lesson.

The curtailment of democratic elements and real federalism is taking its toll on the dynamic of international relations. I cannot force myself to apply the term *democratic* to the state structure of many Russian national republics in the late 1990s and early 2000s. Nevertheless, they were regimes formed by the local elites and capable of controlling interethnic relations within the republic and had influence in the local societies. Attempts to replace them with appointed Moscow puppets sometimes led to the formal state organs of the republic managing and administering nothing. The real process of decisionmaking bypassed them. But where the authorities remain representatives of influential local elites, they can lay the blame on Moscow for any problems that arise. The fact that presidents of autonomous republics are appointed by the federal center is playing into the hands of the nationalists, who can use this as proof that Moscow treats the residents of autonomies not as full-fledged citizens but as conquered entities. A better present for separatists is hard to imagine.

In economic policy, the Russian authorities have learned from the Soviet experience. That is evident in the responsible budget and monetary policy of 2000–2004, in view of the high oil prices and the related high, but not permanent, budget revenues. The budget policy was conservative in order to support a balanced budget, reduce foreign debt that was the legacy of the Soviet Union, and lower the expenses required to service it. In creating a stabilization fund according to well-defined rules, the Russian government and the Russian parliament showed political reasonability and demonstrated an ability to learn from the mistakes of their predecessors, unusual in Russian history.

In 2000–2004, the Russian budget could function without serious excesses or large imbalances with medium-range oil prices for the long term and remain unaffected even with anomalously low prices, such as those in 1986–90 and 1998–99. It is difficult to hold such a responsible fiscal line for long. There is a wealth of world experience to show that.

Today, with unusually high oil prices, discussions about how reasonable it is for Russian leaders to invest the country's stabilization fund in securities of countries whose currencies are seen as reserves is a natural element of the economic and political landscape. Only a lazy Russian politician would not join the competition to propose popular and exotic ideas for spending the money in the stabilization fund. However, if we compare the size of the Russian stabilization fund, which was only 5.7 percent of GDP as of January 1, 2006, with the state oil fund of Norway, which also has to deal with the problem of the "oil curse" (where it was 70.1 percent of GDP as of October 1, 2005), it is clear that the idea that Russia's stabilization fund is too big is an exaggeration. No less popular is the topic of an excess of gold currency reserves (as of January 1, 2006, it represented 24.2 percent of GDP). Talk that only enemies of the homeland would invest so heavily in foreign stocks is cheap on today's political market. Nevertheless China, whose economic policy was held up frequently over the past fifteen years as a model to be emulated by Russia, had 36.3 percent of its GDP in currency reserves.[1]

It was obvious in 2005 that the government's ability to continue the policies that would minimize the risk of a financial and currency crisis after a drop in oil prices was becoming restricted. As noted in chapter 3, it is possible to explain to the public why the state cannot spend money on something when there is no money. To tell people it cannot be done when there *is* money is more difficult, even if one explains that the country's economy might find itself too dependent on unpredictable factors, which would lead to a deep economic crisis, the price for which is incommensurate with the short-term gains.

For now, the steps taken by the government that are financed by additional oil revenues and that increase its budget commitments are relatively few. From 2004 to 2006, budget commitments grew by approximately 3.5 percent of GDP. But in view of the limited size of the stabilization fund, even such modest growth reduces the reliability of the country's fiscal system. Russia's economy, like the USSR's before it, is becoming dependent on keeping oil prices at historically anomalous levels.

Different scenario calculations performed at the Institute for the Economy in Transition show that if prices for oil (Brent type) fall to $25 by 2009, the revenues of the federal budget will be approximately 9 percent less than in 2005. Instead of increasing, GDP will decrease. The deficit of the federal budget will be 7 percent of GDP. The remaining money in the stabilization fund will be zero. The volume of gold currency reserves will be approximately $80 billion less than in 2005. Inflation rates will reach 40 percent.[2]

Naturally, this is not a prognosis, but a scenario calculation. The institute is also looking at scenarios with super-high oil prices and inertia scenarios. Each potential scenario produces different results. But as I have repeated, in countries that are dependent on commodity markets, it is important to soberly evaluate the risks of hard-to-predict developments on the market when one is elaborating economic policy.

Realistic prognoses show that with the present reserves of the stabilization fund, even with negative developments, Russia in 2006–08 will not face a serious financial crisis. The threats lie in the noticeable deceleration of economic growth. However, in discussing long-term risks, it is important to think farther ahead than two to three years. In making economic decisions today, in creating budget commitments, we are defining the outlines within which the Russian government will have to work over the next ten to fifteen years. The reserve of stability guaranteed in the early 1980s by high oil prices gave the Soviet leadership the opportunity to do nothing and still retain power. The problems that began in the late 1970s and early 1980s appeared later, but on a scale that is hard to imagine. The decisions about how to regulate those risks had to be made by others, by the governments of the states that arose from the ruins of the empire. We must do everything possible to prevent Russia from repeating the mistakes of the Soviet Union.

Today, the risks of destabilization in Russia are much lower than those in the USSR in the early 1980s. We call today's political regime soft authoritarianism. It has many elements of freedom and flexibility. That is a hopeful sign. The proportion of ethnic Russians in Russia is much higher than it was in the Soviet Union, and that makes regulating interethnic relations with a reasonable policy possible. The market economy functioning in Russia is incomparably more flexible than the socialist one. It can adapt easily to changes in the world economy. Its logic does not presuppose that all responsibility for changes in economic life belongs to the current leaders. But this does not mean that the risks attendant on an inability to adapt and the growth of the country's dependence on dynamics not controllable by the regime have disappeared. Caution and a sober evaluation of the threats the country might face will be integral components of responsible policymaking.

NOTES

Abbreviations used in notes:

GARF, Gosudarstvennyi Arkhiv Rossiiskoi Federatsii (State Archive of the Russian Federation)

RGAE, Rossiiskii Gosudarstvennyi Arkhiv Economiki (Russian State Archive of the Economy)

RGANI, Rossiiskii Gosudarstvennyi Arkhiv Noveishei Istorii (Russian State Archive of Contemporary History)

F. = Fund	D. = File
Inv. = Inventory	L/Ll. = Sheet/sheets [or Page/pages]
Ob. = Verso	P. = Listing
Op. = Inventory	S. = List

Introduction

1. The attitude of the Soviet leadership toward its East European satellites is illustrated by Leonid Brezhnev's accusation during the negotiations following the invasion of Czechoslovakia by Soviet troops that the arrested first secretary of the Czech Communist Party, Alexander Dubcek, did not show Moscow the drafts of his political reports. According to the Czech authorities, approximately 30 percent of the Ministry of Internal Affairs of Czechoslovakia worked for the KGB. Cf. K. Dawisha, *The Kremlin and the Prague Spring* (University of California Press, 1984), pp. 6, 53.

2. *Komsomol'skaia Pravda,* January 19, 2004.

3. A. Prokhanov, *Gospodin Geksogen* [Mister Hexogen] (Moscow: Ad Marginem Press, 2002), p. 426.

4. A. Dugin, *Osnovy geopolitiki* [Bases of Geopolitics] (Moscow: Ark-tsentr, 2000), p. 195.

5. See, for example, R. Staryer, *Why Did the Soviet Union Collapse? Understanding Historical Change* (New York: M. E. Sharpe, 1998). The authoritative Russian political analyst I. Yakovenko writes: "Beginning with the era of Ivan the Terrible, the Moscow kingdom existed as an empire. At first the imperial idea inspired the Muscovy elite that had created a state. Later, in the course of four centuries, Russian society created an empire, lived in it, received the benefits, and bore the burdens of imperial existence. The imperial consciousness entered the body of the society, penetrated all levels of culture, and impressed itself on the psychology of the masses. By itself, empire is neither good nor bad. It is a special method of political integration of large expanses, consistent with a certain level of historical development. On our Russian expanses, in the given historical era, it has exhausted itself. But that

statement is a dry, analytical judgment. For people of a traditional bent, who grew up in the framework of an imperial lifestyle, the empire is an entire cosmos, way of life, and system of worldview and world perception. The cosmos is organic; they do not know any other and will not accept any other. The traditional person tends to perceive the stable as eternal and unalterable, especially since the state ideology told him the USSR was eternal and indestructible. From that point of view the collapse of the empire is an accident, an unnatural course of events, the result of a conspiracy of hostile elements that found support inside 'our' society." See I. Yakovenko, "Ukraina i Rossiia: suzhety sootnesennosti" [Ukraine and Russia: Topics of Interrelationships], *Vestnik Evropy* XVI: 64.

6. Address of President of the Russian Federation V. Putin to the Federal Assembly of the Russian Federation, April 15, 2005 (http://president.kremlin.ru/text/appears/2005/04/87049.shtml).

7. M. Von Hagen, "Writing the History of Russia as Empire: The Perspective of Federalism," in *Kazan, Moscow, St. Petersburg: Multiple Faces of the Russian Empire* (Moscow: O.G.I., 1997), p. 393.

8. V. I. Dal, *Tolkovyi slovar' zhivogo velikorusskogo yazyka* [Explanatory Dictionary of the Living Russian Language] (Moscow: Russkii yazyk, 1989), vol. 2, p. 42.

9. S. I. Ozhegov, *Slovar' russkogo yazyka* [Dictionary of the Russian Language], AN SSSR, Institut russkogo yazyka (Moscow: Russkii yazyk, 1991), vol. 1, p. 662.

10. *Slovar' russkogo yazyka v4-x t* [Dictionary of the Russian Language in 4 vols.], AN SSSR, Institut russkogo yazyka (Moscow: Russkii yazyk, 1981), p. 248.

11. It is more accurate to speak of colonial empires with overseas territories (as is done above), but the term "overseas empires" has become entrenched, and I use it in this work.

12. G. Arnold, *Britain since 1945: Choice, Conflict, and Change* (London: Blandford, 1989), pp. 41–49.

13. M. Broszat, *Hitler and the Collapse of Weimar Germany* (New York: Berg, 1987), p. 45.

14. Ibid., pp. 55, 56.

15. These materials were published by the German historian F. Fischer only in the 1960s. In the 1920s the Social-Democratic government spent great financial resources to propagandize the thesis of Germany's innocence at the start of World War I. See S. Delmer, *Weimar Germany: Democracy on Trial* (New York: Macdonald, 1972), p. 52.

16. About how a swift and unexpected collapse of an empire is perceived as a catastrophe, but one that can be overcome, see B. Podvintsev, "Postimperskaia adaptatsiia konservativnogo soznaniia: blagopriiatstvuiushchie factory" [Post-imperial Adaptation of the Conservative Consciousness: Beneficial Factors], *POLIS* 3, no. 623 (2001): 25–33.

17. On the dangers to the stability of democratic institutions inherent in radical nationalism born of the post-imperial syndrome, see A. Gerschenkron, *Bread and Democracy in Germany* (University of California Press, 1943). On the link between pro-imperial policies and authoritarian tendencies in contemporary Russia, see also

"Overcoming Postimperial Syndrome," transcript of a discussion on April 21, 2005, as part of the "After the Empire" project of the Liberal Mission Foundation (www. liberal.ru/sitan.asp?Num=549).

18. Yakovenko, "Ukraina i Rossiia," pp. 65, 66.

19. Chapter 8 provides more detail on these events.

20. In May 1926, President P. Hindenburg decreed that both the flag of the republic and the imperial flag would hang over German diplomatic representations abroad.

21. W. Gutmann and P. Meehan, *The Great Inflation: Germany 1919–1923* (London: Gordon and Gremonesi, 1975), p. 237.

22. W. Brustein, *The Logic of Evil: The Social Origins of the Nazi Party, 1925–1933* (Yale University Press, 1996).

23. A significant part of Russian society perceives the Russian Federation as a temporary, transitional formation that will either expand or collapse over time. Only 28.4 percent of those polled by sociologists in 2006 believe that "Russia must remain an independent state, not unifying with anyone." See Yu. Solozobov, "Rossiia v postimperskii period: primenim li postkolonial'nyi opyt Velikobritanii?" [Russia in the Postimperial Period: Is the Post-Colonial Experience of Great Britain Applicable?] (www.ukpolitics.ru/rus/members/9/09.doc).

24. L. Gudkov, "Pamiat' o voine i massosvaia identichnost' rossiian" [Memory of the War and the Mass Identity of Russians], *Neprikosnovennyizapas* 40–41 (2005): 45–57.

Chapter One

1. J. Bryce, *Sviashchennaia Rimskaia imperiia* [The Holy Roman Empire] (Moscow: Tipografiia A. I. Mamontova i K, 1891), p. 71.

2. On preserving the prestige of an imperial title, invested with supreme power, in the eyes of barbarian rulers in Belgium, Spain, Africa, and Italy, see Sh. Dil', *Istoriia Vizantiiskoi imperii* [History of the Byzantine Empire] (Moscow: Gosudarstvennoe izdatel'stvo inostrannoi literatury, 1948), p. 26.

3. G. Barraclough, *The Mediaeval Empire: Idea and Reality* (London: Published for the Historical Association by George Philip & Son, 1950), pp. 9–11.

4. J. H. Elliott, *Spain and Its World, 1500–1700: Selected Essays* (Yale University Press, 1989), p. 9.

5. L. M. Cullen, *A History of Japan, 1582–1941* (Cambridge University Press, 2003), pp. 178–82; E. Ihsanoglu, ed., *History of the Ottoman State, Society and Civilization* (Istanbul: IRCICA, 2001), vol. 1, pp. 73–76, 80; *Mezhdunarodnye otnosheniia na Dal'nem Vostoke* [International Relations in the Far East] (Moscow: Mysl', 1973), vol. 1, pp. 58–62.

6. R. Gopal, *British Rule in India: An Assessment* (London: Asia Publishing House, 1963), pp. 17–19.

7. R. Datt Palm, *Krizis Britanii i Britanskoi imperii* [The Crisis of Britain and the British Empire] (Moscow: Izdatel'stvo inostrannoi literatury, 1954), p. 14.

8. Historical statistics are not precise enough for an accurate estimate. The result calculated using A. Maddison's data is 22.6 percent. See A. Maddison, *The World Economy: Historical Statistics* (Paris: OECD, 2003). A more realistic estimate is 20–25 percent.

9. A. Gerschenkron, *Economic Backwardness in Historical Perspective* (Belknap Press of Harvard University Press, 1962).

10. Ye. Gaidar, *Dolgoe vremia. Rossiia v mire: ocherki ekonomicheskoi istorii* [Long Time: Russia in the World: Sketches in Economic History] (Moscow: Delo, 2005), pp. 36–46.

11. On the inability of the English political elite to adapt to a world in which Britain was no longer a dominant power, as a condition leading to the chain of world wars in the twentieth century, see A. Gamble, *Britain in Decline: Economic Police, Political Strategy and the British State* (Boston: Beacon Press, 1931).

12. On the impact of Russia's defeat in the Russo-Japanese war on developments in the English colonies, see H. G. Rawlinson, *The British Achievement in India* (London: William Hodge & Company, 1948).

13. R. Aron, *France Steadfast and Changing: The Fourth to the Fifth Republic* (Harvard University Press, 1960).

14. Palm, *Krizis Britanii i Britanskoi imperii*, p. 31.

15. On the incompatibility of imperial establishments and democratic organization, see Charles Tilly, "How Empires End," in *After Empire: Multiethnic Societies and Nation-Building: The Soviet Union and the Russian, Ottoman, and Habsburg Empires*, ed. Karen Barkey and Mark von Hagen (Boulder, Colo.: Westview, 1997), p. 3.

16. Edmund von Glaise-Horstenau, *The Collapse of the Austro-Hungarian Empire* (London: J. M. Dent and Sons, 1930).

17. V. Sorgin, *Politicheskaia istoriia sovremennoi Rossii. 1985–1994: ot Gorbacheva do El'tsina* [Political History of Contemporary Russia, 1985–1994: From Gorbachev to Yeltsin] (Moscow: Progress-Akademia, 1994), p. 101.

18. Aron, *France Steadfast and Changing*.

19. W. H. Morris-Jones and Georges Fischer, eds., *Decolonisation and After: The British and French Experience* (London: Frank Cass, 1980), p. 121; D. Goldsworthy, *Colonial Issues in British Politics 1945–1961* (Oxford: Clarendon Press, 1971).

20. Goldsworthy, *Colonial Issues*.

21. England's financial obligations to the United States, accumulated over the course of World War II, gave American authorities the ability to influence England's colonial policy. Ibid.

22. D. L. Rady, *Fascism and Resistance in Portugal: Communists, Liberals and Military Dissidents in the Opposition to Salazar, 1941–1974* (Manchester University Press, 1988); D. Porch, *The Portuguese Armed Forces and the Revolution* (London: Croom Helm, 1977); N. Bruce, *Portugal: The Last Empire* (London: David & Charles, 1975).

23. K. Leontiev, *Vostok, Rossia i slavianstvo*. Sb. st. [The East, Russia, and Slavicism: Collected Articles] (Moscow: Tipo-Litografia I. N. Kushneriova i K, 1885), vol. 1, p. 106.

24. Morris-Jones and Fischer, *Decolonisation and After*.

25. Rawlinson, *The British Achievement in India*, p. 189. Under the new law, half the members of the imperial legislative council were elected. In the provinces the majority of members to legislative councils under governors were elected.

26. W. Churchill, *The Second World War*, 6 vols. (London: Cassell, 1958–54), vol. 5, p. 88.

27. Goldsworthy, *Colonial Issues*.

28. G. Arnold, *Britain since 1945: Choice, Conflict and Change* (London: Blandford, 1989).

29. Morris-Jones and Fischer, *Decolonisation and After*, p. 23.

30. It is possible to explain the painless dissolution of the British Empire only by comparing it with similar political instances in history. The post-imperial syndrome had an impact on English foreign policy of the 1950s and 1960s. For a long time it was impossible to determine the position of the country on European integration.

31. H. G. Ferreira and M. W. Marshall, *Portugal's Revolution: Ten Years On* (Cambridge University Press, 1986).

32. P. P. Cherkasov, *Raspad kolonial'noi imperii Frantsii* [The Collapse of the Colonial Empire of France] (Moscow: Nauka, 1985).

33. Britain's repeal of the system of conscription after World War II was one of the most important factors explaining the relative ease of the bloodless dissolution of the British Empire. In the 1950s it became clear to the English authorities that if the empire were to be preserved by armed force, it would be, at the very least, necessary to resume military conscription. Political considerations made such a course inappropriate.

34. J. Talbott, *The War without a Name: France in Algeria, 1954–1962* (New York: Alfred A. Knopf, 1980), p. 39.

35. Ibid.

36. Ibid., p. 202.

37. P. M. Williams, *Wars, Plots and Scandals in Postwar France* (Cambridge University Press, 1970), p. 151.

38. On the specific ethnic composition of the Austro-Hungarian Empire that made it impossible for it to take the path chosen by England and France, see O. Jaszi, *The Dissolution of the Habsburg Monarchy* (University of Chicago Press, 1961).

39. I. G. Gerder, *Idei k filosofii istorii chelovechestva* [Ideas for a Philosophy of the History of Mankind] (Moscow: Nauka, 1977), pp. 226, 250.

40. E. Solsten, ed., *Portugal: A Country Study* (Washington: Federal Research Division, Library of Congress, 1994), p. 137.

41. Glaise-Horstenau, *The Collapse of the Austro-Hungarian Empire*, p. 270.

42. I. V. Starodubovskaia and V. A. Mei, *Velikiie revolutsii: Ot Kromvelia do Putina* [Great Revolutions: From Cromwell to Putin] (Moscow: Vagrius, 2001), pp. 25–92.

43. M. Hroch, who analyzed national movements in European countries in the nineteenth century, observed that they all underwent three stages: analysis and enlightenment; nationalist revival, during which groups advocating patriotic rebirth viewed their mission as dissemination of national consciousness; and the rise of a mass national movement. See M. Hroch, *Social Preconditions of National Revival in*

Europe: A Comparative Analysis of the Social Composition of Patriotic Groups among the Smaller European Nations (Cambridge University Press, 1985), p. 23.

44. E. I. Rubinshtein, *Krusheniie avstro-vengerskoi monarkhii* [Collapse of the Austro-Hungarian Monarchy] (Moscow: Izdatel'stvo Akademii Nauk SSSR, 1963), p. 325.

45. Jaszi, *The Dissolution of the Habsburg Monarchy*, pp. 7, 11.

46. A. Vishnevskii, *Serp i rubl': konservativnaia modernizatsiia v SSSR* [Sickle and Ruble: Conservative Modernization in the USSR] (Moscow: OGU, 1998), p. 331.

47. W. R. Brubaker, "Postimperskaia situatsia i raz" edinenie narodov v sravnitel'no-istoricheskoi perspective" [The Post-Imperial Situation and Separation of Nations in a Comparative-Historical Perspective] (www.hrights.ru/text/b3/Chapter2.htm).

48. R. D. Robinson, *The First Turkish Republic: A Case Study in National Development* (Harvard University Press, 1963).

49. F. M. Dostoevskii, *"Dnevniki pisatelia" za 1881g.* [Diaries of a Writer for 1881], chap. 3; *Geok-Tepe. Chto takoie Azia?* [Geok-Tepe: What Is Asia?], both in *Polnoe sobranie sochinenii v 30 t.* [Complete Collected Works in 30 volumes] (Leningrad: Mysl', 1984), vol. 27, pp. 26–28.

50. On the role of national factors in the revolution and the Civil War in Russia, see *Rossiia v XX veke: Reformy i revolutsii* [Russia in the Twentieth Century: Reforms and Revolutions], vol. 1, ed. G. N. Sevostianov (Moscow: Nauka, 2002).

51. A. Besançon, *L'empire russe et la domination sovietique: Le concept d'empire* (Paris: PUF, 1980), pp. 367–68.

52. O. Bauer, *Natsional'yi vopros i sotsial-demokratia* [The National Question and Social Democracy] (St. Petersburg: Serp, 1909).

53. R. Serbin, "Lenine et la question Ukrainienne en 1914: le discourse 'separatiste' de Zurich," *Pluriel*, no. 25 (1981): 83–84.

54. "Similar to the communist concept, the nationalist concept had a very high political appeal and ability to unite. It always attracted masses of people who failed to adapt to changes and who were nostalgic about the past, about former ethnic isolation, about an opportunity to have privileges without competition, and so on. The nationalist ideology lent certainty to their vague sentiments, kindled their dissatisfaction, and united them in a longing for unrealizable goals. All that turned nationalism into a serious ideological and political force. Social groups that fought for redistribution of wealth and power could not resist the temptation to form an alliance with it." Vishnevskii, *Serp i rubl'*, p. 317.

55. Brubaker, "Postimperskaia situatsia."

56. Yugoslavia is not a foreign country to me. I spent many years there. I know the Serbo-Croatian language. In the fall of 1994, in Pala, at the height of the Bosnian war, I spent many hours with the future prime minister of Serbia, Z. Jindjic. He was later killed by terrorists as he tried to convince the leader of the Bosnian Serbs, R. Karadjic, of the urgency of reaching a compromise at a time when military success was on the side of the Serbs. He warned that the price of rejecting mutual concessions would be high. In 1999 I was in Belgrade during the bombings. I tried to negotiate the terms of a cease-fire. I am well aware of the development of

events in the tragedy of Yugoslavia. But this book is not a memoir. It is an attempt to understand the mechanisms of the making and collapse of empires and the formation of a post-imperial syndrome. Therefore, when I touch on the problems associated with the collapse of Yugoslavia and the bloody war that followed, I prefer to discuss them without addressing my personal recollections.

57. I. I. Leshchilovskaia, "Istoricheskiie korni ugoslavskogo konflikta" [Historical Roots of the Yugoslav Conflict], *Voprosi istorii*, no. 5 (1994): 40–56.

58. S. A. Romanenko, *Ugoslavia: istoriia vozniknoveniia, krizis, raspad, obrazovaniie nezavisimykh gosudarstv* [Yugoslavia: History of Its Appearance, Crisis, Collapse, and Formation of Independent States] (Moscow: Moskovskii obshchestvennyi nauchnyi fond, 2000), pp. 57–59.

59. E. Yu. Gus'kova, *Istoria ugoslavskogo krizisa (1990–2000)* [History of the Yugoslav Crisis] (Moscow: Izdatel' A. Soloviev, 2001), pp. 53–54.

60. Susan L. Woodward, *Balkan Tragedy: Chaos and Dissolution after the Cold War* (Brookings, 1995), p. 45.

61. B. Ward, "The Firm in Illiria: Market Syndicalism," *American Economic Review* 48, no. 4 (1958): 266–89; B. Ward, *The Socialist Economy: A Study of Organizational Alternatives* (New York: Random House, 1967).

62. Woodward, *Balkan Tragedy*, p. 129.

63. S. Kovacevic and P. Daji, *Hronologija jugoslovenske krize 1942–1993* (Belgrade: IES, 1994), p. 284.

64. See, for example, C. Bennett, *Yugoslavia's Bloody Collapse: Causes, Course and Consequences* (New York: New York University Press, 1995); B. Denitch, *Ethnic Nationalism: The Tragic Death of Yugoslavia* (University of Minnesota Press, 1996); V. Gligorov, *Why Do Countries Break Up? The Case of Yugoslavia* (Uppsala University, 1994); T. Oberschall, "The Fall of Yugoslavia," *Journal of the Budapest University of Economic Sciences* 28, no. 3 (1992).

65. In 1971, Tito forced almost all the leaders of the Croatian Communist Party into retirement after they began to actively promote the idea of nationalism.

66. On the impact of the lack of democratic traditions and the effect of the authoritarian heritage on the development of radical nationalism in Yugoslav republics, see D. Yanich, "Krizis natsional'nogo samoopredeleniia i etnicheskiie stolknoveniia v postkommunisticheskom obshchestve" [Crisis of National Self-Determination and Ethnic Conflict in Postcommunist Society], *Sotsial'nyie konflikty v transformiruushikhsia obshchestvakh* [Social Conflicts in Transforming Societies], Materialy Mezhdunarodnoi konferentsii [Materials of an International Conference], Moscow, May 15–17, 1996, p. 13.

67. K. Mihailovih and V. Krestih, *Memorandum CAHY: Odgovori na kritike* (Belgrade: CAHY, 1995), p. 150.

68. The 2005 election in Iraq is typical of the same sort of problem. There were many political movements with radically different economic and social precepts both among the Shiites and the Sunnis, as well as the Kurds. Nonetheless, the election had the effect of a census that demonstrated who was in the majority in the country, a factor that had previously been ignored by the Iraqi Sunnis. After the election, it was very clear that they were in the minority. The problem is that a census does not eliminate acute interethnic conflicts.

69. V. Meier, *Yugoslavia: A History of Its Demise* (London: Routledge, 1995).

70. R. Dornbusch and S. Edwards, *The Macroeconomics of Populism in Latin America* (University of Chicago Press, 1991).

Chapter Two

1. Constitutional monarchies, in which the head of a country performs ceremonial functions while governance issues, such as executive power, finance, and legislation, are controlled by a parliament, are in essence democratic regimes.

2. It is customary to think of agrarian society as a social organization formed after the Neolithic revolution, after farming and cattle breeding were mastered and widely practiced. Agrarian society was dominant in the world for centuries. It was preeminent in human society up until the emergence of economic growth in the nineteenth century. For greater detail see Ye. Gaidar, *Dolgoe vremia. Rossiia v mire: ocherki ekonomicheskoi istorii* [Long Time. Russia in the World: Sketches in Economic History] (Moscow: Delo, 2005), pp. 127–70.

3. M. Olson, *Power and Prosperity: Outgrowing Communist and Capitalist Dictatorships* (New York: Basic Books, 2000).

4. For greater detail see Gaidar, *Dolgoe vremia,* chap. 7.

5. On the interconnection between the social changes tied to modern economic growth, social mobilization, and the crippling of traditional fundamentals of legitimacy in a social system, see K. W. Deutsch, "Social Mobilization and Political Development," *American Political Science Review* 55 (September 1961): 494, 495; S. N. Eisenstadt, ed., *Comparative Social Problems* (New York: Free Press of Glencoe, 1964); S. M. Lipset, *Political Man* (Garden City, N.Y.: Doubleday, 1960).

6. Paine wrote that if a monarchy humiliates its citizens, the right of inheritance is an obvious insult. In Paine's view, all people are created equal. No one should have the privilege by birthright of an advantage over others. People may earn the respect of their contemporaries, but their heirs should not inherit that honor. See T. Paine, *Common Sense and Other Political Writings* (New York: Putnam, 1983).

7. I use a common definition of *democracy* as a political system, in which those who govern a country are chosen in the course of a competitive election. From this standpoint, democracy is a political system in which the ruling party is not immune from defeat during the next election. See A. Przeworski and others, *Democracy and Development: Political Institutions and Well-Being in the World, 1950–1990* (Cambridge University Press, 2000).

8. Political regimes in which power is passed to a new ruler not on the grounds of rules adopted by the society, not as a rightful succession to the throne, not on the basis of democratic procedure, but rather by force, are called *authoritarian.* Under such regimes, political and civil rights and freedoms hold no sway.

9. It happened in Greece in 1973, in Portugal in 1974, and in Spain in the mid-1970s.

10. The Parliament Act of 1624 in England read, "He who does not have property is not free." See C. Hill, *The Century of Revolution: 1603–1714* (New York: W. W. Norton, 1982), p. 38.

11. S. P. Huntington, *The Third Wave: Democratization in the Twentieth Century* (University of Oklahoma Press, 1993), pp. 16–18.

12. On the succession of medieval establishments in Europe and the development of the concept of a free society, see B. Moore Jr., *Social Origins of Dictatorship and Democracy* (Boston: Beacon Press, 1967), p. 415.

13. K. De Schweinitz Jr., "Industrialization, Labor Controls and Democracy," *Economic Development and Cultural Change* 7, no. 4 (1959): 385–404.

14. A dialogue has come down to us from Thucydides regarding the stability of regimes based on violence that are not accepted by their subjects as legitimate. It is a discussion between the Melians and the Athenians. See Thucydides, *Istoriia* (Moscow: Ladomir; AST, 1999), pp. 344–49.

15. Machiavelli wrote in *The Prince*: "A power, which comes to light from heaven knows where, does not have roots and offshoots, just as everything in nature which grows too fast after it is born. That is why it perishes when bad weather strikes." See N. Makhiavelli, *Izbrannie* (Moscow: Ripol-Klassik, 1999), p. 385.

16. Jean-Jacques Rousseau, *Ob obshchestvennom dogovore: Traktaty* [The Social Contract: Treatises], trans. A. D. Khaiutin and V. S. Alekseiev-Popov (Moscow: KANON-Press; Kuchkovo pole, 1998), p. 18.

17. Classic works dedicated to the functioning of authoritarian regimes include J. Linz, "An Authoritarian Regime: Spain," in *Cleavages, Ideologies and Party Systems: Contributions to Comparative Political Sociology,* ed. E. Allardt and Y. Lettunen (Helsinki: Westermarck Society, 1964), vol. 10, pp. 292–343. See also S. N. Eisenstadt, *Modernization: Protest and Change* (Englewood Cliffs, N.J.: Prentice-Hall, 1966), p. 69.

18. The average life span of authoritarian regimes that had reached the end of their existence by the 1990s was 9.3 years. See Przeworski and others, *Democracy and Development,* p. 50.

19. A. C. Vacs, "Authoritarian Breakdown and Redemocratization in Argentina," in *Authoritarians and Democrats: Regime Transition in Latin America,* ed. J. M. Malloy and M. A. Seligson (University of Pittsburgh Press, 1987), pp. 15–42.

20. The Brazilian military regime that came to power after the coup of 1964 is typical of a government uncertain of its right to lead the country and compelled to solve "the problem of resignation." See S. R. D. Baretta and J. Markoff, "Brazil's Abertura: A Transition from What to What?" in ibid.

21. Olson, *Power and Prosperity,* p. 21.

22. E. Burke, *Reflections on the Revolution in France* (Chicago: Regnery, 1955), p. 92.

23. Gaidar, *Dolgoe vremia,* chap. 15.

24. A totalitarian regime is a political regime that strives to control all spheres of life in society. For specific features of totalitarian regimes see, for example, Minxin Pei, *From Reform to Revolution: The Demise of Communism in China and the Soviet Union* (Harvard University Press, 1994).

25. H. F. Cline, *The United States and Mexico* (Harvard University Press, 1963), p. 52; H. B. Parker, *A History of Mexico* (Boston: Houghton-Mifflin, 1950), p. 308.

26. A. G. Larin, *Dva prezidenta, ili Put' Taivania k demokratii* [Two Presidents, or Taiwan's Path to Democracy] (Moscow: Akademiia, 2000), p. 139.

27. K. Medhurst, "Spain's Evolutionary Pathway from Dictatorship to Democracy," in *The New Mediterranean Democracies: Regime Transition in Spain, Greece and Portugal,* ed. G. Pridham (London: Frank Cass, 1984), pp. 30, 31.

28. S. Kurtua, N. Vert, and others, *Chernaia kniga kommunizma. Prestupleniia, terror, repressii* [The Black Book of Communism: Crimes, Terror, Repression] (Moscow: Tri veka istorii, 1999), p. 433.

29. During student riots in Iran, to the question "Shall we use arms against them?" one of the officers of the shah's Revolutionary Guards answered, "No, we can't. After all, they are our children." See *New York Times,* December 4, 1961, p. 10, quoted in S. P. Huntington, *Political Order in Changing Societies* (Yale University Press, 1968), p. 211. Naturally we can raise the question whether the shah's regime in Iran was still authoritarian at that time. In form it was a traditional monarchy. But it is worth remembering that Shah Reza Pahlavi was not the scion of many generations of Iranian royalty.

30. "Creeping Revolt: Cuba," *Time,* January 7, 1957, p. 33.

31. R. H. Phillips, "Cuba Says Rebels Number Only 50," *New York Times,* March 2, 1957; H. L. Matthews, "Castro Rebels Gain in Face of Offensive by the Cuban Army," *New York Times,* June 9, 1957, pp. 1, 13; "Cuban Rebels," Interview with Fidel Castro by Andrew St. George, *Look,* February 4, 1958, p. 30; R. H. Phillips, "Castro's Power st Peak on Eve of Cuban Vote," *New York Times,* November 2, 1958, p. 4E; "Batista's Drive to Crush Rebels Called Failure," *New York Times,* July 2, 1958, p. 1; "Into the Third Year: Cuba," *Time,* December 1, 1958, p. 32.

32. Che Guevara, *Epizody revolutsionnoi voiny* [Episodes from a Revolutionary War] (Moscow: Voennoie izdatel'stvo Ministerstva oborony SSSR, 1974), pp. 210–17.

33. H. L. Matthews, "Rebel Strength Gaining in Cuba, but Batista Has the Upper Hand," *New York Times,* February 25, 1957; L. Huberman and P. M. Sweezy, *Cuba: Anatomy of a Revolution* (New York: Monthly Review Press, 1960), pp. 59–60.

34. W. H. Sullivan, *Mission to Iran* (New York: W. W. Norton, 1981), p. 156.

35. Przeworski and others, *Democracy and Development.*

36. J. B. DeLong, "International Financial Crises in the 1990s: The Analytics," November 2001 (www.j.-bradford-delong.net); R. Dornbusch, "A Primer on Emerging Market Crises," Working Paper 8326 (Cambridge, Mass.: National Bureau of Economic Research, 2001); M. Goldstein, "Structural Programs," Paper prepared for the NBER Conference on Economic and Financial Crises in Emerging Market Economies, Woodstock, Vermont, October 19–21, 2000.

37. J. Amuzegar, *Managing the Oil Wealth: OPEC's Windfalls and Pitfalls* (London: I. B. Tauris, 1999).

38. R. Benedict and O. G. Anderson, eds., *Violence and the State in Suharto's Indonesia* (Southeast Asia Program Publications, Cornell University, 2001); Hal Hill, "Indonesia: The Strange and Sudden Death of a Tiger Economy," *Development Studies* (Oxford) 28, no. 2 (2000): 117–39.

39. H. Binnedijk, ed., *Authoritarian Regimes in Transition* (Washington: Foreign Service Institute of the U.S. Department of State, 1987).

40. Quite a few people who worked in Cuban government organs after the revolution and who later emigrated told me that they had decided to leave their coun-

try after they understood that Cuba was of no interest to Castro. They saw his short-term plan as a means to launch an anti-American revolution in Latin America; it was a tool to destroy the United States within the framework of his long-term plan.

41. Walter Lippmann noted correctly, "There is nothing more important for a human being than to live in a community which can be governed; it is good if it can be self-governed; it is wonderful if it is well governed, but in any case–governed" (W. Lippmann, *New York Herald Tribune*, December 10, 1963). The last issue of the magazine *Vestnik Evropy* (The Herald of Europe) of January–April 1918, founded by N. Karamzin and continued by M. Stasulevich, clearly demonstrated the misunderstanding, typical among the Russian liberal intellegentsia, that the breakdown of an imperfect and corrupt regime might lead to the collapse of state institutions and chaos in society and the economy, making ordinary and imperfect yet normal life no longer possible. B. Nol'de, "Voprosy vnutrennei zhizni" [Questions of Inner Life], *Vestnik Evropy* (Petrograd) (January–April 1918): 374–96.

42. M. Weber, *Politik als Beruf* (Munich: Duncker and Humboldt, 1919).

43. On the difficulty of stabilizing democratic regimes after the crash of authoritarianism, see G. O'Donnell, P. C. Schmitter, and L. Whitehead, eds., *Transitions from Authoritarian Rule: Tentative Conclusions about Uncertain Democracies* (Johns Hopkins University Press, 1986).

44. J. Maravall, *The Transition to Democracy in Spain* (London: Croom Helm, 1982); D. Gilmour, *The Transformation of Spain: From Franco to the Constitutional Monarchy* (London: Quartet Books, 1985).

45. O'Donnell and Schmitter, *Transitions from Authoritarian Rule*, p. 41.

Chapter Three

1. J. H. Elliott, *Imperial Spain 1469–1716* (London: Edward Arnold, 1965), p. 174.

2. Martin de Azpilicueta, an economist connected to the School of Salamanca, was perhaps the first one in Europe to notice the connection between rising prices and the flow of gold and silver from America. See M. Grice-Hutchinson, *The School of Salamanca: Readings in Spanish Monetary Theory, 1544–1605* (Oxford: Clarendon Press, 1952), pp. 91–96. A classic work on the impact of gold from America on the Spanish economy is E. J. Hamilton's *American Treasure and the Price Revolution in Spain, 1501–1650* (Harvard University Press, 1934). Like many economic analyses of complex issues, it was much criticized. See, for example, J. O. Nadal, "La Revolución los Precios Españoles en el Sigio XVI," *Hispania* 19 (1959): 503–29.) A later analysis demonstrated that the price revolution of the late sixteenth and early seventeenth centuries depended not only on the importation of gold and silver from America. Beginning in the 1460s and the 1470s, Portugal was exporting Sudanese gold to Europe in large quantities. The total exports came to 17 tons from 1470 to 1500. See I. Wilks, "Wangara, Akan and the Portuguese in the Fifteenth and Sixteenth Centuries," in *Forests of Gold: Essays on the Akan and the Kingdom of Asante*, ed. I. Wilks (Ohio University Press, 1993), pp. 1–39. At the end of the fifteenth century, silver mining in southern Germany played a role in the considerable increase

of the silver supply in Europe. See J. Munro, "The Monetary Origins of the 'Price Revolution': South German Silver Mining, Merchant Banking, and Venetian Commerce, 1470–1540," Working Paper 8 (Department of Economics, University of Toronto, June 1990); R. B. Outhwaite, *Inflation in Tudor and Early Stuart England* (London: Macmillan, 1969); P. Burke, ed., *Economy and Society in Early Modern Europe: Essays from Annales* (London: Routledge & Kegan Paul, 1972). John Nef estimated the volume of silver production in southern Germany, Austria, Bohemia, Slovakia, and Hungary in the range of 80 to 90 tons a year in 1526–35. See J. Nef, "Silver Production in Central Europe, 1450–1618," *Journal of Political Economy* 49 (1941): 575–91. All these facts, the subject of an interesting economic-historical discussion, cannot overshadow the main issue: the connection between rising prices in Europe in the sixteenth and seventeenth centuries and the increase in supply of precious metals. See Grice-Hutchison, *The School of Salamanca,* p. 95.

3. On how government-regulated prices, a shortfall in the food supply, and the promotion of imports affected the development of agriculture in Spain, see V. Mau, "Uroki Ispanskoi imperii, ili lovushki resursnogo izobiliia" [Lessons from the Spanish Empire, or Traps in Resource Abundance], *Rossiia v global'noi politike,* no. 1 (2005): 12.

4. M. González de Cellorigo, *Memorial de la Política Necesari y útil Restauración a la República de España* (Valladolid, 1600); Grice-Hutchison, *The School of Salamanca.*

5. A. Ramirez, *Epístolario de Justo Lapsio y los españoles* (Madrid: Castalia, 1966), p. 374. Quoted from J. H. Elliott, *Spain and Its World, 1500–1700: Selected Essays* (Yale University Press, 1989), p. 25.

6. R. T. Davies, *The Golden Century of Spain, 1501–1621* (London: Macmillan, 1954), pp. 263, 264.

7. Elliott, *Imperial Spain 1469–1716.*

8. P. Kennedy, *The Rise and Fall of the Great Powers: Economic Change and Military Conflict from 1500 to 2000* (New York: Random House, 1987), p. 55.

9. The 1621 execution of Rodrigo de Calderon, who was hated by many in Spain, is a typical example. See Elliott, *Imperial Spain.*

10. Elliott, *Spain and Its World,* p. 25.

11. H. Trevor-Roper, *The Crisis of the Seventeenth Century* (New York: Liberty Fund, 1967), p. 51.

12. *World Development Indicators 2000* (Washington: World Bank, 2000).

13. For ways to define countries rich in natural resources, see J. D. Sachs and A. M. Warner, "Economic Convergence and Economic Policy," Working Paper 5039 (Cambridge, Mass.: National Bureau of Economic Research, 1995); A. Wood and K. Berger, "Exporting Manufactures: Human Resources, Natural Resources and Trade Policy," *Journal of Development Studies* 34, no. 1 (1997): 35–59; T. Gylfason, T. T. Herbertsson, and G. Zoega, "A Mixed Blessing: Natural Resources and Economic Growth," *Macroeconomic Dynamics* 3 (1999): 204–25; M. Syrquin and H. B. Chenery, "Patterns of Development, 1950 to 1983," Discussion Paper 41 (Washington: World Bank, 1989).

14. On problems faced by countries rich in natural resources in the course of securing stable economic development, see A. H. Gelb, *Windfall Gains: Blessing or*

Curse? (Oxford University Press, 1988); J. D. Sachs, and A. M. Warner, "Natural Resource Abundance and Economic Growth," Working Paper 5398 (Cambridge, Mass.: National Bureau of Economic Research, 1995); J. D. Sachs and A. M. Warner, "The Big Push, Natural Resource Booms and Growth," *Journal of Development Economics* 59 (1999): 43–76; Gylfason, Herbertsson, and Zoega, "A Mixed Blessing," pp. 204–25. G. Ranis, "The Political Economy of Development Policy Change," in *Politics and Policy Making in Developing Countries: Perspectives on the New Political Economy,* ed. G. M. Meier (San Francisco: ICS Press, 1991; D. Lal and H. Myint, *The Political Economy of Poverty, Equity and Growth* (Oxford: Clarendon Press, 1996).

15. X. Sala-i-Marin and A. Subramanian, "Addressing the Natural Resource Curse: An Illustration from Nigeria," Working Paper 9804 (Cambridge, Mass.: National Bureau of Economic Research, June 2003), p. 4.

16. Some try to prove that institutional weakness, a typical feature of many countries rich in natural resources, is the obstacle to their development. See T. L. Karl, *The Paradox of Plenty: Oil Booms and Petro-States* (University of California Press, 1997).

17. On problems faced by countries whose economy depends on market conditions for raw materials, see M. Cardenas and Z. Partow, "Oil, Coffee and the Dynamic Commons Problem in Colombia" (Washington: Inter-American Development Bank, Office of the Chief Economist, Research Network Document R-335, 1998).

18. As a rule, in countries rich in natural resources, tax revenues unrelated to redistribution of rent are lower than in countries of the same level of development that lack an abundance of natural resources; see Karl, *The Paradox of Plenty.* In Saudi Arabia, the largest oil-producing country in the world, over 90 percent of budget revenue comes from the production and export of oil. See *Kingdom of Saudi Arabia: Achievements of the Development Plans 1970–1986* (Riyadh: Ministry of Planning Press, 1986). The extent to which a state is capable of concentrating proceeds from sales of natural resources plays a significant role in political and economic development of a country rich in those resources. P. Sutela noted that it was difficult to place large reserves of cod, a natural resource of medieval Norway, at the disposal of the state. That explains the lack of problems stemming from the struggle for redistribution of rent in that nation. See P. Sutela, "Eto sladkoe slovo—konkurentosposobnost'" [That Sweet Word—Competitive], in *Pochemu Rossiia ne Finliandia: Sravnitel'nyj analiz konkurentosposobnosti* [Why Russia Is Not Finland: Comparative Analysis of Competitiveness], ed. A. Khelantera and S.-E. Ollus (Moscow: IEPP, 2004).

19. D. C. North, *Institutions, Institutional Change and Economic Performance* (Cambridge University Press, 1990). An Indonesian oil company that covertly financed the country's armed forces provides a clear illustration of how oil and mining companies act in countries without an established tradition of democratic institutions. See H. McDonald, *Suharto's Indonesia* (University of Hawaii Press, 1981).

20. On how an abundance of natural resources affects the quality of national institutions and slows the rates of development in countries so endowed, see Sala-i-Martin and Subramanian, "Addressing the Natural Resource Curse"; H. Mehlun, K. Moene, and R. Torvik, "Institutions and the Resource Curse"

(www.svt.ntnu.no/iso/Ragnar.Torvik/world economy7.pdf [2005]); E. H. Bulte, R. Damania, and R. T. Deacon, "Resource Abundance, Poverty and Development," in *World Development 2005* (www.econ.ucsb.edu/papers/wp21-03.pdf).

21. M. E. Saltykov-Shchedrin, *Sobraniie sochinenii* [Collected Works in 10 volumes] (Moscow: Izdatel'stvo "Pravda," 1988), vol. 7, *Za rubezhom* [Abroad], p. 19.

22. E. E. Leamer, H. Maul, S. Rodriguez, and P. K. Schott, "Does Natural Resource Abundance Increase Latin American Income Inequality?" *Journal of Development Economics* 59, no. 1 (1999): 3–42.

23. J. G. Williamson, "Growth, Distribution and Demography: Some Lessons from History," *Explorations in Economic History* 34, no. 3 (1998): 241–71.

24. A. Krueger, *Foreign Trade Regimes and Economic Development: Liberalization Attempts and Consequences* (Columbia University Press, 1978). On how the struggle for redistribution of rent influences the spread of corruption in countries rich in natural resources, see also A. Tornell and P. Lane, "Voracity and Growth," *American Economic Review* 89 (1999): 22–46; P. Mauro, "Corruption and Growth," *Quarterly Journal of Economics* 90 (1995): 681–712; C. Leite and V. Weidmann, "Does Mother Nature Corrupt? Natural Resources, Corruption and Economic Growth," Working Paper WP/99/85 (Washington: International Monetary Fund, 1999).

25. P. Collier and Hoffler, *Greed and Grievance in African Civil Wars* (Oxford University Press, 2004).

26. T. Gylfason, "Natural Resources; Education and Economic Development," *European Economic Review* 45 (2001): 851.

27. Mau, "Uroki Ispanskoi imperii."

28. J. Sachs and A. M. Warner, "Natural Resource Abundance and Economic Growth," in *Development Policies in Natural Resource Economies,* ed. J. Mayer, B. Chambers, and A. Farooq (Cheltenham-Northampton, U.K.: Edward Elgar, 1999), p. 26.

29. M. Corden and J. P. Neary, "Booming Sector and Dutch Disease Economics: A Survey," *Economic Journal* 92 (December 1982): 826–44; L. Kamas, "Dutch Disease Economics and the Colombian Export Boom," *World Development* (September 1986): 1177–98; G. A. Davies, "Learning to Love the Dutch Disease: Evidence from the Mineral Economies," *World Development* 23, no. 10 (1995): 1765–79; T. Gylfason, "Lessons from the Dutch Disease: Causes, Treatments and Cures," Working Paper 01/06 (Reykjavik: Institute of Economic Studies, August 2001); P. Krugman, "The Narrow Moving Band, the Dutch Disease and the Competitive Consequences of Mrs. Thatcher: Notes on Trade in the Presence of Scale Economies," *Journal of Development Economics* 27 (1987): 41–55. A. Moiseev, "Analysis of Influence of the 'Dutch Disease' and Taxation on Economic Welfare," Working Paper BSP/99/030 (Moscow: New Economic School, 1999); J. J. Struthers, "Nigerian Oil and Exchange Rates: Indicators of Dutch Disease," *Development and Change* 21, no. 2 (1990): 309–41; A. Jazayeri, *Economic Adjustment in Oil-Based Economies* (Aldershot, U.K.: Avebury, 1988).

30. These problems are particularly critical for Russia. Unlike the Arab states of the Persian Gulf, Russia is industrialized. Of course, Russia's processing industry is not highly competitive. That is why problems related to the Dutch disease are so serious. See P. Kadochnikov, S. Sinel'nikov-Murylev, and S. Chetverikov,

Importozameshcheniie v Rossiiskoi Federatsii v 1998–2002 gg. [Import Replacement in the Russian Federation, 1998–2002] (Moscow: IEPP, 2003).

31. J. D. Sachs and A. M. Warner, "The Curse of Natural Resources," *European Economic Review* 45 (2001): 827–38.

32. Gylfason, Herbertsson, and Zoega, "A Mixed Blessing"; T. Gylfason, *Natural Resources, Education and Economic Development,* paper presented at the 15th Annual Congress of the European Economic Association, Bolzano, August–September 2000.

33. T. Gylfason, "Natural Resources and Economic Growth: A Nordic Perspective on the Dutch Disease," Working Paper 167 (Helsinki: World Institute for Development Economics Research, October 1999).

34. R. Prebisch, "International Trade and Payments in an Era of Coexistence: Commercial Policy in Underdeveloped Countries," *American Economic Review* 49, no. 2 (May 1959): 251–73; *Economic Survey of Latin America and the Caribbean* (New York: United Nations, 1968); *La mano de obra y el desarrollo Económico de America Latina en los ultimos años,* Economic Commission for Latin America (New York: United Nations, 1964).

35. P. Cashin, C. J. McDermott, and A. Scott, "The Long-Run Behavior of Commodity Prices: Small Trends and Big Variability," Working Paper (Washington: International Monetary Fund, 2001).

36. I. Skeet, *OPEC: Twenty-Five Years of Prices and Politics* (Cambridge University Press, 1988), p. 195. On the specific nature of the raw materials industry, which complicates the need to cut production when market conditions are unfavorable, see E. T. Dowling and F. G. Hilton, "Oil in the 1980s: An OECD Perspective," in *The Oil Market in the 1980s: A Decade of Decline,* ed. S. Shojai and B. S. Katz (New York: Praeger, 1992), p. 77. For a ratio of capital and current expenses, and on the difficulties of cutting back production when global demand decreases, using copper mining as an example, see R. F. Mikesell, *The World Copper Industry. Structure and Economic Analysis* (Johns Hopkins University Press for Resources for the Future, 1957).

37. L. Pritchett, "Patterns of Economic Growth: Hills, Plateaus, Mountains and Plains," Policy Research Working Paper 1947 (Washington: World Bank, 1998); R. Marbo, "OPEC Behavior 1960–1998: A Review of the Literature," *Journal of Energy Literature* 4, no. 1 (June 1998): 3–27.

38. A. D. Brunner, "El Nino and World Primary Commodity Prices: Warm Water or Hot Air?" Working Paper (Washington: International Monetary Fund, 2000), p. 3.

39. D. K. Backus and M. J. Crucini, "Oil Prices and the Terms of Trade," Working Paper 6697 (Cambridge, Mass.: National Bureau of Economic Research, August 1998), p. 24.

40. J. D. Hamilton, "What Is an Oil Shock?" Working Paper 7755 (Cambridge, Mass.: National Bureau of Economic Research, 2000).

41. M. Falcoff, *Modern Chile 1970–1989: A Critical History* (New Brunswick, N.J.: Transaction, 1989).

42. Skeet, *OPEC,* pp. 157, 158.

43. E. Kanovsky, "Economic Implications for the Region and World Oil Market," in *The Iran-Iraq War: Impact and Implications,* ed. E. Karsh (London: Macmillan, 1989), p. 241.

44. E. Jadresic and R. Zahler, "Chile's Rapid Growth in the 1990s: Good Policies, Good Luck or Political Change?" Working Paper 00/153 (Washington: International Monetary Fund, 2000).

45. D. Rodrik, "Why Do More Open Economies Have Bigger Governments?" *Journal of Political Economy* 106, no. 5 (1998): 997–1032; J. Daniel, "Hedging Government Oil Price Risk," Working Paper (Washington: International Monetary Fund, 2001).

46. J. Amuzegar, *Managing the Oil Wealth: OPEC's Windfalls and Pitfalls* (London: I. B. Tauris, 2001), p. 12.

47. R. A. De Santis, "Crude Oil Price Fluctuation and Saudi Arabian Behavior," Working Paper 1014 (Kiel Institute for the World Economy, October 2000), p. 6.

48. D. Yergin, *The Prize: The Epic Quest for Oil, Money, and Power* (New York: Simon and Schuster, 1992).

49. Amuzegar, *Managing the Oil Wealth*, p. 24.

50. Ibid., p. 25.

51. Skeet, *OPEC*; P. N. Andreasian, *Neft' i arabskiie strany v 1927–1983 gg. Ekonomicheskii i sotsial'nyi analiz* (Moscow: Nauka, 1990), p. 80.

52. E. Penrose, "Oil and the International Economy: Multinational Aspects, 1900–1973," in *Oil in the World Economy*, ed. R. W. Ferrier and A. Fursenko (London: Routledge, 1989), p. 14.

53. Amuzegar, *Managing the Oil Wealth*, p. 28.

54. In the years since 1969 the average oil price, adjusted for inflation as of 2004, was $18.59 ($18.43 in 2000 prices) per barrel. The 1958 oil price was $16.00 per barrel (in 2004 dollars), and it was less than $13.00 per barrel by 1970 (in 2000 dollars, $15.00 and $12.00 respectively). See *Oil Price History and Analysis, 2004* (www.wtrg.com/prices.htm).

55. Yergin, *The Prize*, p. 567.

56. J. Darmstadter and H. H. Landsberg, "The Economic Background," in *The Oil Crisis*, ed. R. Vernon (New York: W. W. Norton, 1976), p. 31.

57. Skeet, *OPEC*, p. 86.

58. T. V. Rybczynski and G. F. Ray, "Historical Background to the World Energy Crisis," in *The Economics of the Oil Crisis*, ed. T. M. Rybczynski (London: Macmillan, 1976), p. 2.

59. R. B. Barsky and L. Kilian, "Do We Really Know That Oil Caused the Great Stagflation? A Monetary Alternative," Working Paper 8389 (Cambridge, Mass.: National Bureau of Economic Research, July 2001), pp. 5, 14.

60. L. A. Sobel, ed., *Energy Crisis*, vol. 1: *1969–1973* (New York: Facts on File, 1974), pp. 199–206.

61. Kanovsky, "Economic Implications," p. 231.

62. Karl, *The Paradox of Plenty*.

63. Andreasian, *Neft' i arabskiie strany*, pp. 124–30.

64. Dowling and Hilton, "Oil in the 1980s," p. 74.

65. Yousaf Hasan J. Mahhamad, "OPEC Strategies for the Monopoly Oil Profits," in *The Oil Market in the 1980s*, ed. Shojai and Katz, p. 37; P. Wickham, "Volatility of Oil Prices," Working Paper (Washington: International Monetary Fund, 1996).

66. Se-Hak Park, "Falling Oil Prices and Exchange Rate Fluctuation," in *The Oil Market in the 1980s,* ed. Shojai and Katz, p. 6.

67. Skeet, *OPEC,* pp. 207, 208.

68. Shojai and Katz, eds., *The Oil Market in the 1980s,* p. xiii.

69. Karl, *The Paradox of Plenty,* p. 32.

70. Amuzegar, *Managing the Oil Wealth,* p. 13.

71. In 1970, the oil deposits of Mexico were estimated at 4 billion barrels; in 1982 at 57 billion barrels. See Dowling and Hilton, "Oil in the 1980s," p. 76. On the rapid growth of the volume of confirmed oil reserves in Mexico in 1976–80, see also F. J. P. Bolio, "Petroleum and Political Change in Mexico," *Latin American Perspective* 9, no. 1: 65–78.

72. S. Everhart and R. Duval-Hernandez, "Management of Oil Windfalls in Mexico: Historical Experience and Policy Opinions for the Future," Policy Research Working Paper 2592 (Washington: World Bank, April 2001), p. 2.

73. R. E. Looney, *Economic Policymaking in Mexico: Factors Underlying the 1982 Crisis* (Duke University Press, 1985), p. 40.

74. O. Guzman, "PEMEX's Finances," in *Energy Policy in Mexico,* ed. O. Guzman and R. Gutierrez (Boulder, Colo.: Westview, 1988).

75. A. Tornell and P. Lane, "Are Windfalls a Curse? A Non-Representative Agent Model of the Current Account and Fiscal Policy," Working Paper 4839 (Cambridge, Mass.: National Bureau of Economic Research, 1994). For the connection between resource rent, the regime of a closed democracy, and the high degree of corruption in Mexico, see E. G. Davies, "The Mexican Experience," in *The Oil Market in the 1980s,* ed. Shojai and Katz, p. 45.

76. W. G. Chislett, "The Causes of Mexico's Final Crisis and the Lessons to Be Learned," ed. G. Philip, *Politics in Mexico* (Sydney: Croom Helm, 2001), pp. 1, 3.

77. Looney, *Economic Policymaking in Mexico,* p. 49.

78. R. M. Auty, "Large Resource-Abundant Countries Squander Their Size Advantage: Mexico and Argentina," in *Resource Abundance and Economic Development,* ed. R. M. Auty (Oxford University Press, 2004), pp. 208–23, 218; A. H. Gelb and associates, *Oil Windfalls: Blessing or Curse?* (Oxford University Press, 1988).

79. R. Hausmann, "Dealing with Negative Oil Shocks: The Venezuelan Experience in the Eighties," Working Paper 307 (Washington: Inter-American Development Bank, 1995), p. 12.

80. Everhart and Duval-Hernandez, "Management of Oil Windfalls in Mexico," p. 5.

81. Calculated using the World Bank's World Development Indicators online database (http://devdata.worldbank.org/dataonline/).

82. R. Hausman, "Venezuela's Growth Implosion: A Neo-Classical Story?" Working Paper (Kennedy School of Government, Harvard University, August 2001), pp. 1–11.

83. Karl, *The Paradox of Plenty,* p. 179.

84. Daniel, "Hedging Government Oil Price Risk."

85. On the reasons that motivate countries rich in natural resources to create stabilization funds, see P. Arrau and S. Claessen, "Commodity Stabilization Funds," Working Paper 835 (Washington: International Monetary Fund, January 1992).

86. U. Fasano, "Review of the Experience with Oil Stabilization and Savings Funds in Selected Countries," Working Paper WP/00/112 (Washington: International Monetary Fund, 2000), p. 3.

87. For problems faced by countries that create stabilization funds see Daniel, "Hedging Government Oil Price Risk," p. 12.

88. S. Montenegro, "Macroeconomic Risk Management in Nigeria: Dealing with External Shocks," *Macroeconomic Risk Management–Issues and Options,* Report 11983 (Washington: Western Africa Department, World Bank, 1994).

89. Karl, *The Paradox of Plenty,* p. 160.

90. Gylfason, "Natural Resources and Economic Growth," p. 33.

Chapter Four

1. V. A. Kozlov, *Massovye besporiadki v SSSR pri Khrushcheve i Brezhneve (1953–nachalo 1980-x gg.)* [Mass Riots in the USSR under Khrushchev and Brezhnev (1953–early 1980s)] (Novosibirsk: Sibirskii khronograf, 1999), p. 8.

2. *Prezidium TsK KPSS: 1954–1964* [Presidium of the Central Committee of the CPSU: 1954–1964]. *Chernovye protokol'nye zapisi zasedanii. Stenogrammy. Postanovleniia.* [Draft Minutes of Meetings. Transcripts. Resolutions], vol. 1, 2nd ed., edited by A. A. Fursenko (Moscow: POSSPEN, 2004), p. 702.

3. Message by Yu. Andropov (Chairman of the KGB under the Council of Ministers of the USSR) to the Central Committee of the CPSU, information analysis "On the nature and causes of negative behavior among high school and college students," December 12, 1976. Here and below we cite V. Bukovsky, who uses materials that at present are not publicly available. We quote them, relying on the trustworthiness of the author. I venture to use these materials because in my opinion the reputation of the person who published them allows me to have no doubt about their authenticity. In the quotes from archived documents of the Soviet period, original spelling and punctuation are used.

4. Memorandum by Yu. Andropov (Chairman of the KGB) to the CC of the CPSU, December 21, 1970, no. 3461-A, "An analysis of samizdat literature for 5 years" (RGANI [Rossiiskii Gosudarstvennyi Arkhiv Noveishei Istorii/Russian State Archive of Contemporary History], F. 89, Op. 55, D. 1, Ll. 2–4).

5. Memorandum by Yu. Andropov, about remarks on human rights in the USSR made by the leaders of the French and Italian communist parties, December 29, 1975, no. 3213-A (www.2ntl.com/archive/pdfs/dis70/kgb75-9.pdf).

6. Kozlov, *Massovye besporiadki,* pp. 401, 404.

7. Address of General Secretary of the CC of the CPSU L. I. Brezhnev to the Plenum of the CC of the CPSU on December 15, 1969: "The principal task of the long-term development of our economy is to rapidly increase efficiency (by roughly 2–2.5 times) in the use of existing labor and material resources and to create new resources. This is the only possible path for us." See RGANI, F. 2, Op. 3, D. 168, P. 11688, L. 42.

8. Resolution of the Central Committee and the Council of Ministers USSR of October 4, 1965, "On the perfection of planning and increasing economic stim-

uli of industrial production," in *Resheniia partii i pravitel'stva po khoziaistvennym voprosam* [Resolutions of the Party and the Government on Economic Issues] (Moscow: Politizdat, 1968), vol. 5, pp. 658–85.

9. E. Ermakov, "Vzgliad v proshloie i budushcheie" [View into the Past and the Future], *Pravda*, January 8, 1988.

10. V. M. Kudrov, *Sovetskaia ekonomika v retrospective* [The Soviet Economy in Retrospect] (Moscow: Nauka, 2003), p. 19.

11. Ye. Gaidar and O. Latsis, "Po karmanu li traty?" [Are the Expenditures Affordable?] *Kommunist*, no. 17 (1988): 26–30. In this chapter and later I use my own articles, published in the magazine *Kommunist*, as the original source for quotations. Under a resolution by the party leadership, first the Central Statistics Department of the USSR, then the State Committee on Statistics of the USSR was instructed to check all statistical data published in *Kommunist*. In this connection, the statistics in *Kommunist* of that time are just as reliable on the situation in the country as the publications of the USSR official organs of statistics.

12. Speech by M. S. Gorbachev, "On the Five-Year Plan for Economic and Social Development of the USSR for 1986–1990 and the Tasks of the Party Organizations in Its Realization," June 16, 1986, in *Resheniia partii i pravitel'stva po khoziaistvennym voprosam* [Resolutions of the Party and the Government on Economic Issues] (Moscow: Politizdat, 1988), vol. 16, part 2, pp. 323, 324.

13. Transcript of the session of the Presidium of the CC of the CPSU on December 23, 1963, *Prezidium TsK KPSS. 1954–1964. Chernovye protokol'nye zapisi zasedanii. Stenogrammy. Postanovleniia* [Draft Minutes of Meetings. Transcripts. Resolutions], vol. 1, 2nd ed., p. 794.

14. Resolution of the CC of the CPSU and the Council of Ministers of the USSR of October 23, 1984, "On a long-term program of land reclamation, improving efficiency of reclaimed land with the purpose of increasing the country's food supply" (transcript), *Resheniia partii i pravitel'stva po khoziaistvennym voprosam* [Resolutions of the Party and the Government on Economic Issues], vol. 15, part 2, p. 113.

15. "In the period 1986–88, over a million hectares of reclaimed land were added annually. Capital investments for that project, including construction of industrial facilities, came to 8 billion rubles. However, a large part of the reclaimed irrigated land was in the zone with an insufficient water supply; for that reason, each year almost a million hectares were not irrigated and were used instead for dry farming. In addition, poor maintenance of irrigation systems and installations, as well as excessive irrigation, led to high soil salinity and turned much of the land into swamp. Today, high salinity is found in one-fifth of the reclaimed land. Large areas of reclaimed land were unusable and had to be written off. For this reason, from 1986 to 1988, about 2 million hectares were removed from agricultural use in the country. . . . The increase in the cost of reclamation, accompanied by low production output, resulted in the rapid decrease of economic effectiveness of irrigated and drained land." See Main Department for Planning and Socioeconomic Development of the Agro-Industrial Complex, "The Socioeconomic Development of Gosagroprom in 1988 and for Three Years of the Twelfth Five-Year Plan," January 20, 1989 (RGAE, F. 650, Op. 1, D. 3848, L. 9).

16. O. Latsis, *Chto s nami bylo, chto s nami budet* [What Has Happened to Us, What Will Happen to Us] (Moscow: Izdatel'stvo "Evraziia," 1995), p. 37.

17. See GARF, November 17, 1988. F. 5446, Op. 149, D. 727, Ll. 137–48.

18. M. Feschbach and A. Friendly, *Ekotsid v SSSR: Zdorovie i priroda na osadnom polozhenii* [Ecocide in the USSR: Health and the Environment under Siege] (Moscow, 1992); A. Yu. Pidzhakov, *Sovetskaia ekologicheskaia politika 1970s-nachala 1990s* [Soviet Ecological Policy] (St. Petersburg: Izdatel'stvo Sankt-Peterburgskogo universiteta ekonomiki i finansov, 1994); L. A. Fedorov and A. V. Yablokov, *Pesticides: The Chemical Weapon That Kills Life (The USSR's Tragic Experience)* (Moscow: Pensoft, 2004); F. L. Yanshin and F. I. Melua, *Uroki ekologicheskikh proschetov* (Moscow: Mysl', 1991).

19. Fedorov and Yablokov, *Pesticides.*

20. RGANI, F. 3, Op. 12, D. 1005, Ll. 21–23, quoted from *Prezidium TsK KPSS. 1954–1964*, vol. 2, 2nd ed., p. 160.

21. G. G. Zaigraiev, "Proschety lobovoi ataki, ili pochemu poterpela neudachu antialkogol'naia kampaniia?" [Errors of a Frontal Attack, or Why the Anti-Alcohol Campaign Failed], *Vestnik Akademii Nauk*, no. 8 (1991): 30, 34.

22. Address of General Secretary of the CC of the CPSU to the Plenum of the CC of the CPSU on December 15, 1969 (RGANI, F. 2, Op. 3, D. 168, P. 11688, L. 58).

23. B. M. Levin and M. B. Levin, "Alkogol'naia reforma v SSSR: uspekhi, problemi, trudnosti" [Alcohol Reform in the USSR: Successes, Problems, Difficulties], in *Effektivnost' alkogol'noi reformi: nekotoryie sotsiologicheskiie aspekty* [The Effectiveness of Alcohol Reform: Some Sociological Aspects], International Conference, Baku, November 1–3, 1988 (Moscow: Institut Sotsiologii AN SSSR, 1988), p. 3.

24. N. K. Baibakov, *Sorok let v pravitel'stve* [Forty Years in Government] (Moscow: Respublika, 1993), pp. 123, 124.

25. For a link between the termination of the mass terror and increasing inefficiency of the Soviet economic-political system, see A. Dallin, "Causes of the Collapse of the USSR," *Post-Soviet Affairs* 8, no. 4 (1992): pp. 282, 283.

26. This term was introduced for the first time by V. Naishul in an unpublished manuscript. Subsequently, it was widely used in economic literature on late socialism. See, for example, P. O. Aven and V. M. Shironin, "Reforma khoziaistvennogo mekhanizma: Real'nost' namechaiemykh preobrazovanii" [Reform of the Economic Mechanism: Reality of Intended Transformations], *Izvestiia Sibirskogo otdeleniia Akademii Nauk SSSR* (Ekonomika i prikladnaia sotsiologiia [Economics and Applied Sociology] series) 3, no. 13 (1987).

27. Ye. Gaidar, *Ekonomicheskiie reformy i ierarkhicheskie struktury* [Economic Reforms and Hierarchical Structures], edited by S. S. Shatalin (Moscow: Nauka, 1990), p. 44.

28. On bargaining in the Soviet economy in the 1930s over which information was disclosed when the Soviet materials were declassified, see P. R. Gregory, ed., *Behind the Façade of Stalin's Command Economy* (Stanford, Calif.: Hoover Institution Press, 2001).

29. On incentives and privileges offered to workers in competing enterprises, see L. A. Voronin (Deputy Chairman of Gosplan) to the Council of Ministers, on

the organization of work to improve financial management (GARF, February 23, 1984, F. 5446, Op. 144, D. 3, L. 44).

30. W. Easterly and S. Fisher, "The Soviet Economic Decline," *World Bank Economic Review* 9, no. 3 (1995): 341–72.

31. Sovietologists believe that, for ten years beginning in the 1950s, GNP declined at an average annual rate of about 1 percent (from 6 percent in the 1950s to 4 percent in the 1970s); they expected that trend to continue in the future. See F. G. Whitehouse and D. R. Kazmer, "Output Trends: Prospects and Problems," in *The Future of the Soviet Economy: 1978–1985*, edited by H. Hunter (Boulder, Colo.: Westview, 1978), p. 9.

32. V. A. Medvedev, *V komande Gorbacheva. Vzgliad iznutri* [On Gorbachev's Team: The Inside View] (Moscow: Bylina, 1994), pp. 6, 7.

33. E. Chazov, chief of the fourth department of the Ministry of Healthcare, who was directly responsible for the health of Soviet leaders, would later write: "In the end the country lost its leadership, not just their ability to solve different urgent organizational problems, but those whose responsibility it was to secure the future development and welfare of society. . . . No need to delve into the cause of the crisis. It is sufficient to know that A. N. Kirilenko, who was nice and pleasant in personal contacts and who, according to our data, suffered from progressive cortical atrophy, about which we repeatedly informed the CC of the CPSU, was elected the third most powerful person in the Party. . . . From the time of the XXV Party Congress, I observed Brezhnev's inability to function as a statesman and the political leader of the country, which led to the emerging crisis of the Party and the country. . . . Today it is difficult to remember how many official messages about Brezhnev's health were sent to the Politburo during the last six to seven years of his life. Perhaps they are stored in some archive. However, Andropov had good reason to be calm: not only was there no reaction to any of the letters, but none of the Politburo members displayed any interest whatsoever in the information they contained." See E. Chazov, *Zdorovie i vlast': Vospominaniia "kremliovskogo vracha"* [Health and the Regime; Memoirs of a "Kremlin Doctor"] (Moscow: Izdatel'stvo "Novosti," 1992), pp. 117, 144, 149.

34. Ya. Kornai, *Ekonomika defitsita* [Deficit Economy] (Moscow: Ekonomika, 1990).

35. K. Marx, "Vosemnadtsatoie briumera Lui Bonaparta" [Eighteenth Brumaire of Louis Bonaparte], in *Collected Works of K. Marx and F. Engels*, 2nd ed. (Moscow: Gospolitizdat, 1961), vol. 16, p. 377.

36. On the role of modern agricultural methods as a prerequisite for industrialization, see, for example, D. G. Johnson, "Role of Agriculture in Economic Development Revisited," *Agricultural Economics* 8 (1993): 421–34.

37. D. G. Johnson, "Agricultural Performance and Potential in the Planned Economies: Historical Perspective," Paper 97 (1) (Office of Agricultural Economic Research, University of Chicago, March 21, 1997), pp. 3, 4.

38. N. S. Khrushchev, "Stroitel'stvo kommunisma v SSSR i razvitie sel'skogo khoziaistva" [Construction of Communism in the USSR and the Development of Agriculture], *Rechi i documenty v 5-ti tomakh* [Speeches and Documents in five volumes] (Moscow: Gospolitizdat, 1962), vol. 1, p. 155.

39. Memorandum from Khrushchev to the Presidium of the CC of the CPSU on January 22, 1954, in ibid., pp. 85, 86.

40. I. E. Zelenin, "Pervaia sovetskaia programma massovogo osvoieniia tselinnykh zemel' (konets 20-x-30-e gody)" [The First Soviet Program of Mass Exploitation of Virgin Lands (late 1920s–1930s), *Otechestvennaia istoriia*, no. 2 (1966): 55, 65.

41. Khrushchev, *Rechi i documenty*, vol. 2, pp. 506, 507; vol. 3, pp. 7, 347, 351.

42. "Sel'skoe khoziastvo SSSR" [USSR Agriculture], *Statisticheskii sbornik* (Moscow: Finansy i statistika, 1988); "Narodnoe khoziaistvo SSSR v 1979g" [USSR Economy in 1979], *Statisticheskii sbornik* (Moscow: Statistika, 1980).

43. On the unprecedented increase in agricultural investment in the Soviet Union between 1960 and 1980, see D. G. Johnson, "Agriculture," in *The Soviet Union Today: An Interpretive Guide*, edited by J. Cracraft (University of Chicago Press, 1983), pp. 195–207. In comparison with the five-year plan of 1961–65, investment in agriculture grew by 62 percent. See P. Hanson, *The Rise and Fall of the Soviet Economy* (London: Longman, 2003), p. 112.

44. I. E. Zelenin, "Agrarnaia politika N. S. Khrushcheva i sel'skoe khoziaistvo strany" [Khrushchev's Agrarian Policy and the Country's Agriculture], *Otechestvennaia istoriia*, no. 1 (2000): 84.

45. Johnson, "Agriculture," p. 5.

46. Ye. Gaidar and O. Latsis, *"Po karmanu li traty?" Kommunist* no. 17 (1988): 26–30.

47. UN Food and Agriculture Organization, FAOSTAT data, 2005.

48. G. Shakhnazarov, *S vozhdiami i bez nikh* [With Rulers and without Them] (Moscow: Vagrius, 2001), pp. 109, 110.

49. O. Latsis, "Lomka, ili koe-chto o prirode tsen" [Breakage, or a Few Things about the Nature of Prices], *Izvestiia*, May 7, 1991.

50. "Address of General Secretary of the CC of the CPSU Comrade L. I. Brezhnev to the Plenum of the CC of the CPSU on December 15, 1969" (RGANI, F. 2, Op. 3, D. 168, P. 11688, Ll. 49–50).

51. By the end of the 1980s, the share of subsidies allocated to support retail prices of agricultural products was 10–12 percent of the GNP. See *Food and Agricultural Policy Reforms in the Former USSR: An Agenda for the Transition* (Washington: World Bank, 1992).

52. "On the brink of the '50s and the '60s, authorities were caught in a vicious circle. It was impossible to solve economic problems without stirring up indignation among the citizens, without creating conditions for the rise of opposing sentiments, without provoking comparisons that were disadvantageous for the authorities between the declared goals of the Party (the building of communism, and so on) and the bleak realities of the economy. The imbalance between wages and prices of consumer goods, particularly food, caused to some extent by concessions to workers in the second half of the '50s, made the traditional Soviet problem of the deficit more acute. As prices for agricultural products fell and wages increased, the deficit approached disaster and prompted grumbling disapproval." See Kozlov, *Massovye bezporiadki*, p. 231.

53. *Prezidium TsK KPSS. 1954–1964*, pp. 176–77.

54. In a conversation between G. Sokolnikov and N. Bukharin on June 11, 1928, Bukharin said: "Stalin's policy leads to civil war. He will have to drown the uprising in blood." At the joint Plenum of the CC of the CPSU and the CCC (the Central Control Commission) of the All-Union Communist Party (Bolsheviks), April 16–23, 1929, A. Mikoyan said: "The Georgian uprising served as a spur of Bukharin's fall over a peasant issue in 1925. Bukharin took the Georgian uprising for Russia's second Kronshtadt signal." See *Kak lomali NEP: Stenogrammy plenumov TsK VKP(b), 16–23 aprelia 1929 goda* [How NEP Was Destroyed: Transcripts of the Plenums of the Central Committee of the All-Russian Communist Party, April 16–23, 1929], 5 vols., edited by A. N. Yakovlev (Moscow: MFD, 2000), vol. 4, pp. 563, 241.

55. I. Matiukha (Chief of the Budget Statistics Division of the Central Statistics Department) to the CC of the CPSU, on the analysis of an ordinary person's budget for nine months of 1962 and the influence of higher retail prices of meat, meat products, and butter on a family budget, December 21, 1962 (RGANI, F. 5, Op. 20, D. 310, Ll. 122, 125–28).

56. D. Mandel', "Novocherkassk 1–3 iiunia 1962. Zabastovka i rasstrel" [Novocherkassk June 1–3, 1962: Strike and Execution], *Rossia*, no. 11–12 (1998): 160; I. Mardar', *Khronika neob"iavlennogo ubiistva* [Chronicle of an Unannounced Murder] (Novocherkassk: Press-Servis, 1992).

57. V. E. Semichastnyi, "Novocherkasskaia tragedia, 1962" [The Novocherkassk Tragedy, 1962], *Istoricheskii arkhiv*, no. 4 (1993): 170.

58. On problems that the Soviet leadership has faced since Khrushchev's time, linked to the policy of stable prices of consumer goods, see J. R. Millar, "An Economic Overview," in *The Soviet Union Today: An Interpretive Guide*, edited by J. Cracraft (University of Chicago Press, 1983), pp. 173–86.

59. "In 1961–1985 the money stock (M2) grew by 10 percent annually. At the beginning of the '60s the rate of growth of the nominal gross national product lagged behind the rate of growth of the money stock by approximately 1.5 times, in the second half of the '60s, and particularly in the '70s by two times, and in the first half of the '80s by three times. A large infusion of money into the economy was reflected in the rapid growth of the ratio of M2 to the gross national product. If in 1961 the aggregate M2 was 22.8 percent of the GNP, in 1970 it was 29.5 percent, and in 1980 44.2 percent. It reached 52.6 percent in 1984. By 1980 the level of prices at *kolkhoz* markets, for a comparable list of products, was 2.57 times state retail prices." See A. Illarionov, *Popytki provedenia politiki finansovoi stabilizatsii v SSSR i v Rossii* [Attempts to Implement a Policy of Financial Stabilization in the USSR and in Russia], 1995 (www.budgetrf.ru/Publications/Magazines/Ve/1995/95-7illarionov/95-7illarionov000.htm). *Kolkhoz* markets were just a small part of the Soviet consumer market. In its other segments, a larger money supply resulted in a commodity deficit.

60. A. Voronov, "O problemakh preodoleniia defitsita i metodakh regulirovaniia potrebitel'skogo rynka" [On the Problems of Overcoming Deficit and Methods of Regulating the Consumer Market], *Voprosy ekonomiki*, no. 1 (1990): 26–32.

61. On the Soviet leadership's understanding of the need for profound changes in the system of price setting and their unwillingness to change the prices of basic

consumer goods, see V. A. Kriuchkov, *Lichnoe delo* [Personal File] (Moscow: Olimp AST, 1996), part 1, pp. 271, 272.

62. B. I. Gostev (Minister of Finance), M. A. Korolev (Chairman of Goskomstat), and V. S. Pavlov (Chairman of Goskomtsen) to the Council of Ministers, on the dynamics of retail prices for food and other products, November 4, 1988 (GARF, F. 5446, Op. 149, D. 304, L. 18).

63. A. Shokhin, A. Guzanova, and L. Liberman, "Tseny glazami naseleniia" [Prices through the Eyes of the Populace], *Literaturnaia gazeta*, no. 37 (1988): 11.

64. Appendix to paragraph 9c of executive order no. 250, K. Yu. Chernenko to the CC of the CPSU, on letters from workers on some issues regarding the supply of bread to the public and the need to be frugal with bread resources, February 17, 1981 (RGANI, F. 89, Op. 43, D. 58, Ll. 4–7).

65. From minutes no. 28a, meetings on July 9 and 12, 1956, dedicated to the situation in Poland: "To give them all the goods, and jute and wool. If they want to have gold, we shall give them gold." Quoted from *Prezidium TsK KPSS. 1954–1964*, p. 148 (RGANI, F. 3, Op. 12, D. 1005, Ll. 1–2 ob.).

66. *Prezidium TsK KPSS. 1954–1964*, p. 778.

67. R. G. Pikhoia, *Sovetskii Soiuz; istoriia vlasti 1945–1991* [The Soviet Union: History of Power] (Moscow: RAGS, 1988), p. 370. The problems linked to the decrease of the gold reserve were discussed by the Presidium of the CC of the CPSU as early as 1956. See *Prezidium TsK KPSS. 1954–1964*, p. 118.

68. *Prezidium TsK KPSS. 1954–1964*, p. 769.

69. Pikhoia, *Sovetskii Soiuz*, p. 370.

70. "Import of Grain: Old and New Problems" (1989), from Ye. T. Gaidar's archive.

71. M. Chadwick, D. Long, and M. Nissanke, *Soviet Oil Exports: Trade Adjustments, Refining Constraints and Market Behavior* (Oxford, U.K.: Oxford Institute for Energy Studies, 1987), pp. 91, 95, 105, 107.

72. V. Kriuchkov writes: "The United States so far can do fairly well without us, but our cursed dependence on their grain has made us, the Soviet Union . . . , a hostage of these relations." See Kriuchkov, *Lichnoe delo*, part 2, p. 95.

73. V. P. Muravlenko, Yu. B. Fain, and others, eds. *Neft' Sibiri* (Moscow: Nedra, 1973), p. 13.

74. M. V. Slavkina, *Triumf i tragediia: razvtie neftegazovogo kompleksa SSSR v 1960–1980-e gody* [Triumph and Tragedy: The Development of the Oil and Gas Complex of the USSR in the 1960s–1980s] (Moscow: Nauka, 2002), pp. 45,70.

75. N. Eronin remembers: "He could brazenly challenge a top executive: 'You are an adventurer. Where are you leading the country? Do you think about the consequences of your proposals?' " See "K 85-letiiu so dnia rozhdeniia V. D. Shashina. Materialy ubileinoi konferentsii" [For the 85th Birthday of V. D. Shashin. Materials of a Jubilee Conference, Moscow, June 22, 2001] (Moscow, 2002), pp. 38, 39.

76. Interview with V. I. Graifer, quoted in Slavkina, *Triumf i tragediia*, p. 143.

77. Kudrov, *Sovetskaia ekonomika v retrospective*, p. 31.

78. In 1977 the CIA published a report that predicted the beginning of a decline in oil production in the USSR in the 1980s. See *The International Energy Situation:*

Outlook to 1985 (Washington: Central Intelligence Agency, April 1977); *Prospects for Soviet Oil Production* (Washington: Central Intelligence Agency, April 1977).

79. On the role of oil proceeds during this temporary conquest of the key contradiction in the Soviet economy—the growing demand for foodstuffs for the urban population and the chronic crisis of agricultural production—see Millar, "An Economic Overview," pp. 173–86.

80. At the session of the Politburo on March 17, 1979, N. Kosygin summed up the results: "We have a unanimous opinion that we cannot give away Afghanistan." However, on March 18, after his conversation with N. Taraki, during which the Afghan leader posed a direct question about the need to bring Soviet troops into Afghanistan immediately, the mood changed. It was clear that it was not simply a question of military-technical and economic aid, but also of the use of Soviet troops. After that A. Gromyko said: "I fully support Comrade Andropov's proposal to rule out bringing our troops into Afghanistan. Their army is unreliable. If we do that, our army will enter Afghanistan as an aggressor. Against whom will it fight? First, it will fight against the Afghan people, and it will be the people whom they will have to shoot at." Yu. Andropov: "I think we should not approve a decision to bring in our troops. To bring in our troops will mean fighting against the people, suppressing the people, shooting at the people. We will look like aggressors, we cannot permit that." See RGANI, F. 89, Op. 25, D. 2, Ll. 10, 15, 24.

All of the above is true, but that did not prevent the Politburo in December 1979 from passing a resolution to send four divisions and four brigades, totaling 150,000 servicemen, into Afghanistan. See V. Bukovskii, *Moskovskii protsess* [Moscow Trial] (Paris, Moscow: Russkaia Mysl', "MIK," 1996), part 2, p. 49 (www. belousenko.com/wrBukovsky.htm). The final decision was made at the meeting conducted by L. Brezhnev on December 26, 1979 (RGANI, F. 89, Op. 25, D. 2, Ll. 1, 2). In accordance with a resolution of the Politburo of January 8, 1980, after the Soviet troops entered Afghanistan, the armed forces of the USSR added 50,000 servicemen to their ranks. See Resolution of the CC of the CPSU and the Council of Ministers of the USSR of January 2, 1980, "About the increase in size of the Armed Forces of the USSR," minutes no. 177 of the session of the Politburo of the CC of the CPSU on January 2, 1980, no. П177\239 (www.2ntl.com/archive/pdfs/afgh/ 177-80-2.pdf). The decision to send troops into Afghanistan would cost the Soviet regime dearly up until the last years of its existence. Privates and officers killed in Afghanistan, their grieving families, the injured—all that against the background of the war, incomprehensible for Soviet society, was an important factor that undermined the fundamentals of the regime's legitimacy. In addition, the war was costly. From the message to the CC: "With the purpose of replenishing ministry losses in the Afghan armed forces, of reinforcing their capability to ward off the onslaught of the implacable opposition . . . a proposal is made to provide special supplies to Afghanistan in 1989 at a cost of about 990 million rubles (of which 200 million rubles worth of tanks, guns, and aircraft will become available through unilateral arms reduction and armaments subject to destruction). The Soviet government found it possible to deliver to Afghanistan in 1989 special supplies at 0.99 billion rubles on top of the previously allocated supplies in 1989 valued at 2.6 billion rubles. . . . Deliveries of special supplies are expected to be made on the previously accepted terms, that is to say, the payment of 25 percent of the cost on credit for 10 years, with annual two percent interest." Minutes of the session of the Politburo of the CC of the CPSU of July 22, 1989, on additional special supplies to the Republic of Afghanistan (RGANI, F. 89, Op. 10, D. 39).

From a memorandum by E. Shevardnadze and V. Kriuchkov of August 11, 1989: "The decision to reinforce the strength of the existing regime requires further broad comprehensive support to the government and president of Afghanistan, including material aid. . . . It will be necessary to help the Afghan friends with foodstuffs, wheat grain in particular, for the armed forces and the population of Kabul. Since the reserve of wheat grain in Hairaton is almost depleted, it is urgently necessary to deliver 15,000 tons of wheat grain there as part of our aid to Afghanistan." Minutes of a session of the Politburo of the CC of the CPSU on August 16, 1989, on the talks in Kabul and possible further actions in regard to Afghanistan (RGANI, F. 89, Op. 10, D. 46).

81. "As estimated by the Chase Manhattan Bank, the balance-of-payments deficit of the Communist bloc countries increased from \$5 billion in 1974 to \$12 billion currently. Out of the entire sum of the general deficit about half is the Soviet Union's share. . . . As estimated by Chase Manhattan Bank, this year the USSR has sold gold valued at \$1 billion; also, its hard currency deposits in Western banks decreased by \$2 billion." The same memorandum states that U.S. banks were reluctant to provide credit to the socialist countries. See letter from K. Nazarkin (Chairman of the Board of the Ministry of Foreign Economic Relations) to Comrade M. A. Lesechko, December 25, 1975 (GARF, F. 5446, Op. 109, D. 60, Ll. 37–39).

82. As early as the 1980s experts were aware of the risks to the oil market of dependence on grain and processing industry equipment imports. See Chadwick, Long, and Nissanke, *Soviet Oil Exports.*

83. N. K. Baibakov, *Sorok let v pravitel'stve* (Moscow: Respublika, 1993), pp. 129–34. "Since we could not fit within the bounds of the old pattern of financing, we had to resort to new, 'nontraditional' methods: money deposited by the general population in savings banks and money from the accounts of enterprises were partially withdrawn and spent for budget needs" (p. 134).

84. G. Crossman, "Roots of Gorbachev's Problems: Private Income and Outlay in the Late 1970s/Gorbachev's Economic Plans," Joint Economic Committee Study Papers, U.S. Congress, vol. 1 (Washington, November 23, 1987), pp. 213–29.

85. On the distribution of aid from the USSR to foreign Communist parties, see minutes no. 8 of the session of the Politburo of the CC of the CPSU of June 24, 1966 (RGANI, F. 89, Op. 51, D. 25, L. 1); minutes no. 73 of the session of the Politburo of the CC of the CPSU of March 4, 1968 (RGANI, F. 89, Op. 51, D. 27, L. 1); excerpt from the minutes no. 230 of the session of the Politburo of the CC of the CPSU of December 29, 1980, no. П230/34 (RGANI, F. 89, Op. 38, D. 47, L. 1). On the request of the Socialist Party of Japan, see excerpt from minutes no. 37, paragraph 46гс of the session of the Secretariat of the CC of the CPSU of October 31, 1967, no. Cт-37/46 (www.2ntl.com/archive/pdfs/non-comm.ct037-67.pdf).

86. Excerpt from minutes no. 225, paragraph 84гс of the Secretariat of the CC (no. Cт-225/84), August 26, 1980 (RGANI, F. 89, Op. 43, D. 26, L. 1).

87. Memorandum from A. Cherniaiev (Deputy Chief of the International Division of the CC of the CPSU) to the CC of the CPSU, December 12, 1980 (RGANI, F. 89, Op. 46, D. 78, L. 2).

88. Excerpt from minutes no. 94 of the session of the Politburo of the CC of the CPSU on January 18, 1983, no. П94/52 (RGANI, F. 89, Op. 51, D. 33, L. 1).

89. The CC of the CPSU, excerpt from the minutes of the session of the Politburo of the CC of the CPSU of November 30, 1987, on the International Division of the CC of the CPSU (RGANI, F. 89, Op. 38, D. 54).

90. Information for the fraternal parties, March 7, 1982. The information about an official visit of the party-government delegation of the Polish People's Republic, headed by W. Jaruzelski, to Moscow on March 1–2, 1982, was presented by Tomasz Mianovicz (www/2ntl.com/archive/pdfs/poland/pol-gdr82.pdf); Resolution of the Secretariat of the CC of the CPSU no. CT-231/5c of October 4, 1980, "About additional measures for organizing propaganda and counter-propaganda in connection with the events in Poland" (RGANI, F. 89, Op. 46, D. 59, Ll. 4–7); Resolution of the Secretariat of the CC of the CPSU no. 242/61гc of December 22, 1980, "About additional measures on oversight of the distribution of Polish printed mass media in the USSR" (RGANI, F. 89, Op. 46, D. 81, Ll. 1–26).

91. The data are drawn from statistical collections for various years, "The People's Economy of the USSR." I am not sure these data are accurate. The official Soviet statistical data in such a sensitive sphere could have been deliberately distorted. However, the given numbers reflect a general picture of the development of events and the speedy growth of oil exports.

92. Memorandum from Yu. Andropov (Chairman of the KGB under the Council of Ministers) to General Secretary of the CC of the CPSU L. Brezhnev, on the secret meeting of a KGB agent with V. Haddad in Lebanon, April 23, 1974, no, 1071-A/OB (www.2ntl.com/archive/pdfs/terr-wd/plo75a.pdf). In another letter to L. Brezhnev about the supply of arms to the People's Liberation Front of Palestine, Andropov called Haddad an agent of the KGB; see a memorandum from Yu. Andropov (Chairman of the KGB under the Council of Ministers) to General Secretary of the CC of the CPSU L. Brezhnev, on handing over a consignment of foreign arms and ammunition to V. Haddad, May 16, 1975, no. 1218-A/OB (www.2ntl.com/archive/pdfs/terr-wd/plo75d.pdf).

93. P. Schweitzer, *Victory: The Reagan Administration's Secret Strategy That Hastened the Collapse of the Soviet Union* (New York: Atlantic Monthly Press, 1994), p. 218.

94. "International solidarity in general and friendship with the Soviet Union in particular are great things all by themselves, but they are especially strong when they are reinforced through supplies of Soviet oil at prices three to four times lower than those on the world market. I happened to hear Nicolae Ceausescu emotionally reproach the Soviet leadership for annually supplying only 5–6 million tons of Soviet oil to Rumania while other countries got two to three times as much. What kind of proletarian internationalism is that!" See Shakhnazarov, *S vozhdiami i bez nikh*, p. 119. See also R. W. Campbell, *Trends in the Soviet Oil and Gas Industry* (Johns Hopkins University Press, 1976), pp. 80, 81.

95. Schweitzer, *Victory*, pp. xxvi, 6–12, 26–32; R. Strayer, *Why Did the Soviet Union Collapse? Understanding Historical Change* (New York: M. E. Sharpe, 1998), p. 127. For the agreement between the United States and Saudi Arabia on cutting oil prices, see V. G. Treml and M. Ellman, "Debate: Why Did the Soviet Economic System Collapse?" Radio Free Europe/Radio Liberty Research Report 2, no. 23 (1993): 53–58.

96. On the financial situation in socialist countries regarding convertible currency (as of mid-1988), see ПП no. 4013 of February 24, 1988 (RGAE, F. 2324, Op. 33, D. 696, Ll. 4, 5).

97. A. P. Alexandrov (President of the Academy of Sciences of the USSR) to Chairman of the Council of Ministers N. A. Tikhonov, a review of "The state of the economy in capitalist countries and the situation in the oil, natural gas and gold markets in the first quarter of 1983," prepared by experts of the Institute of World Economy and International Relations and the Institute of the USA and Canada of the Academy of Sciences of the USSR, January 3, 1984 (GARF, F. 5446, Op. 144, D. 1256, Ll. 5, 6); A. P. Alexandrov (President of the Academy of Sciences) to Chairman of the Council of Ministers N. A. Tikhonov, a review of "The state of the economy of capitalist countries and the situation in the oil, natural gas and gold markets in the first quarter of 1984," prepared by experts of the Institute of World Economy and International Relations and the Institute of the USA and Canada of the AS of the USSR, April 5, 1984 (GARF, F. 5446, Op. 144, D. 1255, Ll. 113, 114). For reviews of the state of the economy of capitalist countries and the situation in the oil, natural gas, and gold markets in the second quarter of 1984, the third quarter of 1984, the fourth quarter of 1985, and the first quarter of 1986, see GARF, F. 5446, Op. 144, D. 1255, Ll. 131–50; GARF, F.5446, Op. 144, D. 1255, L. 46–66; GARF, F. 5446, Op. 147, D. 1079, Ll. 50–69; GARF, F. 5446, Op. 147, D. 1079, Ll. 123–41.

98. Remarks by Senator William Proxmire, Vice Chairman, Subcommittee on International Trade, Finance, and Security Economics, Joint Economic Committee, United States Congress, December 1, 1982, quoted in H. Rowen, "Central Intelligence Briefing on the Soviet Economy," in *The Soviet Policy in the Modern Era*, edited by Erik P. Hoffmann and Robbin F. Laird (New York: Aldine, 1984), p. 417.

99. On the dominant idea in Soviet studies that the Soviet economy was stable, see T. Buck and J. Cole, *Modern Soviet Economic Performance* (Oxford: Basil Blackwell, 1987); Millar, "An Economic Overview," pp. 173–86. On the same thinking about the political stability of the Soviet Union at the beginning of the 1980s, see J. Boffa, *Istoria Sovetskogo Soiuza* [History of the Soviet Union], vol. 2, *Ot otechestvennoi voiny do polozheniia vtoroi mirovoi derzhavy. Stalin i Khrushchev. 1941–1964 gg.* [From the Patriotic War to the Position of Second World Power: Stalin and Khrushchev, 1941–1964] (Moscow: Mezhdunarodniie otnosheniia, 1994), pp. 538–42.

100. A. Shtromas and M. A. Kaplan, eds., *The Soviet Union and the Challenge of the Future,* vol. 1, *Stasis and Change* (New York: Paragon House, 1988).

101. On the collapse of the Soviet Union, unexpected by Western researchers, see, for example, G. Grossman, "The Soviet Economy in Mid-1991: An Overview," in *Dilemmas of Transition: In the Soviet Union and Eastern Europe,* edited by

G. W. Breslauer (International and Area Studies, University of California, Berkeley, 1991), p. 65.

102. On the thinking of Sovietologists who linked the collapse of the Soviet Union to subjective decisions made by the Soviet leadership after 1980, see M. Harrison, "Coercion, Compliance, and the Collapse of the Soviet Command Economy" (Department of Economics, University of Warwick. March 2001); V. Kontorovich, "The Economic Fallacy," *The National Interest* 31 (1993): 44; D. Pryce-Jones, *The War That Never Was: The Fall of the Soviet Empire 1985–1991* (London: Weidenfeld & Nicolson, 1995); S. White, *Gorbachev and After* (Cambridge University Press, 1991). For similar views expressed in Russia, see *Ot katastrofy k vozrozhdeniiu: prichiny i posledstviia razrusheniia SSSR* [From Catastrophe to Renaissance: The Causes and Consequences of the Collapse of the USSR], edited by I. P. Osadchevyi (Moscow: Izdatel'stvo "Bylina," 1999), p. 7.

103. For the views of those who linked the collapse of the USSR with the policies of the Reagan administration, see Schweitzer, *Victory,* p. 198.

104. V. M. Kudrov estimates that Soviet aid to socialist countries was $20 billion a year. N. Ryzhkov's estimates for the period 1986–89 are approximately the same. According to Western analysts, aid to Cuba alone cost the Soviet Union $6–7 billion a year. See Kudrov, *Sovetskaia ekonomika,* p. 59; N. I. Ryzhkov, *Desiat' let velikikh potriasenii* [Ten Years of Great Shocks] (Moscow: Assotsiatsia "Kniga. Prosviashchenie. Miloserdiie," 1995), p. 232. However, it should be recognized that the estimates of aid to the USSR in real dollars are debatable. An important component of aid was the supply of arms and military equipment, for which it was impossible to receive convertible currency.

105. V. Shlykov, "Chto pogubilo Sovetskii Soiuz? Genshtab i ekonomika" [What Destroyed the Soviet Union? The General Staff and the Economy], *Voennyi vestnik,* no. 9 (2002): 192.

106. On the link between the burden of expenditures and slower economic growth, see also A. Dallin, "Causes of the Collapse of the USSR," *Post-Soviet Affairs* 8, no. 4 (1992): 294–96.

107. On the lack of data showing an acceleration of Soviet defense spending in the early 1980s, see, for example, C. D. Blacker, *Hostage to Revolution* (New York: Council on Foreign Relations Press, 1993), p. 28; R. T. Maddock, *The Political Economy of the Soviet Defense Spending* (Basingstoke, U.K.: Macmillan, 1988), pp. 88–90; P. Hanson, *The Rise and Fall of the Soviet Economy* (London: Longman, 2003); R. F. Kaufman, "Soviet Defense Trends: A Staff Study," prepared for the Joint Economic Committee, 1983.

108. W. E. Odom, *The Collapse of the Soviet Military* (Yale University Press, 1998), p. 105.

109. The argument that increasing the military equipment reserve in peacetime was tied to the threat that new military production after the beginning of a war would be impossible is provided by a well-known and authoritative Soviet commander, V. Sokolovsky. See V. D. Sokolovskii, *Voennaia strategiia* [Military Strategy] (Moscow: Voenizdat, 1968), pp. 387, 388. From evidence given by Colonel General (equivalent to a U.S. lieutenant-general) A. Danilevich (former Deputy Chief of General Headquarters): "As to conventional arms, we were considerably

superior. In 1991, we had 63,900 tanks (in addition to the tanks of our allies), 66,900 artillery guns, 76,500 armored carriers and armored infantry carriers, 12,200 aircraft and helicopters, 437 large warships. We had six times as many tanks as NATO." See Shlykov, "Chto pogubilo Sovetskii Soiuz?" p. 21.

110. Shlykov, "Chto pogubilo Sovetskii Soiuz?"

111. See a letter from Yu. A. Ivanov (Chairman of the Board of Vneshtorgbank, the State Foreign Trade Bank) to N. V. Talyzin (Chairman of the Presidium of the USSR Council of Ministers Commission on the Comecon), for information on convertible currency credit relations of the People's Republic of Bulgaria, Cuba, and the Czechoslovakian Socialist Republic with capitalist countries and banks, as well as other issues discussed during talks at Vneshtorgbank of the USSR, April 28, 1984 (GARF, F. 5446, Op. 144, D. 79, Ll. 36, 37).

112. The average age of the Politburo members at the time Stalin died was 55; in 1980 it was over 70. See J. Boffa, *Ot SSSR k Rossii. Istoriia neokonchennogo krizisa* [From the USSR to Russia. The History of an Unfinished Crisis] (Moscow: Mezhdunarodnyie otnosheniia, 1996), p. 110.

Chapter Five

1. Data from the Ministry of Agricultural Production of the Russian Federation.

2. N. I. Ryzhkov, *Desiat' let velikikh potriasenii* (Moscow: Assotsiatsiia "Kniga. Prosviashchenie. Miloserdie," 1995), p. 229.

3. V. Serov, "Proizoshli izmenenia v khudshuiu storonu" [Changes for the Worse Have Taken Place], *Sotsialisticheskaia Industriia*, February 28, 1989.

4. On the views of those who tie the fluctuation in Gorbachev's policies to his personal idiosyncrasies, see, for example, L. M. Zamiatin, *Gorbi i Meggi. Zapiski posla o dvukh izvestnykh politikakh–Mikhaile Gorbacheve i Margaret Tetcher* [Gorby and Maggie: Notes of an Ambassador on Two Famous Politicians—Mikhail Gorbachev and Margaret Thatcher] (Proizvodstvenno-izdatel'skii kombinat VINITI, 1995), p. 115; M. Nenashev, *Poslednee pravitel'stvo SSSR: lichnosti, svidetel'stva, dialogi* [The Last Government of the USSR: Personalities, Accounts, Dialogues] (Moscow: A/O "Krom," 1993).

5. On the prices of meat and meat products bought by populations at various income levels, see A. E. Surinov and V. A. Dybtsina, "O pitanii naseleniia s razlichnym urovnem dokhoda (Po materialam obsledovaniia Goskomstatom SSSR 90 tysiach semeinykh budzhetov i anketnogo obsledovaniia mnenii 30 tysiach grazhdan o tsenakh na tovary i uslugi)" [On the Nourishment of People at Various Income Levels (Based on Materials of Goskomstat's Review of 90,000 Family Budgets and a Survey of 30,000 Citizens on Pricing of Goods and Services)], *Bulleten' sotsiologicheskikh i budzhetnykh obsledovanii*, no. 1 (1991): 62.

6. G. I. Vashchenko (Minister of Trade) to the Council of Ministers of the USSR, on fulfilling development goals for retail trade in the eleventh five-year plan, January 24, 1986 (GARF, F. 5446, Op. 147, D. 958, L. 85).

7. V. L. Kosmarskii, L. A. Khakhulina, and S. P. Shpil'ko, "Obshchestvennoe mnenie o perekhode k rynochnoi ekonomike Nauchnyi doklad" [Public Opinion

on the Transition to a Market Economy: A Scholarly Report] (Moscow: VTsIOM, 1991), p. 17.

8. On the measures for improving the economy, phases of economic reform, and a fundamental approach to the development of the thirteenth five-year plan, see *Doklad Pravitel'stva SSSR vtoromu S"ezdu narodnykh deputatov SSSR* [USSR Government Report to the Second Congress of People's Deputies of the USSR] (Moscow: Izvestiia, 1989), p. 16.

9. N. V. Garetovsky (Chairman of the Board of Gosbank) to the Council of Ministers, a review of the financial situation in socialist countries regarding convertible currency (as of the beginning of 1989), July 13, 1989 (GARF, F. 5446, Op. 150, D. 73, L. 69).

10. Speech by Chairman of the Government N. Ryzhkov at the Plenum of the CC of the CPSU on January 27–28, transcript of the session of the Plenum of the CC of the CPSU (RGANI, F. 2, Op. 5, D. 45, Ll. 22–22 ob.)

11. V. S. Pavlov, *O Gosudarstvennom budzhete SSSR na 1990 god i ob ispolnenii Gosudarstvennogo budzheta SSSR za 1988 god* [On the State Budget of the USSR for 1990 and on the Implementation of the State Budget of the USSR for 1988] (Moscow: Finansy i statistika, 1990), pp. 9, 15.

12. The Convertible Currency-Economic Department of Gosbank of the USSR to the Council of Ministers of the USSR, on the financial situation in socialist countries regarding convertible currency, ПП no. 4013, February 24, 1988 (RGAE, F. 2324, Op. 33, D. 696, Ll. 4, 5).

13. N. V. Garetovsky (Chairman of the Board of Gosbank) to the Council of Ministers, a review of the financial situation in socialist countries (GARF, F. 5446, Op. 150, D. 73, Ll. 74, 75); on the size of the gold reserves as of January 1, 1986 (587 tons of gold), see Ryzhkov, *Desiat' let velikikh potriasenii*, p. 240.

14. Memorandum from Gosbank about the financial situation in socialist countries regarding convertible currency (as of mid-1988), December 8, 1988 (RGAE, F. 2324, Op. 32, D. 3526, L. 150).

15. Plenum of the CC of the CPSU, February 5–7, 1990, on the draft platform of the CC of the CPSU for the XXVIII Party Congress (RGANI, F. 2, Op. 5, D. 403, L. 21).

16. V. M. Serov (Chairman of Gosstroi) to the Council of Ministers, on measures to reduce the stock of uninstalled imported equipment, May 7, 1990 (GARF, F. 5446, Op. 162, D. 1493, L. 113).

17. Letter from Chairman of Vneshekonombank Yu. S. Moskovsky to Chairman of the State Foreign Economic Commission of the Council of Ministers S. A. Sitarian and Deputy Chairman of Gosplan Yu. P. Khomenko, November 22, 1989, no. 392/01, on setting up petrochemical-natural gas-chemical complexes on the basis of joint ventures in the USSR (Ye. T. Gaidar's personal archive).

18. As attested to by M. Gorbachev, Secretary of the Economy of the CC of the CPSU, N. Sliunkov advocated cuts in defense spending under conditions of decreased oil prices. His position was not supported at the session of the Politburo. See D. Muratov, "Vokrug Gorbacheva opiat' bushuiut strasti" [Passions Flaring around Gorbachev Again], *Novaia Gazeta*, February 21, 2005. Judging from official speeches by Chairman of the Government N. Ryzhkov and his subsequent memoir,

it is clear he was the greatest advocate among the Soviet leadership for raising prices as a way to solve the USSR's financial difficulties. Like the decision to cut defense spending, the decision to raise prices was not passed until the country's financial and monetary system had collapsed.

19. The way in which financial issues were discussed by the Soviet leadership in the mid-1980s is vividly reflected in the opening speech by the minister of finance of the USSR, V. Garbuzov, on the 1985 budget at the session of the Supreme Soviet of the USSR. This was the beginning of the acute phase of the country's financial crisis: "It is with a feeling of profound satisfaction that all our people and the progressive world public welcomed the decoration of Comrade K. Yu. Chernenko with the Order of Lenin and his third gold 'Hammer and Sickle' medal. (Applause.) An outstanding politician and statesman, like Lenin, Konstantin Ustinovich Chernenko works selflessly in the highest positions of the Party and the State making his great invaluable personal contribution to the development and practical implementation of the Leninist domestic and foreign policy of the CPSU. This policy enjoys the infinite trust of all the working people of the Soviet Union who view it as their own vital cause." See V. F. Garbuzov, *O Gosudarstvennom budzhete SSSR na 1985 god i ob ispolnenii Gosudarstvennogo budzheta SSSR za 1983 god* [On the State Budget of the USSR for 1985 and the Implementation of the State Budget of the USSR for 1983] (Moscow: Politizdat, 1984), p. 4.

20. M. S. Gorbachev, *Zhizn' i reformy* [Life and Reforms] (Moscow: Novosti, 1995), vol. 1, p. 234.

21. V. A. Kriuchkov, *Lichnoie delo* [Personal file] (Moscow: Olimp AST, 1996), part 1, p. 42.

22. *Prezidium TsK KPSS. 1954–1964. Chernovye protokol'nye zapisi zasedanii. Stenogrammy. Postanovleniia* [Presidium of the Central Committee of the CPSU, 1954–1964. Draft Minutes of Meetings. Transcripts. Resolutions], vol. 1, p. 151.

23. A. D. Chernev, *229 kremliovskikh vozhdei. Politburo. Orgburo. Sekretariat TsK Kommunisticheskoi parti v litsakh i tsifrakh. Spravochnik* [229 Kremlin Leaders: Politburo, Orgburo, and Secretariat of the Communist Party in People and Figures. A Handbook] (Moscow: Redaktsiia zhurnala "Rodina"; Nauchnyi tsentr "Russika," 1996).

24. From a speech by Chairman of the Council of Ministers N. Tikhonov at the meeting of the Politburo of the CC of the CPSU on March 11, 1985: "Lately, I have worked much with Mikhail Sergeevich Gorbachev. We got to know each other particularly well during our work for the Commission on the Improvement of Economic Mechanism. What can I say about Mikhail Sergeevich? He is an outgoing person; one can discuss a variety of issues with him and discuss them at the highest level. He is the first among the Secretaries of the CC who has a good understanding of economics. You can imagine how important this is." See session of the Politburo of the CC on March 11, 1985, transcript, on the General Secretary of the CC of the CPSU (RGANI, F. 89, Op. 36, D. 16, Ll. 1, 2).

25. Session of the CC of the CPSU Plenum on June 29, 1990 (RGANI, F. 2, D. 495 [microfiche 2200685], L. 14).

26. Ryzhkov, *Desiat' let velikikh potriasenii*, pp. 41–87.

27. A. Yakovlev wrote that in 1985 the leadership of the Party did not have any doubts about the stability and progressive nature of the socialist system. See A. N. Yakovlev, *Gor'kaia chasha: bol'shevism i reformatsia Rossii* [Bitter Cup: Bolshevism and the Reformation of Russia] (Yaroslavl': Verkhne-Volzhskoie knizhnoie izd-vo, 1994), pp. 213–39.

28. Transcript of the session of the CC of the CPSU Plenum on January 27–28, 1987 (RGANI, F. 2, Op. 5, D. 33, Ll. 168–70).

29. RGANI, F. 9, Op. 5, D. 33, Ll. 168–70.

30. M. S. Zotov (Chairman of the Board of Promstroibank) to the Council of Ministers, to B. Ye. Shcherbina, on key problems of the 1989 draft plans of economic and social development of branches of the fuel-energy complex, May 26, 1988 (GARF, F. 5446, Op. 149, D. 1439, Ll. 72–94).

31. From an interview with M. Gorbachev on the occasion of the twentieth anniversary of the beginning of perestroika, "We screwed up financial issues," in Muratov, "Vokrug Gorbacheva opiat' bushuiut strasti."

32. N. K. Baibakov, *Sorok let v pravitel'stve* (Moscow: Respublika, 1993), p. 161.

33. Ryzhkov, *Desiat' let velikikh potriasenii,* p. 101.

34. N. T. Glushkov (Chairman of Goskomtsen) to the Council of Ministers, on the fulfillment of the resolution of the CC of the CPSU and the decision of the Council of Ministers of the USSR of July 19, 1986, no. 847, August 1, 1986 (GARF, F. 5446, Op. 147, D. 374, L. 32).

35. V. M. Kudrov, *Sovetskaia ekonomika v retrospective* [The Soviet Economy in Retrospective] (Moscow: Nauka, 2003), p. 102.

36. K. Z. Terekh (Minister of Trade) to the Council of Ministers of the USSR, information about the state of the retail trade in individual goods, December 2, 1987 (GARF, F. 5446, Op. 148, D. 950, Ll. 7, 8).

37. Ibid.

38. A. V. Voilukov (Chief of the Division of the Monetary Circulation of Gosbank of the USSR), information regarding the question of the size of the population's unsatisfied demand for spending, November 22, 1988 (RGAE, F. 2324, Op. 33, D. 741, Ll. 146–54).

39. N. Petrakov, "Monetary Stabilization in Russia: What Is to Be Done?" *Cato Journal* 12, no. 3 (1993): 610–11. As estimated by S. Sinelnikov, the USSR's budget deficit was 94.4 billion rubles and 97.7 billion rubles in 1988 and 1989 respectively, 10–11 percent of the gross national product. See S. G. Sinel'nikov, *Budzhetnyi krizis v Rossii: 1985–1995* [The Budget Crisis in Russia: 1985–1995] (Moscow: Evrazia, 1995).

40. V. S. Pavlov (Minister of Finance of the USSR) and V. N. Kirichenko (Chairman of Goskomstat of the USSR) to the Council of Ministers of the USSR, material on measures to overcome inflation, December 5, 1989 (GARF, F. 5446, Op. 162, D. 289, L. 72); N. Ryzhkov (Chairman of the Council of Ministers), Yu. Masliukov (Chairman of Gosplan), L. Voronin (Chairman of Gossnab) to the CC of the CPSU, proposals for measures to further develop a radically new economic reform (GARF, F. 5446, Op. 149, D. 1, Ll. 39–56).

41. A. V. Voilukov (Chief of the Division of the Monetary Circulation), on the state of monetary circulation (RGAE, F. 2324, Op. 33, D. 741, Ll. 27–31).

42. V. G. Panskov (Deputy Minister of Finance) and S. A. Sitarian (Deputy Chairman of Gosplan) to the Council of Ministers, proposals on procedure and dates for the implementation of a radical restructuring of the financial system, April 12, 1988 (GARF, F. 5446, Op. 149, D. 1, L. 149).

43. Message from Chairman of the Council of Ministers N. Ryzhkov, Chairman of Gosplan Yu. Maslukov, and Chairman of Gossnab L. Voronin to the CC of the CPSU of July 17, 1988 (GARF, F. 5446, Op. 149, D. 1, Ll. 37–56).

44. A. V. Voilukov (Deputy Chairman of the Board of Gosbank) to V. G. Kucherenko, on the country's issuing policy, September 18, 1990 (RGAE, F. 2324, Op. 33, D. 741, L. 166).

45. O. Latsis describes an episode pertaining to this subject in his book: "Along with Gaidar I wrote a detailed message to Gorbachev with which I enclosed some clippings from a magazine, a recent article on the subject. . . . Gorbachev was so interested in the message that he read it at the very beginning of a Politburo meeting that did not even have that subject on its agenda. The discussion lasted two hours, and, as Ivan (I. T. Frolov) told me later, no one could remember whether the Politburo had ever discussed financial and budget issues. . . . Noting the sad fate of our attempt to open the eyes of the country's leadership and of our society to the current situation, I was indignant with Chairman of the Government Nikolai Ryzhkov and with Yuri Masliukov, because I was sure that these protégés of the military-industrial complex sabotaged the Politburo's resolution, leading to the country's economic crash. I was most likely right, but in the whirlwind of the events I did not have time to hit upon the only correct conclusion: the Soviet government machine had lost the ability to fulfill its basic functions. Even in the face of inevitable disaster, of which the entire Politburo, headed by Gorbachev, was aware, our "Titanic" could not escape collision with the iceberg." See O. Latsis, *Tshchatel'no splanirovannie samoubiistvo* [A Well-Planned Suicide] (Moscow: Moskovskaia shkola politicheskikh issledovanii, 2001), pp. 195–97.

46. V. A. Tsareva, "Piteinye obychai v SSSR i Finliandii" [Drinking Habits in the USSR and Finland], in *Effektivnost' alkogol'noi reformy: nekotoryie sotsiologicheskiie aspekty* [The Effectiveness of Alcohol Reform: Some Sociological Aspects] (Moscow: Institut sotsialogii AN SSSR, 1988), p. 16.

47. For examples of some negative occurrences in the struggle against heavy drinking and alcoholism, see *Izvestiia Tsk KPSS*, no. 1 (1989): 48–50.

48. C. D. Blacker, *Hostage to the Revolution* (New York: Council on Foreign Relations Press, 1993), p. 57.

49. M. S. Gorbachev, *Ob osnovnykh napravleniiakh vnutrennei i vneshnei politiki SSSR* [On the Basic Directions of USSR Domestic and Foreign Policy], speech at the Congress of People's Deputies of the USSR, May 30, 1989. Moscow: Politizdat, 1989, p. 8.

50. On measures for the financial improvement of the economy and strengthening of monetary circulation in the country from 1989 to 1990 and during the thirteenth five-year plan, *Izvestiia Tsk KPSS*, no. 5 (1989): 14–16.

51. V. A. Dinkov (Minister of the Oil Industry) to the Council of Ministers, on oil supplies for the people's economy in 1989, June 30, 1989 (GARF, F. 5446, Op. 150, D. 1576, Ll. 106–11).

52. L. I. Filimonov to the Council of Ministers, on the state order for oil production in 1989, August 16, 1989 (GARF, F. 5446, Op. 150, D. 1576, Ll. 43–46).

53. V. Medvedev, *V komande Gorbacheva: Vzgliad iznutri* [On Gorbachev's Team: An Inside View] (Moscow: Bylina, 1994), pp. 87, 103.

54. A. O. Voronov, "O Problemakh preodoleniia defitsita i metodakh regulirovaniia potrebitel'skogo rynka" [On Problems of Overcoming the Deficit and Methods for Regulating the Consumer Market], *Voprosy ekonomiki,* no. 1 (1990): 26–32.

55. Gosbank, material for a report on the country's socioeconomic situation, January 2, 1990 (RGAE, F. 2324, Op. 33, D. 741, Ll. 54–58).

56. Letters from working people on issues pertaining to the implementation of the radical economic reform, *Izvestiia TsK KPSS,* no. 8 (1989): 150.

57. Memorandum from the Agrarian Division of the CC of the Party to the Central Committee of the CPSU, on the sale of foodstuffs in Moscow, July 10, 1989, *Izvestiia TsK KPSS,* no. 9 (1989): 91.

58. M. G. Sheludko, on results of the fulfillment of the economic and social development plan by the Ministry of Bread and Baked Goods in 1988 and for the three years of the twelfth five-year plan, January 26, 1989 (RGAE, F. 8040, Op. 19, D. 4393, Ll. 252, 253).

59. Ibid., L. 252.

60. Minister of Bread and Baked Goods A. D. Budyka to First Deputy Chairman of the Council of Ministers V. V. Nikitin, August 11, 1989, no. 120–272, RGAE, F. 8040, Op. 19, D. 4421, L. 244.

61. P. D. Kondrashev (Deputy Minister of Trade) to the Council of Ministers, on the situation of bread and baked goods supply to the population in the first half of 1989, January 13, 1989 (RGAE, F. 8040, Op. 19, D. 4421, L. 32).

62. V. N. Kirichenko (Chairman of Goskomstat) to the Council of Ministers, on fulfillment of assignments for the production and supply of basic consumer goods from January to September of this year, October 10, 1989 (GARF, F. 5446, Op. 150, D. 288, Ll. 88, 90, 92).

63. Minutes of a meeting of the Presidium of the Council of Ministers of the USSR of November 10, 1989, on the fulfillment of 1989 production assignments for basic consumer goods (GARF, F. 5446, Op. 150, D. 288, L. 113).

64. On measures for improving the economy, phases of economic reform and the principal approach to the development of the thirteenth five-year plan, address of the government of the USSR to the Second Congress of the People's Deputies of the USSR, Moscow, November 1989, p. 5.

65. Garetovsky, a review of the financial situation in socialist countries (GARF, F. 5446, Op. 150, D. 73, Ll. 75, 76).

66. M. I. Goldman, *What Went Wrong with Perestroika* (New York: W. W. Norton, 1992), pp. 159, 160.

67. From a memorandum to the CC of the CPSU, "On regulating the debt of developing countries (with the exception of less developed countries) as a continuation of the position presented in Comrade M. S. Gorbachev's speech to the UN," minutes of the session of the Politburo of the CC of the CPSU, August 23, 1989 (RGANI, F. 89, Op. 9, D. 23, Ll. 3, 4).

68. Yu. A. Borisov (Deputy Chairman of the State Commission for Foodstuffs and Acquisitions) to S. A. Sitarian (Deputy Chairman of the Council of Ministers), on payments for imported foodstuffs, May 30, 1990 (GARF, F. 5446, Op. 162, D. 1495, Ll. 64, 65).

69. V. A. Bykov (Minister of the Medical Industry) to S. A. Sitarian (Deputy Chairman of the Council of Ministers), on paying bills for medicines in convertible currency, April 11, 1990 (GARF, F. 5446, Op. 162, D. 1492, L. 32).

70. Yuri Luzhkov (Deputy Chief of the Main Provisions Department under the Moscow Municipal Executive Committee) to S. A. Sitarian (Deputy Chairman of the Council of Ministers), on supplying raw food materials to Moscow Municipal Executive Committee in 1990, August 6, 1990, GARF, F. 5446, Op. 162, D. 1500, L. 129.

71. Report on the work of the Savings Bank of the USSR in 1989 (RGAE, F. 2324, Op. 33, D. 721, Ll. 1a, 2, 4).

72. Yu. S. Moskovsky (Chairman of the Board of Vneshekonombank) to Chairman of the Council of Ministers N. I. Ryzhkov, on the issuance of bonds on the FRG (Federal Republic of Germany) market, March 22, 1989 (GARF, F. 5446, Op. 150, D. 73, L. 53).

73. Yu. S. Moskovsky (Chairman of the Board of Vneshekonombank) to Chairman of the Council of Ministers N. I. Ryzhkov, on credits given to the Soviet Union, August 8, 1989 (GARF, F. 5446, Op. 150, D. 73, L. 55).

74. A. I. Kachanov (Deputy Minister for Foreign Economic Relations) to the Council of Ministers, on paying for imported goods of ferrous and nonferrous metallurgy against the limit of imported resources for 1990, February 21, 1990 (GARF, F. 5446, Op. 162, D. 1465, L. 18).

75. K. F. Katushev (Minister for Foreign Economic Relations) to S. A. Sitarian (Chairman of the State Foreign Economic Commission of the Council of Ministers), on the delay in payments by the All-Union Export-Import Association for Food Products (Prodintorg), May 28, 1990 (GARF, F. 5446, Op. 162, D. 1463, L. 106).

76. V. N. Vorontsov (Deputy Minister for Foreign Economic Relations) to S. A. Sitarian (Deputy Chairman of the Council of Ministers), on the delay in payments by the All-Union Foreign Trade Agency of the Ministry for Foreign Economic Relations, September 14, 1990 (GARF, F. 5446, Op 162, D. 1464, L. 110).

77. Yu. S. Moskovsky (Chairman of the Board of Vneshekonombank) to S. A. Sitarian (Deputy Chairman of the Council of Ministers), on the work of Vneshekonombank to bring in unrestricted financial resources from the end of 1989 to the beginning of 1990, April 25, 1990 (GARF, F. 5446, Op. 162, D. 1463, Ll. 110–14).

78. S. A. Sitarian (Deputy Chairman of the Council of Ministers) to N. I. Ryzhkov (Chairman of the Council of Ministers), May 3, 1990 (GARF, F. 5446, Op. 162, D. 1464, L. 82).

79. "Bankers Show Caution on the Issue of Giving Credits to the USSR," *International Herald Tribune,* June 5, 1990 (GARF, F. 5446, Op. 162, D. 1464, L. 76).

80. Yu. S. Moskovsky (Chairman of the Board of Vneshekonombank) to the Council of Ministers, on the attitude in Western business circles about giving funds to the Soviet Union, June 14, 1990 (GARF, F. 5446, Op. 162, D. 1464, L. 74).

81. A. I. Kachanov (Deputy Minister of Foreign Economic Relations) to L. I. Voronin (First Deputy Chairman of the Council of Ministers), on additional possibilities for acquisitions abroad, October 25, 1990 (GARF, F. 5446, Op. 162, D. 1465, L. 67).

82. S. I. Sitarian (Deputy Chairman of the Council of Ministers) to N. I. Ryzhkov (Chairman of the Council of Ministers), on M. Gorbachev's statement regarding the need to extend the debt, July 31, 1990 (GARF, F. 5446, Op. 162, D. 1464, Ll. 13, 14).

83. V. Gerashchenko (Chairman of the Board of Gosbank) to S. A. Sitarian (Deputy Chairman of the Council of Ministers), on the possibility of bringing in intermediate-term financial resources on an intergovernmental basis, April 4, 1990 (GARF, F. 5446, Op. 162, D. 1464, Ll. 80, 81).

84. Memorandum regarding E. Shevardnadze's talks with H. Kohl (GARF, F. 5446, Op. 162, D. 1464, Ll. 83, 84).

85. A. N. Yakovlev, *Omut pamiati. Ot Stolypina do Putina* [Deep Waters of Memory. From Stolypin to Putin], 2 vols. (Moscow: Vagrius, 2001), vol. 1, p. 372.

86. Meeting of the Politburo on September 25, 1986, working notes, on people who serve prison terms for political crimes (RGANI, F. 89, Op. 36, D. 20, L. 2).

87. Transcript of the Plenum of the CC of the CPSU, January 27–28, 1987 (RGANI, F. 2, Op. 5, D. 45, L. 3).

88. RGANI, F. 2, Op. 5, D. 45, L. 22.

89. Medvedev, *V komande Gorbacheva*, p. 42.

90. On the reluctance of the USSR's leadership and of the agencies responsible for economic policy with regard to whether price-setting reforms should be carried out in 1989, and on the unwillingness of the Soviet leadership to take upon itself the responsibility for this difficult decision, see ibid., pp. 54, 55. As surveys of the All-Union Center for the Analysis of Public Opinion on socioeconomic issues demonstrated, in 1989–90 the population was essentially in favor of the legalization of private property, but was definitely against price liberalization. The society did not understand that it was impossible to have one without the other. See *Opros obshchestvennogo mneniia "otnoshenii k probleme sobstvennosti"* [Public Opinion Poll "Attitude toward the Property Issue"] (Moscow: VTsIOM, 1989); S. P. Shpil'ko, L. A. Khakhulina, Z. V. Kupriianova, V. V. Bordova, L. G. Zubova, N. P. Kovaliova, M. D. Krasil'nikova, and T. V. Avdeienko, "Otsenka naseleniiem sotsial'no-ekonomicheskoi situatsii v strane (po rezul'tatam sotsiologicheskikh oprosov 1991 goda), Nauchnyi doklad" [Public Opinion on the Socioeconomic Situation in the Country (Based on Results of Sociological Surveys in 1991): A Scholarly Report] (Moscow: VTsIOM, 1991). From the late 1980s to the early 1990s, over half the population of the USSR surveyed on socioeconomic issues was convinced that it was necessary to create a market economy, yet 58 percent of those surveyed found unemployment to be absolutely unacceptable. See V. Kosmarskii, Ekspress-otchet VTsIOM, *"Otnoshenie naseleniia k sokrashcheniiu chasti rabochikh mest i uvol'neniiu zaimaiushchikh ikh rabotnikov"* [Express-Report by VTsIOM, The Popular Attitude toward the Reduction of Jobs and the Firing of Workers in Those Jobs] (Moscow: VTsIOM, July 12, 1989), p. 8.

91. USSR law of November 19, 1986, On Individual Labor Activity, in *Resheniia partii i Pravitel'stva po khoziaistvennym voprosam* [Decisions of the Party and Government on Economic Issues] (Moscow: Politizdat, 1988), vol. 16, part 2, pp. 489–99.

92. L. Pleshakov, "*Ne Delit', a Zarabatyvat*" [Not Share, but Earn], interview with L. I. Abalkin, *Ogonek*, no. 41. (October 1989): 2.

93. *Prezidium Tsk KPSS. 1954–1964*, vol. 1, pp. 638, 639.

94. V. Kossov to D. A. Voronin, on the danger of stagflation in 1990, December 20, 1989 (GARF, F. 5446, Op. 150, D. 17, L. 138).

95. For problems created by the development of cooperatives, see "Potentsial i 'Bolezni Rosta' Kooperatsii" [Potential and Growing Pains of Co-operatives], interview with First Deputy Head of the Socioeconomic Department of the CC CPSU V. P. Mozhin, *Politicheskoe obrazovanie*, no. 16 (1989): 38–43. On the practice of using cooperatives to sell products purchased at fixed prices from state enterprises and sold at market prices, see A. A. Krasnopivtsev (Deputy Chairman of Goskomtsen) to the Council of Ministers, on measures for the prevention of inflation on the basis of holding back unsubstantiated raising of prices, September 8, 1989 (GARF, F. 5446, Op. 150, D. 2066, L. 27).

96. A. Glushetskii, "Kooperativnaia politika: itogi, protivorechiia, napravleniia optimizatsii" [Cooperative Policy: Results, Contradictions, Directions for Optimization], *Ekonomicheskie nauki*, no. 6 (1990): 52–67.

97. Osnovy Zakonodatel'stva Soiuza SSR i Soiuznykh Respublik [Foundations of Legislation of the USSR and Union Republics], no. 810-1, November 23, 1989, "Ob arende" [On Rent], *Zakon SSSR* [Law of the USSR], no. 2015-1, March 7, 1991. The original text of the document was published in *Vedomosti SND i VS SSSR*, no. 25 (1989): 481.

98. *Izvestiia TsK KPSS*, no. 12 (1989): 20.

99. RGAE, F. 2324, Inv. 32, S. 3996A, P. 93.

100. The Department of Commercial and Co-operative Banks to the Board of Gosbank, on the work of commercial banks in 1990, May 7, 1991 (RGAE, F. 2324, Op. 32, D. 3996A, L. 96).

101. V. Bakatin (Minister of Internal Affairs) to First Deputy Chairman of the Council of Ministers Yu. D. Masliukov, on the principal tendencies of the dynamics of crime in the economic sphere in the first half of 1990 and the forecast for possible criminal consequences during the transition to market relations, July 13, 1990 (GARF, F. 5446, Op. 162, D. 1, L. 56).

102. N. Ryzhkov (Chairman of the Council of Ministers), Yu. Masliukov (Chairman of Gosplan), and L. Voronin (Chairman of Gossnab) to the CC of the CPSU, proposals for developing radical economic reform, for delving into it, and for eliminating shortcomings in the course of its implementation, July 17, 1988 (GARF, F. 5446, Op. 149, D. 1, L. 50).

103. Ryzhkov, *Desiat' let velikikh potriasenii*, p. 202.

104. *Rabochee dvizhenie Kuzbassa. Sbornik dokumentov i materialov. Aprel' 1989–mart 1992* [The Workers' Movement in Kuzbass: Collection of Documents and Materials, April 1989–March 1992], compiled by L. N. Lopatin (Kemerovo: Izd-vo "Sovremennaia otechestvennaia kniga," 1993), pp. 39, 40, 68–71.

Chapter Six

1. Transcript of a meeting with Chairman of the Council of Ministers N. I. Ryzhkov, on the supply of oil, natural gas condensate, and oil products to the state in 1991, September 17, 1990 (GARF, F. 5446, Op. 162, D. 379, L. 129).

2. Ibid., Ll. 131–37, 143–49.

3. Memorandum from the Socioeconomic Division of the CC of the CPSU, "On serious shortcomings in creating stability in the national economy for the autumn–winter period of 1990/1991," September 19, 1990 (RGANI, F. 89, Op. 20, D. 8, Ll. 4–6).

4. K. F. Katushev (Minister of Foreign Economic Relations) to Chairman of the Council of Ministers N. I. Ryzhkov, on the export of oil products in the fourth quarter of 1990, October 31, 1990 (GARF, F. 5446, Op. 162, D. 1524, L. 1).

5. Letter from V. N. Kostiunin (Deputy Chairman of Gossnab) and A. A. Troitsky (Deputy Chairman of Gosplan) to Deputy Chairman of the Cabinet of Ministers L. Riabiev, on the supply of fuel and energy for the national economy and the population for autumn–winter 1991–92, May 23, 1991 (GARF, F. 5446, Op. 163, D. 1640, Ll. 60–61).

6. GARF, F. 5446, Op. 163, D. 269, Ll. 17–20.

7. Yu. Bobylev and A. Cherniavsky, "The Economic Impact of the Crisis in Russian Oil Exploration and Production," in *Oil and Gas Development in the Russian Federation* (Alexandria: Legacy International, 1992), pp. 63, 87.

8. Letter from L. D. Churilov (Minister of the Oil and Natural Gas Industry) to Prime Minister V. S. Pavlov, urgent message on the supply of material-technical resources to the Ministry of Oil and Natural Gas Industry, July 12, 1991 (GARF, F. 5446, Op. 163, D. 1446, L. 158).

9. In May 1991, O. Latsis wrote that what happened in the USSR in the spring of 1991 was very similar to events in Poland in 1981, "We now live in Poland of 1981. . . . We are reliving the emergence of and the course of the Polish economic crisis. We have similar overinvestments by irresponsible government departments, similar 'presents' to our people in the form of overconsumption (not in the sense that we are fully satisfied, not in the least, we consume more than the country produces), a similar deficit in the state budget, similar long-term growth of foreign debt and credit dependence, the similar inevitability of free prices and a similar refusal to accept this inevitability, and violent protests by workers. Behind the political disputes, the epidemic of strikes, the grueling Polish disease of the previous decade, looms like a huge shadow." O. Latsis, "Lomka, ili Koe-chto o Prirode Tsen" [Breakage, or a Few Things about the Nature of Prices], *Izvestiia*, May 7,1991.

10. Speaking at the United Nations in December 1988, M. Gorbachev said that the size of the USSR armed forces would be cut back by 500,000 servicemen, the number of tanks in the arsenal by 10,000, the number of aircraft by 820. Taking into account additional activities—the relocation of units of varying sizes—the intention was to cut the number of tanks by 15,000 and aircraft by 860. See *XXVIII s"ezd Kommunisticheskoi Partii Sovetskogo Soiuza, 2–13 iiulia, 1990: Stenograficheskii otchet* [The Twenty-Eighth Congress of the Communist Party of the Soviet Union, July 2–13, 1990] (Moscow: Politizdat, 1991), p. 210.

11. As attested to by U.S. ambassador to the USSR J. Matlock, in November 1989, Gorbachev assured Bush that Soviet troops would not be used to preserve existing regimes in Eastern Europe and that he was ready to give Eastern Europe the freedom to choose a political and economic system. See J. F. Matlock, *Autopsy on an Empire: The American Ambassador's Account of the Soviet Union* (New York: Random House, 1995), p. 272.

12. For the interconnection between the Soviet leadership's more persistent appeals, tied to politically motivated credits, and the changing nature of the dialogue between the USSR and Western countries, see C. D. Blacker, *Hostage to Revolution* (New York: Council on Foreign Relations Press, 1993), p. 5. On limited financial benefits received by the Soviet Union from the West as a payment for the liberation of Eastern Europe, see S. Bialer, "Death of Soviet Communism," *Foreign Affairs* (Winter 1991/1992): 176–77.

13. On the unpreparedness of the Soviet leadership to secure political control over Poland through the direct use of troops and its desire for Polish leaders to do so, see Materialy zasedanii Politburo TsK KPSS v 1980–1981 gg. V. Bukovsky, *Moskovskii protsess* (www.belousenko.com/wr_Bukovsky.htm). G. Shakhnazarov, who was responsible for Polish problems in the CC of the CPSU, wrote in his memoir, "It is necessary to admit that it was Suslov who set the commission's work on the right track from the very beginning. In his first speech he declared that the Soviet Union absolutely could not resort to military intervention in Poland. The same principle was reconfirmed by the next chairman of the commission, Andropov." See G. Shakhnazarov, *S vozhdiami i bez nikh* [With Leaders and without Them]. (Moscow: Vagrius, 2001), p. 250.

14. E. Shevardnadze, A. Yakovlev, D. Yazov, and V. Kriuchkov to the CC of the CPSU, on the situation in Poland, possible versions for its development, and the prospects for Soviet Polish relations, September 20, 1989 (RGANI, F. 89, Op. 9, D. 33, L. 13).

15. On the interconnection between the inability of the Soviet leadership to use unlimited force against its own people and the population of the satellite territories and the collapse of empires and the Soviet system, see J. Hough, *Democratization and Revolution in the USSR, 1985–1991* (Washington: Brookings, 1997).

16. Matlock, *Autopsy on an Empire.*

17. S. U. Alieva, ed., *Tak eto bylo: Natsional'nye repressii v SSSR* [This Is How It Happened: National Repressions in the USSR] (Moscow: Insan, 1993), vol. 1, p. 13.

18. On problems of interethnic relations in the USSR since the 1920s and their potentially explosive character, see A. G. Vishnevskii, *Serp i rubl': konservativnaia modernizatsiia v SSSR* [Sickle and Ruble: Conservative Modernization in the USSR] (Moscow: OGI, 1998).

19. M. S. Gorbachev, *Perestroika i novoe myshlenie dlia nashei strany i dlia vsego mira* [Perestroika and New Thinking for Our Country and the Whole World] (Moscow: Politizdat, 1987), p. 118.

20. *Prezidium TsK KPSS. 1954–1964. Chernovye protokol'nye zapisi zasedanii. Stenogrammy. Postanovleniia* [Presidium of the Central Committee of the CPSU, 1954–1964. Draft Minutes of Meetings. Transcripts. Resolutions], vol. 1, pp. 929, 930.

21. N. Amrekulov, "Inter-Ethnic Conflict and Resolution in Kazakhstan," in R. Z. Sagdeev and S. Eisenhower, eds., *Central Asia: Conflict, Resolution and Change* (Chevy Chase, Md.: CPSS Press, 1995).

22. *Alma-Ata. 1986. December* (Alma-Ata: Kollegiia "Audarma"; Altyn orda, 1991), p. 8.

23. Excerpt from the resolution of the Secretariat of the CC of the CPSU, February 4, 1991, about proposals for the legal, organizational, and economic fundamentals of regulating forced migration (RGANI, F. 89, Op. 20, D. 31).

24. T. Kuzio and A. Wilson, *Ukraine: Perestroika to Independence* (New York: St. Martin's Press, 1994), p. 100.

25. For problems linked to the multiethnic character of the Soviet armed forces, see A. R. Alexiev and R. C. Nurick, *The Soviet Military under Gorbachev: Report on a RAND Workshop* (Santa Monica, Calif.: RAND, February 1990), pp. 21, 22.

26. On the unwillingness of any of the political leaders to take responsibility for using violence in Tbilisi in the spring of 1988, see A. Sobchak, *Tbilisskii izlom, ili krovavoe voskresen'e 1989g* [The Tbilisi Break, or Bloody Sunday 1989] (Moscow, 1993).

27. The riots in the Fergana Valley began on May 23–25, 1989. On the morning of June 3 they assumed a mass nature. Beginning on the morning of June 4, large groups of nationalists armed with knives, axes, and metal rods attacked places where Turks resided and the administrative buildings where they were hiding from reprisals. This is how an eyewitness described these events: "From high above, one could see houses, sometimes whole blocs, in flames in towns, townships, and villages. The oblast center Fergana was covered with blotches of burned-out areas. A few streets in Kokand were burned down completely. The houses of Meskhetian Turks were being burned." See V. Ardaiev, "Fergana: povtoreniie proidennogo" [Fergana: A Repetition of the Past], *VVS Moscow*, May 13, 2005 (http://news8.thdo.bbc.co.uk/hi/russian/news/newsid_4544000/4544787.stm). The events in Fergana killed 103 persons, and injured 1,001; 757 residences and 27 government buildings were burned down and looted. See TsK Kompartii Uzbekistana, "O tragicheskikh sobytiakh v Ferganskoi oblasti i otvetstvennost' partiinykh, sovetskikh i pravookhranitel'nykh organov" [Central Committee of the Uzbekistan Communist Party, On the Tragic Events in Fergana Oblast and the Responsibility of Party, Soviet, and Law Agencies], *Izvestiia TsK KPSS,* 1989, no. 10, p. 95. Only at about 8:00 p.m. on June 4 did troops of the Ministry of Internal Affairs begin decisive action to stop the riots. By the morning of June 5 the number of troops had been increased to 6,000. For the factors that affected the three-day delay in the use of troops in Fergana, see M. Lur'ie and P. Studenikin, *Zapakh gari i goria. Fergana, trevozhnyi iiun' 1989-go* [The Smell of Fire and Grief: Fergana, the Anxious June of 1989] (Moscow: Kniga, 1990), pp. 4, 5.

28. V. Medvedev, *V komande Gorbacheva: Vzgliad iznutri* [On Gorbachev's Team: An Inside View] (Moscow: Bylina, 1994), pp. 85, 86.

29. A. Illesh and V. Rudnev, "Militsia prosit pomoshchi, ei vse trudnei spravit'sia s narastaiushchim valom prestupnosti" [The Police Are Asking for Help, They Can't Handle the Growing Crime Wave], *Izvestiia,* January 5, 1991.

30. Postanovleniie S"ezda Narodnykh Deputatov ot 9 iiunia 1989 g., "Ob osnovnykh napravleniiakh vnutrennei i vneshnei politiki SSSR" [Resolution of the Congress of People's Deputies of June 9, 1989, On the Basic Directions of the Domestic and Foreign Policy of the USSR], *Pravda,* June 25, 1989.

31. Resolution of the Supreme Soviet of the USSR no. 1897-1 of January 12, 1991, on the All-Union forecast by the government of the USSR on the functioning of the country's economy in 1991 and the State plan for the fiscal-social issues for 1991.

32. *Sbornik dokumentov, priniatykh pervym–shestym s"ezdami narodnykh deputatov RF* [Collection of Documents Passed by the First–Sixth Congresses of People's Deputies of the Russian Federation]. Published by the Supreme Soviet of the Russian Federation (Moscow: Respublika, 1992), p. 119.

33. N. Ryzhkov (Chairman of the Council of Ministers) and Yu. Masliukov (Chairman of Gosplan) to the CC of the CPSU, proposals for measures to develop radical economic reform, to delve into it and to eliminate shortcomings disclosed in the course of its implementation, July 17, 1988 (GARF, F. 5446, Op. 149, D. 1, L. 50).

34. Plenum of the CC of the CPSU, February 5–7, 1990, on the draft platform of the CC of the CPSU by the Twenty-Eighth Party Congress (RGANI, F. 2, Op. 5, D. 403, Ll. 17–21).

35. At the beginning of December 1988, the director of the Institute of Economics of the Academy of Sciences of the USSR, L. Abalkin, wrote a letter to the leadership of the country in which he warned that raising retail prices could lead to social unrest and suggested postponing it for two to three years. See L. Abalkin, "Proposals of the Institute of Economics of the USSR Academy of Sciences on improving economic reforms being carried out in the country," December 1, 1988 (GARF, F. 5446, Op. 150, D. 2, Ll. 94–138). In the government's address to the Second Congress of People's Deputies of the USSR in November of 1989 a suggestion was put forward to present the question of retail price reform for nationwide discussion. See *Doklad Pravitel'stva SSSR vtoromu S"iezdu narodnykh deputatov SSSR. O merakh po ozdorovleniiu ekonomiki, etapakh ekonomicheskoi reformy i printsipial'nykh podkhodakh k razrabotke trinadtsatogo piatiletnego plana* [Report by the Government of the USSR to the Second Congress of People's Deputies USSR: On Measures for Improving the Economy, Stages of Economic Reform, and Fundamental Approaches to the Elaboration of the Thirteenth Five-Year Plan] (Moscow, November 1989), p. 21.

36. *XXVIII s"ezd Kommunisticheskoi partii Sovetskogo Soiuza, 2–13 iiulia, 1990,* p. 67.

37. Ibid., p. 126.

38. Ibid.

39. V. K. Senchagov (Chairman of Goskomtsen) to Chairman of the Council of Ministers N. I. Ryzhkov, on managing price setting, December 12, 1990 (GARF, F. 5446, Op. 162, D. 270, L. 149).

40. Speech by Deputy Chairman of the Council of Ministers L. I. Abalkin at the Fourth Session of the Supreme Soviet of the USSR, November 26, 1990, transcript, Part 9, p. 196.

41. *Pravitel'stvennaia programma formirovaniia struktury i mekhanisma reguliruemoi i rynochnoi ekonomiki* [Government Program for the Formation of the Structure and Mechanism of a Regulated and Market Economy] (Moscow, September 1990), p. 5.

42. Plenum of the CC of the CPSU on February 5–7, 1990, on the draft platform of the CC of the CPSU by the Twenty-Eighth Congress of the Party (RGANI, F. 2, Op. 5, D. 403, L. 3).

43. Database of the UN Food and Agriculture Organization, FAOSTAT, 2005.

44. K. F. Katushev (Minister of Foreign Economic Relations) to S. A. Sitarian (Chairman of the State Foreign Economic Commission of the Council of Ministers), on payments for grain, bread, and baked goods, April 13, 1990 (GARF, F. 5446, Op. 162, D. 1515, L. 21).

45. V. Falin (Chief of the International Division of the CC of the CPSU) to the CC of the CPSU, on the work of the International Division of the CC of the CPSU, minutes no. 144 of the meeting of the Politburo of the CC of the CPSU on December 28, 1988, no. P144/129 (RGANI, F. 89, Op. 38, D. 55, Ll. 1–3).

46. S. Sitnin (Deputy Minister of Finance) to the State Foreign Economic Commission of the Council of Ministers, on cutting aid to foreign countries, August 23, 1990 (GARF, F. 5446, Op. 162, D. 1457, L. 140).

47. K. F. Katushev (Minister of Foreign Economic Relations) to L. A. Voronin (First Deputy Chairman of the Council of Ministers), on paying overdue debts of the All-Union Foreign Trade Agency (Prodintorg) under the Ministry of Foreign Economic Relations, October 11, 1990 (GARF, F. 5446, Op. 162, D. 1512, L. 181).

48. A. I. Kachanov (Deputy Minister of Foreign Economic Relations) to L. A. Voronin (First Deputy Chairman of the Council of Ministers), urgent message on supplies of foodstuffs to the USSR in November–December, November 1990 (GARF, F. 5446, Op. 162, D. 1512, Ll. 195–97).

49. V. V. Gerashchenko and Yu. S. Moskovsky to Chairman of the Council of Ministers N. I. Ryzhkov, on issuing guarantees of payment for imported purchases by Vneshekonombank of the USSR, October 1, 1990 (GARF, F. 5446, Op. 162, D. 1457, L. 133).

50. A. I. Kachanov (Deputy Minister of Foreign Economic Relations) and A. M. Belichenko (Deputy Chairman of the State Commission on Foodstuffs and Acquisitions of the Council of Ministers) to L. A. Voronin (First Deputy Chairman of the Council of Ministers), urgent message on the debt of Vneshekonombank, November 28, 1990 (GARF, F. 5446, Op. 162, D. 1512, L. 150).

51. A. K. Krivenko (Chairman of Prodintorg) to N. I. Ryzhkov (Chairman of the Council of Ministers), on the agency's debt to foreign companies, August 15, 1990 (GARF, F. 5446, Op. 162, D. 1514, Ll. 57, 58).

52. V. N. Vorontsov (Deputy Minister of Foreign Economic Relations) to S. A. Sitarian (Chairman of the State Foreign Economic Commission of the Council of Ministers), on the delay of payments by Vneshekonombank to foreign economic agencies, April 10, 1990 (GARF, F. 5446, Op. 162, D. 1495, L. 27).

53. Address by Yu. D. Masliukov to the Fourth Session of the Supreme Soviet of the USSR, November 26, 1990, transcript (Moscow: Verkhovnyi Sovet SSSR, 1990), p. 187.

54. V. V. Gerashchenko to V. G. Kucherenko, Chairman of the Budget-Financial Commission of the Supreme Soviet of the USSR, on monetary circulation in 1990, September 19, 1990 (RGAE, F. 2324, Op. 33, D. 741, Ll. 69–74).

55. I. A. Pogosov (First Deputy Chairman of Goskomstat), on the work of enterprises and organizations regarding sufficient supply of consumer goods for the population in January–October of 1990 (GARF, F. 5446, Op. 162, D. 268, Ll. 109–16).

56. N. I. Ryzhkov, *Desiat' let velikikh potriasenii* (Moscow: Assotsiatsiia "Kniga. Prosviashchenie. Miloserdie," 1995), p. 421.

57. Express report of the All-Union Center for Analysis of Public Opinion (VTsIOM), on the attitude of the population toward possible acceleration in the shift to a market economy, May 22, 1990 (GARF, F. 5446, Op. 162, D. 2, L. 225).

58. V. L. Kosmarskii, L. A. Khakhulina, and S. P. Shpil'ko, "Obshchestvennoie mneniie o perekhode k rynochnoi ekonomikem," in *Nauchnyi doklad* (Moscow: VTsIOM, 1991), p. 8; S. White, *Gorbachev and After* (Cambridge University Press, 1991), pp. 239, 247.

59. White, *Gorbachev and After,* pp. 239, 247.

60. Notes for the introductory speech at the session of the Plenum of the CC of the CPSU on October 8, 1990, not later than October 18, 1990 (Archive of the Gorbachev Foundation, G. Shakhnazariov foundation file, archival no. 15368, p. 14).

61. L. Pleshakov, "Chto dal'she?," interview with G. A. Yavlinsky, *Ogonek,* no. 44 (October 1990): 5.

62. Transcript of the session of the Politburo of the CC of the CPDU on November 16, 1990 (RGANI, F. 89, Op. 42, D. 30, L. 16, 20).

63. K. Z. Terekh (Minister of Trade) to Chairman of the Council of Ministers N. I. Ryzhkov, on consumer goods resources for the first quarter of 1991, December 25, 1990 (GARF, F. 5446, Op. 163, D. 1046, Ll. 138–42).

64. N. G. Belov (First Deputy Chairman of Goskomstat) to Chairman of the Council of Ministers N. I. Ryzhkov, on the prices of consumer goods, August 7, 1990 (GARF, F. 5446, Op. 162, D. 277, L. 29).

65. V. N. Kirichenko (Chairman of Goskomstat) to Prime Minister V. S. Pavlov, on the rates of inflation and the unmet demand of the population in 1990, January 23, 1991 (GARF, F. 5446, Op. 163, D. 185, Ll. 97, 98).

66. Yu. M. Luzhkov (Chairman of the Executive Committee of the Moscow Soviet) to Prime Minister V. S. Pavlov, on the poor supply of consumer goods in Moscow, February 26, 1991 (GARF, F. 5446, Op. 163, D. 1049, Ll. 35, 36).

67. Appeal of the Nizhnii Novgorod City Soviet of People's Deputies to President M. S. Gorbachev, December 1990 (GARF, F. 5446, Op. 163, D. 1047, L. 12).

68. "Sotsial'no-ekonomicheskii konflikt v tiumenskom izmerenii" [The Socio-economic Conflict on the Tyumen Scale], *Moskovskiie Novosti,* no. 13 (1990): 8.

69. The Supreme Soviet of the USSR, appeal to the Soviet people regarding raising retail prices, June 12, 1990 (GARF, F. 5446, Op. 162, D. 777, L. 83).

70. RGANI, F. 89, Op. 8, D. 45.

71. "Iz tupika. Programma pravitel'stva RSFSR po stabilizatsii ekonomiki i perekhodu k rynochnym otnosheniiam" [Out of a Dead End: The RSFSR Govern-

ment Program on Stabilizing the Economy and the Transition to Market Relations], *Komsomol'skaia Pravda,* April 23, 1991.

72. From materials prepared by the Institute of Economic Policy. The Institute of Economic Policy, from which the Institute for the Economy in Transition was subsequently created, was founded between late 1990 and early 1991. Its founders believed the institute's most important task was to forecast and analyze the course of the serious Soviet economic crisis and to prepare recommendations on economic policy. (The author has been head of the institute since its founding.)

73. *Rossiiskaia ekonomika v 1991 godu. Tendentsii i perspektivy,* pp. 38–40.

74. A. Vlasov (Chief of the Division of Agrarian Policy of the CC of the CPSU) and I. Skiba (Chief of the Division of Socioeconomic Policy) to the CC of the CPSU, on the need to intensify the struggle against crimes in the economic sphere, March 18, 1991 (RGANI, F. 89, Op. 20, D. 49, L. 8).

75. Decree by the president of the USSR of January 10, 1991, no. UP-1303, "On urgent measures required to improve the situation regarding foodstuffs in 1991."

76. V. N. Kostunin (Deputy Chairman of Gossnab) to First Deputy Prime Minister V. Kh. Doguzhiiev, on providing oil products for the people's economy in 1991, January 31, 1991 (GARF, F. 5446, Op. 163, D. 267, Ll. 29–31).

77. To Deputy Chairman of the State Fuel-Energy Commission V. V. Maryin from A. A. Troitsky (Deputy Minister for Economic Forecasting) and V. N. Kostiunin (Deputy Minister for Material Resources), on preparation of the national economy for work during the autumn–winter period of 1991/92 (assignment no. JIP-2902 of June 12, 1991), July 23, 1991 (GARF, F. 5446, Op. 163, D. 1640, L. 93).

78. R. I. Viakhirev (Acting Chairman of the Board of Gazprom) to S. A. Sitarian (Deputy Chairman of the Council of Ministers), on convertible currency funding allocated for 1990, June 12, 1990 (GARF, F. 5446, Op. 162, D. 1492, L. 128).

79. Address of Prime Minister V. S. Pavlov to the Fifth Session of the Supreme Soviet of the USSR, April 22, 1991, transcript, p. 84.

80. From a memorandum to the CC of the CPSU of May 27, 1991, on the critical situation in the provision of medicines and medical products to the population and healthcare institutions (RGANI, F. 89, Op. 20, D. 50).

81. Address of Prime Minister Pavlov, April 22, 1991, transcript, p. 88.

82. N. M. Olshansky (Chairman of Agrokhim) to S. A. Sitarian (Chairman of the State Foreign Economic Commission of the Council of Ministers), on State Plan commitments, October 31, 1990 (GARF, F. 5446, Op. 162, D. 15, L. 87).

83. From a letter of the Party Committee of the Ministry of Auto-Agricultural Machine Building of the USSR to Deputy General Secretary of the CC of the CPSU V. A. Ivashko, April 11, 1991 (RGANI, F. 89, Op. 22, D. 32).

84. *Programma deistvii Kabineta Ministrov SSSR po vyvodu ekonomiki iz krizisa. Proekt* [Action Program for the Cabinet of Ministers USSR on Bringing the Economy out of Crisis] (Moscow, April 1991), pp. 5, 6, 15.

85. This document could not be found among presently accessible archival materials. I cite it as it was published in the open press. The reputation of the authors allows me to believe its authenticity. See Ye Al'bats and B. Pauell, "Chernaia Kassa Strany," *Kommersant,* no. 67 (April 1999).

86. From the memorandum "On certain Western opinions of the situation in the USSR and prospects for its evolution," July 31, 1990 (Archive of the Gorbachev Foundation, Cherniaev file, archival no. 8459).

87. A. S. Cherniaev, *1991 god: Dnevnik pomoshchnika Prezidenta SSSR* [1991: Diary of a Presidential Aide] (Moscow: TERRA, Respublika, 1997), p. 125; R. Braithwaite, *Across the Moscow River: The World Turned Upside Down* (Yale University Press, 2002), p. 249; Matlock, *Autopsy on an Empire,* pp. 510, 511.

88. Cherniaev, *1991 god,* p. 115. On M. Gorbachev's attempts to mobilize politically motivated state credits from Germany and the United States, see also Matlock, *Autopsy on an Empire,* pp. 531, 532.

89. S. Sitarian to President Gorbachev, on the talks with H. Teltschik, Chief of the Foreign Policy Division of the Department of the Federal Chancellor, November 27–28 in Moscow, December 7, 1990 (GARF, F. 5446, Op. 163, D. 1192, L. 113).

90. K. F. Katushev (Minister of Foreign Economic Relations) to Prime Minister V. S. Pavlov, on the financial situation of the Ministry of Foreign Economic Relations, April 4, 1991 (GARF, F. 5446, Op. 163, D. 45, Ll. 9–10).

91. Braithwaite, *Across the Moscow River,* p. 206.

92. L. M. Zamiatin, *Gorbi i Meggi. Zapiski posla o dvukh izvestnykh politikakh–Mikhaile Gorbacheve i Margaret Tetcher* [Gorby and Maggie: Notes of an Ambassador on Two Famous Politicians—Mikhail Gorbachev and Margaret Thatcher] (Moscow: Proizvodstvenno-izdatel'skii kombinat VINITI, 1995), p. 110.

93. A. Koval', *41-i Prezident SShA George Bush vernulsia v ukrainskuiu stolitsu spustia 13 let.* [George Bush, 41st President of the USA, Has Returned to the Ukrainian Capital after 13 Years], May 21, 2004 (www.ukrinter.com).

94. Resolution "On extending food and pharmaceutical aid to the Soviet Union," passed by the European Parliament on December 13, 1990 (GARF, F. 5446, Op. 163, D. 1028, Ll. 25–27).

95. Letters from V. Arkhipov (Deputy Minister of Defense) to Chairman of the Central Commission on the Use of Humanitarian Aid L. A. Voronin, on distribution of humanitarian aid, January 16, 1991 and January 19, 1991 (GARF, F. 5446, Op. 163, D. 1028, Ll. 44, 45).

96. M. Leont'iev, "Ia ne imel prava lishat' ludei nadezhdy . . . ," interview with G. Yavlinsky, *Nezavisimaia gazeta,* April 13, 1991.

97. A. A. Sobchak (Chairman of Leningrad City Soviet) to Prime Minister V. S. Pavlov, May 16, 1991 (GARF, F. 5446, Op. 163, D. 1446, L. 19).

98. M. I. Goldman, *What Went Wrong with Perestroika* (New York: W. W. Norton, 1992), p. 14.

99. V. E. Orlov to the Cabinet of Ministers, on the implementation of the Union budget and the fund for stabilization of the economy in 1991 (RGAE, F. 7733, Op. 65, D. 5578, Ll. 99–102).

100. V. A. Durasov (Deputy Minister of the Economy) to the Cabinet of Ministers, regarding a complex of planned and executed measures on the stabilization of the USSR economy and the forecast for its development in 1991, June 20, 1991 (GARF, F. 5446, Op. 163, D. 8, Ll. 182, 183).

101. S. Boguslavskii, "Smeshchenie Plastov" [Shifting Strata], *Literaturnaia gazeta,* March 20, 1991.

102. M. Nenashev, *Poslednee pravitel'stvo SSSR: lichnosti, svidetel'stva, dialogi* [The Last Government of the USSR: Personalities, Accounts, Dialogues] (Moscow: A/O "Krom," 1993), p. 73.

Chapter Seven

1. Address of Prime Minister V. S. Pavlov to the Fifth Session of the Supreme Soviet of the USSR, discussion of the prime minister's address on measures to further stabilize the consumer market and implement a price-setting policy, February 19, 1991, transcript, part 1, p. 94.

2. L. B. Vid (Deputy Chairman of Gosplan) to the Cabinet of Ministers, assessment of the alternatives for development of the people's economy of the USSR in 1991, April 27, 1991 (GARF, F. 5446, Op. 163, D. 8, Ll. 93, 94).

3. V. V. Gerashchenko to President M. S. Gorbachev, on the monetary-credit system, April 8, 1991 (RGAE, F. 2324, Op. 32, D. 4005, Ll. 58–60).

4. V. V. Gerashchenko to Chairman of the Supreme Soviet A. I. Lukianov, on the banking system, April 4, 1991 (RGAE, F. 2324, Op. 32, D. 4005, Ll. 64, 65).

5. V. V. Gerashchenko to President M. S. Gorbachev, on a unified credit-monetary policy, April 11, 1991 (RGAE, F. 2324, Op. 32, D. 4005, L. 69).

6. S. A. Sitarian and K. F. Katushev to Prime Minister V. S. Pavlov, on foreign economic relations of the USSR in 1991, May 14, 1991 (GARF, F. 5446, Op. 163, D. 46, Ll. 98–100).

7. V. A. Durasov (Deputy Minister of the Economy) to Cabinet of Ministers, materials on implemented and planned measures to stabilize the economy of the USSR and forecast its development in 1991, June 20, 1991 (GARF, F. 5446, Op. 163, D. 8, L. 156).

8. R. Grinberg and K. Legai, "Stupeni dezintegratsii: problemy torgovli SSSR s Vostochnoi Evropoi" [Steps toward Disintegration: USSR Trade Problems with Eastern Europe], *Nezavisimaia Gazeta* May 25, 1991.

9. A. I. Kachanov (Deputy Minister of Foreign Economic Relations) to Chairman of the State Foreign Economic Commission of the Council of Ministers S. A. Sitarian, regarding the letter by U.S. Secretary of Commerce R. Mosbacher about overdue debt of Soviet organizations for contracts signed with American companies, December 27, 1990 (GARF, F. 5446, Op. 163, D. 1177, L. 26).

10. T. Sato (President of the Japanese-Soviet Trade Association) to Chairman of the Scientific-Industrial Union A. I. Volsky, on the debt of Soviet foreign trade agencies to member companies of the Japanese-Soviet Trade Association, February 13, 1991 (GARF, F. 5446, Op. 163, D. 1178, L. 69).

11. V. A. Durasov (Deputy Chairman of Gosplan) to the Council of Ministers, on proposals for coordinating new purchase prices of grain with retail prices of bread and baked goods, along with corresponding compensation to the public for additional expenses, June 12, 1990 (GARF, F. 5446, Op. 162, D. 277, Ll. 76, 77).

12. Address of Prime Minister V. S. Pavlov to the Fifth Session of the Supreme Soviet of the USSR, discussion of the Prime Minister's address on measures to further stabilize the consumer market and implement a price-setting policy, February 19, 1991, transcript, part 1, p. 96.

13. Memorandum on food supplies in 1991 from M. L. Timoshishin (Chairman of the State Committee for Purchases of Food Resources) to F. P. Senko (Deputy Prime Minister), April 15, 1991 (GARF, F. 5446, Op. 163, D. 562, L. 17).

14. V. Akulinin (Division of Agricultural-Industrial Branches) to V. S. Pavlov, on a possible emergency situation regarding supply of bread and baked goods to the population, and livestock breeding using concentrated feed, March 18, 1991 (GARF, F. 5446, Op. 163, D. 560, Ll. 16, 17).

15. V. Fokin (Chairman of the Council of Ministers of the Ukrainian SSR) to Prime Minister V. S. Pavlov, on food supplies for the republic, February 5, 1991 (GARF, F. 5446, Op. 163, D. 562, L. 9).

16. I. Polozkov (First Secretary of the CC of the Communist Party of the RSFSR) to President M. S. Gorbachev and Prime Minister V. S. Pavlov, March 21, 1991 (GARF, F. 5446, Op. 163, D. 562, L. 16).

17. A. Kudelia (First Deputy Minister of the Ministry of Bread and Baked Goods of the RSFSR) to the Cabinet of Ministers and F. P. Senko (Deputy Prime Minister), March 15, 1991 (GARF, F. 5446, Op. 163, D. 562, Ll. 57–59).

18. K. Z. Terekh (Minister of Trade of the USSR) to Prime Minister of the USSR V. S. Pavlov, on the need to increase market supplies of flour and cereals for May–June 1991, May 5, 1991 (GARF, F. 5446, Op. 163, D. 562, L. 95).

19. Division of Agricultural Policy of the CC of the CPSU, on intensifying the work of Party committees to overcome difficulties linked to winter care of livestock and preparation for spring, February 12, 1991 (RGANI, F. 89, Op. 20, D. 33).

20. M. L. Timoshishin (Chairman of the State Committee for Purchases of Food Resources of the USSR) to F. P. Senko, on increasing market supplies of flour and cereals for May–June 1991, May 22, 1991 (GARF, F. 5446, Op. 163, D. 562, L. 97).

21. O. Shenin (Secretary of the CC of the CPSU) to General Secretary of the CC of the CPSU M. S. Gorbachev, on financial and material-technical funding, May 21, 1991(GARF, F. 5446, Op. 163, D. 32, Ll. 4, 5).

22. A. S. Cherniaev, *1991 god: Dnevnik pomoshchnika Prezidenta SSSR* [1991: Diary of a Presidential Aide] (Moscow: TERRA, Respublika, 1997), pp. 124–26.

23. From materials of the Institute of Economic Policy of 1991: "In 1991, gradual rejection by the leaders of the USSR and Russia of open and concealed populism (including statements about the possibility of finding the way out of the crisis without worsening the living standard of the people) was under way. In the spring, the Union leadership and, in the fall, the leadership of Russia began developing unpopular measures. One might say that the people were ready for such an unfolding of events. . . . During 1991, the majority of the population was increasingly skeptical; at the same time, the public became increasingly aware that it would be impossible to avoid a deep crisis without considerable social sacrifice. Both in the spring and in the fall, over half of the population (as shown in a survey) expected the economic situation to deteriorate, mainly because of higher prices. In December, two-thirds of the population of Russia did not believe it would be possible to overcome the crisis without a temporary worsening of living conditions, which was evidence that they lacked hope for an 'economic miracle' and that there were no signs of a 'revo-

lution of expectations.'" See *Rossiiskaia ekonomika v 1991 godu. Tendentsii i perspektivy* [The Russian Economy in 1991: Tendencies and Prospects] (Moscow: Institut ekonomicheskoi politiki, 1992), pp. 13, 14.

24. Decree of President of the USSR of March 19, 1991, no. Уп-1666, "On reform of retail prices and social measures to protect the population."

25. V. A. Durasov (Deputy Minister of Economy of the USSR) to the Cabinet of Ministers of the USSR, materials on implemented and planned measures to stabilize the USSR economy and forecast its development in 1991, June 20, 1991 (GARF, F. 5446, Op. 163, D. 8, Ll. 177, 178).

26. "In the 1991 plan and budget, it was assumed that a set of social measures would be implemented, unprecedented in scale, at a cost of 47 billion rubles. . . . The reform envisaged raising prices by 311 billion rubles and spending 266 billion rubles, 85 percent of the proceeds, to compensate people for losses incurred by higher prices. In fact, as a result of the changed ratio of fixed and contractual prices, the increase in tariffs on consumer and other services, and decisions passed outside the inter-republic agreements, the increase in prices is estimated at approximately 450 billion rubles. After April, the governments of both the USSR and the Soviet Union republics passed a number of additional resolutions to increase compensation to the general public. As a result, payments totaled practically as much as proceeds from the higher prices. In addition, people received compensation for losses of 160 billion rubles in bank deposits and securities, of which 40 billion rubles could be used in 1991." See V. A. Raevsky and V. G. Gribov to the Committee for Effective Management of the People's Economy of the USSR, on measures to overcome inflation and to stabilize monetary circulation (k-28, п. 9), September 27, 1991 (GARF, F. 5446, Op. 163, D. 41, Ll. 26, 27).

27. V. L. Kosmarskii, L. A. Khakhulina, and S. P. Shpil'ko, "Obshchestvennoie mneniie o perekhode k rynochnoi ekonomike" [Public Opinion on the Transition to a Market Economy], in *Nauchnyi doklad* (Moscow: VTsIOM, 1991), p. 16.

28. I. Zaramensky (Deputy Director of the Division on Relations with Nongovernmental Political Organizations of the CC of the CPSU) to the CC of the CPSU, on measures to stabilize the sociopolitical situation in the country, April 15, 1991 (RGANI, F. 89, Op. 22, D. 69, Ll. 1, 2).

29. V. Ye. Orlov (Minister of Finance) to the Cabinet of Ministers, on revenue and expenditures of the Union budget for 1991 in conjunction with retail price reform and social measures to protect the people, May 12, 1991 (GARF, F. 5446, Op. 163, D. 35, Ll. 218, 222).

30. A. Illarionov, *Popytki provedenia politiki finansovoi stabilizatsii v SSSR i v Rossii* [Attempts to Implement a Policy of Financial Stabilization in the USSR and in Russia] (www.budgetrf.ru/Publications/Magazines/Ve/1995/95-7illarionov/95-7illarionov000.htm).

31. I. A. Pogosov (First Deputy Chairman of Goskomstat) to V. I. Shcherbakov, on the volume of sales and prices on the "black" market, August 2, 1991 (GARF, F. 5446, Op. 163, D. 185, L. 66).

32. V. Konovalov, "Budem li zimoi s ovoshchami i kartoshkoi?" [Will We Have Vegetables and Potatoes This Winter?] *Izvestiia,* May 31, 1991.

33. K. F. Katushev (Minister of Foreign Economic Relations) to Prime Minister V. S. Pavlov, on payment of debts to Greek companies, June 26, 1991 (GARF, F. 5446, Op. 103, D. 1504, L. 28).

34. These withdrawals included funds M. Gorbachev received for publication of his works abroad. He himself most likely did not know about that.

35. Memorandum from V. Ivashko to V. S. Pavlov, on payment of debt to the company of the Finnish Communist Party, June 5, 1991 (RGANI, F. 89, Op. 22, D. 39, Ll. 2–5).

36. R. Braithwaite, *Across the Moscow River: The World Turned Upside Down* (Yale University Press, 2002), p. 299.

37. A. Blunden, *Stalinism: Its Origins and Culture,* vol. 4, *Collapse. 1. The Collapse of Eastern Europe* (http://home.mira.net/~and/lbs/bs4-1a.htm#3-9).

38. S. Kiselev, "Shagi komandora" [The Commander's Steps], *Moskovskie Novosti,* January 13, 1991; E. Ger, "Litva: God nezavisimosti v sostave SSSR" [Lithuania: A Year of Independence within the USSR], *Moskovskie Novosti,* March 24, 1991.

39. M. Sokolov, "Litva: paskhal'nyi podarok Prezidenta," *Kommersant,* April 23, 1990.

40. G. A. Yavlinsky, M. M. Zadornov, A. Yu. Mikhailov, N. Ya. Petrakov, B. G. Fedorov, S. S. Shatalin, T. V. Yarygina, and others, *Perekhod k rynku* [Transition to the Market] (Moscow: EPItsentr, 1990), p. 221.

41. From an interview with Minister of Internal Affairs B. K. Pugo about the killing of Latvian customs officers by unidentified persons: "About a month ago I analyzed the events in the Baltic region and possible measures to liquidate illegal armed groups. I realized that the problem of the local customs had also become urgent. I will speak about just one side of this issue. On seizing smuggled commodities at the national border of the USSR, local customs officials turn over seized commodities not to the Union budget, as they should, but to the republican budget. But these goods were brought there from all over the country, often from places quite far away from the Baltic region! (Correspondent): Perhaps you are right. But as we see, the situation in the Baltic region is dealt with by barbarian methods . . . (B. K. Pugo): I am amazed and upset about such a turn of events myself. Blood was shed, and if the circumstances continue to develop like that, there will be more bloodshed and even more severe consequences." I. Andreev, "Posle podzhogov na granitse" [After Arson on the Border], interview with B. K. Pugo, *Izvestiia,* May 27, 1991.

42. I. Andreev, V. Rudnev, and S. Mostovshchikov, "Iz kompetentnykh istochnikov" [From a Reliable Source], *Izvestiia,* January 21, 1991.

43. M. Sokolov, "Litva: Shevardnadze, mezhdu prochim, preduprezhdal" [Lithuania: Shevardnadze Warned Us, by the Way], *Kommersant,* January 14, 1991.

44. V. Mikhailov (Chief of the Division for Ethnic Policy of the CC of the CPSU) to the CC of the CPSU, on events in Lithuania, January 11, 1991 (RGANI, F. 89, Op. 28, D. 31, L. 1).

45. On the role of General Varennikov in the Baltic region events, see Braithwaite, *Across the Moscow River,* p. 206.

46. M. Sokolov, "Litovskii krizis: teper' vse zavisit ot Rossii" [The Lithuanian Crisis: Now Everything Depends on Russia], *Kommersant,* January 21, 1991.

47. Yu. Shchekochikhin, "Neupravliaemaia armiia?" [An Ungovernable Army?], *Literaturnaia Gazeta*, January 16, 1991.

48. Memorandum by A. S. Cherniaev of January 15, 1991 (Archive of the Gorbachev Foundation, archival no. 8780).

49. *Rossiiskaia ekonomika v 1991 godu*, p. 8.

Chapter Eight

1. V. Kriuchkov, *Lichnoe delo* [Personal File] (Moscow: Olimp AST, 1996), part 1, pp. 184–200.

2. A. S. Barsenkov and A. Yu. Shadrin, "Politicheskii krisiz v SSSR 19–21 avgusta 1991 g." [The Political Crisis in the USSR August 19–21, 1991], *Vestnik Moskovskogo Universiteta*, ser. 8, no. 3 (2001): 50. On the reasons for the failure of the August 1991 coup, see also V. Medvedev, "Avgust 1991," *Svobodnaia mysl'*, no. 12 (1993): 67–77.

3. G. S. Shakhnazarov, *S vozhdiami i bez nikh* [With Leaders and without Them] (Moscow: Vagrius, 2001), p. 440.

4. On February 25, 1917, in Petrograd the number of strikers reached 200,000. At nine in the evening on the same day Lieutenant-General S. Khabalov received a telegram sent through direct lines to the general headquarters: "I command you to stop riots in the capital tomorrow. They are impermissible during this hard time of the war against Germany and Austria. Nicholas." At ten in the morning, Khabalov, after reading the telegram to senior officers, ordered them to open fire if the mob became aggressive. Starting on the morning of February 27, the majority of troops refused to shoot at people. Here's how Khabalov himself describes the situation at 8:00 a.m. on February 28: "(1) I have the main building of the Admiralty, four units of the Guards, five squadrons and companies, and two batteries at my disposal. Other troops have either taken the side of revolutionaries or agreed to remain neutral. Single soldiers and gangs wander around the city shooting at passersby and disarming officers; (2) all railroad stations are in the hands of revolutionaries who guard them closely; (3) the entire city is in the hands of the revolutionaries, telephones are not working, there is no communication with other parts of the city." By noon it was clear to Khabalov that it was impossible to resist. Soon he was arrested by soldiers who were inspecting the Admiralty building. See A. Blok, "Poslednie dni starogo rezhima" [Final Days of the Old Regime], in *Arkhiv russkoi revolutsii* (Berlin, 1922), vol. 4, pp. 5–54. (The poet wrote the cited article using materials collected by the Extraordinary Commission of the Provisional Government during the investigation of illegal actions of former ministers.)

5. M. Sokolov, "Slava Bogu, perestroika konchilas'" [Thank God Perestroika Is Over], *Kommersant*, August 26, 1991.

6. M. S. Gorbachev, "O bezotlagatel'nykh merakh po uvelicheniiu proizvodstva tovarov i uslug dlia naseleniia" [On Immediate Measures to Increase Production of Goods and Services for the Population], *Izvestiia*, August 5, 1991.

7. V. V. Gerashchenko to Prime Minister V. S. Pavlov, on price differences between agricultural raw materials and other products, June 26, 1991 (RGAE, F. 2324, Op. 32, D. 4005, Ll. 125–27).

8. O. Latsis, "Signal bedy, poslannyi nikuda. Chego opasalos' pravitel'stvo SSSR za tri dnia do konchiny" [SOS Sent Nowhere: What the USSR Government Feared Three Days before the End], *Izvestiia,* June 28, 1996.

9. This is how G. Yavlinsky and M. Zadornov evaluated the convertible currency situation in the USSR in May of 1991: "At the beginning of 1990 the USSR still had convertible currency reserves—about $15 billion in accounts in foreign banks. By the end of the year the sum of debts to foreign partners for already-delivered goods ranged from $3–5 billion." See G. I. Yavlinsky, and M. Zadornov, "Plius 'Bolshaia semerka': programma organizovannogo vozvrashcheniia v bol'shuiu ekonomiku" [Plus the G-7: A Program for an Organized Return to Big Economics], *Izvestiia,* May 20, 1991.

10. Memorandum prepared by the Division of Socioeconomic Policy of the CC of the CPSU on January 28, 1991, for M. S. Gorbachev, "On Unsatisfactory Supply of Raw Materials for the Economy in 1991" (RGANI, F. 89, Op. 22, D. 9, Ll. 2–4).

11. O. Latsis, "Kogda nachalsia krizis. O chem govorit spravka KGB SSSR, napisannaia v sentiabre 1991 goda" [When the Crisis Began: What a Note Written by the KGB in September 1991 Tells Us], *Izvestiia,* April 15, 1993.

12. A. Illarionov estimates the aggregate deficit of Russia's budget, Russia's share of the Union budget in 1991, as 31.9 percent of GNP. Average monthly rates of growth of the money supply from May through December 1991 increased up to 8.1 percent, and the ratio of M2 to GNP increased to a record 76.5 percent. From May to December 1991, the M2 was 60.7 percent of Russia's GNP for the corresponding period. See A. Illarionov, *Popytki provedeniia politiki finansovoi stabilizatsii v SSSR i v Rossii. 1995g* [Attempts to Implement a Policy of Financial Stabilization in the USSR and Russia] (www.budgetrf.ru). By S. Alexashenko's calculations, the size of the 1991 budget deficit was approximately 34 percent of GNP, in accordance with international methodology. See S. Alexashenko, "The Collapse of the Soviet Fiscal System: What Should Be Done?" *Review of Economies in Transition* 4 (1992): 39, 40. The World Bank estimated the share of the 1991 deficit of GNP (taking into account forced savings) at 30.9 percent. See *Russian Economic Reform: Crossing the Threshold of Structural Change* (Washington: World Bank, 1992).

13. V. Medvedev, *V komande Gorbacheva. Vzgliad iznutri* [On Gorbachev's Team: An Inside View] (Moscow: Bylina, 1994), p. 195.

14. From the memoir of Chairman of the KGB of the USSR V. Kriuchkov: "Pavlov spoke in detail about the economic situation, about a deep crisis that had already hit the country and that would grow in scope in the near future. He emphasized that we could not rely on credits; we simply could not get them because we were insolvent. The Soviet Union did not even have funds to pay interest on previously received credits." See Kriuchkov, *Lichnoie delo,* p. 151. On the prime minister's stroke related to his abuse of alcohol, see p. 182.

15. The following question was put to a vote: "Do you think it is necessary to preserve the USSR as a new federation of equal sovereign republics in which rights and freedoms of people of every ethnicity will be guaranteed to the full extent?" Of those who voted, 76.4 percent answered yes. The referendum was not conducted in six Union republics.

16. M. Sokolov, "Referendum: bros'te, nichego strashnogo" [Referendum: Drop It, It's Nothing], *Kommersant,* March 4, 1991.

17. A. S. Cherniaev, assistant to President M. Gorbachev, "The armed forces of Ukraine declared that all armed units on its territory and all the property are to be placed under their jurisdiction. It's sheer madness!" A. S. Cherniaev, *1991 god: Dnevnik pomoshchnika Prezidenta SSSR* [1991: Diary of a Presidential Aide] (Moscow: TERRA, Respublika, 1997), p. 235.

18. In the fall of 1991, M. Gorbachev, while presenting arguments in favor of preserving the Union to leaders of the republics said quite reasonably: "There are no physical borders inside the country. We only have administrative borders. It did not occur to anyone to install border posts. Besides, 70 percent of the borders between the republics have been established under resolutions of regional executive committees and rural soviets. . . . Shall we also divide the armed forces?" However, as usually happens when a territorially integrated empire collapses, such words could not convince anyone. See *Soiuz mozhno bylo sokhranit'. Belaia kniga. Dokumenty i fakty o politike M. S. Gorbacheva po reformirovaniiu i sokhraneniiu mnogonatsional'nogo gosudarstva* [The Union Could Have Been Preserved. White Paper. Documents and Facts about Gorbachev's Policy on Reforming and Preserving a Multiethnic State], edited by A. B. Veber (Moscow: "Aprel'-85" Publishing House, 1995), p. 296.

19. M. Sokolov, "Soiuz razvalilsia respublik svobodnykh" [The Union of Free Republics Has Collapsed], *Kommersant,* September 9, 1991.

20. On L. Kravchuk's position during the first days of the coup, see T. Kuzio, *Ukraine: Perestroika to Independence* (New York: St. Martin's Press, 1994), pp. 171–72.

21. *Soiuz mozhno bylo sokhranit'*, p. 245.

22. On economic policy in the former Union republics in 1991, see working materials of the government (Ye. T. Gaidar's personal archive).

23. L. I. Abalkin, *K tseli cherez krizis. Spustia god . . .* [To the Goal through a Crisis: A Year Later] (Moscow: Luch, 1992), p. 176.

24. G. S. Shakhnazarov, *S vozhdiami i bez nikh* (Moscow: Vagrius, 2001), p. 482.

25. Letter from V. V. Gerashchenko (Chairman of Gosbank) to President M. S. Gorbachev, August 9, 1991 (Archive of the Gorbachev Foundation, Shakhnazarov file, archival no. 10811, L. 27).

26. The Sixth Congress of People's Deputies of the Russian Federation, April 6–21, 1992, transcript (Moscow: Respublika, 1992), vol. 1, p. 151.

27. V. A. Raevsky (Deputy Minister of Finance) and V. G. Gribov (Deputy Minister of the Economy and Economic Forecasting) to Committee for Effective Management of the Economy of the USSR, on measures to overcome inflation and to stabilize monetary circulation (k-28, P. 9), September 27, 1991 (GARF, F. 5446, Op. 163, D. 41, Ll. 28, 29, 30, 33, 34).

28. V. A. Raevsky (Deputy Minister of Finance) and V. G. Gribov (Deputy Minister of Economy and Economic Forecasting) to Committee for Effective Management of the Economy of the USSR, on an emergency Union budget and funds outside the budget for the fourth quarter of 1991, October 23, 1991 (GARF, F. 5446, Op. 163, D. 41, Ll. 49, 62).

29. S. G. Sinel'nikov, *Budzhetnii krizis v Rossii* [The Budget Crisis in Russia] (Moscow: Evraziia, 1995).

30. Letter from V. V. Gerashchenko (Chairman of Gosbank of the USSR) to the State Council of the USSR, on monetary circulation in 1991, October 24, 1991 (RGAE, F. 2324, Op. 32, D. 4006, Ll. 65–68).

31. S. P. Shpil'ko, L. A. Khakhulina, Z. V. Kupriianova, V. V. Bordova, L. G. Zubova, N. P. Kovaliova, M. D. Krasil'nikova, and T. V. Avdeienko, "Otsenka naseleniiem sotsial'noekonomicheskoi situatsii v strane (po rezul'tatam sotsiologicheskikh oprosov 1991goda), Nauchnyi doklad" [Public Opinion on the Socio-economic Situation in the Country (Based on Results of Sociological Surveys in 1991): A Scholarly Report] (Moscow: VTsIOM, 1991), pp. 55, 56.

32. A. Orlov (Chairman of the Control Chamber) to Chairman of the Inter-Republic Economic Committee I. S. Silayev, materials on control and analysis of implementation of Union budget and funds outside the budget for nine months of 1991 (GARF, F. 5446, Op. 163, D. 31, Ll. 66–75).

33. V. V. Gerashchenko (Chairman of Gosbank) and Yu. S. Moskovsky (Chairman of the Board of Vneshekonombank) to I. S. Silayev (Chief of Committee for Effective Management of the Economy), urgent message on the use of credit given by Riyadh Bank (Saudi Arabia), October 25, 1991 (GARF, F. 5446, Op. 163, D. 47, L. 7).

34. Yu. V. Poletaev (Deputy Chairman of the Board of Vnesheconombank) to the Chairman of the Committee for Effective Management of the Economy I. S. Silayev, on funding the purchase of grain from the USA under a guarantee of the U.S. Department of Agriculture, September 11, 1991 (GARF, F. 5446, Op. 163, D. 1436, L. 12).

35. I. Silayev to President M. S. Gorbachev, materials on the emergency budget for the fourth quarter of 1991 to be discussed at the Supreme Soviet of the USSR, October 19, 1991 (GARF, F. 5446, Op. 163, D. 41, Ll. 101–06).

36. A. Orlov (Chairman of the Control Chamber) to Chairman of Inter-Republic Economic Committee I. S. Silayev, on the Union budget and legislative procedures for funding expenditures, reducing the deficit in the fourth quarter of 1991, and principles of forming the federal budget for 1992, October 1, 1991 (GARF, F. 5446, Op. 163, D. 41, Ll. 35, 37, 38).

37. I. Silayev, Committee for Effective Management of the Economy, "On monetary circulation," October 1991 (GARF, F. 5446, Op. 163, D. 41, L. 40).

38. V. N. Kulikov (First Deputy Chairman of Gosbank) to Inter-Republic Economic Committee, Comrade I. S. Silayev, on the situation with monetary circulation (assignment of the Committee on Effective Management of the Economy, k-28, P. 9), September 24, 1991 (GARF, F. 5446, Op. 163, D. 41, Ll. 13–15).

39. Letter from I. S. Silayev to M. S. Gorbachev, October 3, 1991 (GARF, F. 5446, Op. 163, D. 36, L. 118).

40. Letter from V. A. Raevsky (Deputy Minister of Finance) to the Committee for Effective Management of the Economy, as addendum to the October 3, 1991, letter of the Minister of Finance of the USSR, no. 01-01/121-1, October 8, 1991 (GARF, F. 5446, Op. 163, D. 36, L. 119).

41. V. V. Gerashchenko to the Inter-Government Economic Committee, on Union budget allocations, February 3, 1991 (RGAE, F. 2324, Op. 32, D. 4006, L. 99).

42. V. V. Gerashchenko to the Council of Heads of Governments—Members of the Economic Commonwealth, on monetary circulation, December 9, 1991 (RGAE, F. 2324, Op. 32, D. 4006, Ll. 103–104).

43. V. V. Gerashchenko to President M. S. Gorbachev, on issuing money in 1991, November 13, 1991 (RGAE, F. 2324, Op. 32, D. 4006, Ll. 84–88).

44. Cherniaev, *1991 god,* p. 280.

45. Shpil'ko and others, "Otsenka naseleniiem sotsial'no-ekonomicheskoi situatsii v strane" [People's Evaluation of the Country's Socioeconomic Situation], pp. 6, 20, 21.

46. V. A. Mangazeev (Minister of Foreign Economic Relations) to Chairman of the Committee for Effective Management of the Economy I. S. Silayev, on payments for deliveries of purchased grain, August 29, 1991 (GARF, F. 5446, Op. 163, D. 1436, L. 4).

47. R. Braithwaite, *Across the Moscow River: The World Turned Upside Down* (Yale University Press, 2002), p. 249.

48. V. V. Gerashchenko to President M. S. Gorbachev, on gold reserves of Gosbank, November 15, 1991 (RGAE, F. 2324, Op. 32, D. 4006, L. 90, 91).

49. Memorandum prepared by A. A. Butin (Acting Financial Director of Mosnarbank) prepared for negotiations with the Bank of England on the question of preserving a branch of Mosnarbank in London, January 23, 1992 (Ye. T. Gaidar's personal archive).

50. Directors of commercial banks to President of the RSFSR B. N. Yeltsin, on Russia's commercial banks abroad, December 19, 1991 (RGAE, F. 2324, Op 32, D. 4006, L. 110–12.

51. Cherniaev, *1991 god,* p. 260.

52. G. Yavlinsky, *Pereferiinyi kapitalizm. Lektsii ob ekonomicheskoi sisteme Rossii na rubezhe XX–XXI vekov* [Peripheral Capitalism: Lecture on Russia's Economic System at the Turn of the Twenty-First Century] (Moscow: EPItsentr Integral-Inform, 2003), pp. 24, 25.

53. RGAE, F. 692, Op. 1, D. 5, L. 32.

54. V. I. Akulinin (First Deputy Chairman of the Committee for Purchase of Food Resources) to Comrade I. S. Silayev, Committee on Effective Management of the Economy, on purchasing grain with convertible currency, August 28, 1991 (GARF, F. 5446, Op. 163, D. 1438, L. 57).

55. V. I. Akulinin (First Deputy Chairman of the Committee for Purchase of Food Resources) to I. S. Silayev, Committee on Effective Management of the Economy, on the volume of imported wheat and purchase of soybean paste, September 27, 1991 (GARF, F. 5446, Op. 163, D. 1439, L. 75).

56. Resolution of the Committee on Effective Management of the Economy of August 31, 1991, no. 4, "On urgent measures to provide the population with foodstuffs."

57. V. B. Turbin (Deputy Minister of MVD) to I. S. Silayev (Chairman of Inter-Government Economic Committee), on providing bread and other basic foodstuffs to the population, November 8, 1991 (GARF, F. 5446, Op. 163, D. 562, L. 141).

58. Working group of the City Soviet (Gorsovet), on Russia's relations with other republics, in preparation for a session of the Gorsovet under the President

of the RSFSR, "Arkhangelskoye," October 24, 1991 (Ye. T. Gaidar's personal archive).

59. Shpil'ko and others, "Otsenka naseleniiem sotsial'no-ekonomicheskoi situatsii v strane" [People's Evaluation of the Country's Socioeconomic Situation], p. 49.

60. Resolution of the government of the RSFSR of December 19, 1991, no. 57, "On emergency measures for supplies of bread and baked goods to the RSFSR."

61. Executive order of the government of the RSFSR of December 28, 1991, no. 244-p, "On additional measures for unconditional supplies of bread and baked goods to the RSFSR."

62. D. A. Rustow, "Transitions to Democracy: Toward a Dynamic Model," *Comparative Politics* 2, no. 3 (April 1970): 350, 351; J. Linz and A. Stepan, *Problems of Democratic Transition and Consolidation: Southern Europe, South America, and Post-Communist Europe* (Johns Hopkins University Press, 1996), p. 17.

63. A memorandum prepared in October 1991 recognized the policy of Great Britain from 1940 to the early 1960s, which managed to carry out a relatively bloodless dissolution of the empire and to adjust to new world realities, as an example to be followed by the leadership of Russia. See "Strategy of Russia in transitional period," October 1991 (Ye. T. Gaidar's personal archive).

64. E. Todd, *Posle imperii. Pax Americana–nachalo kontsa* [After the Empire: The Breakdown of the American Order] (Moscow: Mezhdunarodnye otnosheniia, 2004), pp. 173–76.

65. On the possibility that commanders of military districts might decide to use tactical and operational-tactical nuclear weapons, see K. Sorokin, "Strategicheskoe nasledie SSSR" [The USSR's Strategic Legacy], *Mirovaia ekonomika i mezhdunarodnye otnosheniia*, no. 2 (1992): 51–65.

66. On Moscow's lack of efficient control over individual components of tactical nuclear weapons, particularly outdated models, see also *Ezhegodnik SIPRI. 2002* (Moscow: Nauka, 2002), p. 572.

67. M. Sokolov, "Sud'ba Soiuza: 'N+0' ili '9–9' " [Fate of the Union: N+0 or 9–9], *Kommersant*, September 2, 1991.

68. V. Portnikov, "Yel'tsin obsuzhdal s voennymi vozmozhnost' yadernogo udara po Ukraine . . ." [Yeltsin Discussed the Possibility of a Nuclear Strike against Ukraine with the Army . . .], *Nezavisimaia Gazeta*, October 24, 1991.

69. Memorandum on Russia's immediate actions in the field of military construction, disarmament, and outer space; withdrawal of nuclear weapons from former Union republics, 1991 (Ye. T. Gaidar's personal archive).

70. Agreement on joint measures regarding nuclear weapons, see Resolution of the Supreme Soviet of the RSFSR of December 12, 1991, no. 2014-1, "On ratification of the agreement for establishment of commonwealth of independent states." On the withdrawal of tactical nuclear weapons to central preproduction bases by June 1, 1992, for dismantling under joint control, see V. F. Davydov, "Raspad SSSR i nerasprostraneniie yadernogo oruzhiia" [Disintegration of the USSR and the Nonproliferation of Nuclear Weapons], *SShA: ekonomika, politika, ideologiia*, no. 3 (267) (1992): 25, 29; S. M. Rogov, "Povorotnyi punkt v yadernoi konfrontatsii" [Turning Point in the Nuclear Confrontation], *SShA: ekonomika, politika, ideologiia*, no. 1 (265) (1992). On the concern of Western analysts, turning occasion-

ally into open panic, about the fate of Russia's tactical nuclear weapons if the Soviet Union should collapse, see G. Milkhollin, and D. Yait, "Razval sovetskoi yadernoi moshchi—blago ili ugroza?" [Collapse of Soviet Nuclear Power—Good or Threat?] *Mezhdunarodnaia Zhizn'*, no. 1 (1992): 43–55.

71. *Priroda i zakomonernost' mezhdunadornykh otnoshenii. Sovremennye mezhdunarodnye otnosheniia* [The Nature and Order of International Relations: Contemporary International Relations], edited by A. V. Torkunov (Moscow: ROSSPEN, 2000).

72. On August 8, 1996, Lukashenko addressed the Parliament with an offer to conduct a referendum in regard to introducing changes in the Constitution. The Constitutional Court admitted that a referendum on such serious questions could not be compulsory, but only consultative. The government of Belarus pretended it was not aware of the decision of the Supreme Court of the country. On November 15, the head of the country removed Victor Gobchar, the chairman of the Central Election Commission, from office. Chairman of the Government of Russia Victor Chernomyrdin, Chairman of the State Duma Gennady Seleznev, and Chairman of the Council of the Federation Yegor Stroiev, who were traveling outside Belarus on business, suddenly changed their route and landed in the capital of Belarus on the night of November 21, 1996. The Russian authorities gave a clear signal to the Belarus elite and society that they would not support the opposition against A. Lukashenko's regime. Alexander Lukashenko did not attend the celebration on the occasion of withdrawal of the last Russian strategic missile from the territory of Belarus, which was held on November 27, 1996 (after the referendum). See P. Sheremet and S. Kalinkina, *Sluchainyi president* [Accidental President] (St. Petersburg: Limbus Press, 2004).

73. On December 25, 1991, M. Gorbachev signed a decree that stripped him of his authority as president of the USSR. At 7:38 p.m. Moscow time, the red flag was lowered at the Kremlin and the tricolor flag of Russia was raised.

74. In January of 1992, a survey of officers who participated in an all-army meeting showed that 73 percent of officers thought it natural that, on all issues regarding the future of the armed forces, decisions should rest with the military. On the USSR armed forces that could not be controlled and loss of control over troops by the Union leadership after August 1991, see *Rossiia segodnia. Politicheskii portret v documentakh* [Russia Today: Political Portrait in Documents], edited by B. I. Koval', issue 2, 1991–1992; *Stanovleniie gosudarstvennosti. Armia i politika. Novye partii. Tserkov' i obshchestvo* [Formation of Statehood. The Army and Politics. New Parties. The Church and Society] (Moscow: Mezhdunarodnye otnosheniia, 1993), p. 81.

75. The position of the author, and of leading specialists of the Institute for the Economy in Transition who hold views similar to his on key issues of the postsocialist transition in Russia, is described in detail in the following works: Ye. T. Gaidar, *Dni porazhenii i pobed. Soch* [Days of Defeat and Victory: Essays] (Moscow: Evraziia, 1997), vol. 1; *Ekonomika perekhodnogo perioda: ocherki ekonomicheskoi politiki postkommunisticheskoi Rossii 1991–1997* [Economy of the Transitional Period: Sketches of the Economic Policy of Post-Communist Russia 1991–1997] (Moscow: IEPP, 1998); *Ekonomika perekhodnogo perioda. Ocherki ekonomicheskoi politiki*

postkommunisticheskoi Rossii. 1998–2002 [Economy of the Transitional Period: Sketches of the Economic Policy of Post-Communist Russia 1998–2002] (Moscow: Delo, 2003).

Afterword

1. www.odin.dep.no/fin/English/topic/pension_fund/p10001683/bn.html, International Financial Statistics (IMF); www.gks., www.minfin.ru; www.dbresearch.com/servlet/reweb2.ReWEB; jsessionid=590%3A440c32ca%3A3d8f8df7alleb31?rwkey=u1562160&%24rwframe=0; www.cbr.ru, www.gks.ru.

2. The macroeconomic and financial forecast and the federal budget indicators of the Russian Federation for 2006–10 are based on a structural econometric model of Russia's economy developed at the Institute for the Economy in Transition. The model is a system of structural econometric equations that reflect a link between principal macroeconomic variables. This model, based on exogenous dynamics of some variables, allows for the creation of a forecast for the remaining variables. Each equation allows one to understand the degree of influence of separate *explanatory* factors on the described variable. The equations were derived in the course of evaluating an individual property of an analyzed structure of time series, the order of integration, the statistical significance of individual lag values of variables, seasonal influences, and separate shocks.

LIST OF ABBREVIATIONS

CC	Central Committee
CCC	Central Control Commission
Comecon	Council for Mutual Economic Assistance
CPSU	Communist Party of the Soviet Union
GARF	Gosudarstvennyi Arkhiv Rossiiskoi Federatsii (State Archive of the Russian Federation)
GATT	General Agreement on Tariffs and Trade
GKChP	State Emergency Committee
Glavtyumenneftegaz	Agency for Oil and Gas in Tyumen
Gosbank	State Bank
Goskomstat	State Committee for Statistics
Goskomtsen	State Committee on Pricing
Gosplan	Soviet State Planning Commission
Gossnab	State Committee for Material Technical Supply
Gosstroi	State Commission on Construction and Architecture
Goznak	State Mint
IMF	International Monetary Fund
MVD	Interior Ministry
Prodintorg	All-Union Export-Import Association for Food Products

Promstroibank	Industrial and Construction Bank
RGAE	Rossiiskii Gosudarstvennyi Arkhiv Ekonomiki (Russian State Archive of the Economy)
RGANI	Rossiiskii Gosudarstvennyi Arkhiv Noveishei Istorii (Russian State Archive of Contemporary History)
RSFSR	Russian Socialist Federal Soviet Republic
RUIE	Russian Union of Industrialists and Entrepreneurs
Sberbank	State Savings Bank
Vneshtorgbank	State Foreign Trade Bank
Vneshekonombank	State Foreign Economic Bank
VTsIOM	All-Russia Public Opinion Research Center
ZSNGP	Western-Siberian Oil and Gas Province

INDEX

Abalkin, Leonid, 158, 179–80, 186, 228, 298n35
Abkhazia, ethnic conflicts, 74, 174
Academy of Sciences, 108–09
Administrative rent, 45
Aeroflot, 196, 239
Afghanistan, Soviet war in, 102, 106, 170, 171, 281–82n80
Agrarian states, 13, 27–28, 264n2
Agriculture: in advanced economies, 83; agrarian revolution, 80–81; in North America, 81
Agriculture, in Soviet Union, 82–88; collectivization, 80, 82, 85; effects of currency crisis, 194; exports, 74; fertilizer supplies, 194; fuel required, 164; good harvests, 125, 205; individual farming legalized, 157; inefficiency, 89; investment, 86–87, 121, 129, 205, 275n15; *kolkhoz* (collective farms), 83, 85, 88, 187, 188, 209; labor, 82, 83; land reclamation, 75–76, 275n15; migration from countryside, 84; pesticide use, 77; production, 87; productivity, 83, 119, 121; resources shifted to industry, 74, 82; soil amelioration, 75–76; *sovkhoz* (state farm) sector, 85, 88, 187, 209; subsidies, 119, 121; technology, 194, 210; unreliable harvests, 86, 88, 95, 103, 125; virgin land development, 85–86, 125. *See also* Food supply; Grain
Akulinin, Viktor, 206, 239–40

Alcohol: alcoholism, 77–78; anti-alcohol campaign, 133, 134, 136–37, 138–39; illicit production, 138–39; revenues from sales, 134
Algeria, 6–7, 8, 11–12, 13, 14, 56
Alibegov, T. I., 182
All-Union Scientific Research Institute, 141
Aluminum production, 189
Andropov, Yuri, 87, 106, 131, 277n33, 281n80, 283n92
Animal feed, 88, 95, 119, 124, 207, 208–09
Arab-Israeli war (*1973*), 49, 57, 112
Argentina, 36
Arkhipov, Vladimir, 197
Armenia, 74, 174
Arms limitation talks, 169. *See also* Nuclear weapons
Attlee, Clement, 6
Austro-Hungarian Empire: collapse, 14, 15, 17–19, 243–44; ethnic groups, x, 13, 15, 18–19; nationalism, 15, 17–18; Sudeten Germans, x, 16; suffrage restrictions, 6
Authoritarian regimes: characteristics, 26, 264n8; collapses, 15, 23–24, 35–38; corruption, 31–32, 35, 37; deaths of leaders, 35, 38; differences from totalitarian regimes, 32; duration, 265n18; effects of economic modernization, 33, 34–35, 36–37; in Europe, 29–30; focus on economic development, 33; forma-